ADVANCED

SS

on

Ian Rendell & Julian Mott

HODDER
EDUCATION
AN HACHETTE UK COMPANY

The Publishers would like to thank the following for permission to reproduce copyright material:

Photo credits: p.237, 238 and **261** © TNT Magazine/Alamy; **p.243** and **265** Steve Bardens/Actionplus; **p.250** l © Kim Karpeles/Alamy; **p.250** r, **257, 258** and **270** © Mode Images Limited/Alamy; **p.260** l © ImageState/Alamy, r Laurence Griffiths/Getty Images; **p.262** t © Foodfolio/Alamy, b © Food, drink and diet/Mark Sykes/Alamy; **p.263** © ArkReligion.com/Alamy; **p.266** © Ron Evans/Alamy; **p.267** © Gary Roebuck/Alamy; **p.268** © The Photolibrary Wales/Alamy; **p.271** tr © Stockdisc<u>ª</u> (www.stockdisc.com), br © Niall McDiarmid/Alamy, l Chris Jackson/Getty Images; **p.272** © Peter Titmuss/Alamy; **p.273** tl Isopix/Rex Features br Chris Ladd/Getty Images.

Acknowledgements: p.237, 240, 241, 242 and **261** Bounce-a-Lot logo; **p.269** Chris Kemp.

Every effort has been made to trace all copyright holders, but if any have been inadvertently overlooked the Publishers will be pleased to make the necessary arrangements at the first opportunity.

t = top, b = bottom, l = left, r = right, c = centre

Although every effort has been made to ensure that website addresses are correct at time of going to press, Hodder Education cannot be held responsible for the content of any website mentioned in this book. It is sometimes possible to find a relocated web page by typing in the address of the home page for a website in the URL window of your browser.

Hachette's policy is to use papers that are natural, renewable and recyclable products and made from wood grown in sustainable forests. The logging and manufacturing processes are expected to conform to the environmental regulations of the country of origin.

Orders: please contact Bookpoint Ltd, 130 Milton Park, Abingdon, Oxon OX14 4SB. Telephone: (44) 01235 827720. Fax: (44) 01235 400454. Lines are open 9.00 – 5.00, Monday to Saturday, with a 24-hour message answering service. Visit our website at www.hoddereducation.co.uk

All of the files on the CD-ROM in this book can also be downloaded from www.hodderictcoursework.co.uk.

© Ian Rendell and Julian Mott 2008
First published in 2008 by
Hodder Education
An Hachette UK Company
338 Euston Road
London NW1 3BH

Impression number   5   4   3
Year   2012   2011   2010   2009

Cover photo Zefa/Jupiter Images
Illustrations by Barking Dog Art
Typeset in 10 point Goudy Old Style by Tech-Set Ltd, Gateshead
Printed in Italy

A catalogue record for this title is available from the British Library

ISBN-13: 978 0340 929254

Contents

Introduction   I

Part One   **The development of a system**   **5**

    1 The Pass IT Driving School   5
    2 Getting started   7
    3 Setting up the tables   12
    4 Entering the data   23
    5 Defining the relationships   31
    6 Select queries   36
    7 Further queries   46
    8 Setting up multi-table queries   52
    9 Setting up forms using the Form Wizard   59
    10 Working in Form Design View   65
    11 Taking form design further   77
    12 Setting up reports   92
    13 Further reports   107
    14 Macros   119
    15 Adding a switchboard   124
    16 Using SubForms   132
    17 Setting up search and sort options   146
    18 Calculations in reports   153
    19 Using action queries   166
    20 Finishing touches   173

Part Two   **Access tricks and tips**   **188**

    1 Tables   190
    2 Queries   195
    3 Forms   202
    4 Reports   214
    5 Macros   219
    6 Others   224

Part Three   **Starting points**   **237**

    1 Bouncy Castle Hire   237
    2 Cricket Bat Orders   243
    3 The Stationery Store   250

Part Four   **Project ideas**   **259**

    1 Abbey Window Cleaning Services   259
    2 Albion Away Travel   260
    3 Bouncy Castle Hire   261
    4 Cake Making   262
    5 Charity Xmas Cards   263
    6 Conferences @ The Bird in the Hand Hotel   264
    7 Cricket Bat Orders   265
    8 The Derwentdale Fun Run   266
    9 Hair on the Move   267
   10 Hotel Room Booking @ The Broadway Hotel   268
   11 Peak Cycle Hire   269
   12 School Stationery Orders   270
   13 Village Hall Auctions   271
   14 Westford Community Bus   272
   15 Westford Toy Library   273

Part Five   **Project documentation**
(all materials in Part Five are on the CD-ROM)

    1 Problem specification
    2 Design
    3 Test plans
    4 Implementation
    5 Testing
    6 Evaluation
    7 User guide
    8 Presenting documentation

Part Six   **Finding project ideas**
(all materials in Part Six are on the CD-ROM)

    1 Finding a project
    2 Project ideas

Introduction

Aims

This book is aimed at a number of Advanced courses of study within the National Qualifications Framework currently available in schools and colleges.

The book covers all the key software skills required in practical components of ICT and Computing specifications where a study of databases using Microsoft Access is required.

The materials and approach used in the book are also applicable to students on many Computing and ICT related courses in further and higher education where a study of databases through Microsoft Access is necessary.

Features of Access covered in this book

The main units take students through the following features in Access:
- tables and data types
- simple input masks and data validation
- related tables
- select, parameter and multi-table queries
- calculated fields
- data entry using fully customised forms
- list boxes or combo boxes to facilitate data entry
- basic reports
- macros to automate commonly used features
- switchboards and start-up screens
- subforms to display information in related tables
- update, append and delete queries
- forms and reports based on multi-table queries
- customised reports with use of logos, headers and footers to show grouped data and calculated totals
- customised menus and interfaces by removing toolbars and automating features.

The **Tricks and Tips** section provides many further features in Access.

How to use this book

The book assumes students have a working knowledge of Windows and Windows-based software. It is expected that students will be familiar with the concept of files, records and fields and will have practical experience of simple searching and sorting techniques.

It is also assumed that students will have studied the design of relational databases through a theory component in their course of study.

The book can be used as a formal teaching aid by lecturers and teachers, or students can work independently through the self-study units in class or away from the classroom.

Part 1 takes the student through the development of a system with each unit building on the range of features in Access. The system is based around a driving school, is fictitious and has been designed to incorporate as many features as is possible for demonstration purposes only. The units are best worked through in sequence.

Units 1 to 15 set up a working system, using features which might be expected from students working at this level. The system at this point forms the basis for the electronic support materials offering advice on documenting solutions. Units 16–20 show how to develop this system further.

Teachers and lecturers will clearly use the units in different ways and offer their own input during lessons. However it is expected that the units will take no more than 15–20 hours of study time.

Part 2 offers a range of useful tips and features in Access to support the units and should provide interesting reading. These could be used as further activities for students.

Part 3 provides 3 'Starting points'. These are brief activities each of 1–2 hours' duration. The tables and data are downloaded from the support website as well as the accompanying CD-ROM. Students set up the relationships and forms using just the Wizards. They are then taken through a key process or two in each activity.

- Bouncy Castle Hire focuses on the process of hiring and returning castles. A common project at this level is DVD rentals. Many students forget that once you have taken out a DVD/video, it has to come back! This involves more than just deleting its record from a loans table. This offers a starter but no more!
- Cricket Bat Orders focuses on the IIf function, form referencing and producing customised output.
- Stationery Store deals with the situation where you need to order more than one item. It revises in detail the use of main form/subform approaches.

Each starting point offers good revision, new skills and hopefully will open up project potential and ideas for the student.

Part 4 provides 15 ideas for students' projects. Students could adapt a problem or undertake a similar problem to meet the demands of a real user. Three of the topics are repeated from the starting points in Part 3. This is so that the student can develop their starting point to a finishing point, if they wish.

Further ideas for projects are on the support website and CD-ROM that comes with the book.

Submitting a driving school as coursework for an examination

A number of schools and colleges have steered students away from choosing a driving school for their choice of project. This should not really be the case but students choosing this option do need to proceed with a little common sense. The easiest thing to do is just to throw the book away and start from scratch!

A student who sets about this type of project with a real user will very quickly come up with a significantly different solution. They will find that:

- the driving school may only have one instructor
- the user wants to keep progress records on students
- lessons are block-booked with a variety of discounts on offer
- payments for lessons need to be managed
- different management reports are required
- the organisation of practical and theory tests need to become part of the solution.

Database Projects in Access – differences between the 2nd and 3rd editions

The support file called **DrivingSchoolData** now offers 105 lessons pre-set up for students. This will not only save time entering data but enable students to explore reporting in greater detail. The file offers greater scope for sorting, grouping, forcing page breaks and producing meaningful management reports.

The **Tricks and Tips** section has been significantly added to in a way that offers extension work to the units and stretches the student wishing to move through the materials at pace.

 Students, teachers and lecturers should find no significant differences in working with the second edition alongside the third edition in the classroom. On the website www.hodderictcoursework.co.uk all of the resources for the third edition are contained in zip folders in the right-hand column.

Compatibility issues

All software manufacturers bring out new versions every few years, tweaking the features a little and adding new ones. Microsoft Access is no exception.

It is not necessary to have the latest software version. Although toolbars and dialogue boxes look slightly different in different software versions, all the materials in this book work in all versions of Access.

Access is also backwards compatible so that a more recent version can open files set up in an older version. This is exceptionally useful if students have an older version of the software at home from the version in school or college.

A note to students and lecturers using the materials for external examination

It is important to note that the system used in the text is not being put forward for a particular grade at any level. The system is fictitious and is aimed at showing the student the potential of Microsoft Access and how software features can be incorporated to produce a working ICT system.

All exam boards provide exemplar materials, support and training. It is vital that students in conjunction with their tutors are guided by the specifications.

A word of real caution. Students must on no account copy materials in text books and submit them for examination. Moderators, examiners and the exam boards are very aware of published exemplar materials.

Database Projects in Access Support CD-ROM

The CD-ROM provided offers a number of support files.

Units 1–20 are supported with an end of unit file. This will enable students to pick up the solution at any point in the development.

A file for each trick and tip is included where appropriate. This hopefully will save development time, particularly for teachers/lecturers wanting to demonstrate a particular feature in Access.

A range of Powerpoint files offer advice and support to assist students in documenting the systems they have developed and also allow teachers/lecturers to explain the key issues.

Further files are available offering ideas for project work.

Ian Rendell and Julian Mott have written two coursework books:

- Advanced Spreadsheet Projects in Excel
- Advanced Database Projects in Access

The development of a system

Unit 1: The Pass IT Driving School

The system covered by this book is based on a local driving school. The driving school caters for many students in the surrounding villages. The school has a number of full-time and part-time instructors.

The driving school offers different types of lesson: Introductory, Standard, Pass Plus or the Driving Test. Fees are charged depending on the type of lesson booked.

When a student starts a course of lessons they are issued with a student record card and allocated an instructor. The record card stores the personal contact details of the student driver and can be used by them to keep records of their lessons and the progress they are making.

Students can book lessons through their instructor or by phoning the driving school office. Students usually book lessons of one or two hours though they can book longer sessions if they wish. The driving school organises the practical and theory test for the students; if successful they can go on to do the Pass Plus course.

The driving school office keeps contact detail record cards on each of its instructors. Each instructor is also issued with lesson record sheets on which are kept details of student progress. These are handed into the office at the end of each day.

The system implemented will allow the user to book, cancel and cost driving lessons. Details of all students and their test dates will be stored, enabling quick access and easy editing. Contact details for instructors working for the school will also be stored.

A range of search options will allow the user quickly to locate details of students and/or lessons. Full reporting menus will offer a range of management information including weekly or daily lesson timetables for specified instructors. Further options will include the automatic:

- processing of students who leave the school after passing their test
- filing of all lessons taken for later reference
- analysis of lessons taken

All user interfaces will be fully customised with user-friendly menus.

Individual student lesson progress and lesson payments will not be implemented, enabling the reader to research and develop that side of the solution. Further ideas are discussed in the Introduction.

The system will have four related tables: Student, Instructor, Lesson and LessonType. Details are shown in Figure 1.1.1.

Figure 1.1.1 ▶

Student Table
StudentID
Title
Surname
Forename
Address1
Address2
Address3
Address4
TelNo
DateOfBirth
Sex
TheoryTestDate
PassedTheoryTest
PracticalTestDate
PassedPracticalTest

Instructor Table
InstructorID
Title
Surname
Forename
Address1
Address2
Address3
Address4
HomeTelNo
MobileNo

Lesson Table
LessonNo
StudentID
InstructorID
Date
StartTime
LengthOfLesson
CollectionPoint
DropOffPoint
LessonType

Lesson Type Table
LessonType
Cost

■ Unit 2: Getting started

Microsoft Access is a database management system. It allows the user to store and manipulate data.

The main components of an Access database are:

■ tables
■ queries
■ forms
■ reports
■ macros
■ pages
■ modules

The Pages component allows data to be saved in Web format for publishing on the Web. The Modules component gives the developer access to Visual Basic for Applications. Neither component is covered in this book.

Tables

Access stores data in tables. A table is organised in rows (called records) and columns (called fields).

For example, in a student table a row would store the information about one particular student. This is called a record. Each column would contain details about each student such as forename, surname, etc. These are called fields.

Figure 1.2.1 ▶

Library No	Surname	Forename	Sex	Year	Form
1	Sahota	Sanjot	Female	11	S
2	Gillanders	Mark	Male	13	R
3	Randall	David	Male	11	T
4	Smith	Paul	Male	11	T
5	Webster	Stephanie	Female	10	H
6	Askham	Stephanie	Female	12	T
7	Dayaram	Sunil	Male	13	O
8	Holland	Amanda	Female	11	N
9	Mace	Rebecca	Female	11	N
10	Cooper	Harry	Male	13	J
11	Dilkes	Gemma	Female	13	J
12	Payne	Karen	Female	12	O
13	Pearson	Kathryn	Female	10	P

tblStudent : Table — Record: 1 of 13

Typically a system will consist of more than one table. For example, in a school library the database might be made up of a student table, a book table and a loan table. The student table is shown in Figure 1.2.1.

Access is often referred to as a relational database. Relationships can be defined between tables and used to support the searching and processing of data. A relational database will have at least two tables that are linked together.

Queries

A query is a way of asking questions about the data in your tables according to certain criteria. The user may wish to display a list of appointments for a particular day or output customers who owe payments. In the example shown in Figure 1.2.2 a query has produced a list of students in Year 11. This is known as a **Select Query**.

Figure 1.2.2 ▶

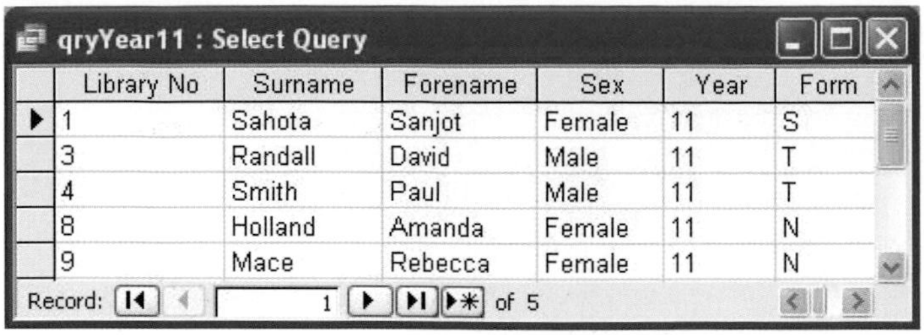

Library No	Surname	Forename	Sex	Year	Form
1	Sahota	Sanjot	Female	11	S
3	Randall	David	Male	11	T
4	Smith	Paul	Male	11	T
8	Holland	Amanda	Female	11	N
9	Mace	Rebecca	Female	11	N

You will notice that there are five records in the output from this query. In the original table there were 13 records. Five of the 13 students are in Year 11.

Queries in Access offer a powerful processing tool. Later you will meet action and parameter queries. Queries can also be used to take data from more than one table and perform calculations on data.

Forms

Forms are used mainly to display the records in a table in a user-friendly way. Through a form you can enter and edit records more easily.

Figure 1.2.3 ▶

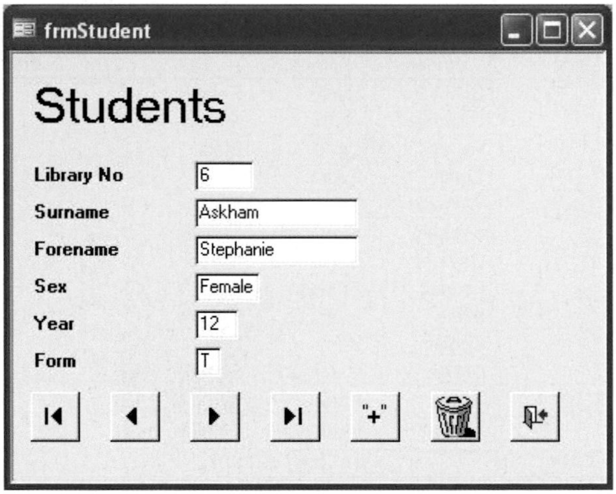

Forms are fully customisable. You can add buttons and controls, edit the appearance and include images (see Figure 1.2.3).

Reports

Reports are used to print information from your database. They provide professional-looking output from a table or query. They can be fully customised and can display summary information (see Figure 1.2.4).

Figure 1.2.4 ►

Year 11 Students

Library No	Surname	Forename	Sex	Year	Form
1	Sahota	Sanjot	Female	11	S
3	Randall	David	Male	11	T
4	Smith	Paul	Male	11	T
8	Holland	Amanda	Female	11	N
9	Mace	Rebecca	Female	11	N

Macros

A macro is a set of one or more actions that perform a particular operation. You can use macros to add buttons to print a report, open a form and other commonly used tasks. Macros help you to fully automate and customise your system.

Starting Access

■ Load **Microsoft Access 2003**. The Microsoft Access application window appears as shown in Figure 1.2.5.

Figure 1.2.5 ▼

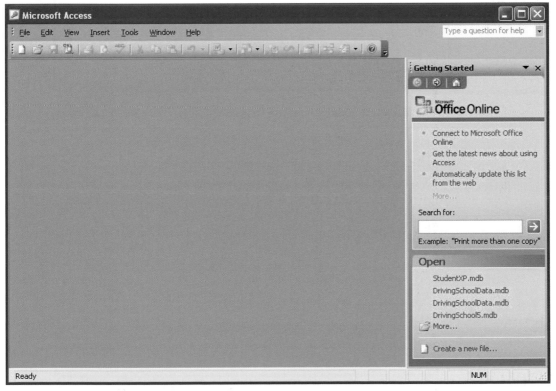

On the right of the screen is the task pane. From here you can either open an existing database, create a new database or use a range of pre-defined databases.

The databases you have most recently used appear in the lower half of the pane. Clicking **Create a new file** or the right arrow in the task pane will display further options.

The Database Window

When you open an Access database the **Database Window** is displayed. The **Database Window** is the control centre of your application.

In Access 2003 the Database Window looks very similar to that shown in Figure 1.2.6. It has a slightly different feel from the Database Window in other versions of Access but has all the same features and functions.

Figure 1.2.6 ▶

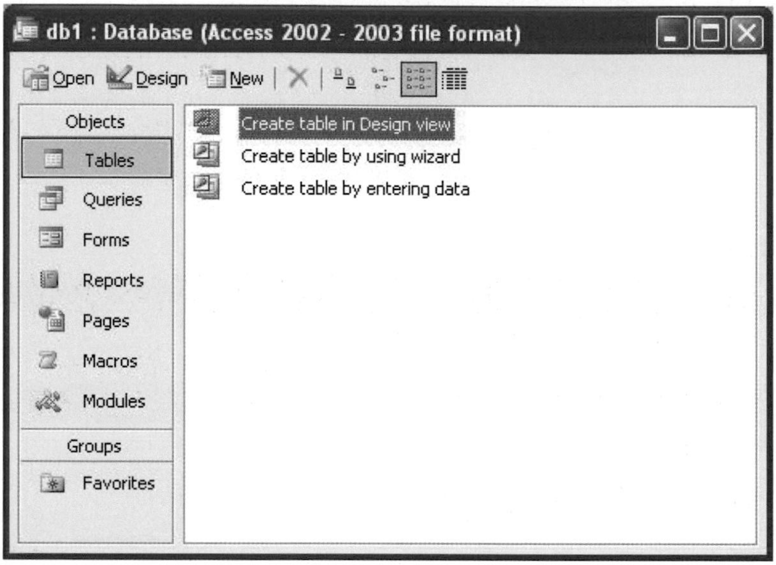

	db1 : Database (Access 2002 - 2003 file format)	
Open	Design	New	×	...
Objects	Create table in Design view
Tables	Create table by using wizard
Queries	Create table by entering data
Forms	
Reports	
Pages	
Macros	
Modules	
Groups	
Favorites	

The Database Window operates in a very similar way whichever version of the software you use.

From the Database Window you can access any of the components in your database by clicking on the Objects tab. For example, in the screen shot in Figure 1.2.6 the Tables tab is selected ready to create a new table.

You would also click on this tab to open an existing table or edit an existing table.

Similarly, by clicking on the **Queries**, **Forms**, **Reports**, **Macros** or **Modules** tabs, you can open, edit or create queries, forms, reports, macros or modules.

The Database Window Toolbar

Figure 1.2.7 ▶

db1 : Database (Access 2002 - 2003 file format)

Open Design New × ...

- **Open** allows you to open a table, query or form.
- **Design** allows you to enter Design View to set up a table, query, form, report or macro.

- **New** allows you to set up a new table, query, form, report or macro.
- **Delete** allows you to delete an object in the Database Window.
- The remaining icons offer display options in the Database Window.

Toolbars

The toolbars in Access change dynamically, depending on which mode you are working in.

For example, if you are designing a table, there is a **Table Design** toolbar as in Figure 1.2.8.

Figure 1.2.8 ▶

If you are viewing a form, there is a **Form View** toolbar. If the toolbar is not on the screen, click on **View**, **Toolbars** and choose from the menu (see Figure 1.2.9).

Figure 1.2.9 ▼

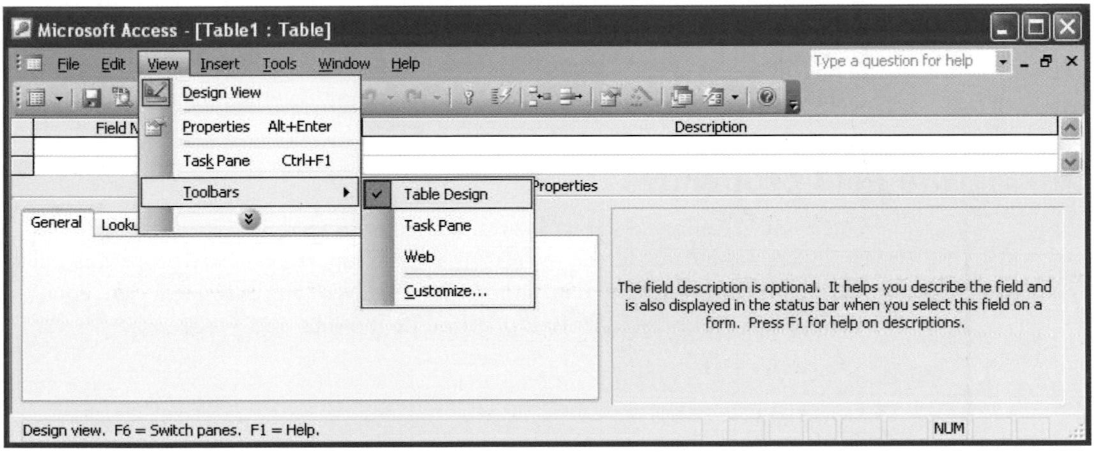

Unit 3: Setting up the tables

In Units 3 and 4 you will learn how to set up the tables that are needed to store the data for the Pass IT Driving School. The Driving School system is based on four tables:

- **Student**
- **Instructor**
- **Lesson**
- **Lesson Type**

In this Unit you will set up the **Student table**. In Unit 4 you will enter the data and set up the remaining tables.

There are two stages to designing a table:

- Define the field names that make up the table and declare the data type for each.
- Set the field properties for each field name.

Defining the field names and data types

Access needs to know the name of each field in each table and what sort of data to expect. For example in the Student table, the Student's telephone number might have as its **Field Name**: TelNo. You also need to tell Access whether the **Data Type** is number, text, date/time, currency, etc. In this case it is text.

Setting the field properties

Once you have named the table and defined each field with its data type, you can control the fields further by setting **Field Properties**. These properties tell Access how you want the data stored and displayed. For example a date could be displayed 19/06/94, 19th June 1994 or 19-Jun-94.

Setting up the Student table

1 Load **Microsoft Access**. Click on **Create a new file …**
2 Select **Blank Database** in the task pane (see Figure 1.3.1).

Figure 1.3.1 ▼

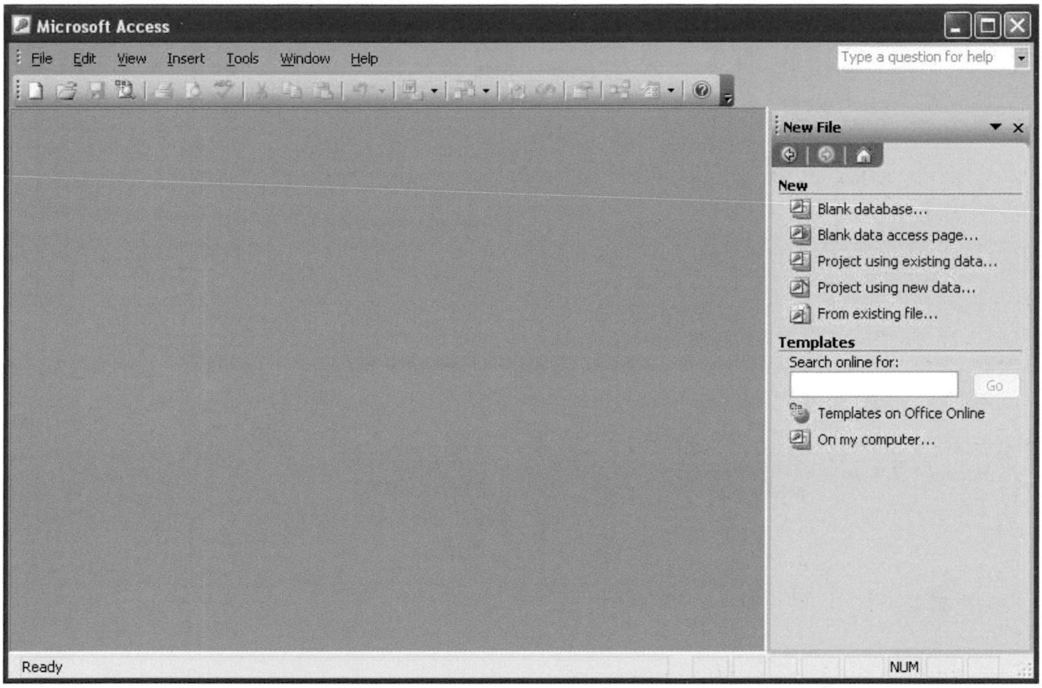

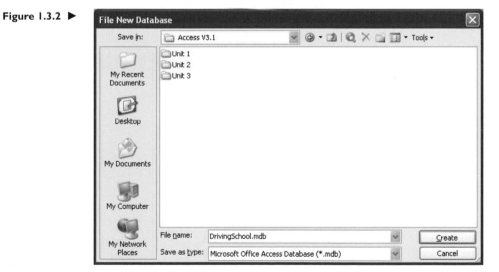

The **File New Database** Window appears as in Figure 1.3.2

Figure 1.3.2 ►

3 Use the **Save in** drop-down box to locate where you want to save your database. Name the file **DrivingSchool** and click on **Create**.

The Database Window loads, this is the control centre from which you can design tables, queries, forms, reports and macros. See Figure 1.3.3.

Figure 1.3.3 ▶

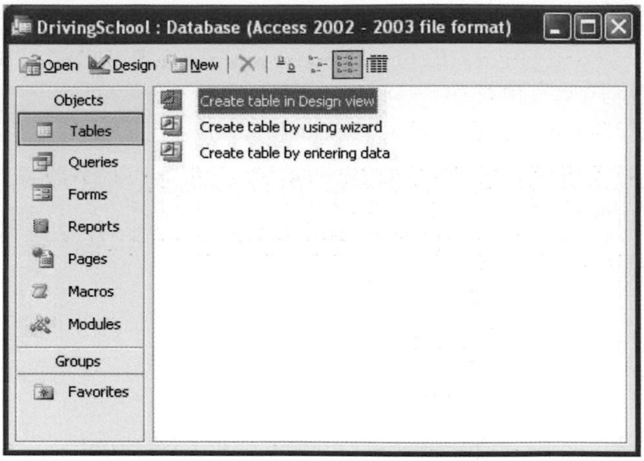

4 Click on **Tables** (it should already be selected) and click on **New**. The **New Table** window will appear. See Figure 1.3.4.

Figure 1.3.4 ▶

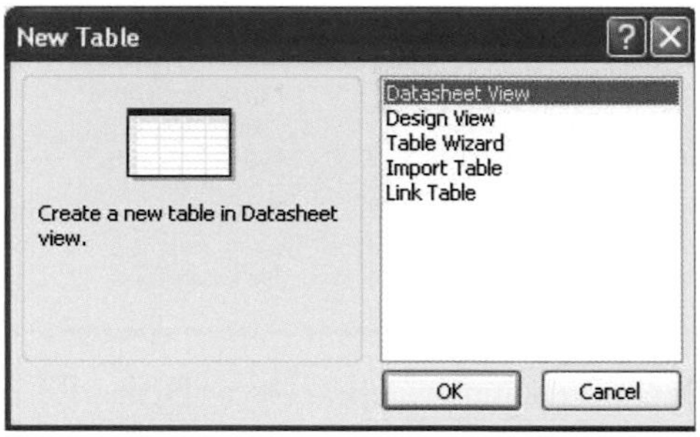

5 Click on **Design View** and click on **OK**.
The **Table Design** window appears as shown in Figure 1.3.5.

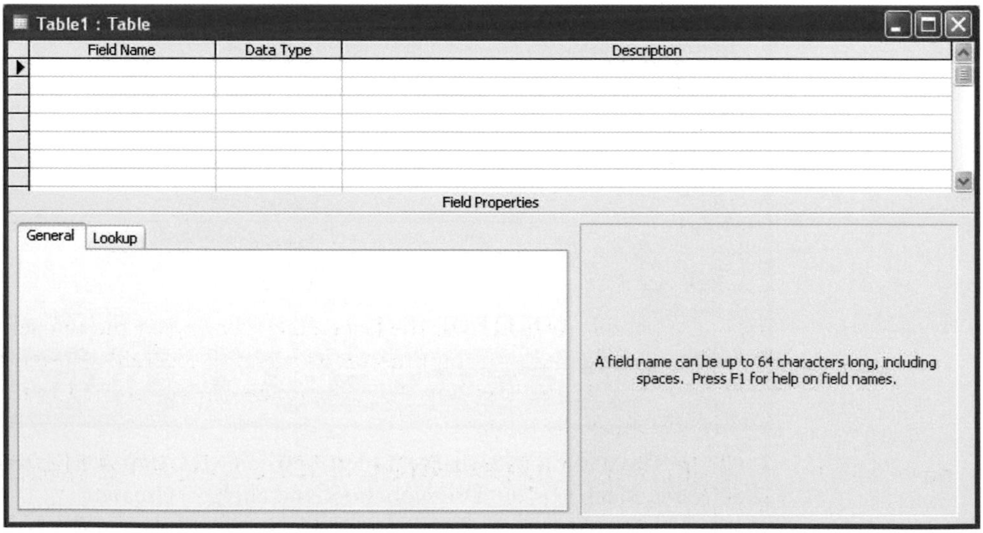

Figure 1.3.5 ▲

Once you are in Table Design view you can start entering the details of the fields needed in the table.

Defining the field names and data types

1 Enter the first Field Name: **StudentID** and press TAB or RETURN to move to the **Data Type** field.

After entering the Field Name you will notice Field Properties are displayed in the lower half of the window, we will enter these later.

2 Click on the drop-down and select **AutoNumber** (see Figure 1.3.6).

Figure 1.3.6 ▶

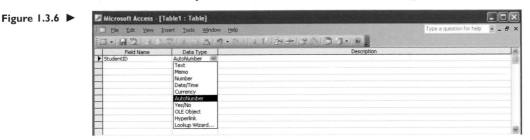

3 In the **Description** field enter **Student's ID number**. This is optional and only for information.

4 Complete the Field Names and Data Types as shown below for the Student table.

Field Name	Data Type
StudentID	AutoNumber
Title	Text
Surname	Text
Forename	Text
Address1	Text
Address2	Text
Address3	Text
Address4	Text
TelNo	Text
DateOfBirth	Date/Time
Sex	Text
TheoryTestDate	Date/Time
PassedTheoryTest	Yes/No
PracticalTestDate	Date/Time
PassedPracticalTest	Yes/No

5 Set the StudentID field to be the key field by clicking on the row selector for this field and clicking on the **Primary Key** icon of the **Table Design** toolbar or click on **Edit, Primary Key**. A small picture of a key appears to the left of the Field Name (see Figure 1.3.7).

Figure 1.3.7 ▶

6 Your **Table Design** window should appear as in Figure 1.3.8. Save the table by closing the window or by choosing **File, Save**. The **Save As** dialogue box will appear, name the table **tblStudent**.

Figure 1.3.8 ▼

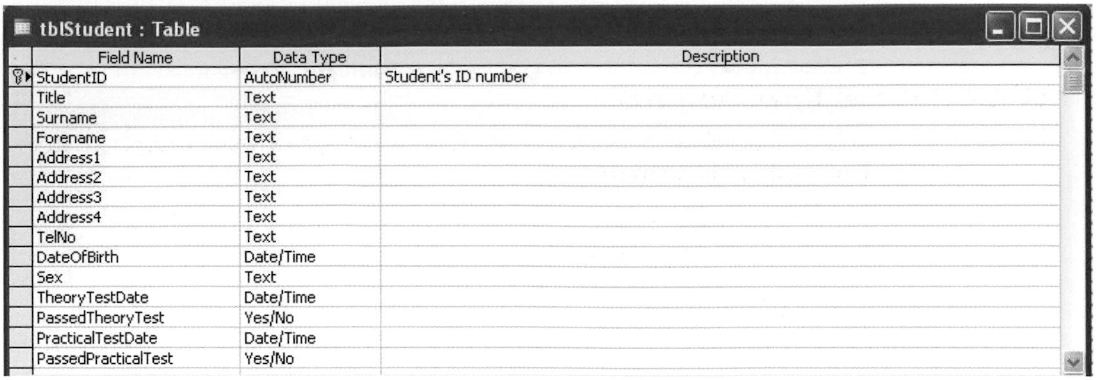

Field Name	Data Type	Description
StudentID	AutoNumber	Student's ID number
Title	Text	
Surname	Text	
Forename	Text	
Address1	Text	
Address2	Text	
Address3	Text	
Address4	Text	
TelNo	Text	
DateOfBirth	Date/Time	
Sex	Text	
TheoryTestDate	Date/Time	
PassedTheoryTest	Yes/No	
PracticalTestDate	Date/Time	
PassedPracticalTest	Yes/No	

Note When saving tables some Access users like to start the name with tbl, e.g. tblstudent. They would start queries with qry, forms with frm, reports with rpt and macros with mcr. You may wish to consider using this naming convention.

Editing the table structure

If the **Table Design** toolbar is not already on the screen insert it by clicking **View, Toolbars, Table Design** (see Figure 1.3.9).

Figure 1.3.9 ▶

During the course of setting up the table it is probable you will make a mistake or decide to make a change to your table's structure. You have a number of editing options available.

Inserting a field

Click on the row selector of the field below the insertion point.

Press the INSERT key on the keyboard or click the **Insert Rows** icon on the toolbar.

Deleting a field

Click on the row selector of the field to delete.

Press the DELETE key on the keyboard or click the **Delete Rows** icon on the toolbar.

Moving a field

Click on the row selector of the field you wish to move.

Click again and drag it to its new position – a black line marks the insertion point.

Changing the primary key field

You can only have one primary key. If you have set the wrong field as the primary key, remove it as follows:

■ Click on the row selector of the correct field.
■ Click on **Edit, Primary Key** or click the **Primary Key** icon on the toolbar.

Setting the field properties

When you click on a field in Design View its field properties are displayed in the lower half of the window.

We will go through each field in the Student table and set its field properties including input masks where appropriate.

StudentID

1 From the Database Window click on **Tables**, select **tblStudent** and click on **Design**.
2 The StudentID field should be the one selected. If not, click in the row selector for StudentID.
3 In the Field Properties set **Field Size** to **Long Integer** (it probably already is). See Figure 1.3.10.

Figure 1.3.10 ▶

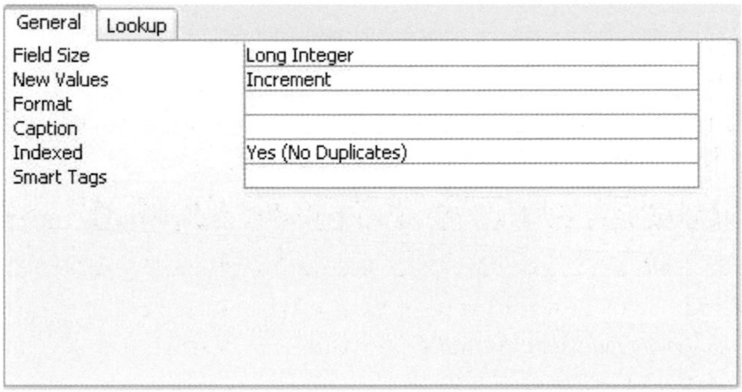

General	Lookup	
Field Size	Long Integer	
New Values	Increment	
Format		
Caption		
Indexed	Yes (No Duplicates)	
Smart Tags		

Title

The Title field can only have the values Mr, Mrs, Miss and Ms. We can use the Lookup Wizard whenever we want to restrict the data entered into a field to certain values.

1 Click on the **Title** field name.

Figure 1.3.11 ▼ 2 In the **Data Type** column click on **Lookup Wizard**. See Figure 1.3.11.

Field Name	Data Type	Description
StudentID	AutoNumber	Student's ID Number
Title	Text	
Surname	Text	
Forename	Memo	
Address1	Number	
Address2	Date/Time	
Address3	Currency	
Address4	AutoNumber	
TelNo	Yes/No	
DateOfBirth	OLE Object	
Sex	Hyperlink	
TheoryTestDate	Lookup Wizard...	
PassedTheoryTest	Yes/No	
PracticalTestDate	Date/Time	
PassedPracticalTest	Yes/No	

tblStudent : Table

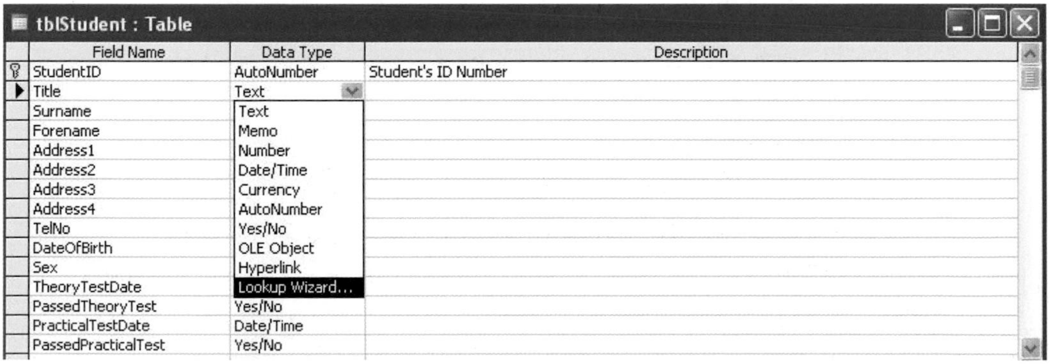

3 Click on **'I will type in the values that I want.'** and click on **Next**. See Figure 1.3.12.

Figure 1.3.12 ▶

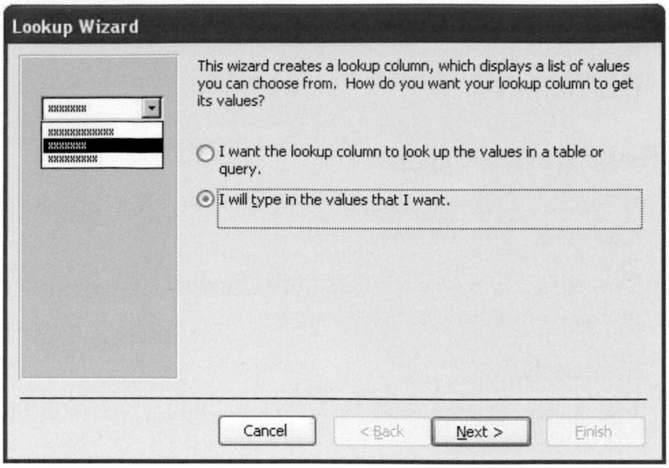

4 Enter **Mr, Mrs, Miss** and **Ms** into the column, press TAB to move to the next row. See Figure 1.3.13.

Figure 1.3.13 ▶

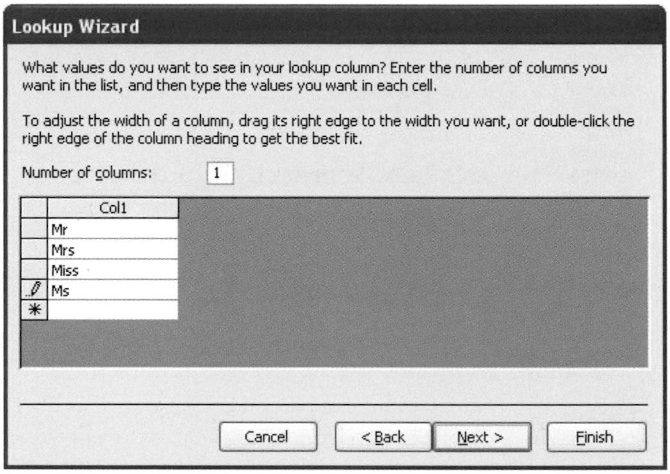

5 Click on **Next** and then click on **Finish**.

Figure 1.3.14 ▶

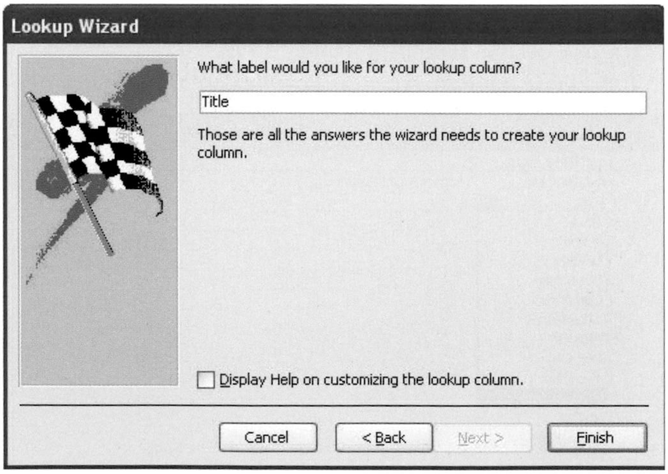

6 In the **Field Properties** set the Field Size to 6. See Figure 1.3.15.

Figure 1.3.15 ▶

General	Lookup
Field Size	6
Format	
Input Mask	
Caption	
Default Value	
Validation Rule	
Validation Text	
Required	No
Allow Zero Length	Yes
Indexed	No
Unicode Compression	No
IME Mode	No Control
IME Sentence Mode	None
Smart Tags	

7 If you click on the **Lookup** tab you will see the screen shown in Figure 1.3.16

Figure 1.3.16 ▶

General	Lookup
Display Control	Combo Box
Row Source Type	Value List
Row Source	"Mr";"Mrs";"Miss";"Ms"
Bound Column	1
Column Count	1
Column Heads	No
Column Widths	2.54cm
List Rows	8
List Width	2.54cm
Limit To List	No

When you wish to enter data into this field a combo box (drop-down box) will give you the choice of Mr, Mrs, Miss or Ms.

Surname, Forename, Address1 and Address2

1 Select the Field Name: **Surname** and set the Field Size to 20, repeat for **Forename**.

2 Select the Field Name: **Address1** and set the Field Size to 30, repeat for **Address2**.

Address3

The Pass IT Driving School is based in Westford. It is likely that students will live in Westford. It will save time if we set the default value for the Address3 field to Westford.

1 Click on the **Address3** field.

2 In the **Default Value** box of the Field Properties, enter **Westford**. Access inserts speech marks around the text.

3 Set the Field Size to 20. See Figure 1.3.17.

Figure 1.3.17 ▶

General	Lookup
Field Size	20
Format	
Input Mask	
Caption	
Default Value	"Westford"
Validation Rule	
Validation Text	
Required	No
Allow Zero Length	Yes
Indexed	No
Unicode Compression	No
IME Mode	No Control
IME Sentence Mode	None
Smart Tags	

Note More information on Default Values can be found at the end of Unit 4.

Address4

The Address4 field is the student's postcode.

1 Click on the **Address4** field name.

2 Set the Field Size to 10.

3 Click on the **Format** property box and enter > as shown in Figure 1.3.18.

This will convert any lower case letters entered into upper case, e.g. we34 2qy will become WE34 2QY.

Later you will see how to set an Input Mask to make entering postcodes easier.

Figure 1.3.18 ▶

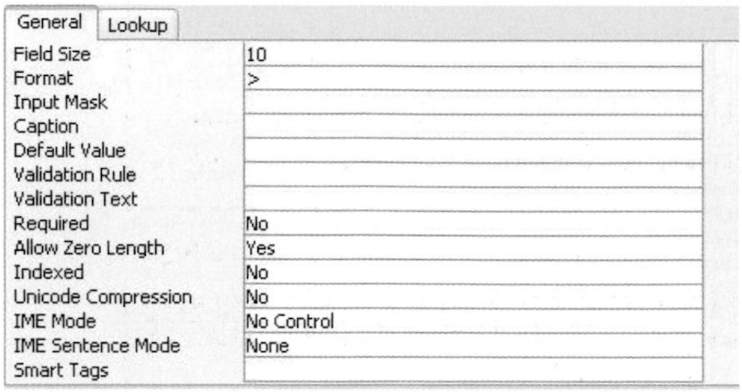

General	Lookup	
Field Size	10	
Format	>	
Input Mask		
Caption		
Default Value		
Validation Rule		
Validation Text		
Required	No	
Allow Zero Length	Yes	
Indexed	No	
Unicode Compression	No	
IME Mode	No Control	
IME Sentence Mode	None	
Smart Tags		

TelNo

Select the Field Name: **TelNo** and set the Field Size to 15.

Note Telephone numbers cannot be a number field as they are likely to include a space, brackets or a preceding zero.

DateOfBirth

The student table uses three Date/Time fields. We will use the Short Date format for each, e.g. 19/06/94.

1 Select the **DateOfBirth** field.

2 Click on the **Format** box in the Field Properties.

3 A drop-down list appears. Choose **Short Date**. See Figure 1.3.19.

Figure 1.3.19 ▶

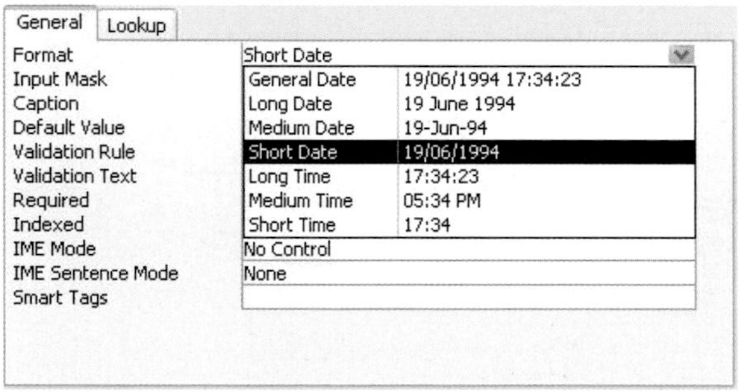

General	Lookup	
Format	Short Date	⌄
Input Mask	General Date	19/06/1994 17:34:23
Caption	Long Date	19 June 1994
Default Value	Medium Date	19-Jun-94
Validation Rule	Short Date	19/06/1994
Validation Text	Long Time	17:34:23
Required	Medium Time	05:34 PM
Indexed	Short Time	17:34
IME Mode	No Control	
IME Sentence Mode	None	
Smart Tags		

It is also possible to use the Input Mask wizard to set a placeholder _ _ / _ _ / _ _ _ _ for each date entered.

4 Click in the **Input Mask** property box and click the three dots icon at the end of the row or the **Build** icon on the **Table Design** toolbar, you will be asked to save your table first. The Input Mask Wizard window is shown as in Figure 1.3.20.

Figure 1.3.20 ▶

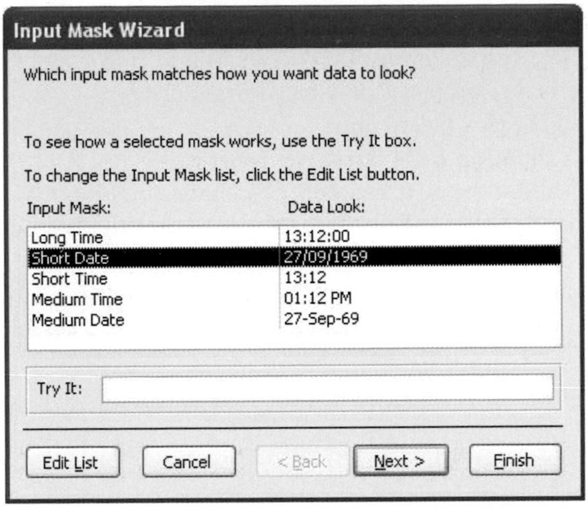

Input Mask Wizard

Which input mask matches how you want data to look?

To see how a selected mask works, use the Try It box.

To change the Input Mask list, click the Edit List button.

Input Mask:	Data Look:
Long Time	13:12:00
Short Date	27/09/1969
Short Time	13:12
Medium Time	01:12 PM
Medium Date	27-Sep-69

Try It: [   ]

[Edit List] [Cancel] [< Back] [Next >] [Finish]

5 Select the **Short Date** option and click on **Next**.

Figure 1.3.21 ▶

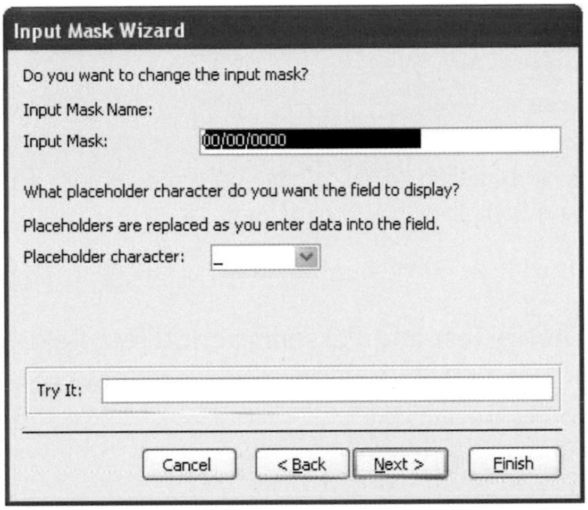

Input Mask Wizard

Do you want to change the input mask?

Input Mask Name:

Input Mask: [00/00/0000]

What placeholder character do you want the field to display?

Placeholders are replaced as you enter data into the field.

Placeholder character: [_ ▾]

Try It: [   ]

[Cancel] [< Back] [Next >] [Finish]

6 A choice of placeholders is offered. Click on **Next** and then click on **Finish** (see Figure 1.3.21).

The field properties are set as shown in Figure 1.3.22.

Figure 1.3.22 ▶

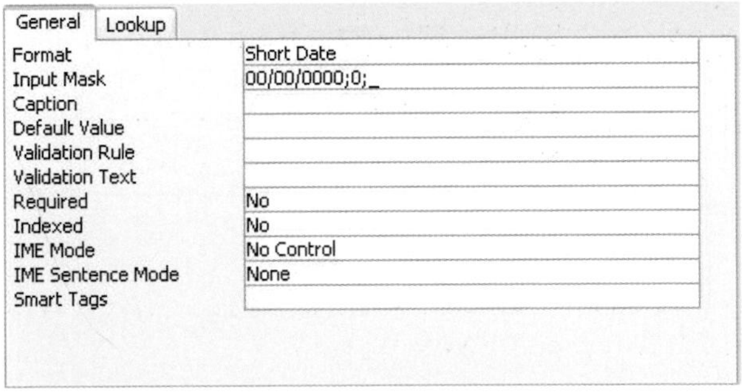

General	Lookup
Format	Short Date
Input Mask	00/00/0000;0;_
Caption	
Default Value	
Validation Rule	
Validation Text	
Required	No
Indexed	No
IME Mode	No Control
IME Sentence Mode	None
Smart Tags	

7 Repeat this for the other two Date/Time fields, **TheoryTestDate** and **PracticalTestDate**.

Note More information on Input Masks can be found at the end of Unit 4.

Sex

The Sex field can only have the values M and F. We can use the Validation Rule box in the Field Properties only to allow M or F.

1 Click on the **Sex** Field Name.

2 In the **Validation Rule** box enter **M or F**.

3 In the **Validation Text** box enter **Sex must be either M or F**. This is the error message that will appear if the user tries to enter anything other than M or F into this field.

4 Save your table as **tblStudent**.

The field properties will appear as shown in Figure 1.3.23.

Figure 1.3.23 ▶

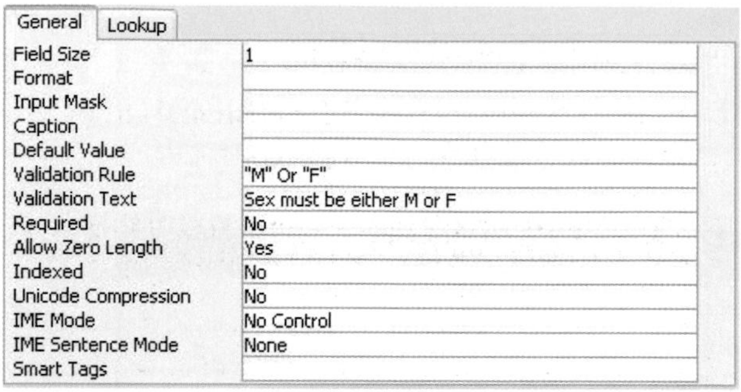

General	Lookup
Field Size	1
Format	
Input Mask	
Caption	
Default Value	
Validation Rule	"M" Or "F"
Validation Text	Sex must be either M or F
Required	No
Allow Zero Length	Yes
Indexed	No
Unicode Compression	No
IME Mode	No Control
IME Sentence Mode	None
Smart Tags	

It is of course equally possible to have used the Lookup Wizard for this field property and limit the choices to M or F.

Note More information on Validation Rules can be found at the end of Unit 4.

PassedTheoryTest and PassedPracticalTest fields.

All the above fields have already been set to **Yes/No** Field types and no further field properties are required.

Unit 4: Entering the data

In this unit we are going to enter the data into the table tblStudent and set up the remaining tables needed to complete the system.

There are two modes for working with tables, so far we have worked in **Design View**.

Design View is used to set up new tables, to edit the structure and to define validation checks and input masks.

To enter new data you have to switch to **Datasheet View**.

Entering data into the Student table

In the **Database Window** select **tblStudent** and click **Open** on the toolbar to open the table in **Datasheet View** as shown in Figure 1.4.1.

Figure 1.4.1 ▼

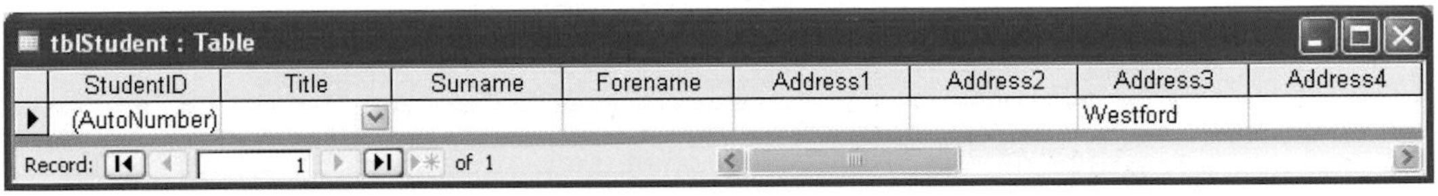

You can switch between modes by selecting **View, Design View** from the menu.

Enter details of the first student, Robert Brammer, as given below. Use TAB or ENTER to move between fields.

StudentID	Title	Surname	Forename	Address1	Address2	Address3	Address4	TelNo
1	Mr	Brammer	Robert	10 Plymouth Drive	Crickham	Westford	WE28 9LO	01993 885304

DateOfBirth	Sex	TheoryTestDate	PassedTheoryTest	PracticalTestDate	PassedPracticalTest
12/05/1991	M	17/07/2008	Yes	17/08/2008	Yes

You will notice a number of features as you enter the data.

- The StudentID which is an AutoNumber field is entered automatically.
- The Title field has a drop-down box set up by the lookup table wizard (see Figure 1.4.2).

Figure 1.4.2 ▼

- Data entered into the Sex field is] validated and any invalid entries rejected (see Figure 1.4.3).

Figure 1.4.3 ▶

	Address2	Address3	Address4	TelNo	DateOfBirth	Sex	TheoryTestDate
	Crickham	Westford	WE28 9LO	U1993 885304	12/05/1991	B	17/07/2008
		Westford					

tblStudent : Table

Microsoft Office Access

⚠ Sex must be either M or F

OK   Help

Record: I◀ ◀ [1] ▶ ▶I ▶* of 1

- Placeholders appear in the fields where you have set input masks to make data entry easier.
- Enter data into Yes/No fields by ticking the check box for Yes and leaving unchecked for No (see Figure 1.4.4).

Figure 1.4.4 ▼

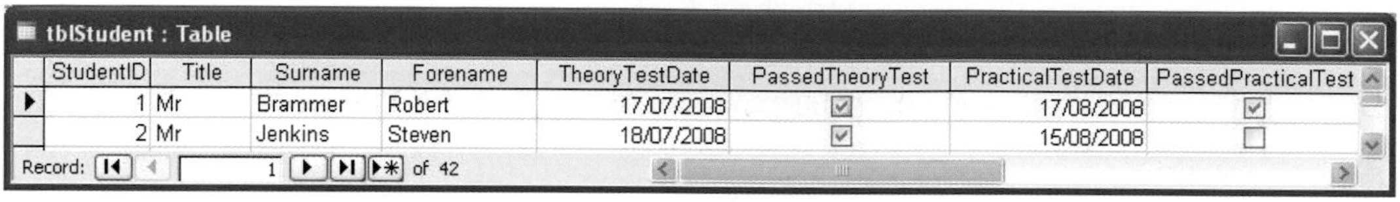

tblStudent : Table

	StudentID	Title	Surname	Forename	TheoryTestDate	PassedTheoryTest	PracticalTestDate	PassedPracticalTest
▶	1	Mr	Brammer	Robert	17/07/2008	☑	17/08/2008	☑
	2	Mr	Jenkins	Steven	18/07/2008	☑	15/08/2008	☐

Record: I◀ ◀ [1] ▶ ▶I ▶* of 42

- When you have entered the last field in a record, a blank record appears underneath to enter the next record. Don't worry if your table finishes with a blank record. Microsoft Access will ignore it.
- When a new record is created, the Address3 field is set to Westford. This can still be edited.
- Data is saved as soon as it is entered. Adjust the column widths by dragging out the column dividers.
- Navigation buttons appear at the bottom of the screen allowing you to scroll through the records (see Figure 1.4.5).

Figure 1.4.5 ▼

Record: I◀ ◀ [1] ▶ ▶I ▶* of 41   T

Complete the table tblStudent by entering the following data.

StudentID	Title	Surname	Forename	Address1	Address2	Address3	Address4	TelNo
2	Mr	Jenkins	Steven	37 Woodfield Close	Pilton	Westford	WE49 5PQ	01993 539264
3	Miss	Fowler	Sarah	19 Sea View Road	Theale	Westford	WE34 8NT	01993 293751

DateOfBirth	Sex	TheoryTestDate	PassedTheoryTest	PracticalTestDate	PassedPracticalTest
14/05/1991	M	18/07/2008	Yes	15/08/2008	No
05/06/1990	F	11/07/2008	Yes	14/08/2008	No

When you have finished entering the data, close the table by clicking on the Close icon (see Figure 1.4.6). You will return to the Database Window with the name of the table highlighted.

Figure 1.4.6 ▶

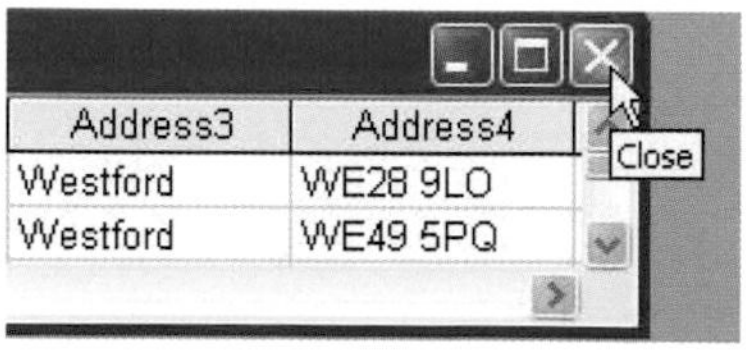

Address3	Address4
Westford	WE28 9LO
Westford	WE49 5PQ

Close

Useful keys for entering data

Key	Action
TAB key, ENTER or right arrow	Move to next field
SHIFT + TAB key or left arrow	Move to previous field
Down arrow	Move to next record
Up arrow	Move to previous record
HOME	Move to start of field
END	Move to end of field

Undo

Press ESC to quit editing a record.

Use the **Undo** icon to undo the last action.

Deleting records

To delete a record, click on the record selector and press delete.

Setting up the Instructor table

You now need to set up a second table called **tblInstructor** to store the details of the instructors. Set it up with the following structure:

Field name	Data type	Other information
InstructorID	AutoNumber	Set as Primary Key field
Title	Text	Lookup table values: Mr, Mrs, Ms, Miss Field Size 6
Surname	Text	Field Size 20
Forename	Text	Field Size 20
Address1	Text	Field Size 30
Address2	Text	Field Size 30
Address3	Text	Default Value = "Westford" Field Size 20
Address4	Text	Field Size 10 and set Format to >
HomeTelNo	Text	Field Size 15
MobileNo	Text	Field Size 15

Save the table as **tblInstructor** and switch to **Datasheet View** mode to enter this data.

InstructorID	Title	Surname	Forename	Address1	Address2	Address3	Address4	HomeTelNo	MobileNo
1	Mr	Jones	Derek	45 Grange Road	Pilton	Westford	WE49 5FG	01993 212541	07720 521478
2	Mr	Batchelor	Andrew	13 Abbey Close	Pilton	Westford	WE49 5FH	01993 255247	07980 352145
3	Mr	Smith	Tony	5 Sunhill Road	Blakeway	Westford	WE44 4ED	01993 252452	07980 525214

Setting up the Lesson Type table

The third table will be the table **tblLessonType**, storing details of the lessons and the cost of each lesson. This is the structure:

Field name	Data type	Other information
LessonType	Text	Set as Primary Key field. Field Size 25
Cost	Currency	

Save the table as **tblLessonType** and enter this data.

Lesson Type	Cost
Introductory	£16.00
Pass Plus	£17.00
Standard	£24.00
Test	£22.00

Setting up the Lesson table

The fourth table will be the **Lesson** table. This is the table that links all the other tables together and stores details of lessons booked with the Driving School. It has the following structure:

Field name	Data type	Other information
LessonNo	AutoNumber	Set as Primary Key field
StudentID	Number	Long Integer
InstructorID	Number	Long Integer
Date	Date/Time	Format: Short Date and set Input Mask
StartTime	Date/Time	Format: Short Time and set Input Mask
LengthOfLesson	Number	Integer and set validation rule as: Between 1 and 8. Text - Please enter a number between 1 and 8. Set the Default Value = 1
CollectionPoint	Text	Default value = "Home Address" Field Size 30
DropOffPoint	Text	Default value = "Home Address" Field Size 30
LessonType	Text	Lookup table values (see below): Introductory, Standard, Pass Plus, Test Field Size 25

Hint When you run the Lookup Wizard choose to type the values in but you could look up the values from the table Lesson Type. For help on Validation see later in this unit.

Save the table as **tblLesson** and enter this data:

LessonNo	StudentID	InstructorID	Date	StartTime	LengthOfLesson	CollectionPoint	DropOffPoint	LessonType
1	1	1	28/07/2008	09:00	1	Home Address	Home Address	Standard
2	2	1	28/07/2008	11:00	2	Home Address	Home Address	Standard
3	3	1	28/07/2008	14:00	1	Home Address	Home Address	Standard

We do not need to store the name of the student or the name of the instructor in the Lesson table. These are already stored elsewhere. The next unit shows you how to link these tables together.

Note You can move straight to Unit 5 and return to this unit if you need further information about setting up tables.

Further information on setting up tables

This section provides a little more detail on a number of the functions you met during setting up the Student table. In particular:

■ Data Types
■ Field Properties
■ Input Masks
■ Format field properties
■ Default field properties
■ Validation Rules

Data types

Access has different data types available to store different kinds of data. They are as follows:

Data type	Meaning
Text	This is the default setting. Used for shorter text entries. Can be a combination of text, numbers, spaces and symbols. Maximum length 255 characters but you can set it to less using the Field Size property.
Memo	Used for longer text entries. Maximum length 65,535 characters!
Number	Used to store numeric data.
Date/Time	This stores a date or a time or a date and the time. There are several formats for a date/time field.
Currency	Monetary values. Normally in the UK this will be set to pounds and work to 2 decimal places.
AutoNumber	An AutoNumber field will number records automatically as you enter more data. The field acts as a counter. Duplicates are avoided and so AutoNumber fields are ideal as the key field. An AutoNumber cannot be edited and when an AutoNumber record is deleted Access does not allow you to go back and reuse this number.
Yes/No	Only allows logical values such as Yes/No, True/False
OLE Object	An object linked to or embedded in a Microsoft Access table. This might be an image or a sound or a file created in another package such as Microsoft Excel or Microsoft Word.
Hyperlink	A hyperlink address. This can be linked to: An object in your Access file e.g. another table Another locally stored file A Web page An email address.
Lookup Wizard	This data type creates a lookup table so that you can choose a value from a drop-down box

Field properties

The following table describes the range of field properties:

Property	Description
Field Size	This is used to fix the maximum length of a text field. The default value is 50 characters. The maximum length is 255.
Format	This fixes how data can be displayed, for example dates can be displayed in many different forms such as 13/01/01 or 13 Jan 01 or 13 January 2001.
Input Mask	This sets a pattern for the data to be entered into this field.
Caption	This is the field label in a form or report. You are not likely to need to use this property.
Default Value	This is the value entered into the field when the record is created. It is usually left blank but can be very powerful.
Validation Rule	This defines the data entry rules.
Validation Text	This is the error message if data is invalid.
Required	This indicates whether an entry must be made or not. If an entry is required, it is best not to set this property until the database is fully working.
Indexed	This allows data to be stored in the order of this field which speeds up searches.
Allow Zero Length	This is used with text fields to decide whether records in that field are allowed to contain zero length or empty text strings.
Unicode Compression	This is a method of compressing the data entered in this field.
IME Mode	Input Method Editor, allows special character input.
IME Sentence Mode	Allows special character input.
Smart Tags	Access 2003 option. See Help.

Setting input masks

Input masks make data entry easier. They display on screen a pattern for the data to be entered into a field.

For example you maybe given the prompt _ _ / _ _ / _ _ to enter the date.

They are suitable for data that always has the same pattern such as dates, times, currency and also for codes like National Insurance numbers, stock numbers or postcodes.

Characters for input masks you are likely to use are as follows:

0	A number (0–9) must be entered
9	A number (0–9) may be entered
#	A number, + or – sign or space may be entered
L	A letter A–Z must be entered
?	A letter A–Z may be entered
A	A letter or digit must be entered
a	A letter or digit may be entered
&	Any character or space must be entered
C	Any character or space may be entered
<	All characters to the right are changed to lower case
>	All characters to the right are changed to upper case

Examples of input masks

A **National Insurance number** in the UK must be in the form **AB123456C**. All letters are in capitals.
Its input mask would be >**LL000000L**. (It must be 2 letters followed by 6 numbers and 1 letter.)

A **postcode** consists of one or two letters, then one or two numbers, then a space, a number and two letters. All the letters must be capital letters. Examples are **B1 1BB** or **DE13 0LL**.
The input mask would be >**L?09 0LL**.

Car registration numbers such as FW57 STZ could have >**LL00 LLL** as an input mask.

A **driving licence number** in the form BESWO150282 MB9BM could have >**LLLLL#000000#LL0LL** as an input mask.

Product Codes of the format A2C-123-4567 A possible input mask might be **AAA-000-0000**.

Input masks are very powerful and need a lot of thought. It is possible to use the Input Mask Wizard to set up an input mask for a field. At this stage you may wish to ignore input masks unless you know the exact format of the input data.

The Format field property

The formats supplied with Access will suit practically all your needs. However, it is possible to set a custom format of your own. Two commonly used examples follow:

> will change text entered in the field to upper case
< will change text entered in the field to lower case

Note There is a significant difference between the Format and Input Mask field property. The Format property affects the data in the field after it is entered, e.g. if you enter 14/0//99 into a Long Date format field, it will appear as 14th July 1999. The Input Mask property controls and restricts data entry. An Input Mask set to _ _ / _ _ / _ _ will only accept dates in the format 14/07/99.

The Default field property

Default values are added automatically when you add a new record. For example in a table of names and addresses you might set the County field to Derbyshire. Derbyshire then appears automatically each time a new record is added and the user can either leave it or change it to something else.

You can also use expressions in this field property. Typically =**Date()** will return the current date from your PC.

In a Library Book Loaning system, the default value for the **Date of Loan** field could be set to =**Date()** and similarly for the **Date of Return**, the default value could be set to =**Date()+14** (assuming a 14 day loan period).

Setting validation rules

Validation rules allow you to control the values that can be entered into a field.

By setting the validation text property you can choose the message that is displayed if the validation rule is broken.

You set up a validation rule by typing an expression into the field properties (see Figure 1.4.7).

Figure 1.4.7 ▶

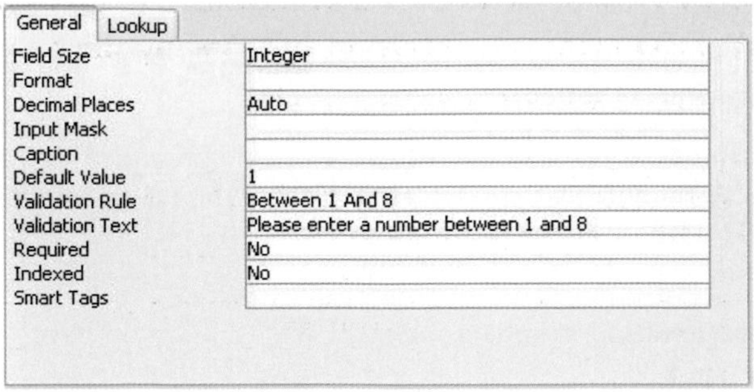

In the example above the user will be forced to only enter numbers between (and including) 1 and 8.

If they do not the Validation Text message is displayed as shown in Figure 1.4.8.

Figure 1.4.8 ▶

A number of comparison operators are available in Access:

Operator	Meaning
<	Less than
<=	Less than or equal to
>	Greater than
>=	Greater than or equal to
=	Equal to
<>	Not equal to
IN	Test for 'equal to' any item in a list
BETWEEN	Test for a range of values; the two values separated by the AND operator
LIKE	Tests a Text or Memo field to match a pattern string of characters

Examples of Validation Rule Settings	Possible Validation Text
>8000	Please enter a salary greater than £8000
<#01/01/01#	You must enter dates before January 1st 2001
>Date()	The date returned must be after today's date!
"S" or "M" or "L"	Sizes can only be S, M or L
Between 0 and 36	Goals scored cannot be greater than 36!
Like "A????"	Code must be 5 characters beginning with A
<20	Age of student must be less than 20
IN("A","B","C")	Grades must be A, B or C

Unit 5: Defining the relationships

In this unit we will define and create the relationships linking the four tables.

The links that need setting up are shown in Figure 1.5.1.

Figure 1.5.1 ▶

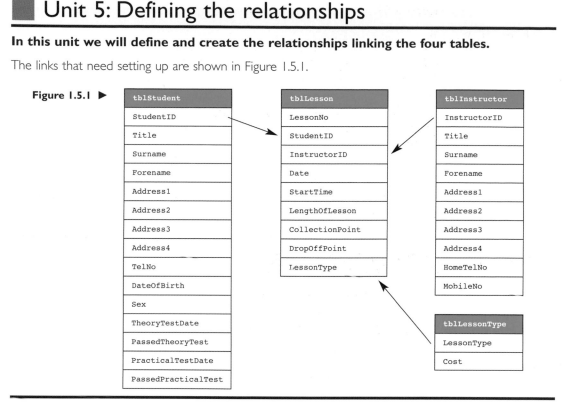

Adding the tables

1 In the Database Window open the **Relationships** window by any of these three methods:

- Right click anywhere in the window and select **Relationships**.
- Click on the **Relationships** icon on the **Database** toolbar if showing (see Figure 1.5.2).
- Click on **Tools**, **Relationships** from the menu bar.

Figure 1.5.2 ▼

If it is the first time you've established a relationship then the Show Table dialogue box will appear (see Figure 1.5.3).

Figure 1.5.3 ▶

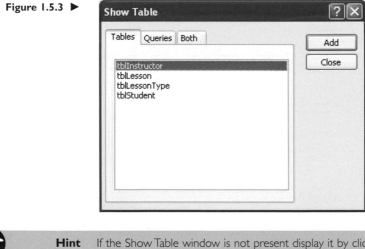

Hint If the Show Table window is not present display it by clicking on **Relationships**, **Show Table** from the menu or click on the **Show Table** icon.

2 Click on **tblInstructor** and click on **Add**.
3 Add the other three tables and then **Close** the window.
4 In the **Relationships** window rearrange the position of the tables by dragging and resizing the table windows (see Figure 1.5.4).

Figure 1.5.4 ▶

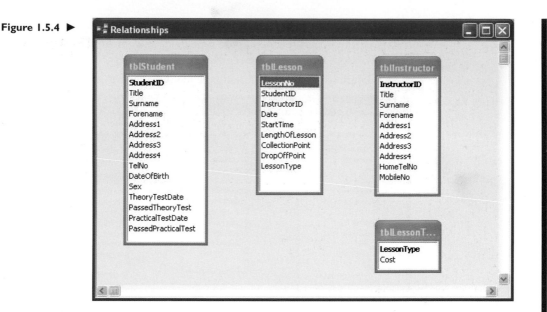

Setting the links

1 Click on **InstructorID** in **tblInstructor**.

2 Drag it on top of **InstructorID** in **tblLesson** and let go. The **Edit Relationships** dialogue box appears (see Figure 1.5.5).

Figure 1.5.5 ▶

3 Check the **Enforce Referential Integrity** box but DO NOT check the **Cascade Delete Related Records** box. Click on **Create**.

A link called the **Relationship Line** is set up between the two tables.

Note If you had checked **Cascade Delete Related Records** and you chose to delete an Instructor from **tblInstructor** then all the lessons for that instructor would be deleted from the Lesson table. We will revisit this in later units and explain why this might not be an option just yet in the development of this solution.

4 Click on the **StudentID** field in **tblStudent** and drag it on top of the **StudentID** field in **tblLesson**.

5 Check the **Enforce Referential Integrity** box and click on **Create**.

Repeat the process for the **LessonType** field, dragging it from **tblLessonType** to **tblLesson** and check **Enforce Referential Integrity**.

The Relationship window should now look like Figure 1.5.6.

Figure 1.5.6 ▶

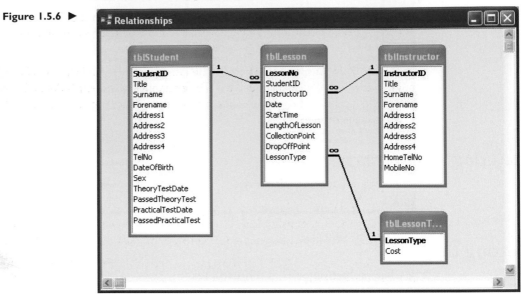

The number 1 and the infinity symbol mean that all three relationships are one-to-many. A **StudentID** can appear only *one* time in **tblStudent** as it is a unique ID. However a **StudentID** can appear *many* times in **tblLesson** as the student will need many lessons.

Similarly the **InstructorID** can only appear once in **tblInstructor** but many times in **tblLesson**. The **LessonType** can appear only once in **tblLessonType** but many times in **tblLesson**.

6 Save your layout by clicking **File**, **Save** from the menu and confirming the option as shown in Figure 1.5.7.

Figure 1.5.7 ▶

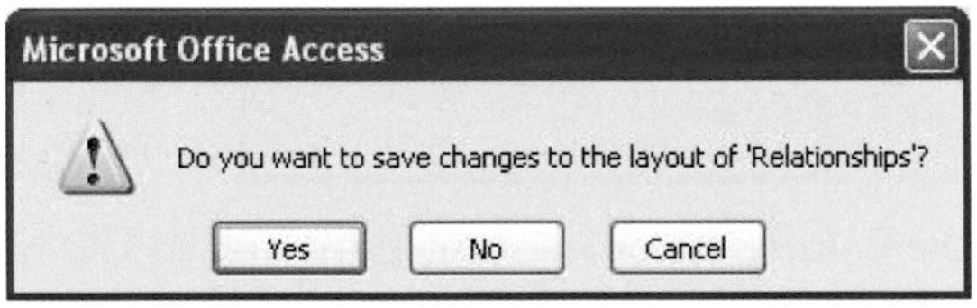

Microsoft Office Access ☒

⚠ Do you want to save changes to the layout of 'Relationships'?

[Yes] [No] [Cancel]

Note As a rule the field you use to create a relationship must be of the same type. However, when you create a relationship between tables using an AutoNumber field, the related field must be Numeric and set to Long Integer.

Referential integrity

Referential integrity is a system of rules that Microsoft Access uses to ensure that relationships between records in related tables are valid and that you don't accidentally delete or change related data.

For example with Referential Integrity set you would not be able to book a lesson for a Student ID 46 as no student with ID number 46 appears in the

Student table. Similarly you could not book a lesson for an Instructor who was not present in the Instructor table.

Cascading updates and deletes

Cascading updates and deletes affect what Access does with the data when you update or delete a record in a table that is related to other records in other tables.

If cascade delete is set, then when you delete a record in the Primary table all related data in other tables is deleted. For example if a student is deleted from the Student table then all related records for that student in the Lesson table would also be deleted.

Deleting relationships

If you wish to delete a relationship:

1 Open the Relationship window as before.
2 Click on the Relationship Line of the relationship you wish to delete and press the delete key. Alternatively you can right click on it and choose delete.

If you wish to delete a field that contains a relationship, you will have to delete the relationship first.

Editing relationships

You can edit relationships by going to the Relationship window and double clicking on the Relationship Line of the relationship you wish to edit.

Tricks and Tips numbers 1 and 5 may help you with some of the problems found when setting up tables and relationships. **Tricks and Tips** numbers 8 and 9 show you how to import data from an Excel file.

Note The Advanced Database Projects in Access CD-ROM has a file named **DrivingSchoolData**. It is the working solution produced at Unit 5 in this book. It contains records of over 100 lessons over the period of a fortnight in July 2008. Students are advised to use this file to start Unit 6. If you are working in a college it would be advisable to make the file available across the college network.

Unit 6: Select queries

In the previous units you set up tables to store information about the students, instructors and lesson bookings in the Pass IT Driving School.

In this unit you will use queries to search and sort the data in your tables according to certain criteria. Queries provide an easy way of asking questions of your database and producing useful information.

For example we might want to:
- find details of lessons booked on a given date
- find contact details for students who have not passed the theory test
- view details of instructors' names and addresses.

There are a number of different types of query available in Access:
- Select Query
- Parameter Query
- Multi-Table Query
- Action Query
- Crosstab Query

We will start by taking you through basic select and parameter queries, progressing to a query involving more than one table. You will meet the other query types as you work through the units.

As with many other parts of Microsoft Access, there is a wizard to help you design simple queries. We shall first look at setting up a query without the wizard.

Query 1   Finding details of lessons booked on a given day

There are usually five steps involved in planning a query:
- choosing which tables to use
- choosing the fields needed in your query
- setting the criteria to produce the output required
- running the query
- saving and/or printing the results

1 Load the **DrivingSchool** database.
2 In the Database Window click on **Queries** and select **New** (see Figure 1.6.1).

Figure 1.6.1 ▶

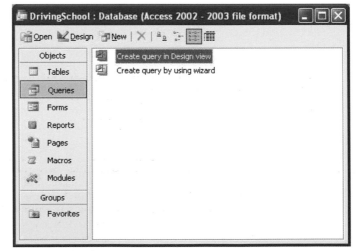

In the **New Query** window select **Design View** and click on **OK** (see Figure 1.6.2).

Figure 1.6.2 ▶

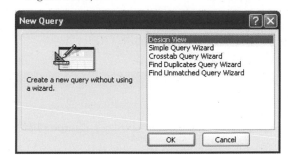

3 In the **Show Table** window select **tblLesson**, click on **Add** and then **Close** the window (see Figure 1.6.3).

Figure 1.6.3 ▶

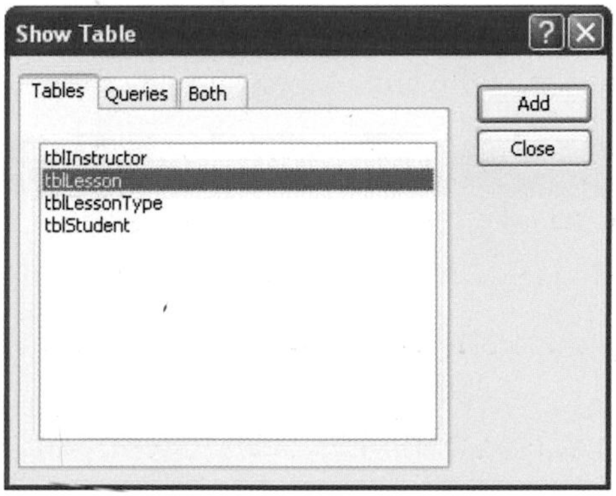

The **Query Design View** window is now shown.

The window is in two sections. The upper section contains the field list for the table used in the query and the lower section contains the QBE (Query by Example) grid where you design the query. Primarily it consists of five rows (see Figure 1.6.4).

Figure 1.6.4 ▼

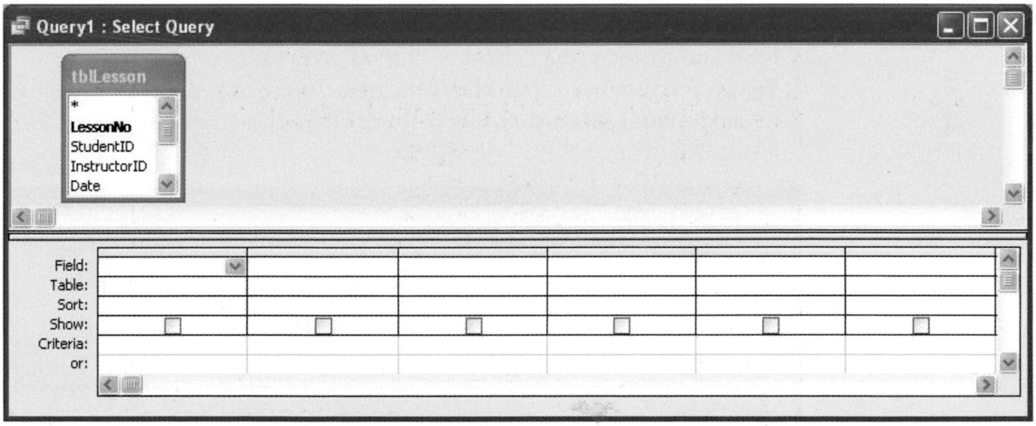

Field   Contains the names of the fields needed for your query.
Table   Holds the name of the table containing the selected field.
Sort   Offers ascending, descending sort options.
Show   Allows you to hide fields from the output.
Criteria This is where you enter the criteria for your search.

You can maximise the window and use the scroll bars in the usual way. You can resize the upper/lower panes by dragging the dividing line between them up or down.

4 If the Query Design toolbar is not showing, click on **View, Toolbars, Query Design** (see Figure 1.6.5).

Figure 1.6.5 ▼

The next stage is to select the fields needed in our query.

5 Double click on **LessonNo** in the table **tblLesson** field list. Then double click on each of the next five fields in turn: **StudentID, InstructorID, Date, StartTime, LengthOfLesson**. The fieldnames will appear in the grid as shown in Figure 1.6.6.

6 Now select the criteria by entering **31/07/08** in the criteria row of the fourth (Date) column of the QBE grid. Access surrounds the data with a #.

Figure 1.6.6 ▼

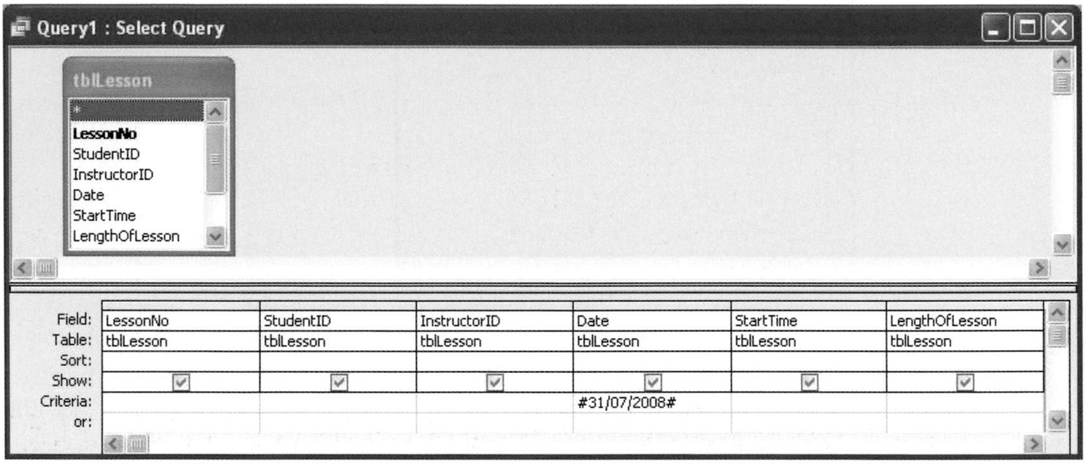

If you have added a field by mistake, click at the top of the column in the QBE grid to select the column and then press DELETE.

7 To run your query click on the **Datasheet View** icon, the **Run Query** icon or choose from the menu **Query, Run**. There should be ten lessons (see Figure 1.6.7).

Figure 1.6.7 ▶

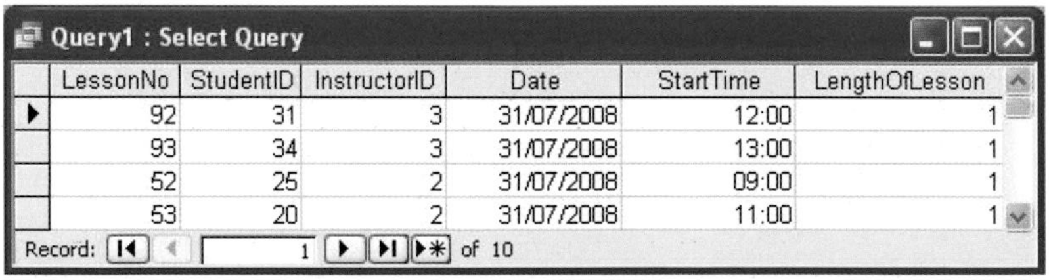

8 Once the query has been run it can be printed using **File, Print**.

9 Save the query as **qryLessonsOnDate** by clicking on the **Save** icon on the toolbar.

Selecting fields in Query Design View

There are a number of other ways of selecting a field from the Field List in the Query Design window. You need to select the one that suits you best.

- In each field cell on the grid is a drop-down list from which fields can be chosen.
- Double click on the title bar in the Field List table. This highlights all the field names. Click on any one (not the *) and drag them to the field cell on the grid. On releasing the mouse button all fields will be entered into the grid.
- Highlight the field in the Field List table and drag it to the field cell on the grid.

Query 2   Finding the contact details for students who have not passed the theory test

1 In the Database Window click on **Queries** and select **New**.
2 In the **New Query** window select **Design View** and click on **OK**.
3 In the **Show Table** window select **tblStudent**, click on **Add** and then **Close** the window.
   The next stage is to select the fields needed in our query. We will add them to the QBE grid by dragging and dropping each field.
4 Select **StudentID** in **tblStudent** and drag it to the field cell.
5 Drag and drop the fields **Forename**, **Surname**, **TelNo** and **PassedTheoryTest** in the same way. The fieldnames will appear in the grid as below (see Figure 1.6.8).
6 Now select the criteria by entering **No** in the criteria row of the **PassedTheoryTest** column. Searching Yes/No fields is just a case of entering Yes or No in the criteria cell.

Figure 1.6.8 ▼

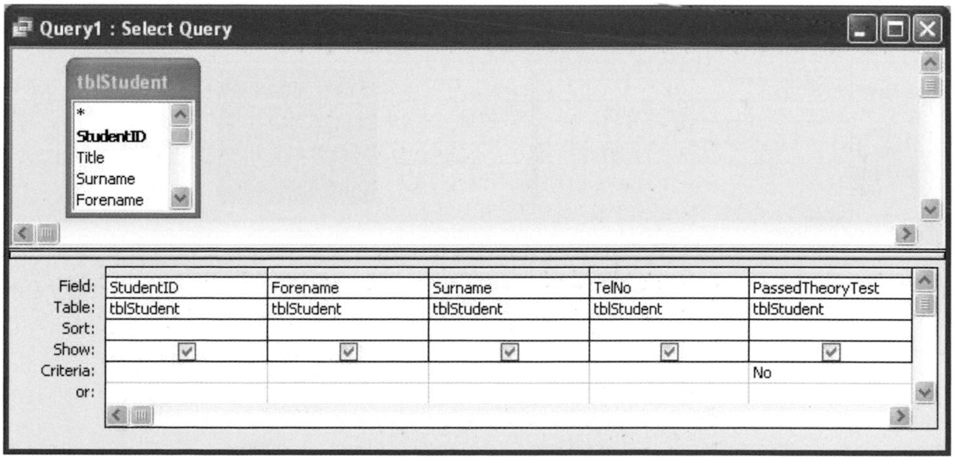

7 To run your query click on the **Datasheet View** icon, the **Run Query** icon or from the menu, select **Query, Run**. The details are shown below (see Figure 1.6.9). There are 7 records.

Figure 1.6.9 ▶

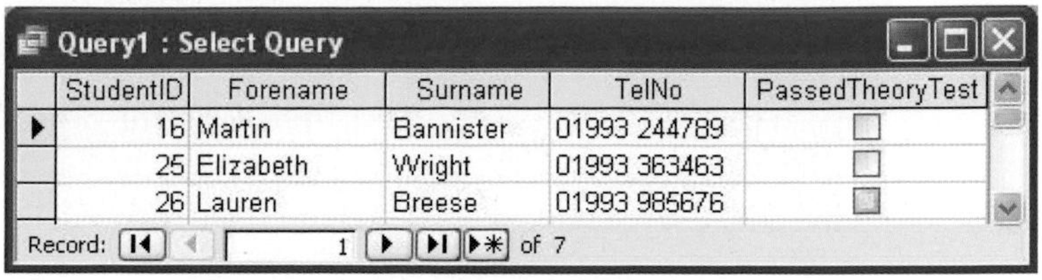

	StudentID	Forename	Surname	TelNo	PassedTheoryTest
▶	16	Martin	Bannister	01993 244789	☐
	25	Elizabeth	Wright	01993 363463	☐
	26	Lauren	Breese	01993 985676	☐

Query1 : Select Query

Record: |◀ ◀| 1 |▶ ▶| |▶*| of 7

8 Save your query as **qryNotPassTheory**.

Some further hints

Adding and removing tables

- To remove a table from the Query Design grid, double click the title bar of the field list box and press DELETE.
- To add a table to the Query Design grid click on the **Show Table** icon or select from the menu, **Query, Show Table** and add the tables required.
- To clear the QBE grid from the menu select **Edit, Clear Grid**.

Renaming the field headings

You can give a different name to the column titles in the query grid.

In the field row, click the start of the field name, type in the new name followed by a colon, e.g. **Telephone number: TelNo**.

Changing the order of the fields chosen

Click the field selector at the top of the column.

Drag the field to the new location (see Figure 1.6.10).

Figure 1.6.10 ▼

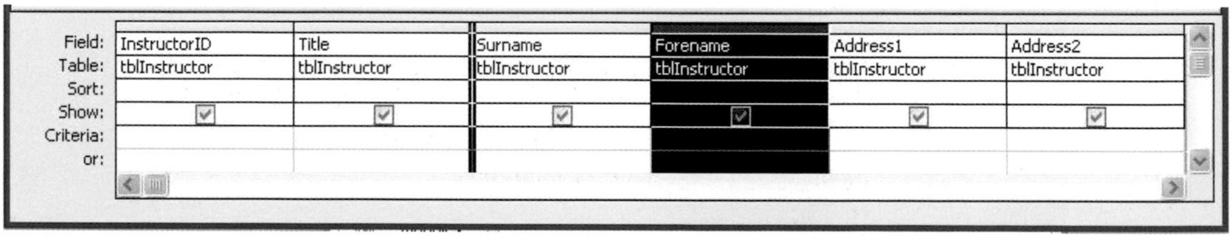

Field:	InstructorID	Title	Surname	Forename	Address1	Address2
Table:	tblInstructor	tblInstructor	tblInstructor	tblInstructor	tblInstructor	tblInstructor
Sort:						
Show:	☑	☑	☑	☑	☑	☑
Criteria:						
or:						

As you drag the field a solid bar appears showing where the relocated field will appear.

Deleting a query

Queries that are only used once are not really worth saving.

In the Database Window select the query to delete and press the DELETE key.

Query 3   Producing a list of instructors' names and addresses

We will use the Query Wizard to design the next query.

1 In the Database Window click on **Queries** and select **New**.
2 In the **New Query** window select **Simple Query Wizard** and click on **OK**. The Simple Query Wizard dialogue box is displayed.
3 Select **tblInstructor** from the Tables/Queries drop-down list.
4 Select the field **InstructorID** in the Available Fields and then click the right arrow >.
5 Repeat this process for the fields **Surname, Forename, Address1, Address2, Address3** and **Address4** as shown below (see Figure 1.6.11).

Figure 1.6.11 ▶

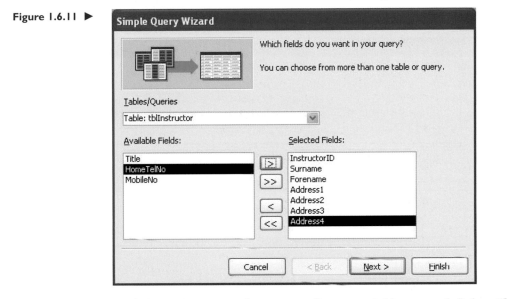

6 Click on **Next**, name the query **qryInstructorAddresses** and click on **Finish** (see Figure 1.6.12).

Figure 1.6.12 ▶

The resulting query opens in Datasheet View as shown in Figure 1.6.13, giving the details of the Instructors' names and addresses.

Figure 1.6.13 ▼

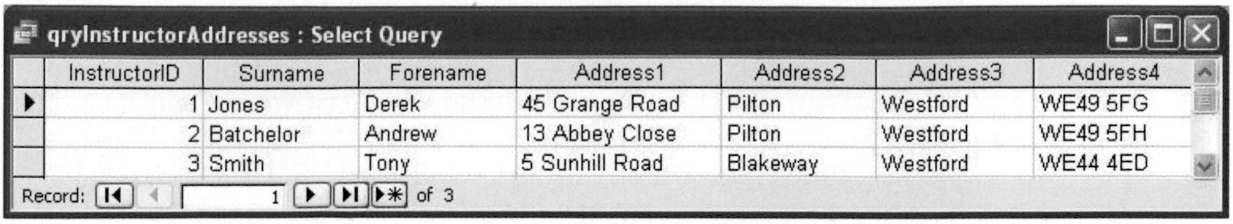

	InstructorID	Surname	Forename	Address1	Address2	Address3	Address4
▶	1	Jones	Derek	45 Grange Road	Pilton	Westford	WE49 5FG
	2	Batchelor	Andrew	13 Abbey Close	Pilton	Westford	WE49 5FH
	3	Smith	Tony	5 Sunhill Road	Blakeway	Westford	WE44 4ED

Record: ◄◄ ◄ 1 ► ►► ►* of 3

From the menu you can now select **View, Design View** to show the QBE grid (see Figure 1.6.14) and refine your query if needed. For example click on the drop-down list in the Sort cell of the Surname field to choose either ascending or descending sort order.

Figure 1.6.14 ▼

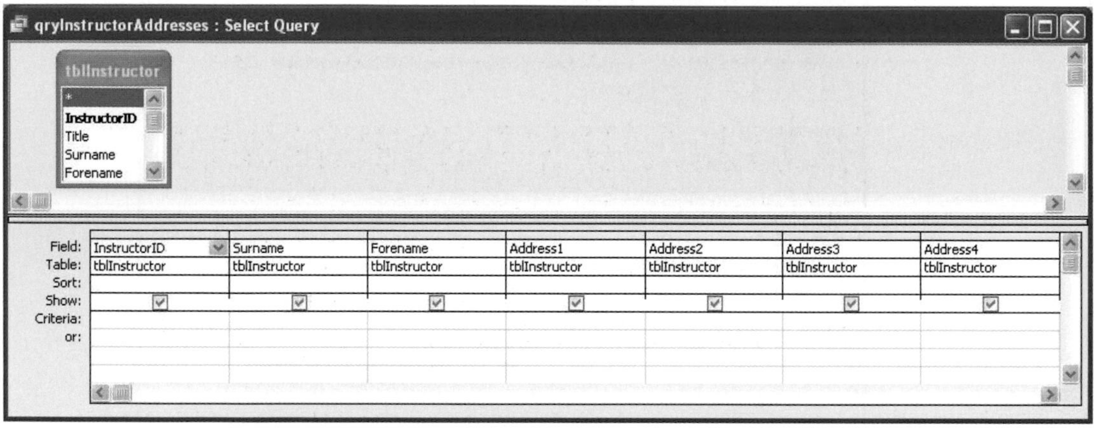

qryInstructorAddresses : Select Query

tblInstructor
*
InstructorID
Title
Surname
Forename

Field:	InstructorID	Surname	Forename	Address1	Address2	Address3	Address4
Table:	tblInstructor	tblInstructor	tblInstructor	tblInstructor	tblInstructor	tblInstructor	tblInstructor
Sort:							
Show:	☑	☑	☑	☑	☑	☑	☑
Criteria:							
or:							

Query 4   Finding lessons between dates

Suppose you wish to view lessons between certain dates or to print a list of lessons for the coming week.

You can select a range of records using the operators < , > , <= , >= , + , – , BETWEEN, AND, NOT.

1 In the Database Window click on **Queries** and select **New**.
2 In the **New Query** window select **Design View** and click on **OK**.
3 In the **Show Table** window select **tblLesson**, click on **Add** and then **Close** the window.
4 Add the fields **LessonNo, StudentID, InstructorID, Date** and **CollectionPoint**.
5 In the criteria row of the **Date** column enter **>30/07/08 and <02/08/08** as shown in Figure 1.6.15.

Figure 1.6.15 ▼

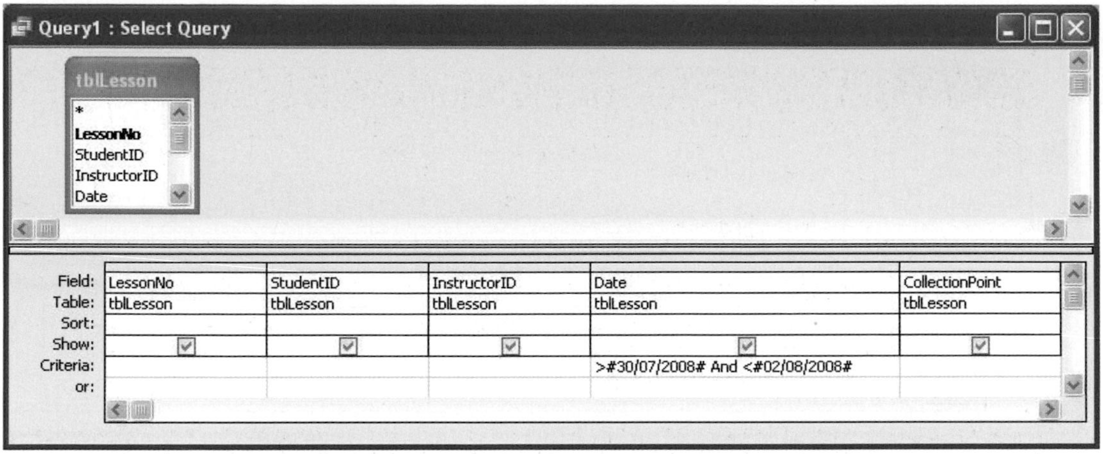

6 Run the query to view the records and then save the query as
qryBetweenDates (see Figure 1.6.16).

Figure 1.6.16 ►

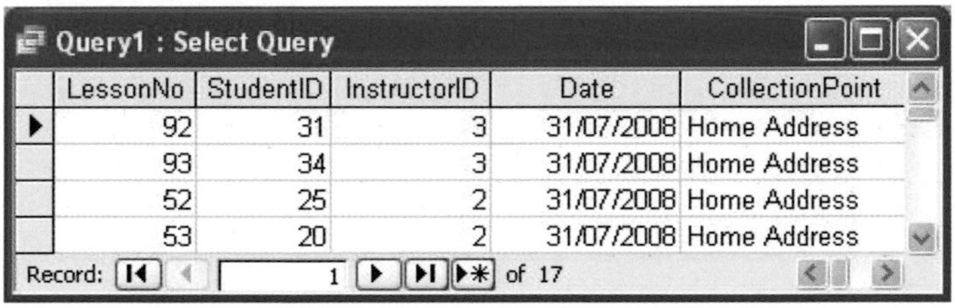

Note This query could also have been designed by entering the expression **Between 31/07/08 and
01/08/08** in the criteria row of the **Date** field cell. The expression includes the stated dates.

Query 5   Finding lessons for an instructor on a given date

It is possible to specify criteria in more than one field. For example you may
want to see details of a specific instructor's lessons on a certain date. This is
sometimes known as an AND search because it involves the InstructorID field
and the Date field.

1 In the Database Window click on **Queries** and select **New**.
2 In the **New Query** window select **Design View** and click on **OK**.
3 In the **Show Table** window select **tblLesson**, click on **Add** and then **Close**
the window.
4 Add the fields **StudentID**, **InstructorID**, **Date**, **StartTime**, **CollectionPoint**
and **LessonType** (see Figure 1.6.17).
5 In the criteria row of the **InstructorID** column enter **2** and enter 31/07/2008
in the criteria cell for **Date**.

Figure 1.6.17 ▼

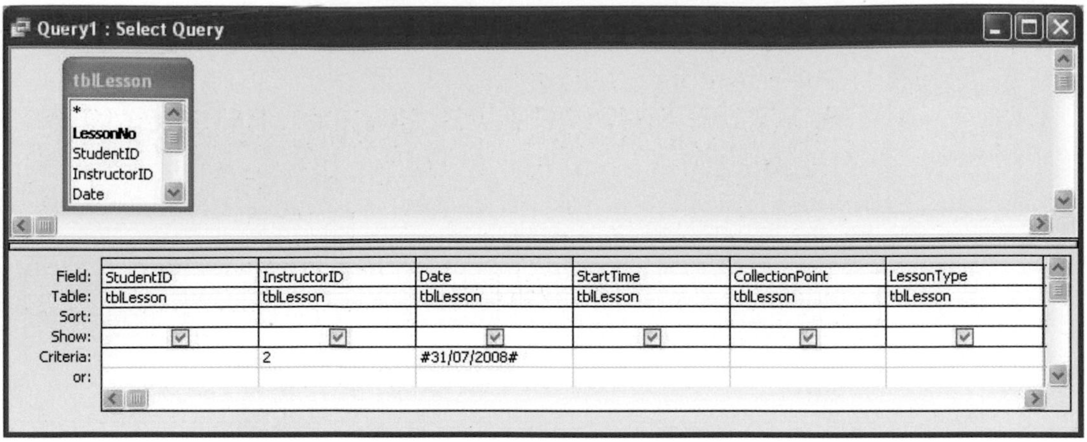

6 Run the query to view the records shown in Figure 1.6.18. Save your query as **qryInstructorAndDate**.

Figure 1.6.18 ▶

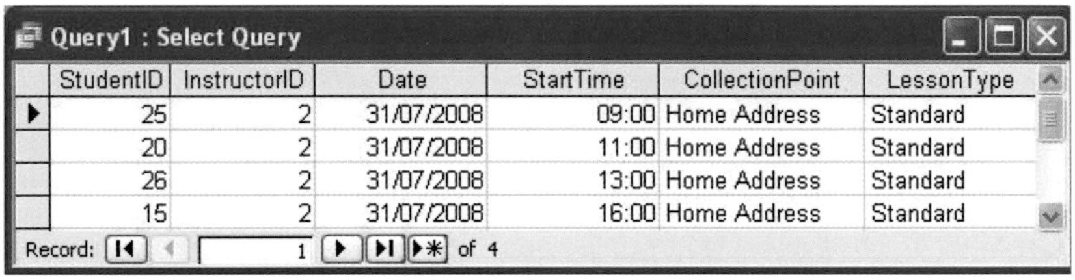

You may wish to look for records which meet one criterion OR another. For example you may wish to view lessons on one day or another. This is sometimes known as an OR search.

1 In the Database Window click on **Queries** and select **New**.
2 In the **New Query** window select **Design View** and click on **OK**.
3 In the **Show Table** window select **tblLesson**, click on **Add** and then **Close** the window.
4 Add the fields **StudentID, InstructorID, Date, StartTime, CollectionPoint** and **LessonType** as shown in Figure 1.6.19.

Figure 1.6.19 ▼

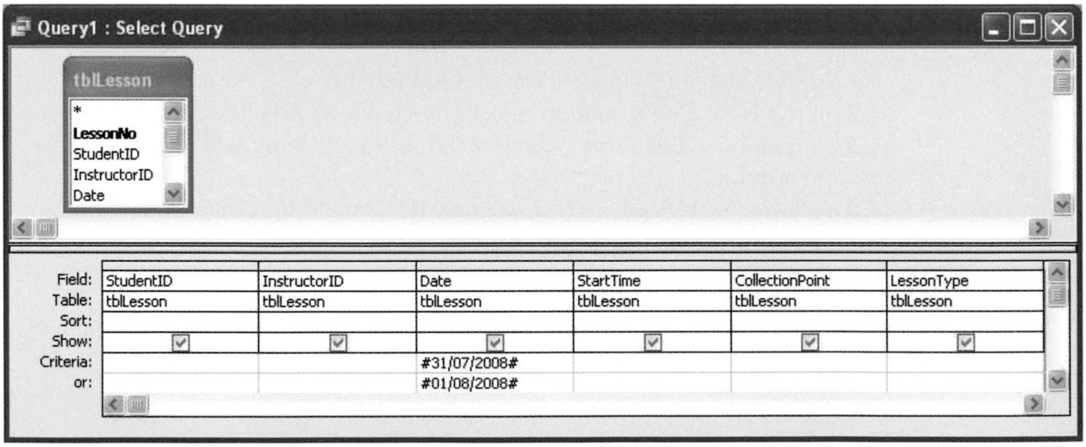

5 In the criteria row of the **Date** column enter **31/07/08** and enter **01/08/08** in the row below.

6 Run the query to view the records (there are 17) and then save as **qryOrDates** (see Figure 1.6.20).

Figure 1.6.20 ▶

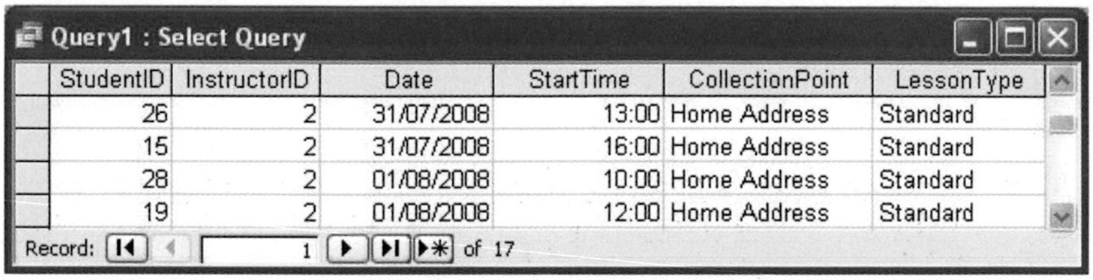

StudentID	InstructorID	Date	StartTime	CollectionPoint	LessonType
26	2	31/07/2008	13:00	Home Address	Standard
15	2	31/07/2008	16:00	Home Address	Standard
28	2	01/08/2008	10:00	Home Address	Standard
19	2	01/08/2008	12:00	Home Address	Standard

Query1 : Select Query
Record: 1 of 17

Note All the queries set up in Unit 6 were only for demonstration purposes. They are not needed as part of the Pass IT Driving School System. It is a good idea to go to the Database Window and **delete** them now.

Unit 7: Further queries

All the queries so far have been select queries. Select queries are not very useful if you have to run the query frequently and use different criteria each time.

In this unit you will be shown how to use the **Date()** function and will be introduced to **Parameter queries**.

Parameter queries overcome the problem by allowing you to enter the criteria each time the query is run.

On running the query a dialogue box will appear asking you to enter the details (see Figure 1.7.1).

Figure 1.7.1 ▶

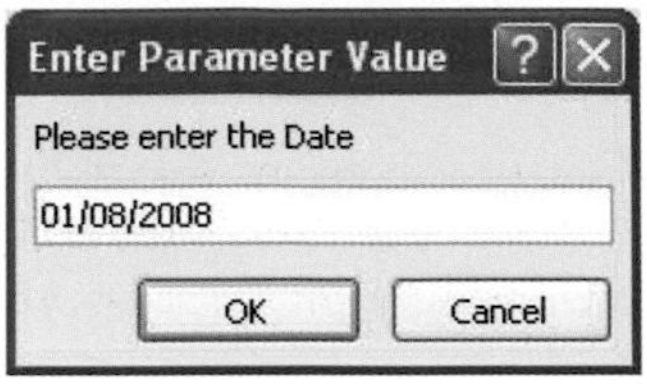

Enter Parameter Value [?][X]

Please enter the Date

01/08/2008

OK   Cancel

In the example shown you would enter the date and the records matching the criteria shown would be displayed.

Query 1   Looking up a student's details

1 Load the **DrivingSchool** database.
2 In the Database Window click on **Queries** and select **New**.
3 In the **New Query** window select **Design View** and click on **OK**.
4 In the **Show Table** window select **tblStudent**, click on **Add** and then **Close** the window.
5 Select **StudentID** in **tblStudent** and drag it on to the QBE grid.
6 Drag and drop the fields **Surname, Forename, Address1, Address2, Address3, Address4, TelNo, DateOfBirth** and **Sex** in the same way. The fieldnames will appear as in Figure 1.7.2.

Figure 1.7.2 ▼

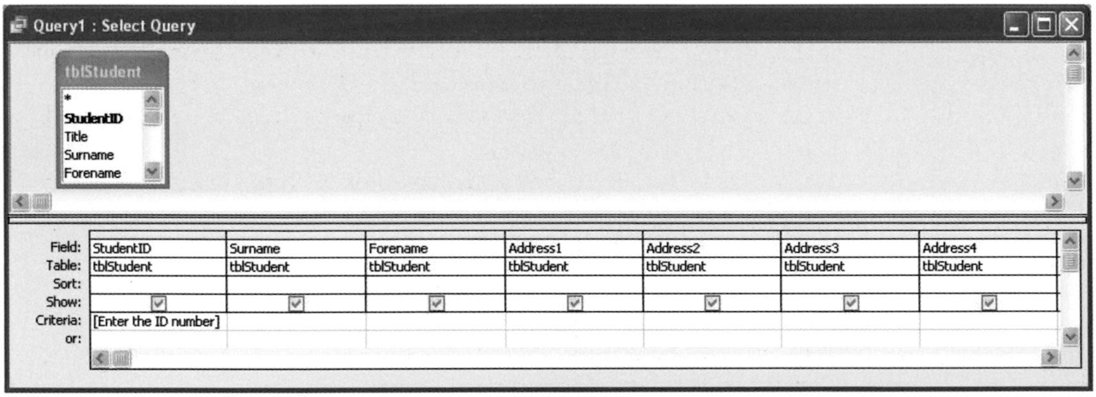

Field:	StudentID	Surname	Forename	Address1	Address2	Address3	Address4
Table:	tblStudent	tblStudent	tblStudent	tblStudent	tblStudent	tblStudent	tblStudent
Sort:							
Show:	✓	✓	✓	✓	✓	✓	✓
Criteria:	[Enter the ID number]						
or:							

7 In the criteria cell for the **StudentID** field type in [**Enter the ID number**] The square brackets are required.

8 Run the query and enter **2** in the dialogue box as shown in Figure 1.7.3.

Figure 1.7.3 ►

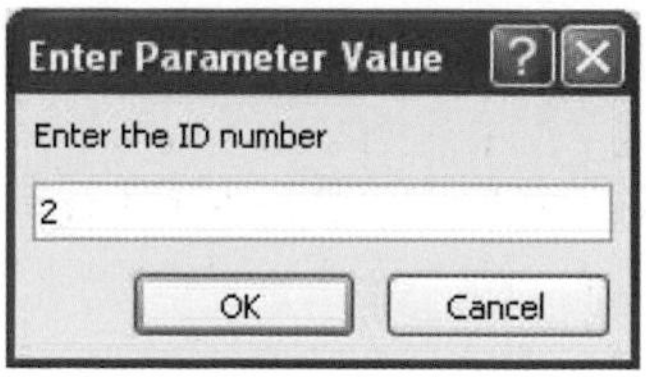

Enter Parameter Value ? X

Enter the ID number

2

OK   Cancel

9 The query will display the details of Student number 2. Save your query as **qrySearchStudentID**.

Query 2   Looking up a student's lessons

1 In the Database Window click on **Queries** and select **New**.
2 In the **New Query** window select **Design View** and click on **OK**.
3 In the **Show Table** window select **tblLesson**, click on **Add** and then **Close** the window.
4 Select **StudentID** in **tblLesson** and drag it on to the field cell (see Figure 1.7.4).

Figure 1.7.4 ►

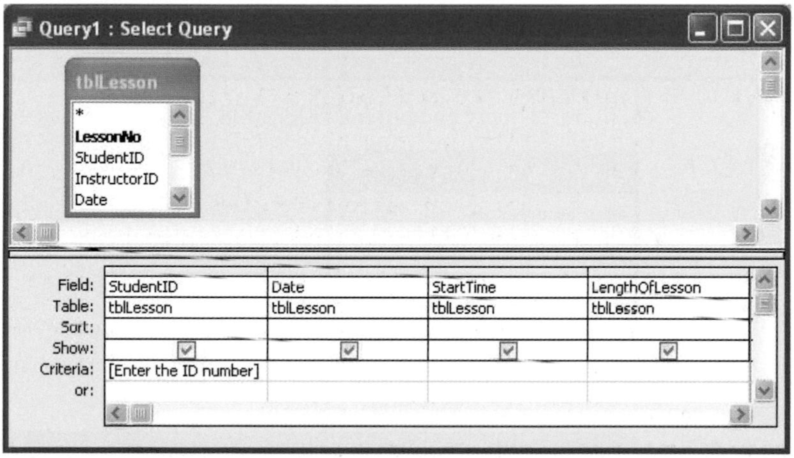

Query1 : Select Query   _ □ X

tblLesson

*
LessonNo
StudentID
InstructorID
Date

Field:	StudentID	Date	StartTime	LengthOfLesson
Table:	tblLesson	tblLesson	tblLesson	tblLesson
Sort:				
Show:	☑	☑	☑	☑
Criteria:	[Enter the ID number]			
or:				

5 Drag and drop the fields **Date**, **StartTime** and **LengthOfLesson** in the same way. The fieldnames will appear in the grid as in Figure 1.7.4.
6 In the criteria cell for the **StudentID** field type in **[Enter the ID number]**. The square brackets are required.
7 Run the query and enter **2** in the dialogue box as shown in Figure 1.7.5.

Figure 1.7.5 ►

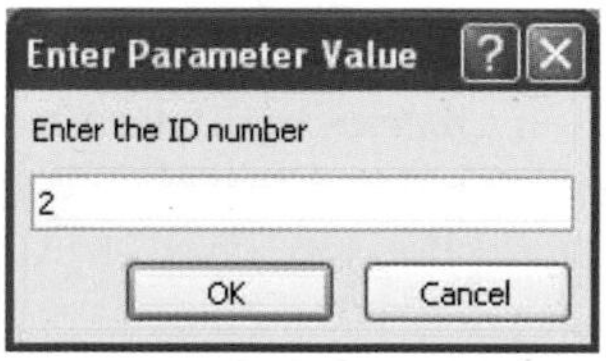

Enter Parameter Value ? X

Enter the ID number

2

OK   Cancel

The query will display the lessons for Student number 2. Save your query as **qryStudentLesson**.

Query 3   Searching for lessons on any date

1 In the Database Window click on **Queries** and select **New**.
2 In the **New Query** window select **Design View** and click on **OK**.
3 In the **Show Table** window select **tblLesson**, click on **Add** and then **Close** the window.
4 Add the fields to the QBE grid as shown in Figure 1.7.6.
5 In the criteria row of the **Date** column type in **[Please enter the Date]**. The square brackets here are vital.

Figure 1.7.6 ▼

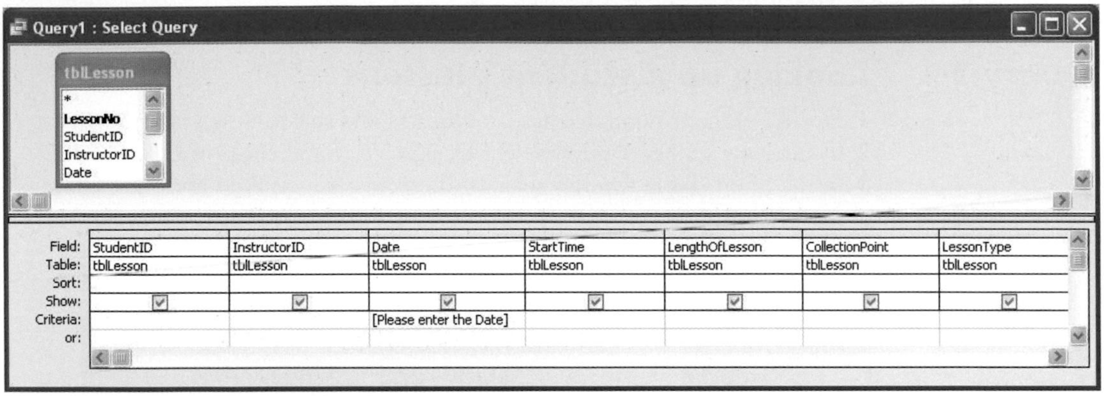

Field:	StudentID	InstructorID	Date	StartTime	LengthOfLesson	CollectionPoint	LessonType
Table:	tblLesson	tblLesson	tblLesson	tblLesson	tblLesson	tblLesson	tblLesson
Sort:							
Show:	☑	☑	☑	☑	☑	☑	☑
Criteria:			[Please enter the Date]				
or:							

6 Run the query and enter **01/08/2008** in the dialogue box (see Figure 1.7.7).

Figure 1.7.7 ►

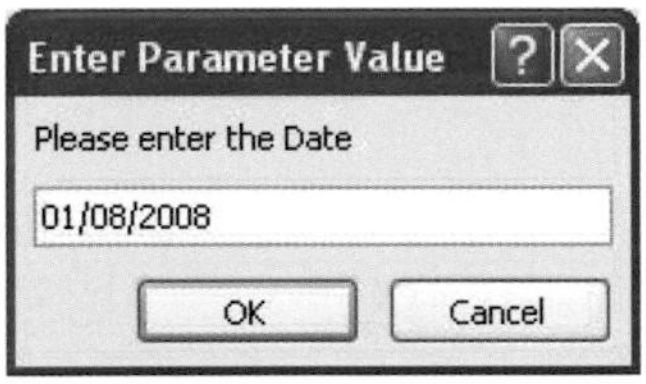

7 The result of the query is shown in Figure 1.7.8. Save your query as **qrySearchLessonDate**.

Figure 1.7.8 ►

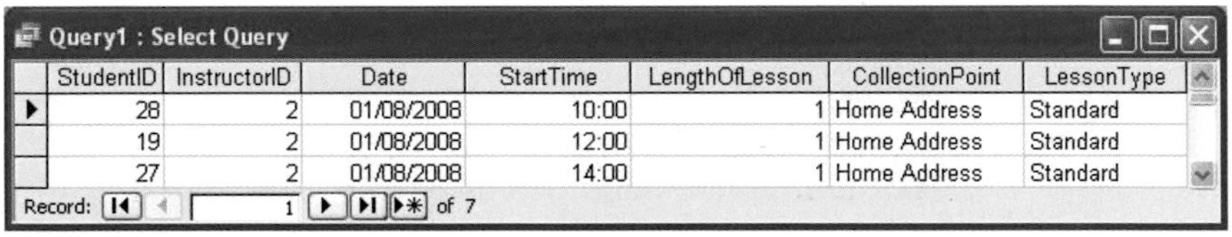

	StudentID	InstructorID	Date	StartTime	LengthOfLesson	CollectionPoint	LessonType
▶	28	2	01/08/2008	10:00	1	Home Address	Standard
	19	2	01/08/2008	12:00	1	Home Address	Standard
	27	2	01/08/2008	14:00	1	Home Address	Standard

Record: 1 of 7

Query 4   Searching for an instructor's lessons by date

1 In the Database Window click on **Queries** and select **New**.
2 In the **New Query** window select **Design View** and click on **OK**.
3 In the **Show Table** window select **tblLesson**, click on **Add** and then **Close** the window.

4 Add all the fields to the grid by double clicking the title bar of the **Field List** table and dragging the highlighted fields to the field cell (see Figure 1.7.9).

Figure 1.7.9 ▼

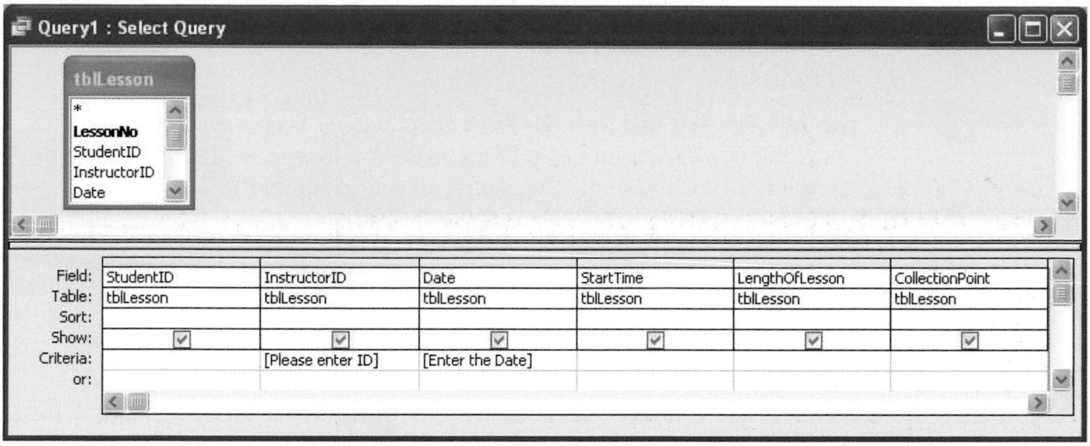

5 Remove fields **LessonNo**, **DropOffPoint** and **LessonType** by clicking the column selector and selecting from the menu **Edit, Delete Columns**.
6 In the criteria cell for the field **InstructorID** type in **[Please enter ID]**.
7 In the criteria cell for the field **Date** type in **[Enter the Date]**.
8 Run the query and enter **1** for the **InstructorID** (see Figure 1.7.10).

Figure 1.7.10 ▶

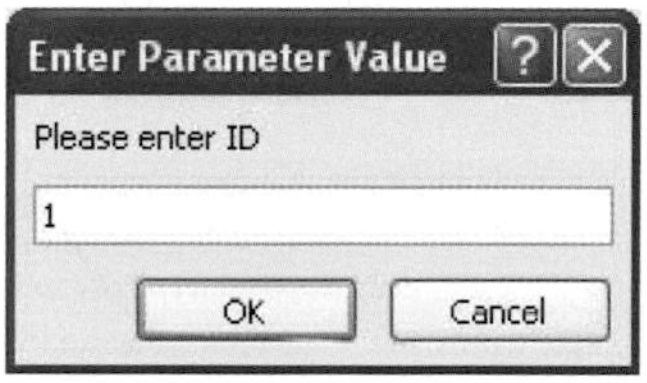

9 Enter **31/07/08** for the date (see Figure 1.7.11).

Figure 1.7.11 ▶

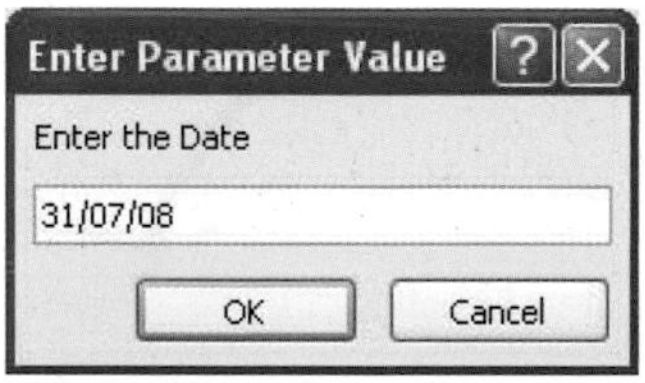

10 The result of the query is shown in Figure 1.7.12.

Figure 1.7.12 ▶

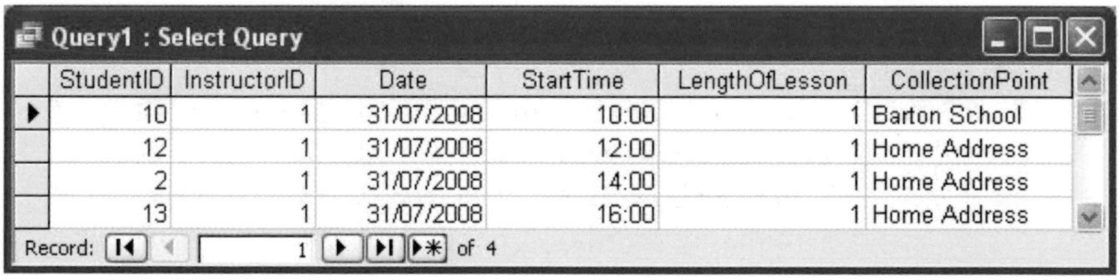

11 Save your query as **qryInstructorLessonsDate**.

Query 5 Finding today's lessons and using the Date() function

You will often want to search for records with the current date. For example you may want to view today's lessons at the driving school or issue weekly timetables to instructors.

The data files supplied with this book cover lessons from week beginning 28/07/08 to 01/08/08 and 04/08/08 to 08/08/08. To work with the data supplied you will need to change the time clock on your computer to 28/07/08.

If you do not have access rights to do this you will need to use Search and Replace to replace 28/07/08 with today's date as shown here. It might be advisable to make a copy of your database and work with the copy.

1 In the Database Window click on **tblLesson** and select **Open**. Place the cursor at the start of the Date column.
2 Select **Edit**, **Replace** from the menu. In the **Find and Replace** dialogue box, enter 28/07/2008 in **Find What** and today's date in **Replace With** for example 23/09/2009
3 Select **Date** from the **Look In** drop-down and **Whole Field** in the **Match** drop-down.
4 Click **Find Next** to find the date that needs replacing and **Replace** to carry out the change as shown below in Figure 1.7.13.
5 For the purposes of this query you only need to change the one date but all the dates can be updated by simply repeating this process.

Figure 1.7.13 ▼

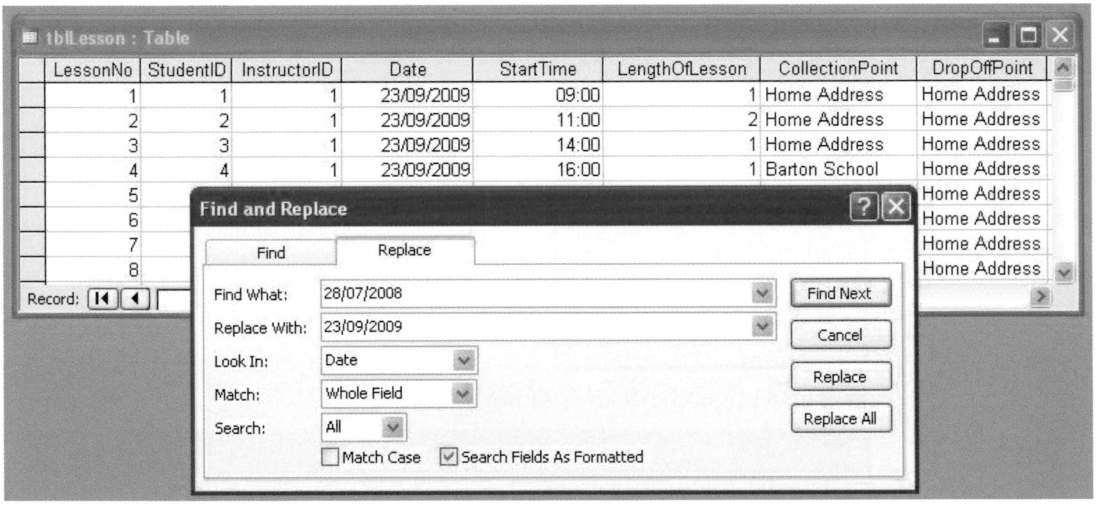

Setting up the query

1 In the Database Window click on **Queries** and select **New**.
2 In the **New Query** window select **Design View** and click on **OK**.
3 In the **Show Table** window select **tblLesson**, click on **Add** and then **Close** the window.
4 Add the fields **LessonNo**, **StudentID**, **InstructorID**, **Date** and **StartTime** as shown in Figure 1.7.14.
5 In the criteria row of the **Date** column enter **=Date()**.

Figure 1.7.14 ▼

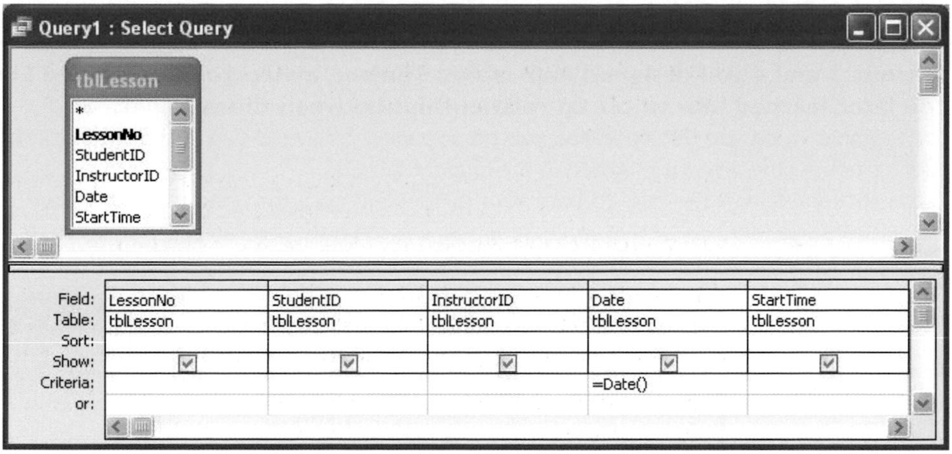

Query1 : Select Query

tblLesson
*
LessonNo
StudentID
InstructorID
Date
StartTime

Field:	LessonNo	StudentID	InstructorID	Date	StartTime
Table:	tblLesson	tblLesson	tblLesson	tblLesson	tblLesson
Sort:					
Show:	✓	✓	✓	✓	✓
Criteria:				=Date()	
or:					

6 Run the query to view the records and save it as **qryTodaysLessons**.

Hint Remember to use the Find and Replace option to restore your dates to their original state.

The date function is a powerful tool in query work and will form the basis of a number of queries later in the units.

Hint Use **Tricks and Tips** numbers 10 and 11 to explore queries further.

Unit 8: Setting up multi-table queries

In Units 3 and 4 you designed four tables: Student, Instructor, Lesson and Lesson Type. You later learned how to set up relationships between those tables.

For example when you book a lesson you do not want to have to key in the student's name and address every time when it is stored in the student table.

In this section you will see how to base your queries on more than one table and start to use the relationships you have set up. In addition you will see how you can use queries to do calculations.

Figure 1.8.1 ▶

	LessonNo	StudentID	InstructorID	Date	StartTime	LengthOfLesson
▶	92	31	3	31/07/2008	12:00	1
	93	34	3	31/07/2008	13:00	1
	52	25	2	31/07/2008	09:00	1
	53	20	2	31/07/2008	11:00	1

qryLessonsOnDate : Select Query

Record: 1 of 10

At the start of Unit 6 you set up a query called **qryLessonsOnDate** to output the lessons booked on a given date.

The output is shown in Figure 1.8.1 based on the table **tblLesson**. If we wanted the output to include the students' names we would have to base the query on the table **tblLesson** (which stores the details of the lessons, dates and ID numbers) and the **tblStudent** (where the students' names are stored).

Query 1

To produce a list of lessons together with student names

1 Load the **DrivingSchool** database.
2 In the Database Window click on **Queries** and select **New**.
3 In the **New Query** window select **Design View** and click on **OK** (see Figure 1.8.2).

Figure 1.8.2 ▶

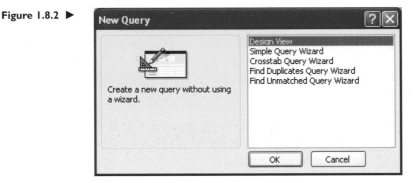

New Query

Design View
Simple Query Wizard
Crosstab Query Wizard
Find Duplicates Query Wizard
Find Unmatched Query Wizard

Create a new query without using a wizard.

OK   Cancel

4 In the **Show Table** window select **tblLesson** and click on **Add** (see Figure 1.8.3).

Figure 1.8.3 ▶

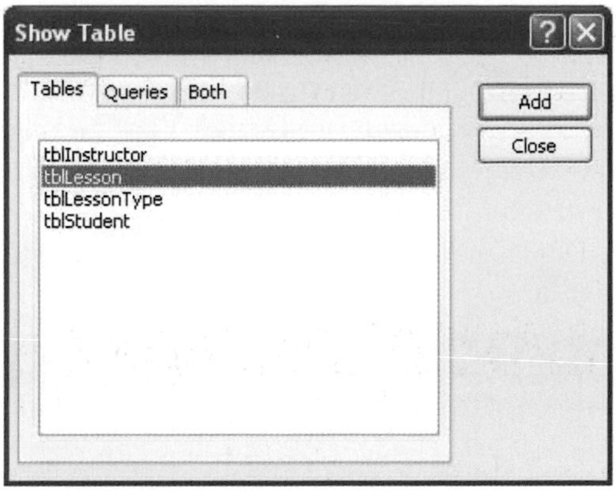

5 Select **tblStudent**, click on **Add** and then **Close** the window.

6 The **Query Design View** window is shown in Figure 1.8.4 with the two tables and their relationships.

Figure 1.8.4 ▼

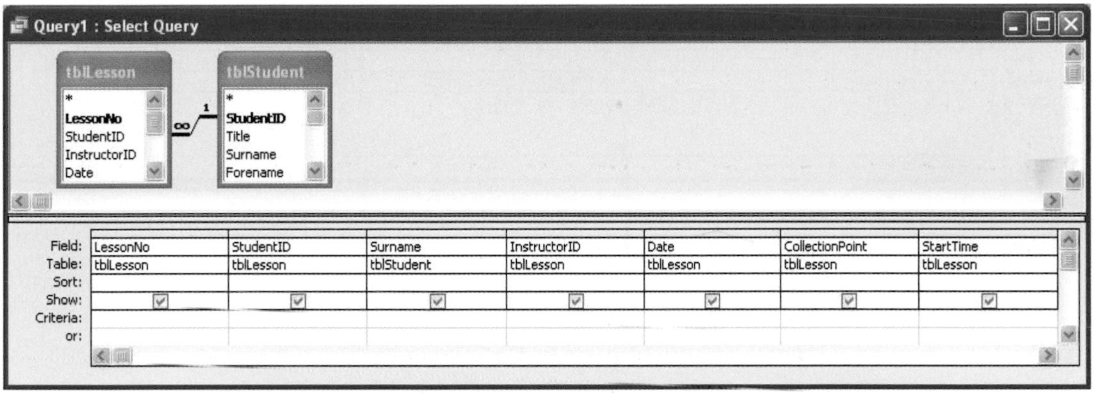

Query1 : Select Query

tblLesson
*
LessonNo
StudentID
InstructorID
Date

tblStudent
*
StudentID
Title
Surname
Forename

Field:	LessonNo	StudentID	Surname	InstructorID	Date	CollectionPoint	StartTime
Table:	tblLesson	tblLesson	tblStudent	tblLesson	tblLesson	tblLesson	tblLesson
Sort:							
Show:	☑	☑	☑	☑	☑	☑	☑
Criteria:							
or:							

7 From **tblLesson** drag and drop the fields **LessonNo**, **StudentID**, **InstructorID**, **Date**, **CollectionPoint** and **StartTime** into the field cells.

8 From **tblStudent** drag and drop the **Surname** field.

9 Move its position by clicking on the column header and dragging to a position after the **StudentID** column. Alternatively you could have entered the fields in the order shown.

10 Run the query and save it as **qryLessonAndNames**.

11 The results of your query are shown in Figure 1.8.5.

Figure 1.8.5 ▼

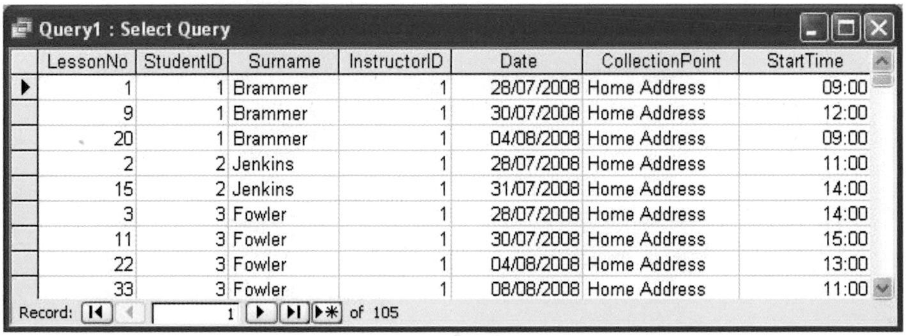

Query1 : Select Query

LessonNo	StudentID	Surname	InstructorID	Date	CollectionPoint	StartTime
1	1	Brammer	1	28/07/2008	Home Address	09:00
9	1	Brammer	1	30/07/2008	Home Address	12:00
20	1	Brammer	1	04/08/2008	Home Address	09:00
2	2	Jenkins	1	28/07/2008	Home Address	11:00
15	2	Jenkins	1	31/07/2008	Home Address	14:00
3	3	Fowler	1	28/07/2008	Home Address	14:00
11	3	Fowler	1	30/07/2008	Home Address	15:00
22	3	Fowler	1	04/08/2008	Home Address	13:00
33	3	Fowler	1	08/08/2008	Home Address	11:00

Record: |◄| ◄ | 1 | ► | ►| | ►* | of 105

Query 2 Searching for an instructor's lessons

This query will enable us to key in an Instructor ID and find all the instructor's lessons.

1 In the Database Window click on **Queries** and select **New**.
2 In the **New Query** window select **Design View** and click on **OK**.
3 In the **Show Table** window select **tblLesson** and click on **Add**.
4 Select **tblInstructor**, click on **Add** and then **Close** the window.
5 The Query Design grid is shown in Figure 1.8.6 with the two tables and their relationships.

Figure 1.8.6 ▼

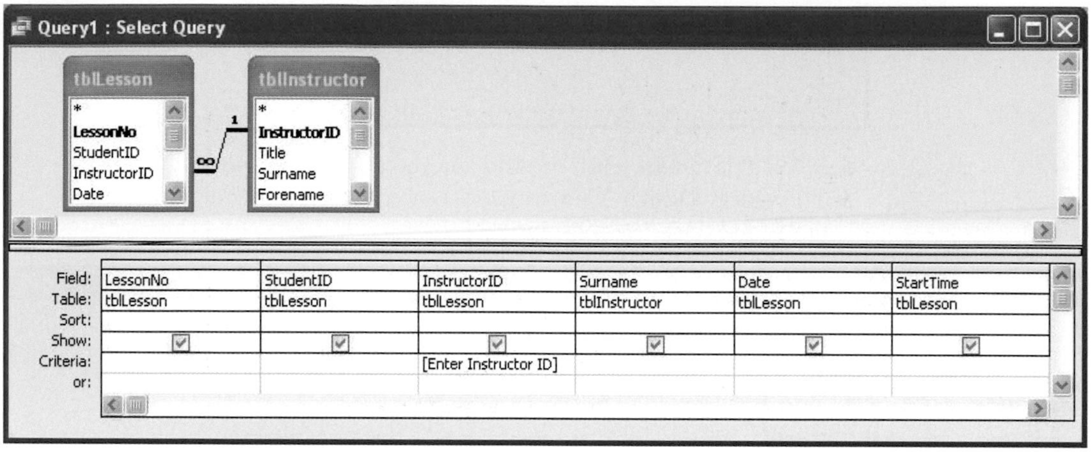

6 From **tblLesson** drag and drop the fields **LessonNo**, **StudentID**, **InstructorID**, **Date** and **StartTime**.
7 From **tblInstructor** drag and drop the **Surname** field.
8 Move its position by clicking on the column header and dragging to a position after the **InstructorID** column.
9 In the criteria cell of the **InstructorID** type **[Enter Instructor ID]**.
10 Run the query and enter **2** in the dialogue box (see Figure 1.8.7).

Figure 1.8.7 ▶

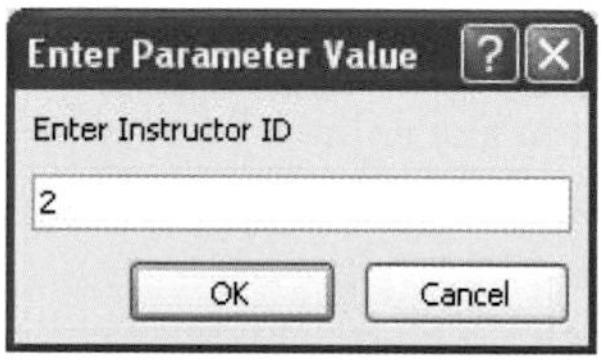

11 The query produces a list of lessons for Instructor ID 2 as shown in Figure 1.8.8.

Figure 1.8.8 ▶

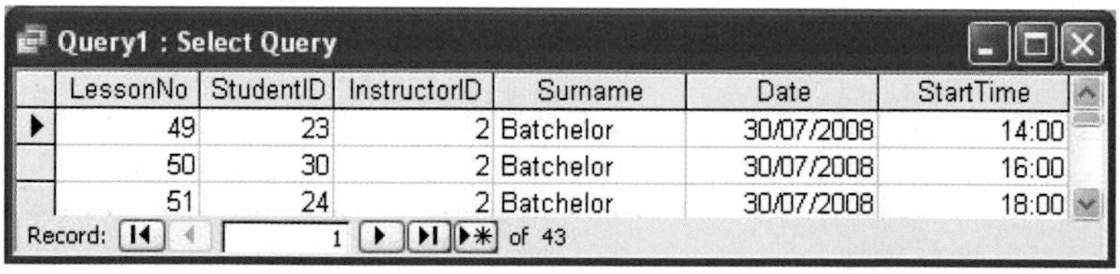

LessonNo	StudentID	InstructorID	Surname	Date	StartTime
49	23	2	Batchelor	30/07/2008	14:00
50	30	2	Batchelor	30/07/2008	16:00
51	24	2	Batchelor	30/07/2008	18:00

12 Save the query as **qryInstructorLessons**.

Query 3 Viewing all lessons with full details of instructor and student names

We will use the Query Wizard to design the next query.

1 In the Database Window click on **Queries** and select **New**.
2 In the **New Query** window select **Simple Query Wizard** and click on **OK**. The Simple Query Wizard dialogue box is displayed.
3 Select **tblLesson** from the Tables/Queries drop-down box.
4 Click the double right arrow >> to put all the fields in the Selected Fields area (see Figure 1.8.9).

Figure 1.8.9 ▶

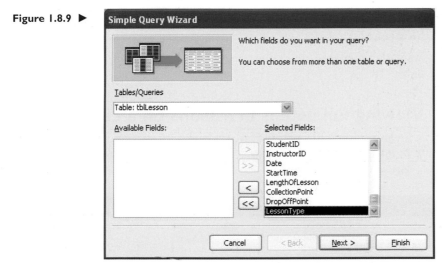

5 Select **tblInstructor** from the Tables/Queries drop-down.
6 Select fields **Surname** and **Forename** and add to the selected fields by clicking the right arrow >.

Figure 1.8.10 ▶

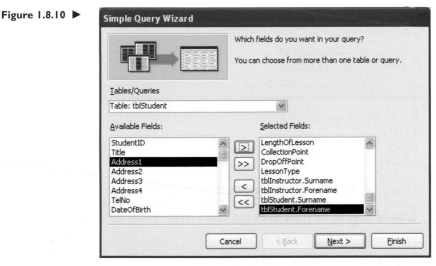

7 Select **tblStudent** from the Tables/Queries drop-down and add the fields **Surname** and **Forename** to the selected fields (see Figure 1.8.10).
8 Click on **Next**, choose **Detail**, click on **Next** again, call the query **qryFullDetails** and click on **Finish**.

The resulting query opens in Datasheet View (see Figure 1.8.11), giving full details of the lessons, the students and instructors along with their names. (You will need to drop into Design View to position names alongside IDs.)

Figure 1.8.11 ▼

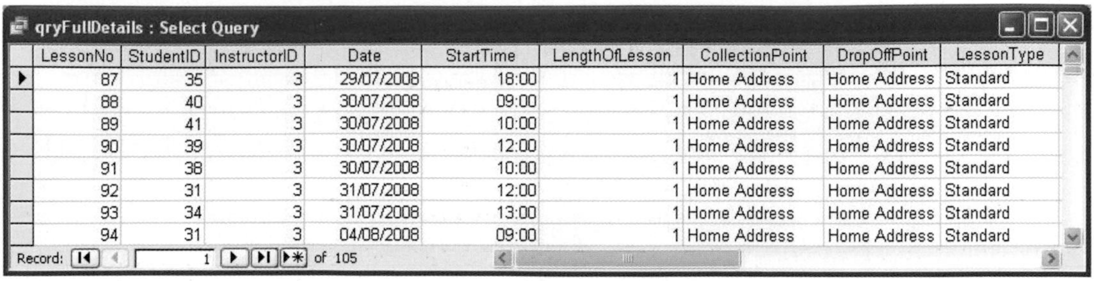

LessonNo	StudentID	InstructorID	Date	StartTime	LengthOfLesson	CollectionPoint	DropOffPoint	LessonType
87	35	3	29/07/2008	18:00	1	Home Address	Home Address	Standard
88	40	3	30/07/2008	09:00	1	Home Address	Home Address	Standard
89	41	3	30/07/2008	10:00	1	Home Address	Home Address	Standard
90	39	3	30/07/2008	12:00	1	Home Address	Home Address	Standard
91	38	3	30/07/2008	10:00	1	Home Address	Home Address	Standard
92	31	3	31/07/2008	12:00	1	Home Address	Home Address	Standard
93	34	3	31/07/2008	13:00	1	Home Address	Home Address	Standard
94	31	3	04/08/2008	09:00	1	Home Address	Home Address	Standard

Record: ◄ ◄ 1 ► ►I ►* of 105

We are now going to develop two more queries which will be used later in these units.

Query 4   Viewing full details of lessons on a certain date

1 Open the **qryFullDetails** in Design View.
2 In the criteria row of the **Date** column, type **[Please enter the Date]** (see Figure 1.8.12).

Figure 1.8.12 ▼

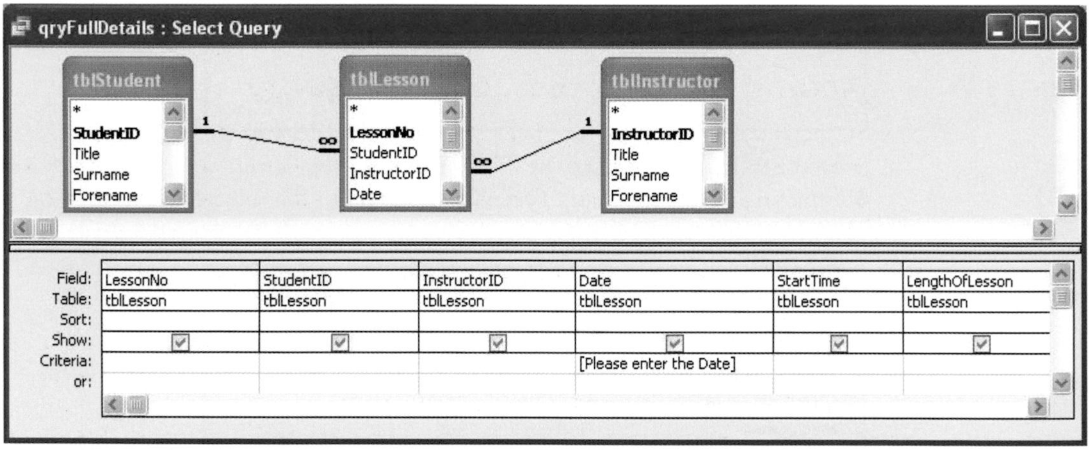

3 Use **File**, **Save As** to save the query as **qryFullDetailsByDate**.

When you run this query you will be prompted for a date. Access will display full details of the lessons on that date along with the names of the students and instructors.

Query 5   Viewing full details of lessons this week

This query uses the Date() function again. The data files supplied with this book cover lessons from week beginning 28/07/08 to 01/08/08 and 04/08/08 to 08/08/08. You will have to use Find and Replace to switch the data to a two-week period starting with today's date. See Unit 7. It is easier of course to just change the time clock on your computer to 28/07/08.

1 Open the **qryFullDetailsByDate** in Design View again.
2 In the criteria row of the **Date** column enter **Between Date() and Date()+7**. This will return all lessons booked in the next 7 days starting from the current date (see Figure 1.8.13).

Figure 1.8.13 ▼

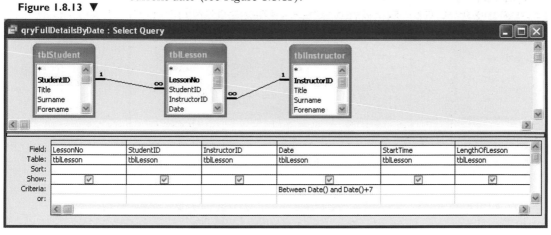

3 Use **File, Save As** to save the query as **qryNextWeeksLessons**.
4 Open the query in Design View again and edit the criteria to Date(). Save As **qryTodayLessons**.

Remember to return your data to its original state.

Query 6   Adding a calculated field to a query

A calculated field is an added field in a query that displays the results of a calculation. For example, if we multiply together the hourly rate for each lesson and the length of each lesson, we can use the query to work out the cost of each lesson.

1 In the Database Window click on **Queries** and select **New**.
2 Select the **Simple Query Wizard** and click on **OK**.
3 Click on **tblLesson** and click on the double arrow >> to select every field.
4 Select **tblLessonType** table and click on the field **Cost**. Click on the single arrow > to select just this field.
5 Select **tblInstructor** and click on the field **Forename**. Click on the single arrow to select just this field. Add the **Surname** field also.
6 Select **tblStudent** and click on the field **Forename**. Click on the single arrow to select just this field. Then add the **Surname**, **Address1** and **Address2** fields as well.
7 Click on **Next**. Click on **Next** again and call the query **qryLessonCost**. Click on **Finish**.
8 Switch to **Design View**. You will need to rearrange the tables by dragging to more suitable positions (see Figure 1.8.14).

Figure 1.8.14 ▼

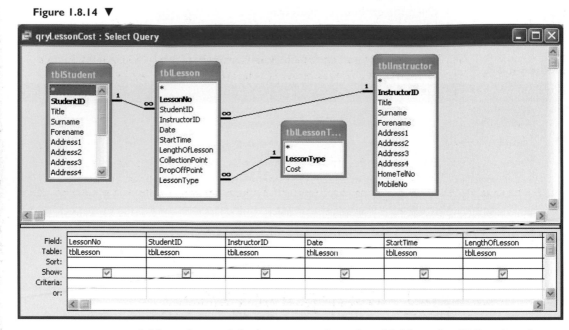

9 Using drag and drop, rearrange the order of fields in the QBE grid so that InstructorID comes after LessonNo, followed by Instructor Forename and Surname, then StudentID followed by Student Forename, Surname, Address1 and Address2.

10 Scroll to the right and find the first blank column of the QBE grid. If there is no blank column, select the last field and click on **Insert, Columns**.

11 In the field row of the blank column enter **TotalCost: [LengthOfLesson]*[Cost]** (see Figure 1.8.15).

Figure 1.8.15 ▼

Field:	LengthOfLesson	CollectionPoint	DropOffPoint	LessonType	Cost	TotalCost: [LengthOfLesson]*[Cost]
Table:	tblLesson	tblLesson	tblLesson	tblLesson	tblLessonType	
Sort:						
Show:	✓	✓	✓	✓	✓	✓
Criteria:						
or:						

12 Save the query again (by closing the window) as **qryLessonCost**.

13 Run the query, to test the calculations are correct (see Figure 1.8.16).

Figure 1.8.16 ▼

qryLessonCost : Select Query

StartTime	LengthOfLesson	CollectionPoint	DropOffPoint	LessonType	Cost	TotalCost
10:00	1	Home Address	Home Address	Standard	£24.00	£24.00
12:00	1	Home Address	Home Address	Introductory	£16.00	£16.00
14:00	2	Home Address	Home Address	Test	£22.00	£44.00
09:00	1	Home Address	Home Address	Standard	£24.00	£24.00
11:00	1	Home Address	Home Address	Standard	£24.00	£24.00
12:00	1	Home Address	Home Address	Standard	£24.00	£24.00
14:00	2	Home Address	Home Address	Standard	£24.00	£48.00
10:00	1	Home Address	Home Address	Standard	£24.00	£24.00

Record: |◄| ◄ | 1 | ► |►|| ►* | of 105

Hint Use **Tricks and Tips** numbers 13, 14, 15 and 16 to explore queries further.

Unit 9: Setting up forms using the Form Wizard

In this unit you will learn how to set up the forms to enter, edit and view data in the Pass IT Driving School database. Forms provide a user-friendly on screen interface.

Initially we will set up three forms:

- A Student form
- An Instructor form
- A Lesson type form

Wizards can again be used to set up the forms. It is usually easier and common practice to use the wizard to set up a form but then to use Design View to customise the form to your requirements.

Setting up the Student form using AutoForm

1 In the Database Window select **Forms** and click on **New**.
2 In the **New Form** window select **AutoForm: Columnar** (see Figure 1.9.1).

Figure 1.9.1 ►

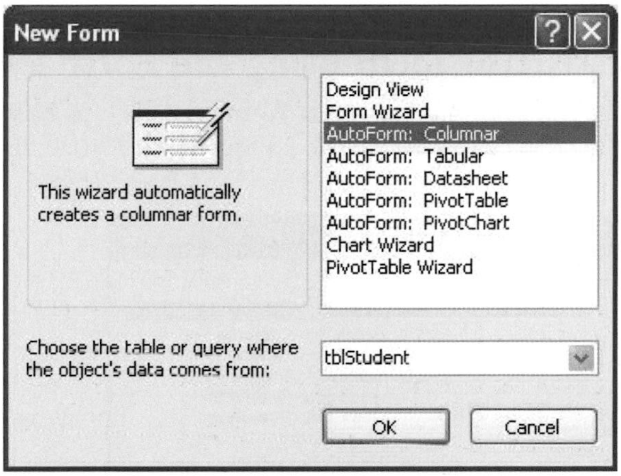

3 Select **tblStudent** from the drop-down list and click on **OK**.
4 The form is generated automatically. If the form is maximised and uses the full screen, click on the **Restore Window** icon (see Figure 1.9.2).

Figure 1.9.2 ►

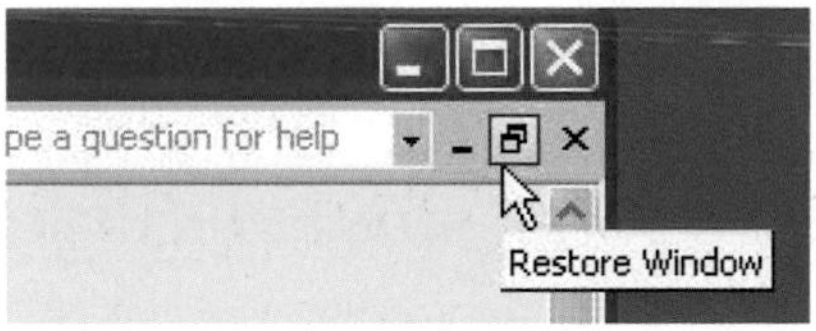

5 To ensure that the form is the correct size, click on **Window, Size to Fit Form**.
6 Save by closing the form and calling it **frmStudent**.

Note Size to Fit Form is not available if the window is maximised. When you next open the form it will open at its saved size.

The form is shown in Figure 1.9.3.

Figure 1.9.3 ▶

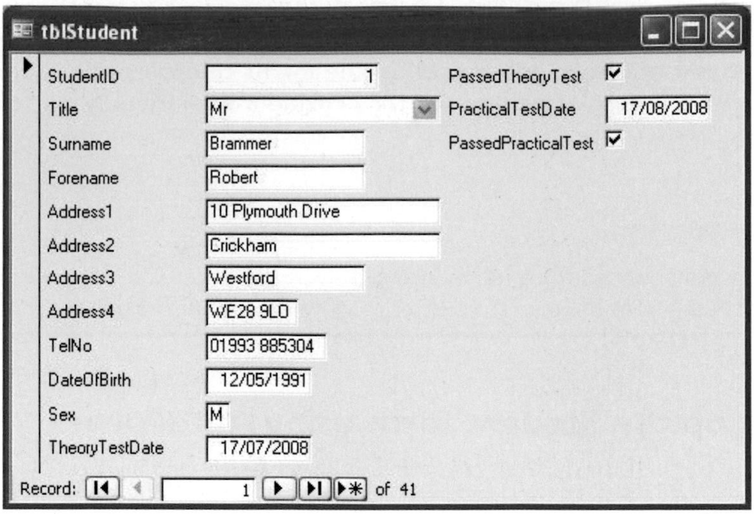

Setting up the Instructor form using the Form Wizard

1 In the Database Window select **Forms** and click on **New**.
2 In the **New Form** window select **Form Wizard**, select **tblInstructor** from the Tables/Queries drop-down and click on **OK** (see Figure 1.9.4).

Figure 1.9.4 ▶

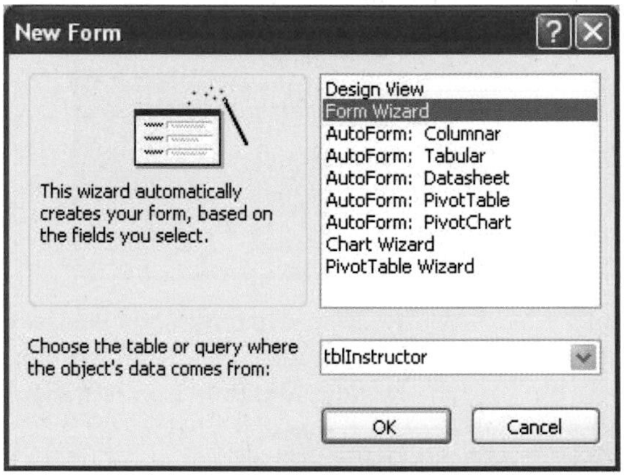

3 The **Form Wizard** window opens with the available fields (Figure 1.9.5). Click the double arrow >> to put all available fields across to the selected fields and click on **Next**.

Hint The single arrow allows you to select one field at a time and the left arrows allow you to deselect fields. Use the single arrow to choose selected fields in a different order from that shown.

Figure 1.9.5 ▶

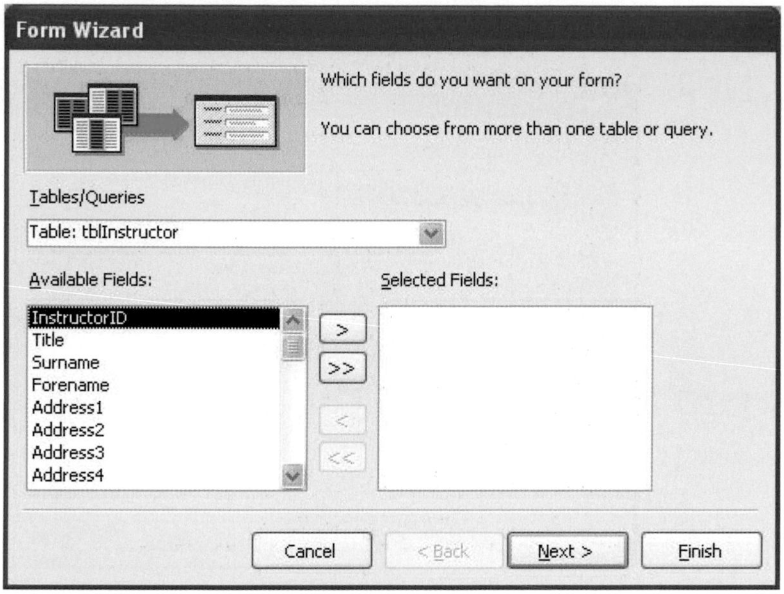

Form Wizard

Which fields do you want on your form?

You can choose from more than one table or query.

Tables/Queries

Table: tblInstructor

Available Fields:

InstructorID
Title
Surname
Forename
Address1
Address2
Address3
Address4

Selected Fields:

>
>>
<
<<

Cancel | < Back | Next > | Finish

4 Select **Columnar** from the range of layouts shown and click on **Next** (see Figure 1.9.6).

Figure 1.9.6 ▶

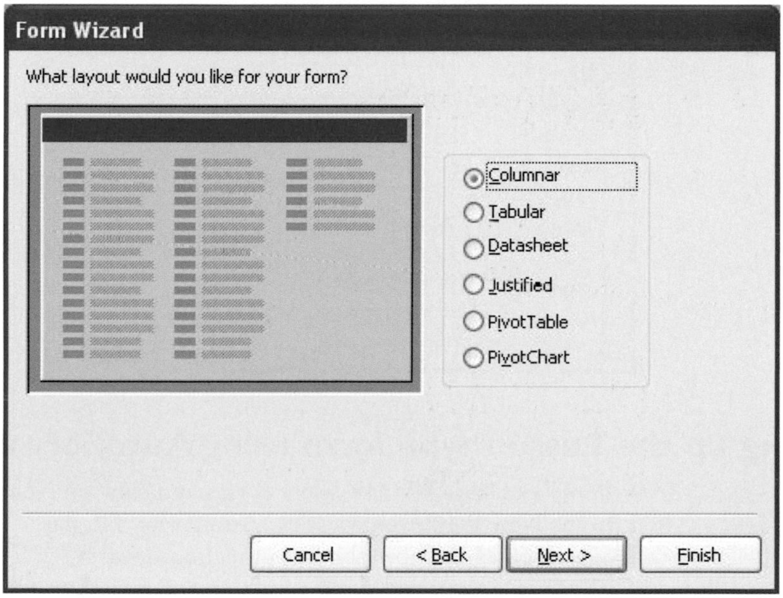

Form Wizard

What layout would you like for your form?

○ Columnar
○ Tabular
○ Datasheet
○ Justified
○ PivotTable
○ PivotChart

Cancel | < Back | Next > | Finish

5 Select **Standard** style from the next **Form Wizard** window and click on **Next** (see Figure 1.9.7).

Figure 1.9.7 ▶

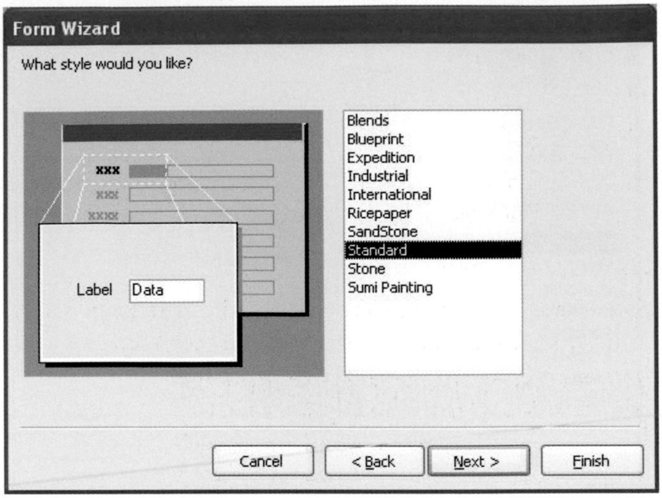

6 Save your form as **frmInstructor** and click on **Finish**. The form will open in **Form View** as shown in Figure 1.9.8.

Figure 1.9.8 ▶

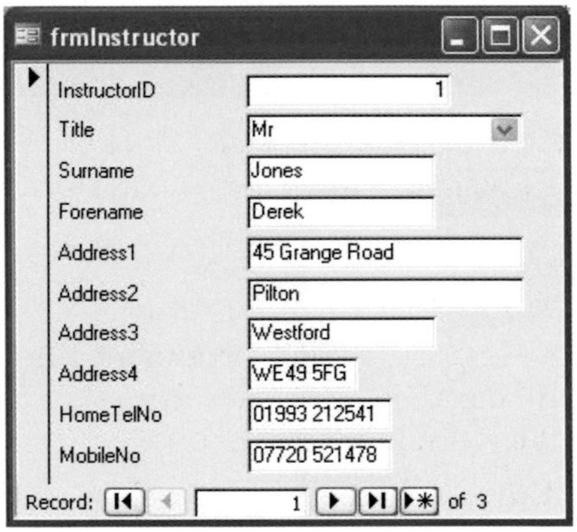

Setting up the Lesson type form using AutoForm: Tabular

1 In the Database Window select **Forms** and click on **New**.
2 In the **New Form** window select **AutoForm: Tabular**.
3 Select **tblLessonType** table from the drop-down list and click on **OK**.
4 The form is generated automatically and opens in **Form View** as shown below. Save the form in the usual way calling it **frmLessonType** (see Figure 1.9.9).

Figure 1.9.9 ▶

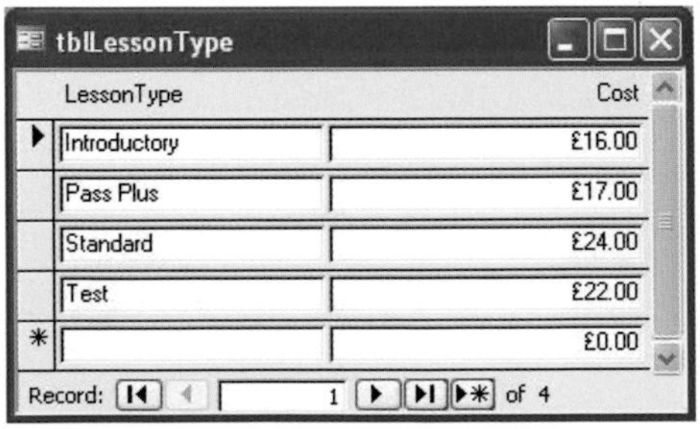

The different Form Views

There are three different views to a form:

- Form View
- Datasheet View
- Design View

Form View

Form View allows you to view and edit records one at a time. Enter Form View from the Database Window by selecting the form and clicking on Open.

Datasheet View

Datasheet View allows you to view and edit the records all on one screen. The form **frmLessonType** is shown in Datasheet View (see Figure 1.9.10).

Figure 1.9.10 ▶

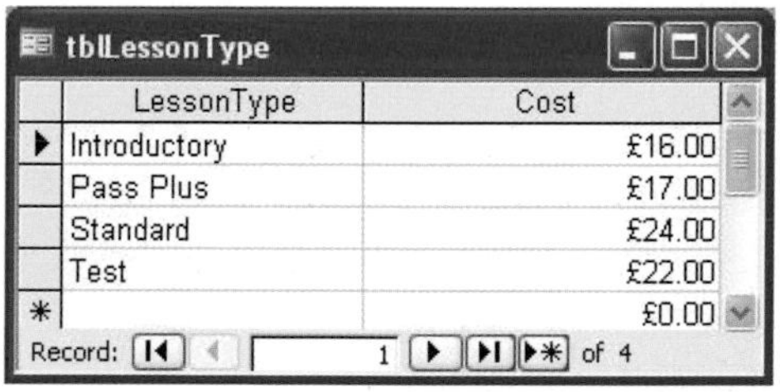

tblLessonType

	LessonType	Cost
▶	Introductory	£16.00
	Pass Plus	£17.00
	Standard	£24.00
	Test	£22.00
*		£0.00

Record: 1 of 4

Design View

Design View allows you to edit the form and is described in Unit 10. Enter Design View from the Database Window by selecting the form and clicking on Design.

Switching between views

There are a number of ways of switching between the Form View, Design View and Datasheet View windows.The easiest way is to select from one of the first three options on the **View** menu (see Figure 1.9.11).

Figure 1.9.11 ▶

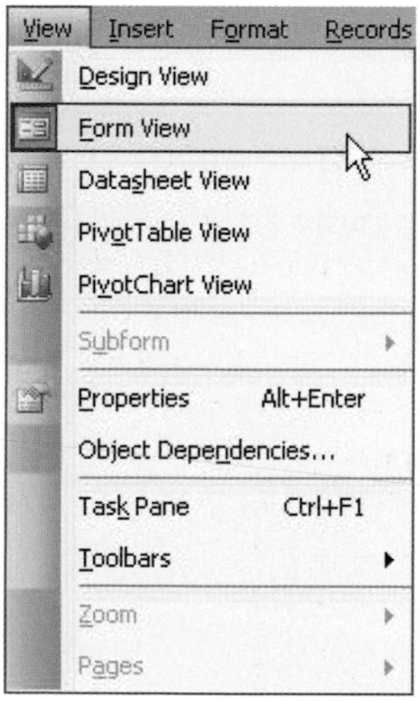

Entering data in Form View

1 Open **frmStudent** in Form View.
2 Use the Record navigation bar shown below to scroll through the records.

Figure 1.9.12 ▶

Record: |◀ ◀ [1] ▶ ▶| ▶* of 41

3 Click on the last icon to add a new record.
4 Add the details of some more students to practise entering data into a form.

Alternatively you can use the Page Up and Page Down keys to display Next and Previous records.

Unit 10: Working in Form Design View

The forms you have produced so far are all standard in layout. Form Design View allows you to customise a form to suit your requirements.

In this unit you will learn how to:
- find your way around a form in Design View
- move, align and edit controls
- edit the appearance of your form

Form Design View

You will grasp the concepts more easily by practising and experimenting with the tasks in this unit. We will start by working on a copy of a form so that if you make a mistake it will not affect the final system.

1 In the Database Window click on **Forms** and select **frmStudent**. From the menu choose **Edit, Copy**.

2 Click in the Database Window and choose **Edit, Paste**. Name the form **frmStudentCopy**.

3 Open **frmStudentCopy** in Design View as shown in Figure 1.10.1 by selecting **frmStudentCopy** and clicking on **Design**.

Figure 1.10.1 ▼

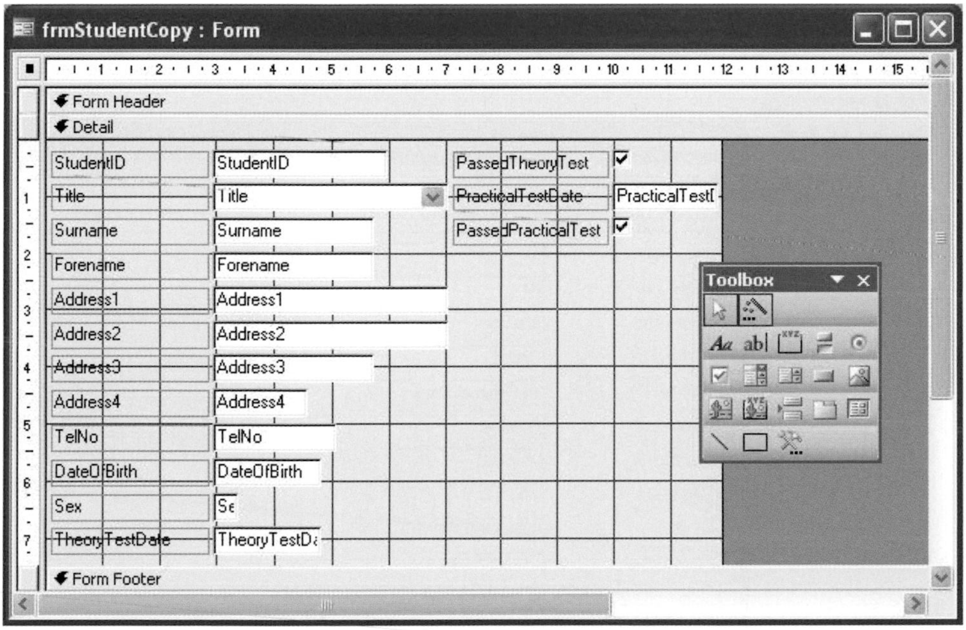

The form opens with the following features showing:

- A **Form Header** section – this area can contain text, headings, titles and graphics. Toggle the **Form Header** off and back on by choosing from the menu **View, Form Header**.
- A **Detail** section – this contains the **controls** that display the data in your tables.

- A number of **Controls** each made up of a **Label** containing the field name and a text box which will contain the data in **Form View**.
- A **Toolbox** from which you can add text, lines, shapes, controls, buttons and other features. Toggle the **Toolbox** on and off by choosing from the menu **View, Toolbox**.
- A **Form Footer** section which can be used in the same way as the Header.
- A **Right Margin** which can be dragged wider using the mouse.
- A **Ruler** and **Grid** to help you with the layout of your form. Toggle these features on and off by choosing from the menu **View, Ruler** or **View, Grid**.
- You may also notice the **Page Header/Footer** options which can be added. They will print at the top and bottom of each page in any printout.

Getting a feel for your working area

1 With **frmStudentCopy** open in **Design View** and maximised as shown in Figure 1.10.1 move the mouse over the right margin until it turns into a cross and drag the margin wider by about 2 cm. You can use the ruler as a guide.
2 Move the mouse over the border between the **Detail** section and the **Form Header** and drag the **Detail** section down by about 1 cm.
3 In the same way move the **Form Footer** section down toward the foot of the screen.
4 Switch to **Form View** by selecting **View, Form View** from the menu.
5 If the form is maximised, click on the **Restore Window** icon. Click on **Window, Size to Fit Form**. Access will give a best fit to your form as shown in Figure 1.10.2. It is **NOT** necessary to save this form.

Figure 1.10.2 ▶

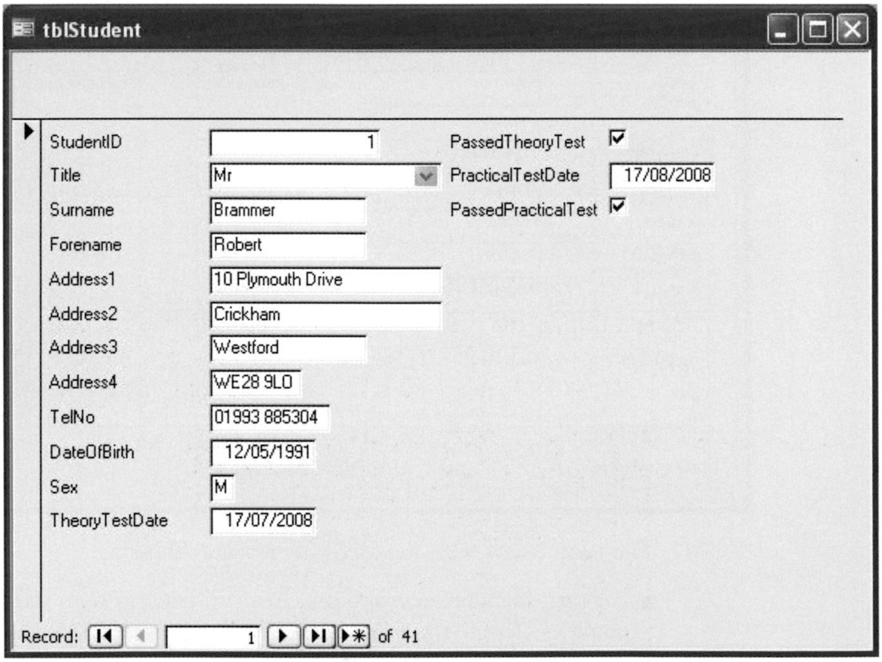

Working with controls

The **Detail** section is initially made up of controls which display the data from your tables. The controls are made up of text boxes, check boxes and attached labels.

In the Database Window click on **Forms** and select **frmStudentCopy** again. Click on **Design** to open the form in **Design View**.

It is worth practising all the following steps on the currently opened **frmStudentCopy** until you feel confident and competent with handling controls.

Selecting controls

- To resize, move, delete, copy or change the properties of a control, first you must select it.
- Simply click anywhere on the control and it will be highlighted with *sizing handles* as shown in Figure 1.10.3.

Figure 1.10.3 ▶

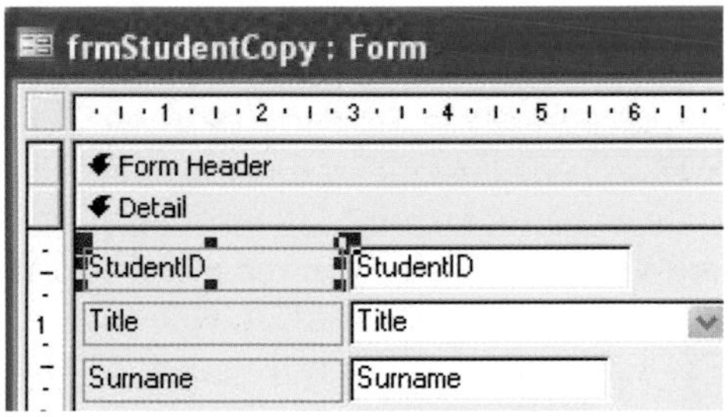

- To select more than one control, simply drag out a rectangle across the controls you wish to select or
- Select the first control and hold down SHIFT while selecting further controls.

Resizing controls

- Click on the control to select it and then drag the resizing handles in or out to resize it.

Moving controls

- Click on the control to select it. To move the control and its label, move the pointer to the border of the control. The pointer turns into an open hand as shown in Figure 1.10.4. Drag the control to a new position.

Figure 1.10.4 ▶

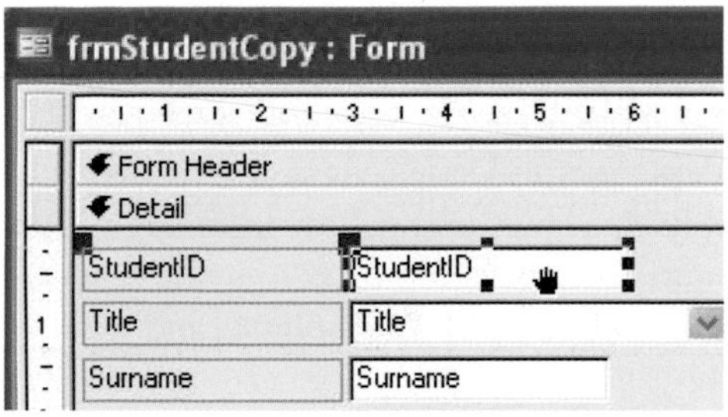

- To move the control without its label, place the pointer over the *move handle* in the top left corner of the control. The pointer changes to a pointing finger as shown in Figure 1.10.5. Drag the control to a new position.

Figure 1.10.5 ▶

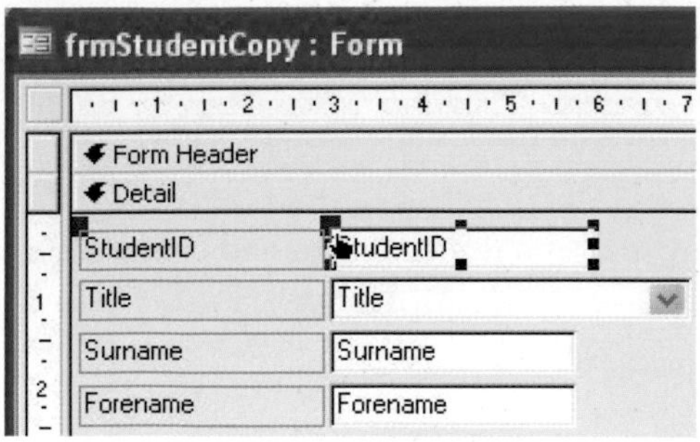

You can select more than one control as outlined earlier and move them at the same time.

Deleting controls

- To delete a control simply select the control and press the DELETE key.

Adding a control

- If you want to add a control for a field, for example because you have already deleted it choose **View**, **Field List** from the menu (see Figure 1.10.6).

Figure 1.10.6 ▶

The Field list will appear on the screen and you can highlight the field and drag and drop it to the required position.

Developing a form

1 Open **frmStudentCopy** in Design View.
2 Drag the Form Footer down and right margin out a little. Move each control in the left column down by about 2 cm to make room for a heading.
3 Select all the controls in the second column and move them down a little further.
4 Select the **TheoryTestDate** control at the foot of the first column and move the control to the top of the second column.

Your controls should now be arranged something like Figure 1.10.7. Do not worry about accuracy. Access provides a number of formatting tools to help you.

Figure 1.10.7 ▼

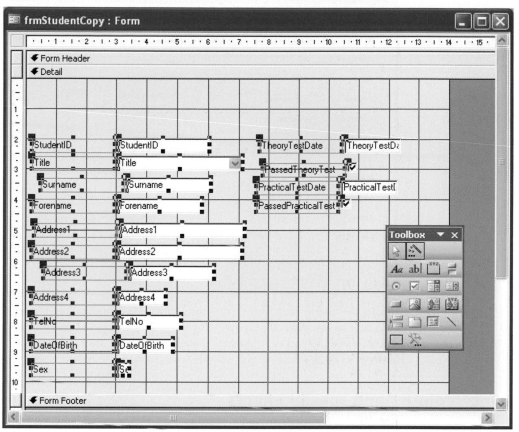

It is probable you will have to use the following steps to align all controls correctly. There is no set way but the following steps should ensure accuracy. Remember you can use the Undo option!

1 Highlight the labels in the first column of controls by dragging over them and select **Format, Align, Left**.
2 Highlight the text boxes in the first column of controls by dragging over them and select **Format, Align, Left**.
3 Repeat the same steps for the controls in the right hand column.
4 Align the control **StudentID** with **TheoryTestDate** to establish the uppermost position for each column.
5 Highlight the first column of controls and select **Format, Vertical Spacing, Make Equal**. There are **Increase** and **Decrease** options to help further.
6 Highlight the second column of controls and select **Format, Vertical Spacing, Make Equal**.
7 When you are happy with your design switch to **Form View**, click on the **Restore Window** icon if the form is maximised and select **Window, Size to Fit Form**.

8 Save your form. It should appear as shown in Figure 1.10.8.

Figure 1.10.8 ▶

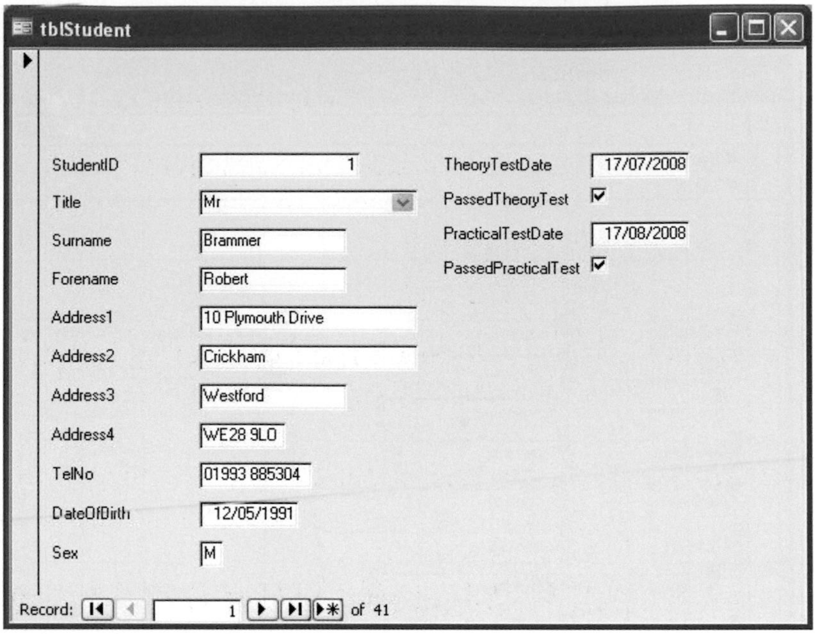

During the course of the next exercises you will be introduced to a number of ways of improving the appearance of your form. Throughout this unit do not be afraid to practise and experiment – remember you can always delete it and start again or as a last resort get the wizards to do it again!

Fonts, colours and special effects

1 Open the **frmStudentCopy** in Design View.
2 Ensure the **Formatting** toolbar is available by clicking on **View, Toolbars, Formatting (Form/Report)**. See Figure 1.10.9.

Figure 1.10.9 ▼

Most of the options here will be familiar to students who have a working knowledge of Windows software.

3 Click on the **Detail** area and click the **Fill/Back Colour** drop-down on the Formatting toolbar to show the colour palette below. See Figure 1.10.10.

Figure 1.10.10 ▶

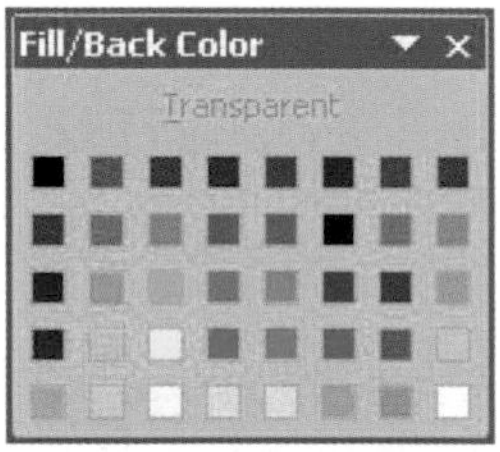

4 Select a suitable colour for the background to your form.
5 Select the labels of all the controls and set the font to **Arial Black** (or one of your choice) by clicking the **Font** drop-down on the **Formatting** toolbar and then clicking on **Bold**.

You will probably have to spend some time resizing the labels or click **Edit**, **Undo** to try another font.

6 Select all the labels again and click the **Fill/Back Colour** drop-down on the **Formatting** toolbar.

7 Choose a colour to make your labels stand out from the background colour of the form.

8 With labels still selected click the **Special Effect** drop-down and choose **Raised** from the **Special Effect** window shown in Figure 1.10.11.

Figure 1.10.11 ▶

Hint If you right click in the Detail area or on any control you will get a menu from which a number of toolbar options are offered.

Using the Toolbox to add a text box, rectangle and lines

The Toolbox offers a number of features many of which you will meet later in this book (see Figure 1.10.12).

Figure 1.10.12 ▶

1 Click on the **Label** icon and drag out a rectangle near the top of your form.
2 Type in a suitable heading and press return.
3 Set the font, background colour and special effect as required.
4 Select the **Rectangle** tool and drag out a box around the controls.
5 Select the box and choose a style from the **Line/Border Width** drop-down on the **Formatting** toolbar (see Figure 1.10.13).

Figure 1.10.13 ▶

Note There is no need to save your form. The next section starts on the Student Form.

Making a start on the Student Form

We now need to go back to our original Student Form and develop it for later use.

Figure 1.10.14 ▶

The Toolbox (see Figure 1.10.14) should appear when you are in Design View. It allows you to add control objects to your forms. If it is not visible, click **View**, **Toolbox** from the menu.

Hint Some of the functions available can be set up using wizards. If you wish to use the wizards you must ensure the Control Wizards icon is selected as shown.

1 Open the **frmStudent** in Design View. Make sure the Toolbox is displayed.
2 Drag the upper border of the **Detail** section down about 1.5 cm to make room for a heading in the **Form Header** section.

3 Move the controls **TelNo**, **DateOfBirth**, **Sex** and **TheoryTestDate** to the top of the right column. Align the **TelNo** field to the **Title** field as shown in Figure 1.10.15.

Figure 1.10.15 ▼

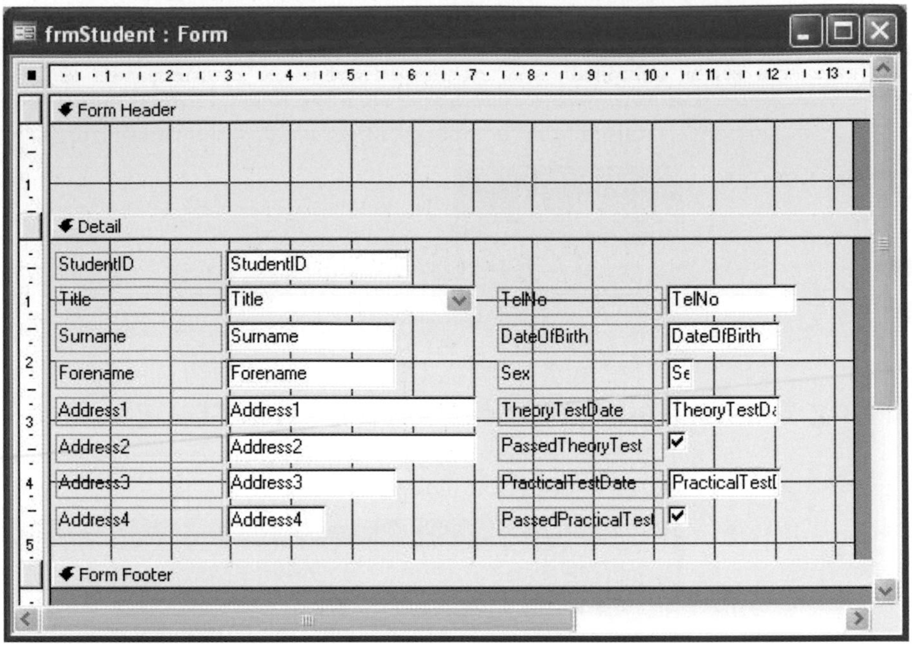

4 In **Design View** click on the **Label** icon in the Toolbox (see Figure 1.10.16).

Figure 1.10.16 ▶

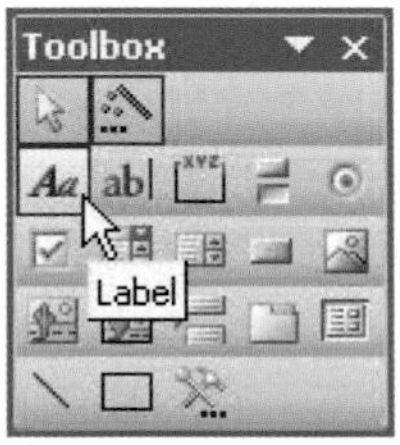

5 Drag out a **Label** in the Form Header section, type in the text **Pass IT Driving School** and press return (see Figure 1.10.17).

Figure 1.10.17 ▼

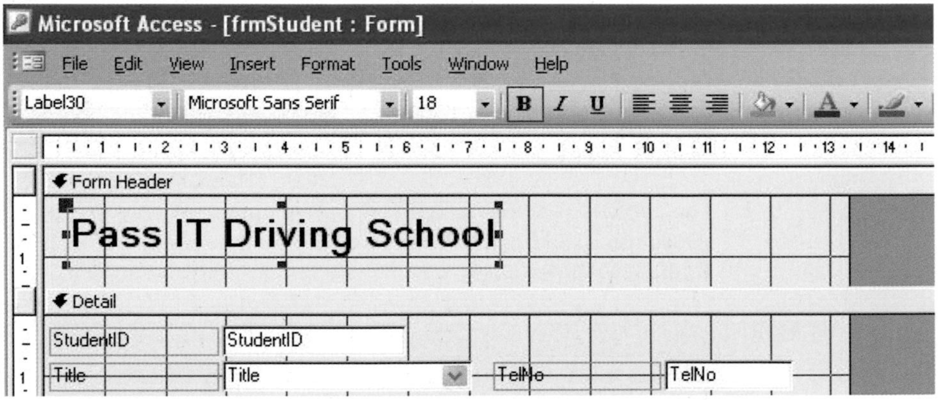

6 With the new control selected set the font, font size, foreground colour and border colour as required using the **Formatting** toolbar. We have chosen to set the **Font Colour** to **Black** and **Font** to **18 pt, Bold, Microsoft Sans Serif**.

Setting control properties

You can customise any control on a form by opening its Property Sheet. With the control selected as shown in Figure 1.10.17, click **View, Properties** or right click and select **Properties** from the menu.

Hint Pressing F4 is a useful short cut.

Figure 1.10.18 shows the Properties for the control in the Form Header with the **Font Name, Font Size** and **Font Weight** set to **Microsoft Sans Serif, 18 pt, Bold**. You might wish to explore some of the other options.

Figure 1.10.18 ▶

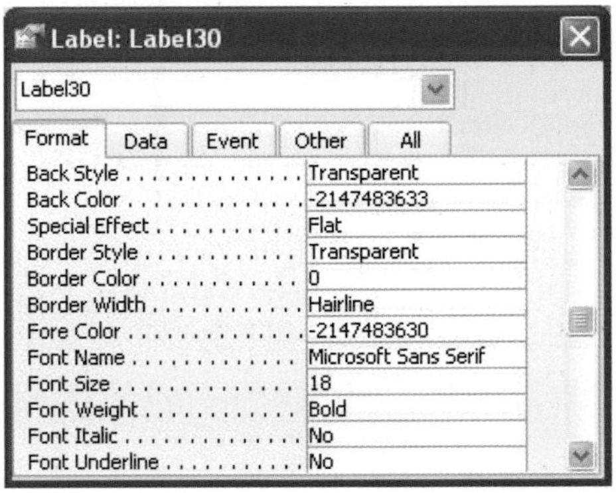

We are now going to put a simple frame around our controls.

7 Click on the **Rectangle** icon in the Toolbox and drag a rectangle around all the controls in the **Detail** section. You will need to create a little room to do this by repositioning all the controls. See Figure 1.10.19. Display the Property Sheet for the control and ensure the **Special Effect** property is set to **Etched**.

8 Repeat the process by placing a rectangle around the title in the **Form Header** section.

Figure 1.10.19 ▶

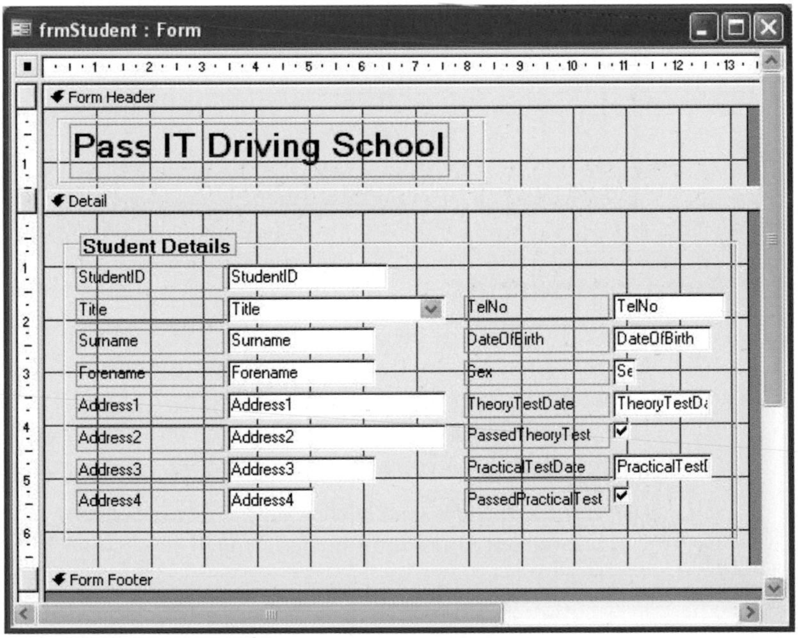

9 Add a Label with the text **Student Details**. Display the Property Sheet (Figure 1.10.20) and set the **Back Style** to **Normal** with the **Font Name**, **Font Size** and **Font Weight** set to **Microsoft Sans Serif, 10 pt** and **Bold**.

Figure 1.10.20 ▶

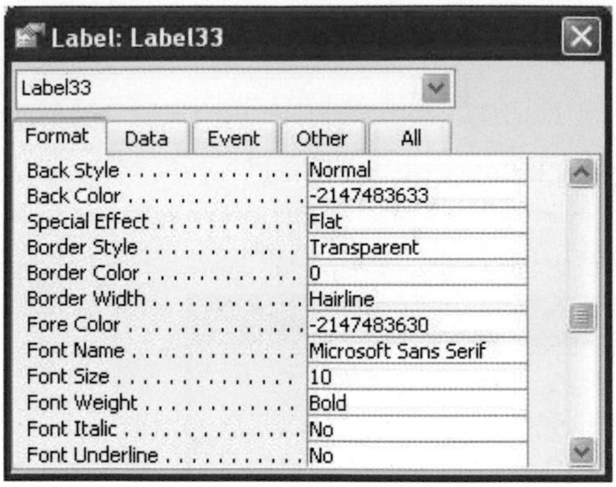

10 Save your form as **frmStudent**. It should appear as in Figure 1.10.21. The form contains a Dividing Line, Record Selector and Navigation Buttons. The next step will explain how to customise those features.

Figure 1.10.21 ▶

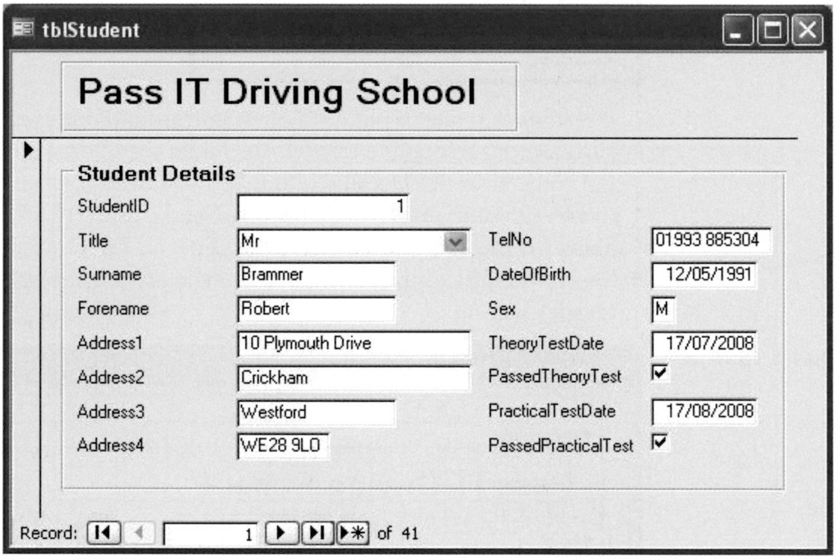

Setting form properties

You can control the behaviour and appearance of your form by setting the form's properties. In the Student Form you have just completed it may look better without a number of features. It still has the Record Selector, the Record Navigation Controls, Maximize, Minimize and Close buttons. These can be removed using the Form Properties window.

I In Design View, double click on the **Form Selector** (see Figure 1.10.22) at the top left of the form in Design View or click on **View, Properties**.

Figure 1.10.22 ▶

2 This displays the **Form Properties** window (see Figure 1.10.23). There are far too many properties to cover all the available options here. You will meet some later in the units but Microsoft Help will give details of all the available options.

The properties are grouped for easier access. Clicking on the Format tab will give a range of options covering the appearance of your form.

Figure 1.10.23 ▶

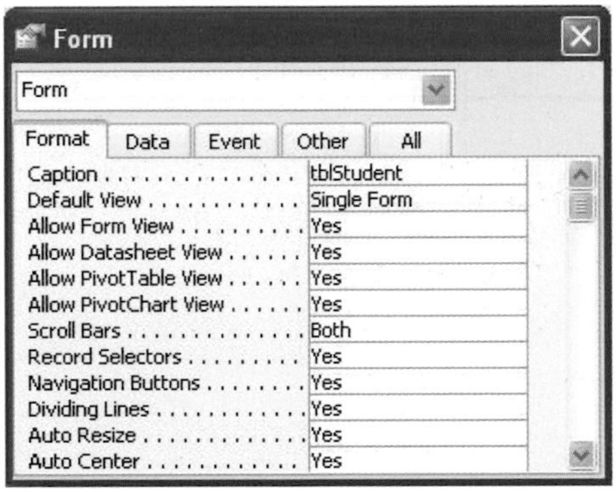

3 Change the form caption using the **Caption** property to **Student Details**.

4 Remove the scroll bars at the bottom and right hand side of the form by setting the **Scroll Bars** property to **Neither**.

5 Remove the record selector on the form by setting the **Record Selectors** property to **No**.

6 We will leave the navigation buttons at the bottom of the form but they can be removed by setting the **Navigation Buttons** property to **No**.

7 Remove the dividing lines by setting the **Dividing Lines** property to **No**.

8 Make the form appear in the middle of the screen by setting the **Auto Center** property to **Yes**.

9 Remove the maximize and minimize buttons from a form by setting the **Min Max Buttons** property to **None**.

10 While in Design View edit the Labels to be more user-friendly, e.g. DateOfBirth to Date of Birth. Edit the Label directly or double click the Label and edit the Caption property.

Note The record selector is a column on the left hand side of a form used to select a whole record in a form; for example you may use this to delete a record rather than just delete one field.

Your finished form should appear as in Figure 1.10.24.

Figure 1.10.24 ▶

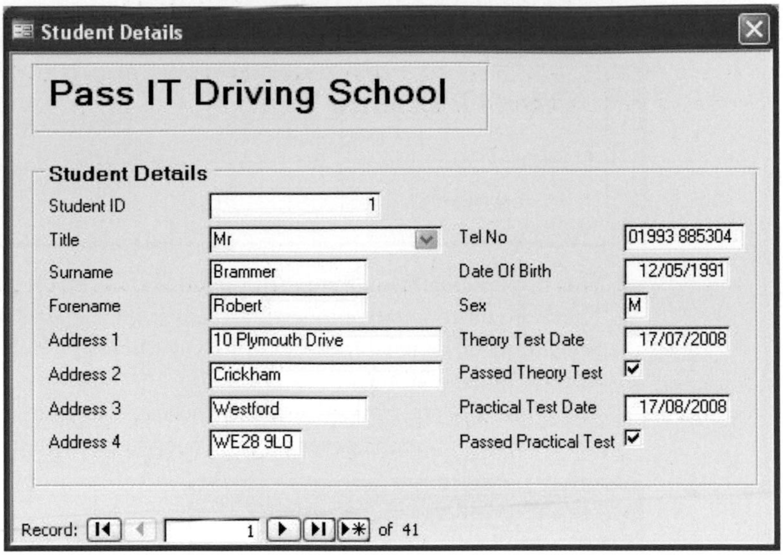

Figure 1.10.24

Unit 11: Taking form design further

This unit describes some of the additional features that you can add to your forms to create a professional feel to your system.

You will learn how to:
- add graphics
- add command buttons
- add combo boxes
- create forms to display data from more than one table

Adding graphics to the form

Graphics can easily be added to your form using copy and paste. The graphic appears in an unbound object frame, enabling you to move or size the frame as needed.

Alternatively, follow these steps.

1 Ensure the image is already saved in a format that Access can recognise e.g. **jpg**, **gif** or **bmp**. Our image is the PASS IT logo (see Figure 1.11.1).

Figure 1.11.1 ▶

PA55 IT

2 Open **frmStudent** in **Design View**.
3 Select the **Image** icon in the Toolbox (see Figure 1.11.2).

Figure 1.11.2 ▶

4 Drag out a rectangle in the Form Header section.
5 Select the image you wish to add to the form from the Insert Picture dialogue box. If the image does not fit the frame then right click on the image, select **Properties** and set the **Size Mode** to **Zoom**.
6 Set the **Special Effect** property of the image to **Flat** and place a rectangle around it in the same way as you did for the header in Unit 10.

7 Save your form as **frmStudent**. It should appear as in Figure 1.11.3. Some of the text boxes have been aligned and resized to give a smarter feel.

Figure 1.11.3 ▶

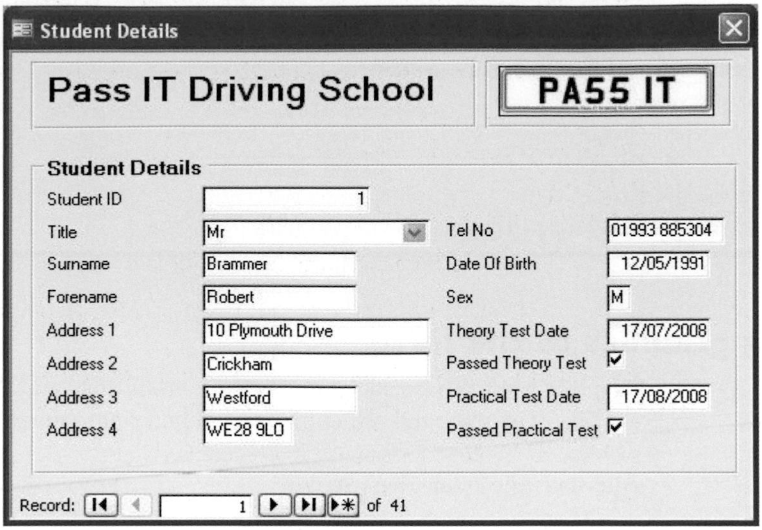

The Instructor form

In exactly the same way as you developed the Student form, you now need to set up the Instructor form to look as shown in Figure 1.11.4.

You will notice Pass IT has been removed from the header and replaced with the logo. The Special Effect property of the logo has been set to Raised. You may experiment and come up with a better design but importantly all forms should have the same layout. We will show you how to add the command buttons in the next section.

Figure 1.11.4 ▶

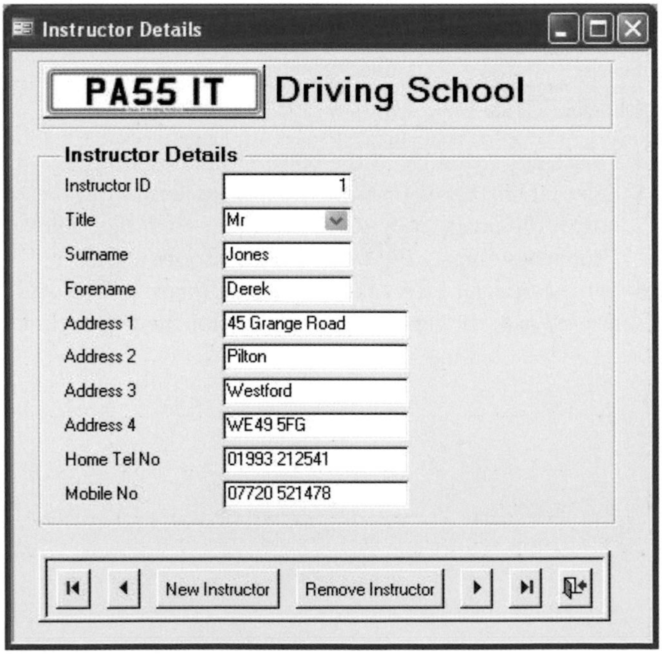

Adding command buttons

Access allows you to automate tasks by creating command buttons and placing them on your form.

Command buttons can be added to deal with a number of operations including:

- Record navigation
- Opening forms and reports
- Printing
- Other commonly used operations

You can set up a command button in one of two ways:

- Use the Command Button Wizard to set up the button and attach the operation.
- Create the button without the Wizard and attach it to a macro or code.

We will be dealing with macros later. We will start by using the Wizards to set up buttons to move between the records, add/delete records and quit the application from our Student form (see Figure 1.11.3).

1 Open **frmStudent** in Design View.
2 We are going to add the buttons to the lower section of the form so you will have to drag down the Form Footer area to create a little room. See Figure 1.11.5
3 Make sure the Toolbox is showing and the **Control Wizards** tool is selected.

Figure 1.11.5 ▶

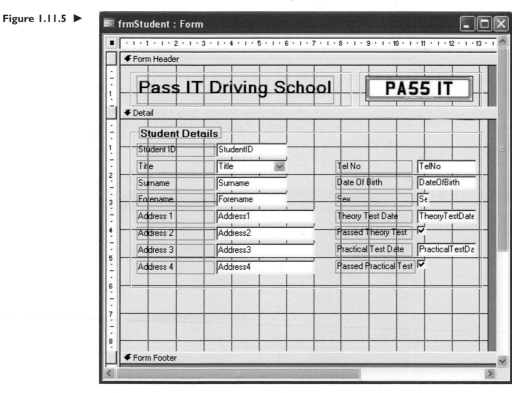

Figure 1.11.6 ►

4 Select the **Command Button** tool (see Figure 1.11.6) and drag out a button on your form.
This displays the Command Button Wizard dialogue box (see Figure 1.11.7).

Figure 1.11.7 ►

5 In the Categories list select **Record Operations**.
6 In the Actions list select **Add New Record** and click on **Next**.
The next window offers you a choice of putting pictures or text on the button. If you choose text you can type in the text you want to go on the button.
If you choose picture you can select from a list or browse the file area to find one of your own (see Figure 1.11.8).

Figure 1.11.8 ►

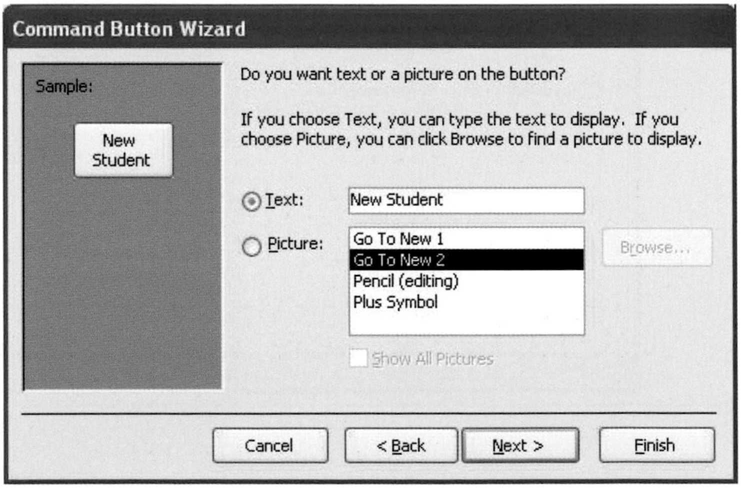

7 We are going to use text and pictures, so choose the **Text** option, enter **New Student** and click on **Next**.

Figure 1.11.9 ▶

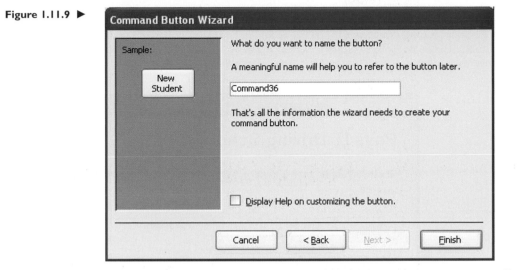

8 Give your button a sensible name and click on **Finish** (see Figure 1.11.9). The lower half of your form should look something like Figure 1.11.10 with the **New Student** button positioned as shown.

Figure 1.11.10 ▼

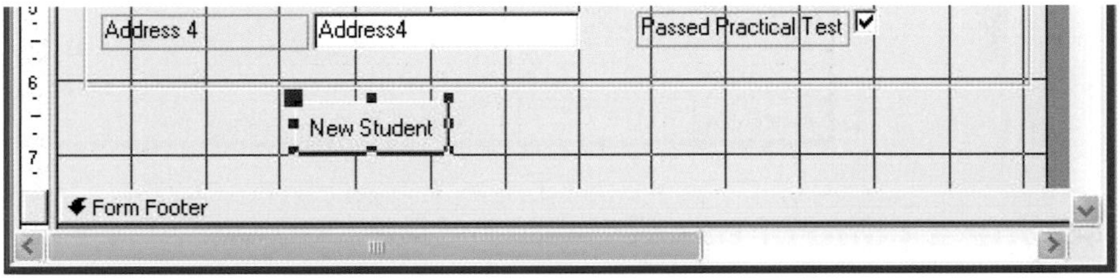

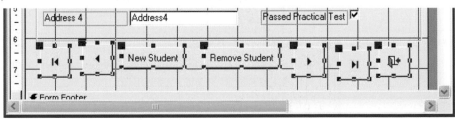

9 Add another button from the **Record Operations** to **Delete a Record** and label it **Remove Student**.

10 Add extra buttons from the **Record Navigation Category** using the actions **Go To First Record, Go To Previous Record, Go To Next Record** and **Go To Last Record.** Don't worry about aligning the buttons yet.

11 Add the **Close Form** button from the **Form Operations** category. You need to arrange the buttons in the order shown in Figure 1.11.11.

Figure 1.11.11 ▼

12 Select all the buttons and align with **Format, Align, Top**.

13 Distribute the buttons evenly by again selecting all and choosing from the menu **Format, Horizontal Spacing, Make Equal**.

14 You may wish to make the buttons smaller and use the **Format, Size** option to make all buttons the same size as shown in Figure 1.11.12. We will remove the Navigation Buttons later now that we no longer need them.

Note Remember you will not be able to use the option Remove Student because of Referential Integrity, the Cascade Delete option has not been checked. Removing records at this point will remove related records in the Lesson table. We will discuss this later in the units.

Figure 1.11.12 ▶

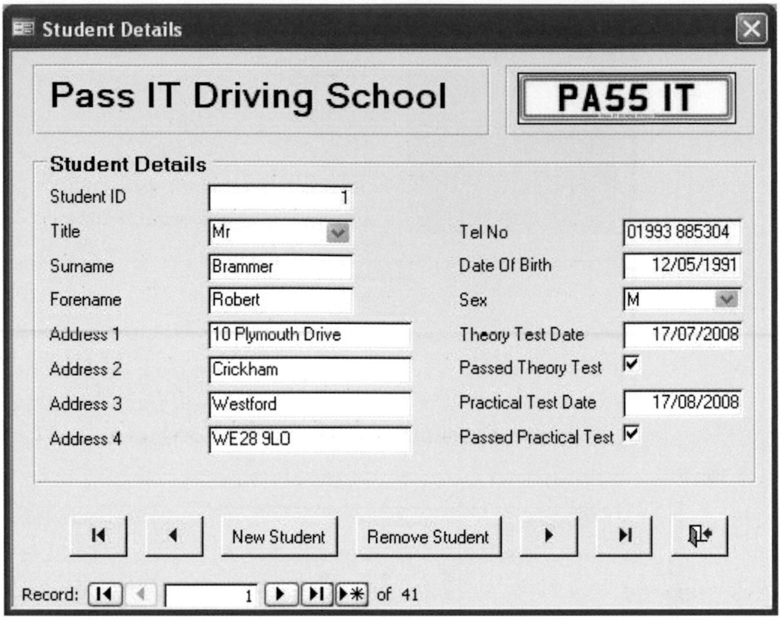

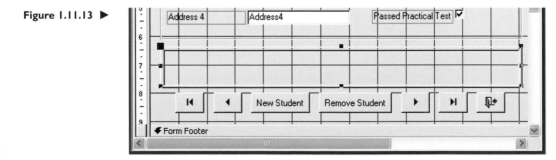

Adding a control panel

It is common practice to keep user buttons away from data entry areas. We are going to add a background to give a control panel effect.

1 From the Toolbox drag out a rectangle big enough to cover the buttons.
2 Select the rectangle and set its **Special Effect** to **Sunken**.
3 Select the rectangle and use copy and paste to make a copy of it. Use the resizing handles to make it slightly larger than the first and set its **Special Effect** to **Raised**.
4 Position the smaller rectangle over the larger and centre the buttons on the panel. If the buttons are hidden by the rectangles you may need to use **Format, Bring to Front** (see Figure 1.11.13).

Figure 1.11.13 ▶

5 Go into the Form Properties and set the **Navigation Buttons** property to **No**. You may wish to set the **Fill Colour** property of the rectangle to make it stand out. Your form should now appear as in Figure 1.11.14.

Figure 1.11.14 ▶

Student Details

Pass IT Driving School   PA55 IT

Student Details

Student ID	1		
Title	Mr	Tel No	01993 885304
Surname	Brammer	Date Of Birth	12/05/1991
Forename	Robert	Sex	M
Address 1	10 Plymouth Drive	Theory Test Date	17/07/2008
Address 2	Crickham	Passed Theory Test	✔
Address 3	Westford	Practical Test Date	17/08/2008
Address 4	WE28 9LO	Passed Practical Test	✔

[◄◄] [◄]   New Student   Remove Student   [►] [►►]   [↵]

You now need to set up a control panel and buttons in exactly the same way on the **frmInstructor**.

Combo boxes

Combo boxes are drop-down boxes which allow the user to select data from a list of choices or type in a data entry of their own. We will set up a combo box on the Student Form so that users can simply enter M or F in the Sex field from a drop-down box.

Adding a combo box to enter student details

1 Open the form **frmStudent** in Design View.
2 Select the **Sex** control and press the DELETE key.
3 Click on the **Combo Box** tool in the Toolbox (see Figure 1.11.15).

Figure 1.11.15 ▶

4 Drag out a small rectangle where the Sex control was.

5 The **Combo Box Wizard** dialogue box is displayed. Check **"I will type in the values that I want"** and click on **Next** (see Figure 1.11.16).

Figure 1.11.16 ▶

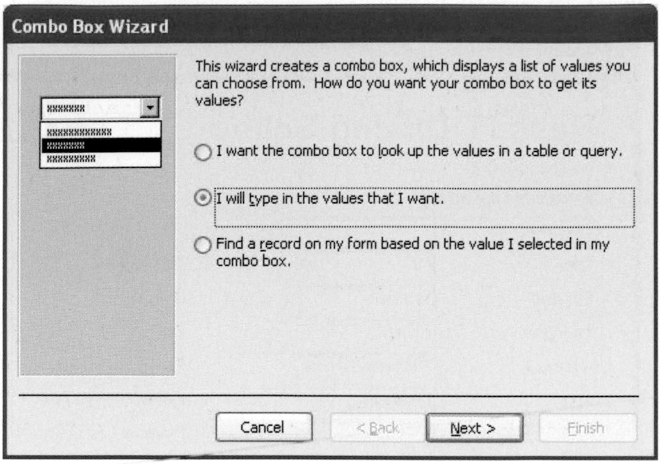

6 Enter **M** and then **F** pressing TAB in between entries and click on **Next** (see Figure 1.11.17).

Figure 1.11.17 ▶

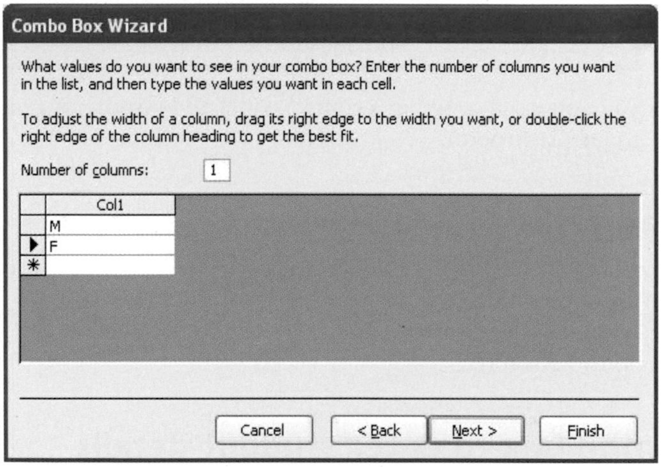

7 Check the **"Store that value in this field"** option and select **Sex** from the drop-down box. Click **Next** (see Figure 1.11.18).

Figure 1.11.18 ▶

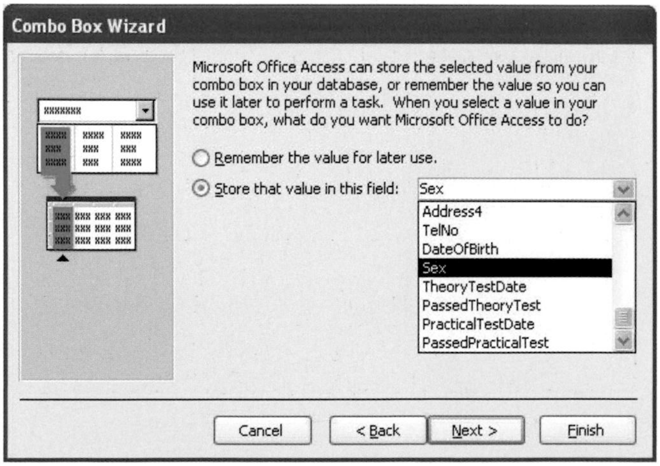

8 Set the label to **Sex** and click on **Finish**. You will need to align the control with the others.

9 Save your form as **frmStudent**. The combo box should appear as in Figure 1.11.19. We will add the Find Record combo box in the next section.

Figure 1.11.19 ▶

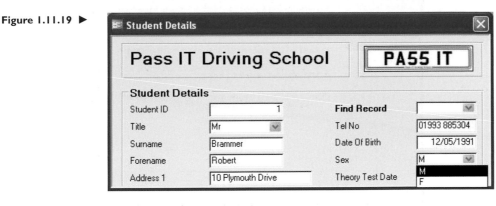

List boxes

List boxes can also be used on forms when a user can only select from a set of predefined choices. They can be added to the form from the Toolbox in the same way as combo boxes.

Using Option Buttons and Option Groups are other methods Access offers for entering data on a form. Further information on this can be found in the **Tricks and Tips** section: "Using option buttons..........." and "Using option groups".

Adding a combo box to look up student details

We are going to set up a combo box to display the names of all our students.

When a student is selected in the combo box, their details will appear on the form.

1 Open **frmStudent** in Design View.

2 Click on the **Combo Box** tool in the Toolbox.

3 Drag out a rectangle above the second column of controls to start the **Combo Box Wizard**. You may have to group the controls and move them a little to create room (see Figure 1.11.20).

Figure 1.11.20 ▶

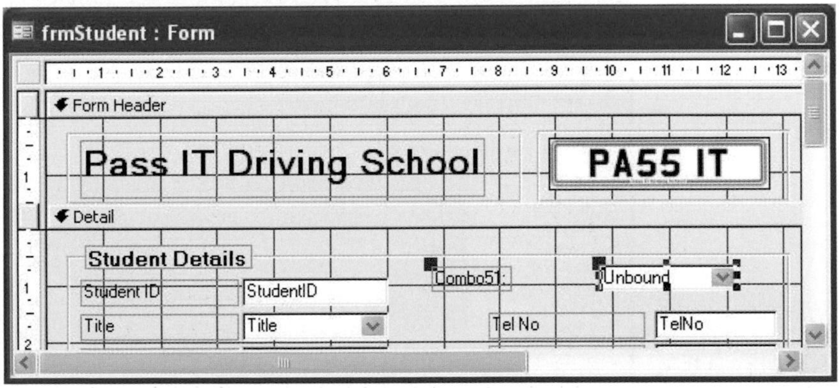

4 Click on **"Find a record on my form based on a value I selected in my combo box"**. Click on **Next** (see Figure 1.11.21).

Figure 1.11.21 ▶

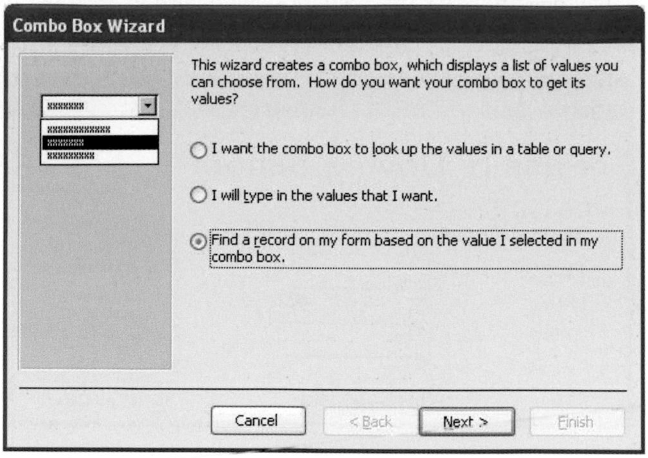

5 Click on the **Surname** field and select it with the > icon. Click on **Next** (see Figure 1.11.22).

Figure 1.11.22 ▶

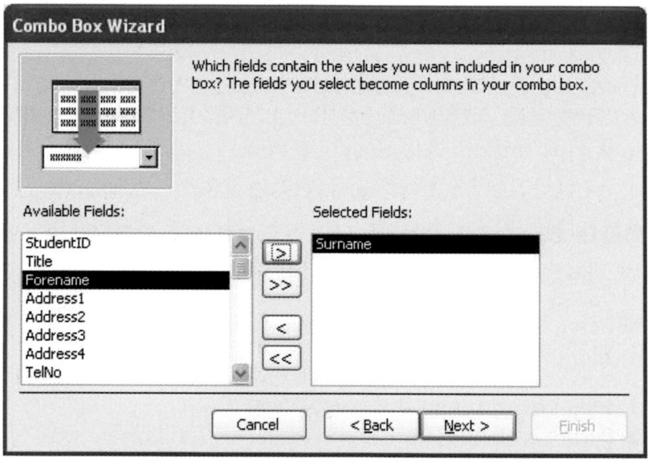

6 The **Combo Box Wizard** dialogue box then displays the names. Click on **Next** again (see Figure 1.11.23).

Figure 1.11.23 ▶

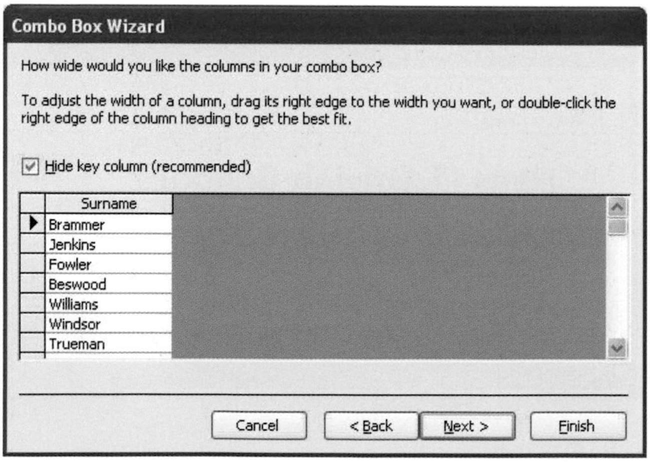

7 Give the combo box the name **Find Record** and click on **Finish**.

8 Switch to **Form View**; **frmStudent** should appear as in Figure 1.11.24. You will need to align and size the control with its label set to bold.

Figure 1.11.24 ▶

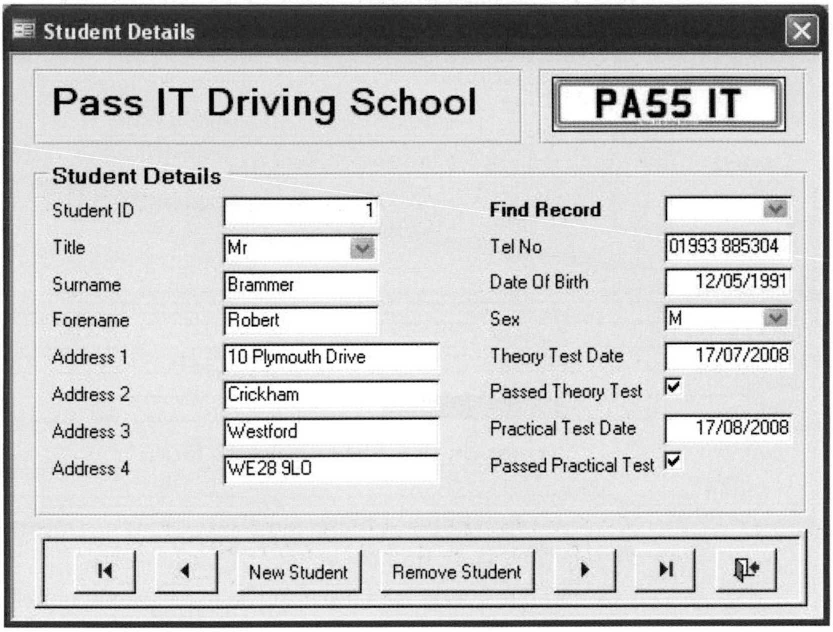

Displaying the names in the combo box in alphabetical order

The names in the drop-down list from the combo box on the Student form are in Student ID order and not alphabetical order. To sort these names into alphabetical order:

1 Open **frmStudent** in Design View and select the **Find Record** Combo box.

2 Click on the **Properties** icon or right click the combo box and click on **Properties**. Click on the **Data** tab.

3 Click on **Row Source** and click on the three dots icon (see Figure 1.11.25).

Figure 1.11.25 ▶

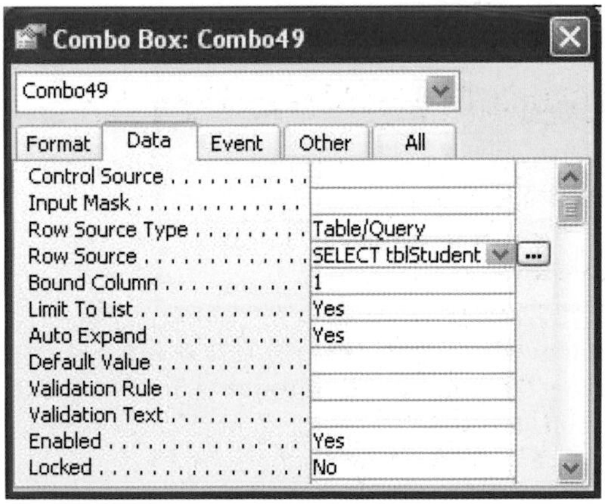

4 The SQL Statement Query Builder window opens (see Figure 1.11.26). It looks similar to Query Design View. In the **Surname** column of the QBE grid, select **Ascending** in the Sort row.

Figure 1.11.26 ▼

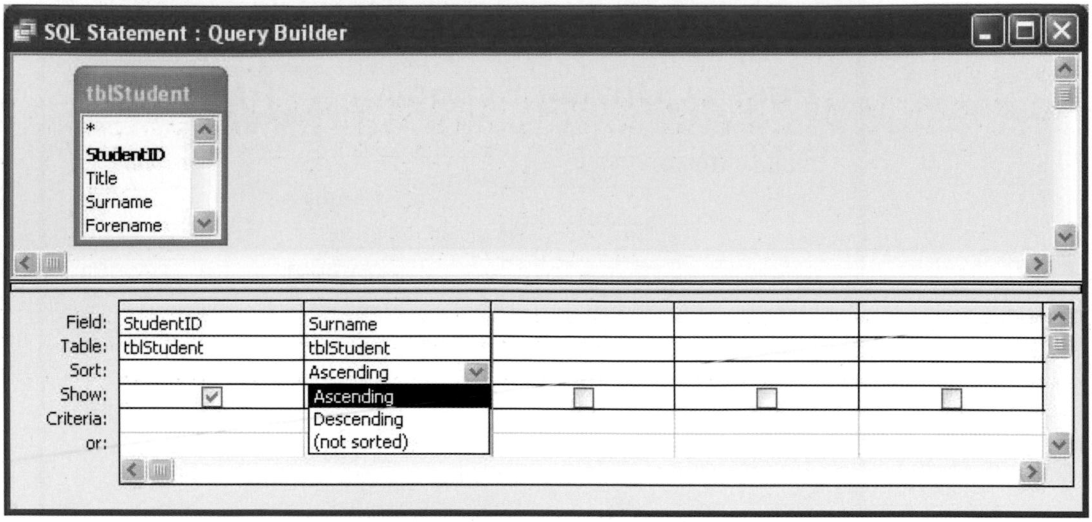

5 Close the **Query Builder** window and save the changes.
6 Go into Form View and test that the names are in alphabetical order.

Create a form to display data from more than one table

In Unit 9 we used the wizards to design simple Student and Instructor forms. We could also have designed a form to book lessons as shown in Figure 1.11.27. The form is based on the table tblLesson.

Figure 1.11.27 ▶

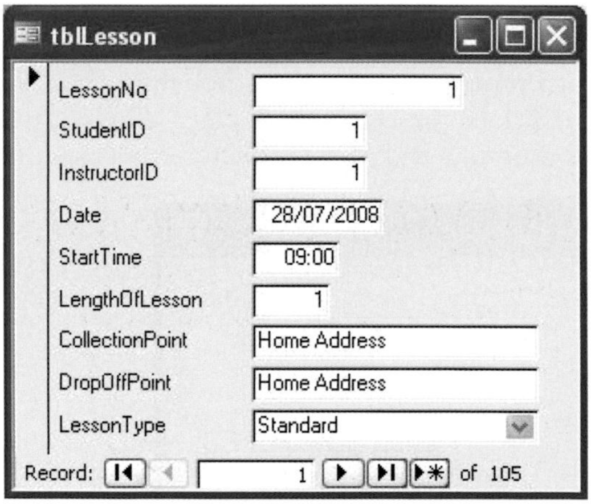

In the real system it is probable the student would not know their ID number and the operator booking their lesson would like to confirm an ID by seeing the student name on screen.

In this section we will set up the Lesson Booking form. You will find out how to base a form on a query. This will enable us to key in the Student ID on the Booking form and Access will find the student's name in the Student table.

Creating the Lesson Booking form

1 In the Database Window click on **Queries**, select **qryLessonCost** and click **Open** to run the Query.

The output in Figure 1.11.28 shows the query bringing in the information from all the tables (some of the columns have been hidden to fit the screen). This is the information that will be displayed in your form.

Figure 1.11.28 ▼

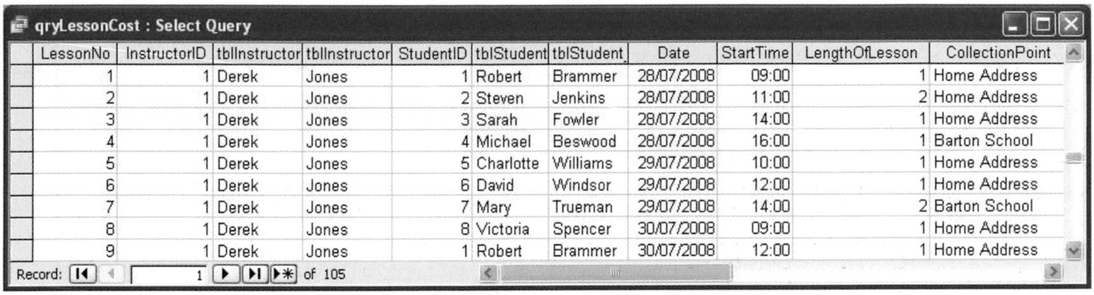

LessonNo	InstructorID	tblInstructor	tblInstructor	StudentID	tblStudent	tblStudent	Date	StartTime	LengthOfLesson	CollectionPoint
1	1	Derek	Jones	1	Robert	Brammer	28/07/2008	09:00	1	Home Address
2	1	Derek	Jones	2	Steven	Jenkins	28/07/2008	11:00	2	Home Address
3	1	Derek	Jones	3	Sarah	Fowler	28/07/2008	14:00	1	Home Address
4	1	Derek	Jones	4	Michael	Beswood	28/07/2008	16:00	1	Barton School
5	1	Derek	Jones	5	Charlotte	Williams	29/07/2008	10:00	1	Home Address
6	1	Derek	Jones	6	David	Windsor	29/07/2008	12:00	1	Home Address
7	1	Derek	Jones	7	Mary	Trueman	29/07/2008	14:00	2	Barton School
8	1	Derek	Jones	8	Victoria	Spencer	30/07/2008	09:00	1	Home Address
9	1	Derek	Jones	1	Robert	Brammer	30/07/2008	12:00	1	Home Address

Record: 1 of 105

2 Close the Query, select **Forms** and click on **New**.

3 In the **New Form** window select the **Form Wizard** and choose **qryLessonCost** from the drop-down list. Click on **OK** (see Figure 1.11.29).

Figure 1.11.29 ▶

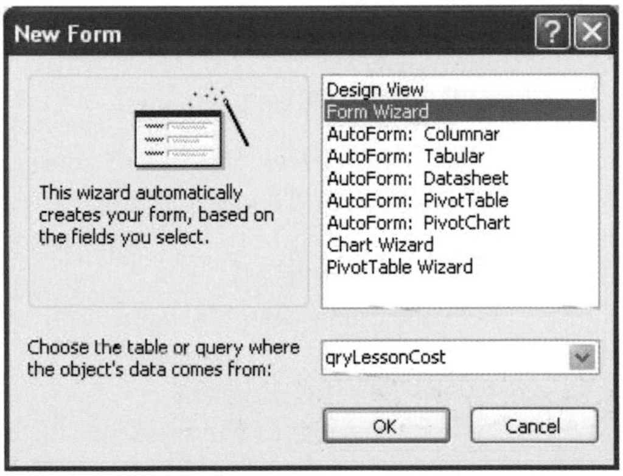

New Form

This wizard automatically creates your form, based on the fields you select.

- Design View
- Form Wizard
- AutoForm: Columnar
- AutoForm: Tabular
- AutoForm: Datasheet
- AutoForm: PivotTable
- AutoForm: PivotChart
- Chart Wizard
- PivotTable Wizard

Choose the table or query where the object's data comes from:

qryLessonCost

OK   Cancel

4 Click the double arrow >> to select all fields as shown in Figure 1.11.30 and click on **Next**.

Figure 1.11.30 ▶

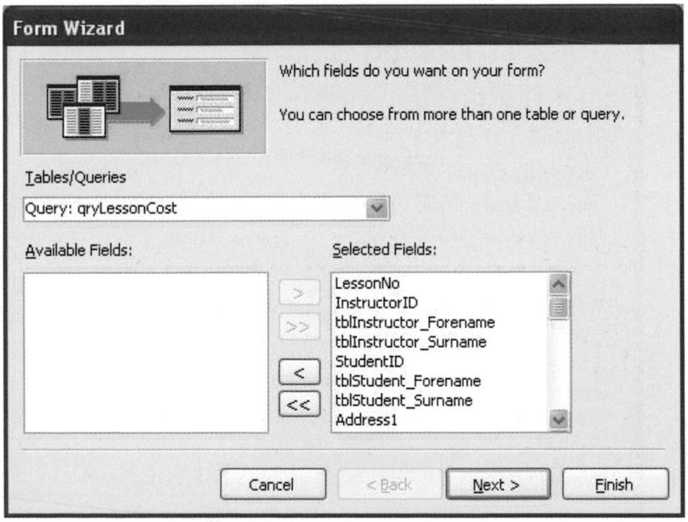

Form Wizard

Which fields do you want on your form?

You can choose from more than one table or query.

Tables/Queries

Query: qryLessonCost

Available Fields:

Selected Fields:

- LessonNo
- InstructorID
- tblInstructor_Forename
- tblInstructor_Surname
- StudentID
- tblStudent_Forename
- tblStudent_Surname
- Address1

Cancel   < Back   Next >   Finish

5 Select **Columnar** and click on **Next**.
6 Select **Standard** and click on **Next**.
7 Name the form **frmLessonBooking** and click on **Finish**.
8 Open the form and **Size to Fit**. It should appear as in Figure 1.11.31.

Figure 1.11.31 ▶

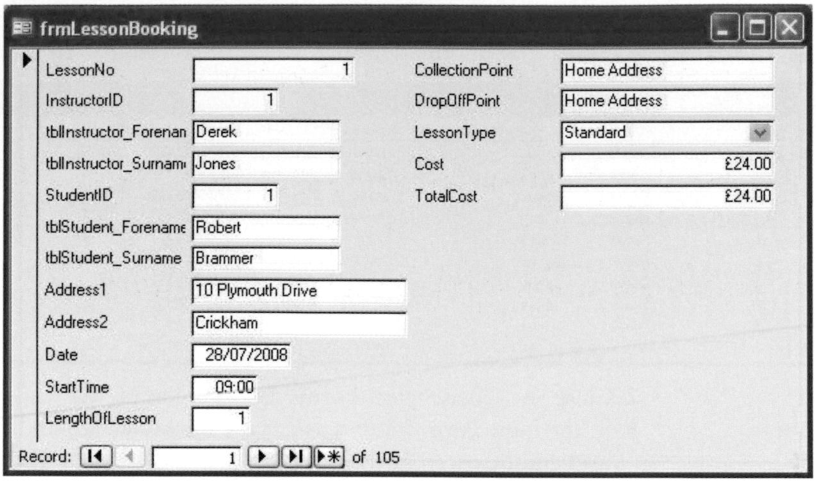

We now need to customise the form to give it the same look and feel as the Student and Instructor forms.

In Form Design View make the following changes:

- Add a Header to the Form Header section in the same font, font size and colour and add the PASS IT logo. You can use copy and paste.
- Edit the labels for the Instructor and Student name control by removing the tbl and underscore. Tidy all other labels.
- Add the control panel (not the buttons) by using copy and paste from one of the other forms.
- Add the buttons using the Wizards as before.
- Set the form properties to the same as the Student and Instructor forms.

Your finished Lesson Booking form should appear as in Figure 1.11.32.

Figure 1.11.32 ▶

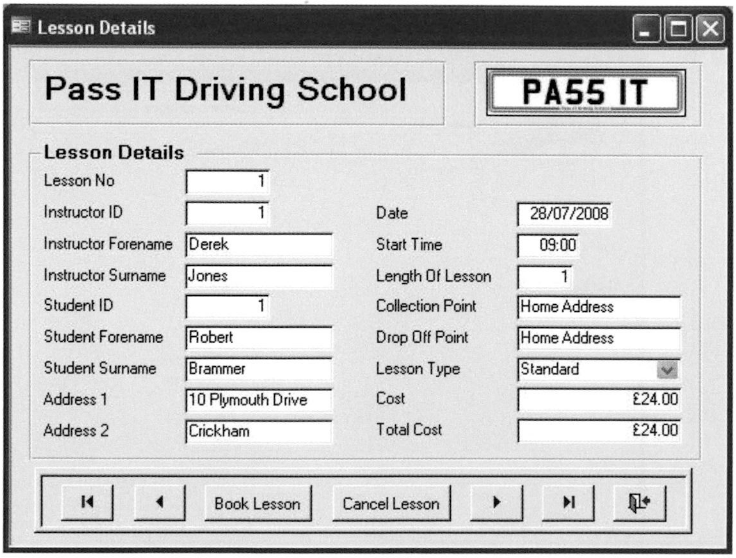

When you book a lesson and enter an Instructor ID number, click on another control or press the TAB key, the instructor's forename and surname will appear.

Similarly after you enter the Student ID, click on another control or press the TAB key, the student's forename, surname and address will appear.

Note To save time we have not developed a **Lesson Type** form but one has been included in the files available for download.

Hint Use **Tricks and Tips** numbers 27, 34, 35 and 37 to explore further how to customise your forms.

Hint Use **Tricks and Tips** numbers 62 and 63 to add a Calendar and Spinner control.

Unit 12: Setting up reports

In this unit you will learn how to set up reports to output information from the Pass IT Driving School database.

A report is a way of presenting data on screen or in printed format. Reports can be based on either a table or a query.

Like a form, a report can be fully customised to suit the user's requirements. Output from a report can include images, text can be positioned where required and the font, size and colour of text can be formatted as shown in Figure 1.12.1.

Figure 1.12.1 ▼

As with forms and queries, wizards can be used to create reports.

It will be normal practice to use the Wizard to set up a report and then to use the Design View window to customise the report to your requirements.

In this section we will set up two reports:

■ a report to show all instructor contact details
■ a report to show details of student lessons

Report 1: Setting up a report to display instructor contact details

We want to set up a report to show a list of all instructors and their contact details. This report will be based on the Instructor table.

1 At the Database Window click on **Reports** and click on **New**.
2 Click on **AutoReport: Tabular** and in the drop-down list click on **tblInstructor**. Click on **OK** (see Figure 1.12.2).

Figure 1.12.2 ▶

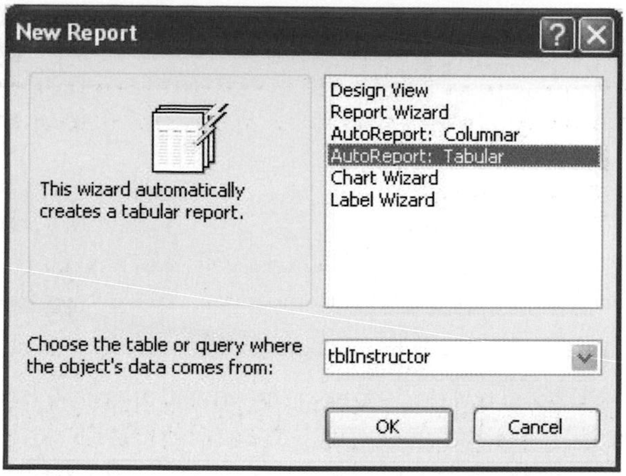

3 The wizard generates the report which is shown in Figure 1.12.3.

Figure 1.12.3 ▼

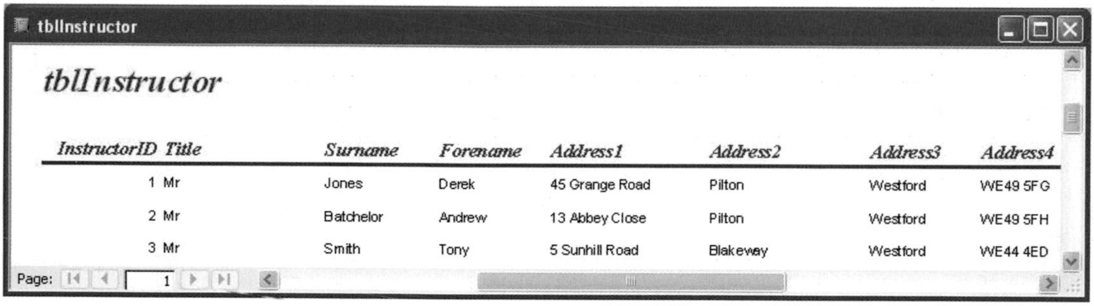

If you scroll down to the bottom of the report, you will see that the Wizard automatically inserts the date and the page number.

4 Close the report and save it as **rptInstructor**.

If you are familiar with the report options you may wish to move quickly to the section called Customising the Instructor Contact Details Report.

The different report views

There are three different views to a report:

■ Print Preview
■ Design View
■ Layout Preview

Print preview

The Print Preview window allows you to see what the report will look like when you print it out. Figure 1.12.5 shows the Print Preview window of the Instructor report.

As the cursor moves over the report it turns into a magnifying glass. Click once to zoom out to see the whole page. Click again to zoom in to actual size as shown in Figure 1.12.4.

Figure 1.12.4 ▼

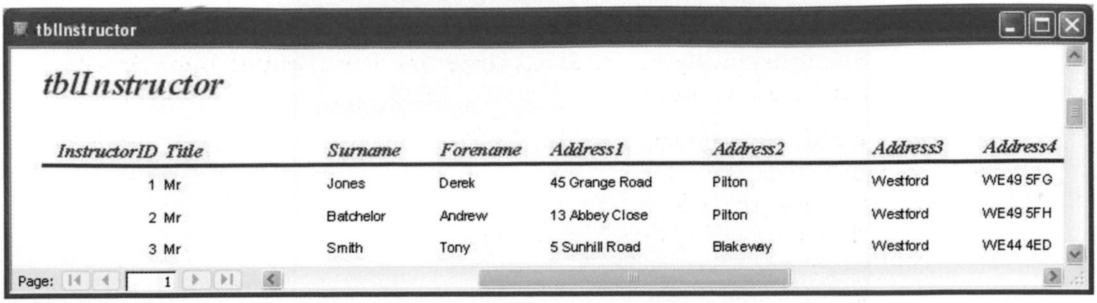
tblInstructor
tblInstructor
InstructorID Title Surname Forename Address1 Address2 Address3 Address4
1 Mr Jones Derek 45 Grange Road Pilton Westford WE49 5FG
2 Mr Batchelor Andrew 13 Abbey Close Pilton Westford WE49 5FH
3 Mr Smith Tony 5 Sunhill Road Blakeway Westford WE44 4ED
Page: 1

When you zoom out the Instructor report will appear as in Figure 1.12.5.

Figure 1.12.5 ▼

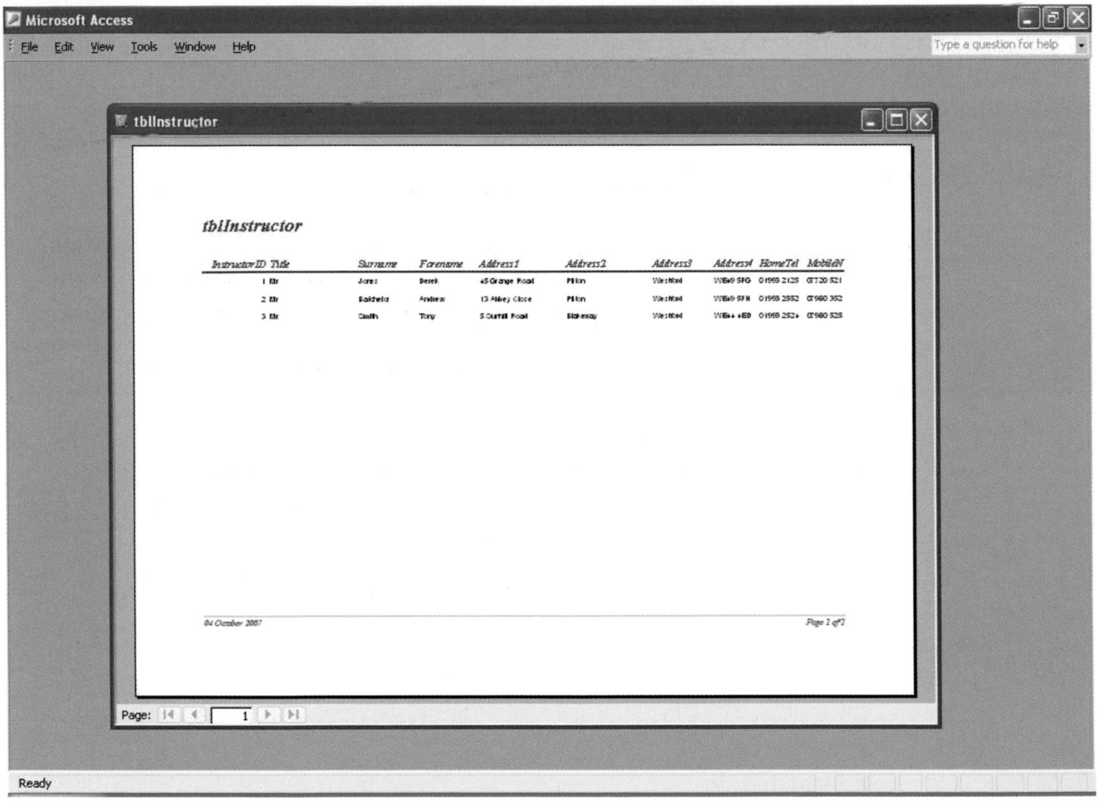
Microsoft Access
File Edit View Tools Window Help
Type a question for help
tblInstructor
tblInstructor
Page: 1
Ready

There is a Print Preview toolbar (see Figure 1.12.6).

Figure 1.12.6 ▶

Print Preview
Fit
Close
Setup

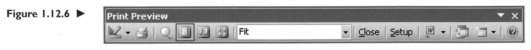

If this toolbar is not displayed, click on **View, Toolbars, Print Preview**.

If there is more than one page in the report you can use the page navigation bar shown at the foot of Figure 1.12.5 to scroll through the pages.

To print a report, simply open the report at the Database Window in Print Preview and click on the Print icon.

Design View

The Design View window allows you to customise your report to suit your requirements. Reports are edited in the same way as editing forms. As with forms it is possible to:

- add, edit and remove fields
- add text and titles
- change the style and layout
- change the font format and colours
- add controls and command buttons
- add images

Click on **View, Design View** to see the Instructor report in Design View (see Figure 1.12.7).

Figure 1.12.7 ▼

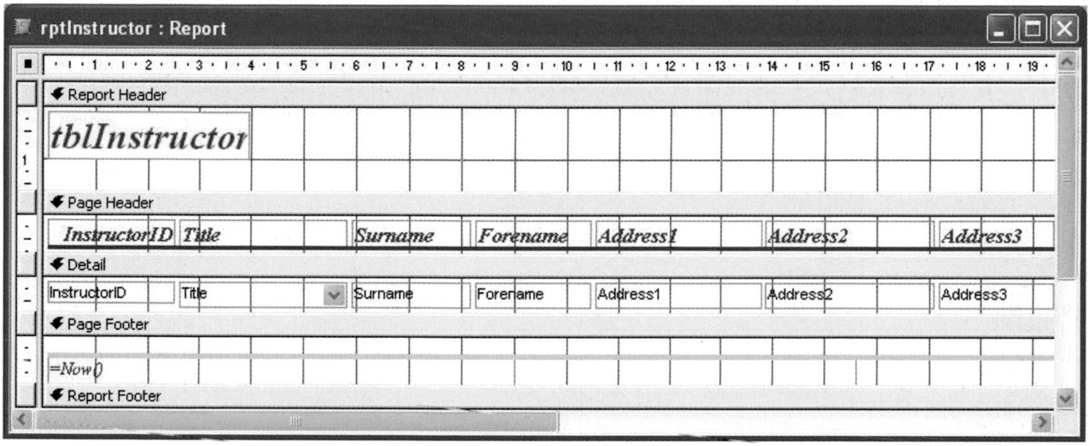

The top part of the report is the **Report Header**. Controls in the Report Header appear only once at the beginning of the report. It is suitable for titles.

The second part of the report is the **Page Header**. Controls in the Page Header appear at the top of every page. It is suitable for column headings.

The third part of the report is the **Detail**. This is used for the data in the report.

The fourth part of the report is the **Page Footer**. Controls in the Page Footer appear at the bottom of every page. It is here the wizard has inserted the page number and the date.

The final part of the report is the **Report Footer**. Controls in the Report Footer appear only once at the end of the report.

We will use Design View to customise the appearance of the Instructor report.

Toolbars

There are two toolbars used in designing reports, the Report Design toolbar (Figure 1.12.8). and the Formatting (Form/Report) toolbar (Figure 1.12.9).

Always ensure these toolbars are displayed when in Report Design View by clicking on **View, Toolbars, Report Design** and **View, Toolbars, Formatting (Form/Report)**.

Figure 1.12.8 ▼

Report Design

Figure 1.12.9 ▼

Formatting (Form/Report)

Label20 | Times New Roman | 20 | **B** *I* <u>U</u>

Two other useful features of Report Design View are the Field List and the Toolbox. If they are not showing they can be found on the View menu.

Right Click menu

If you right click on an object in Report Design View, you get a short-cut menu. Different options are available depending on the object chosen. From this menu you can control the properties of objects on your report (see Figure 1.12.10).

Figure 1.12.10 ▶

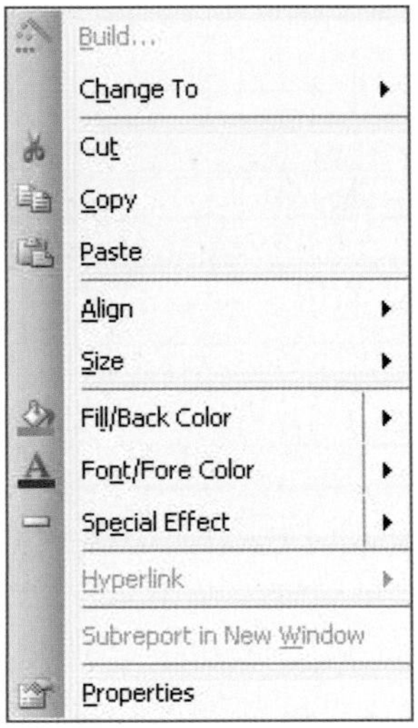

Build...
Change To ▶
Cut
Copy
Paste
Align ▶
Size ▶
Fill/Back Color ▶
Font/Fore Color ▶
Special Effect ▶
Hyperlink ▶
Subreport in New Window
Properties

Orientation of a report

In Design View you can also set a report to be in either portrait or landscape format. Landscape format is often better when the report has many fields in columns.

Click on **File, Page Setup** and click on the **Page** tab to set the orientation of a report to portrait or landscape (see Figure 1.12.11).

Figure 1.12.11 ►

Layout Preview

The Layout Preview window provides a quick way of seeing the layout of a report when you are in Design View to check that it appears how you want it to. However if your report is based on a query, Layout Preview may not include all the data in the report.

There are a number of ways of switching between the Print Preview, Design View and Layout Preview windows. The easiest is to select from the options on the View menu.

Note You cannot switch from Layout Preview to Print Preview or from Print Preview to Layout Preview. To go between these windows, you must first switch to Design View.

Customising the Instructor Contact Details report

We are going to edit the Instructor report, some of the columns (e.g. Title) are too wide and some (e.g. Mobile No) are too narrow.

1 Open the report in **Design View**.
2 Click on the title in the **Report Header**, then drag the resizing handles out to increase the size of the control and change the text in the control to **Instructor Contact Details** (see Figure 1.12.12).

Figure 1.12.12 ▼

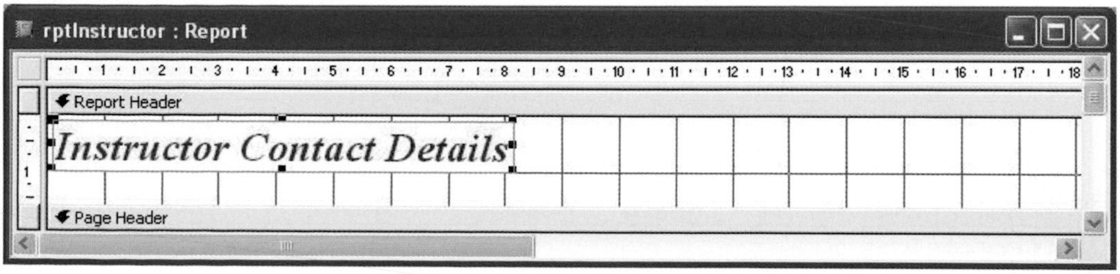

3 Select the **Title** control in the **Detail** section and holding the SHIFT key down select the **Title** control in the **Page Header** section (see Figure 1.12.13).

Figure 1.12.13 ▼

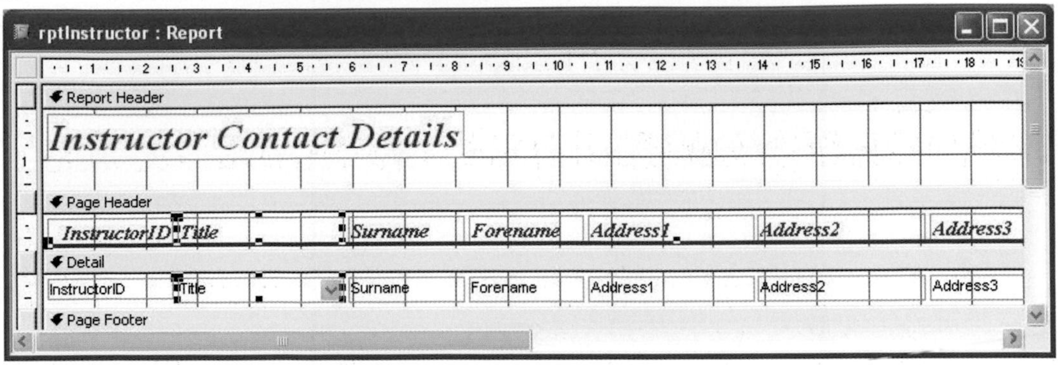

4 Drag the resizing handles in to make one of the controls smaller. The other control will also be resized (see Figure 1.12.14).

Figure 1.12.14 ▼

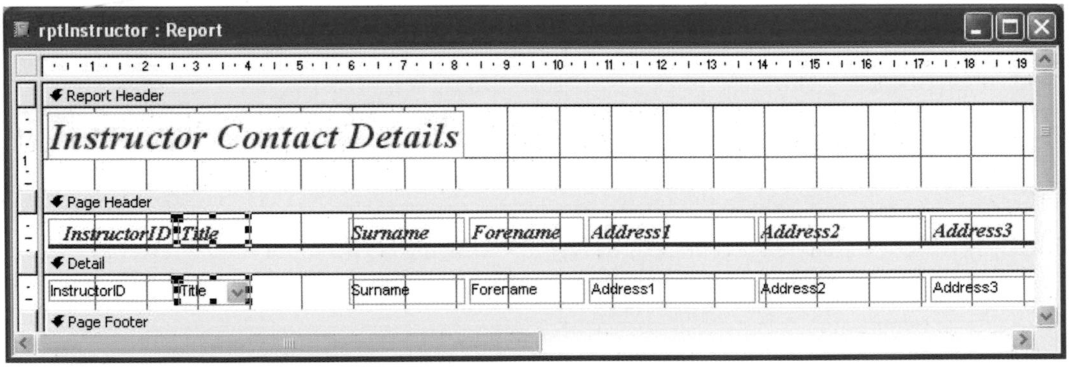

5 Select all the other controls to the right of **Title** in the **Page Header** and the **Detail** sections. (Click on one, then hold down the SHIFT key and click on each of the others in turn.) With care you may find it easier to drag out a rectangle across the controls.

Hint All the controls on a report can be selected with CTRL+A, then it is sometimes quicker to deselect by simply clicking on the controls not required with the SHIFT key held down.

6 Using the 'open hand,' slide all these controls to the left (see Figure 1.12.15).

Figure 1.12.15 ▼

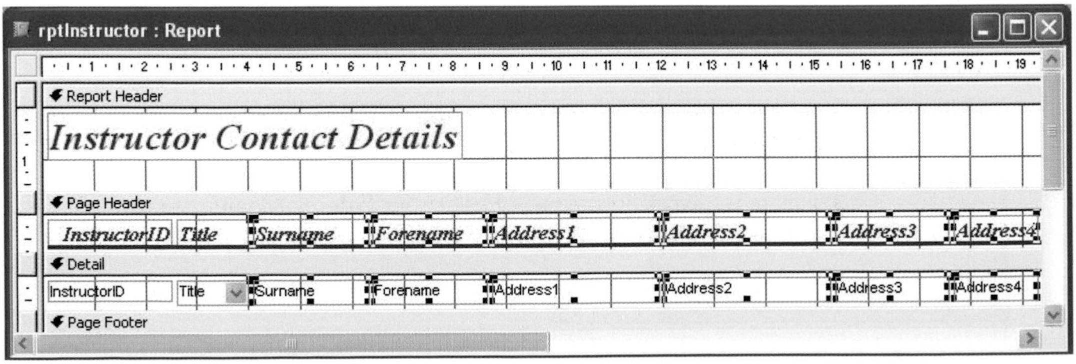

7 Insert spaces in the Header controls for **InstructorID**, **Address1**, **Address2** etc. Select the control for the **Mobile No** and use the resizing handles to enlarge it. You will also have to resize the **Home Tel No** control.

8 Click on **View, Layout Preview** to view your report in Layout Preview mode (see Figure 1.12.16). You may also have to align some of the data controls in the Detail section.

Figure 1.12.16 ▼

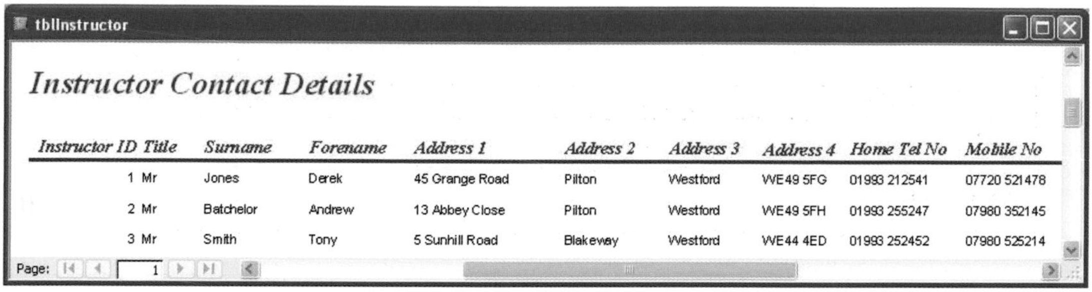
tblInstructor
Instructor Contact Details
Instructor ID Title Surname Forename Address 1 Address 2 Address 3 Address 4 Home Tel No Mobile No
1 Mr Jones Derek 45 Grange Road Pilton Westford WE49 5FG 01993 212541 07720 521478
2 Mr Batchelor Andrew 13 Abbey Close Pilton Westford WE49 5FH 01993 255247 07980 352145
3 Mr Smith Tony 5 Sunhill Road Blakeway Westford WE44 4ED 01993 252452 07980 525214
Page: 1

We can further improve our report as follows:

1 Switch back to Design View and expand the detail area as shown in Figure 1.12.17.

Figure 1.12.17 ▼

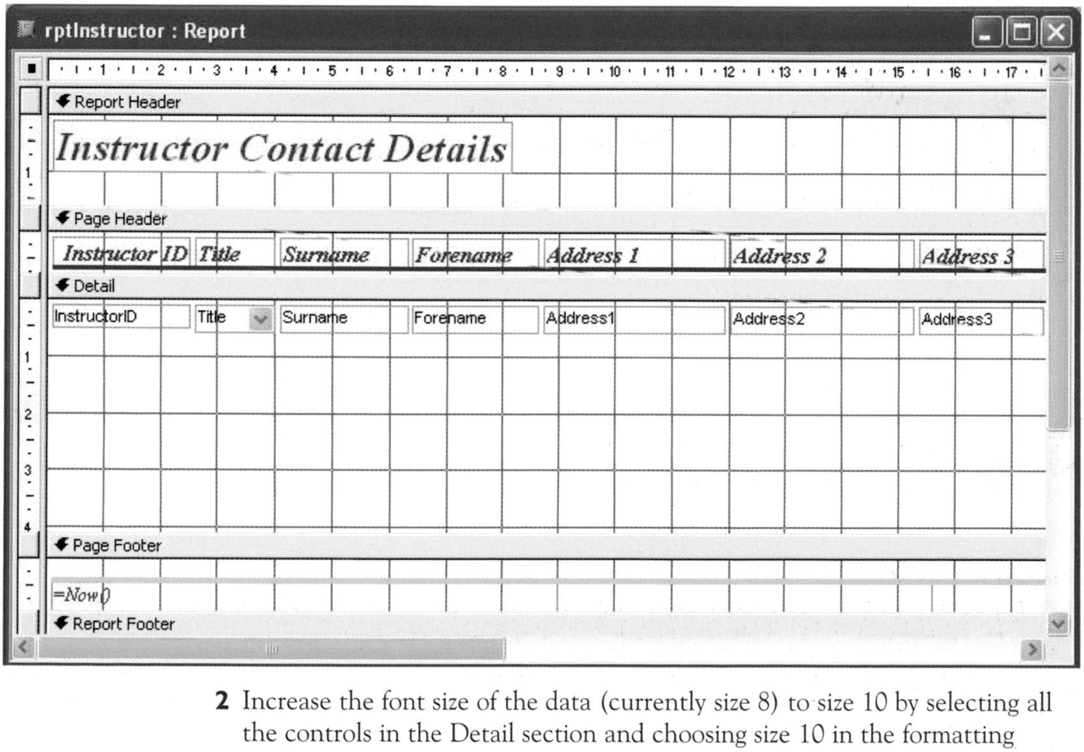
rptInstructor : Report
Report Header
Instructor Contact Details
Page Header
Instructor ID Title Surname Forename Address 1 Address 2 Address 3
Detail
InstructorID Title Surname Forename Address1 Address2 Address3
Page Footer
=Now()
Report Footer

2 Increase the font size of the data (currently size 8) to size 10 by selecting all the controls in the Detail section and choosing size 10 in the formatting toolbar.

3 Delete the labels in the Page Header for **Title, Forename, Address 2, Address 3, Address 4** and **Mobile No.** (Select each label in turn and press delete).

4 Edit the remaining labels to read **Instructor ID, Name, Address** and **Phone** (see Figure 1.12.18).

Figure 1.12.18 ▼

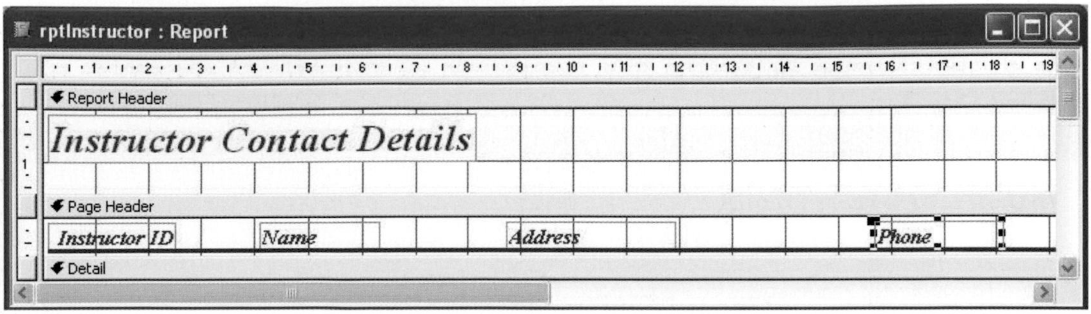

5 Move the controls in the Detail section to look roughly like the report below in Figure 1.12.19.

Figure 1.12.19 ▼

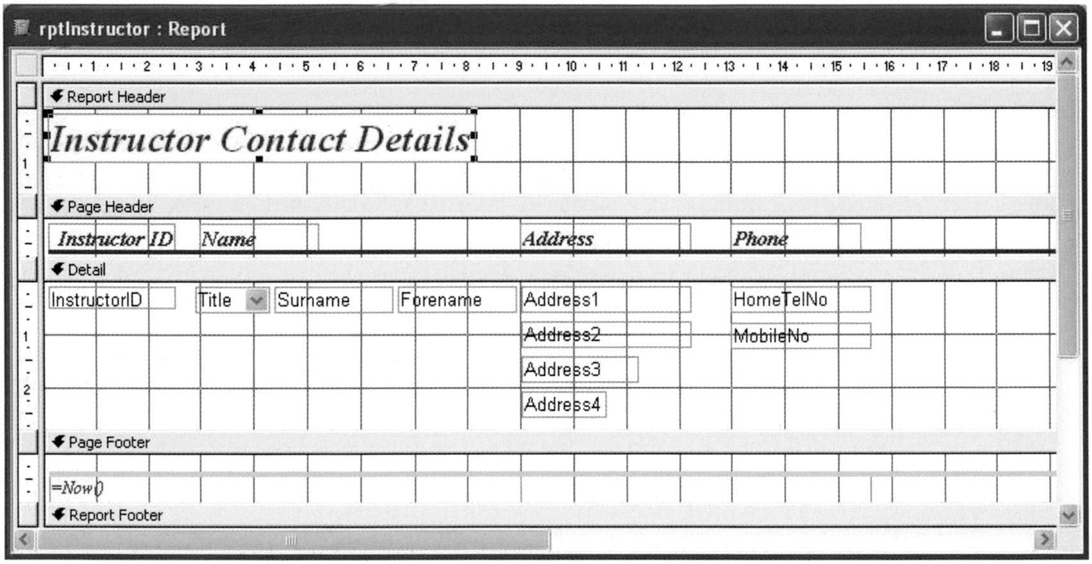

6 Select all the address controls and then click on **Format, Align, Left** to get the controls in a straight line. Click on **Format, Vertical Spacing, Make Equal** to space the controls equally. Format the **InstructorID** control to centre from the formatting toolbar.

7 Switch to **Layout Preview** to see the finished report as in Figure 1.12.20.

Figure 1.12.20 ▶

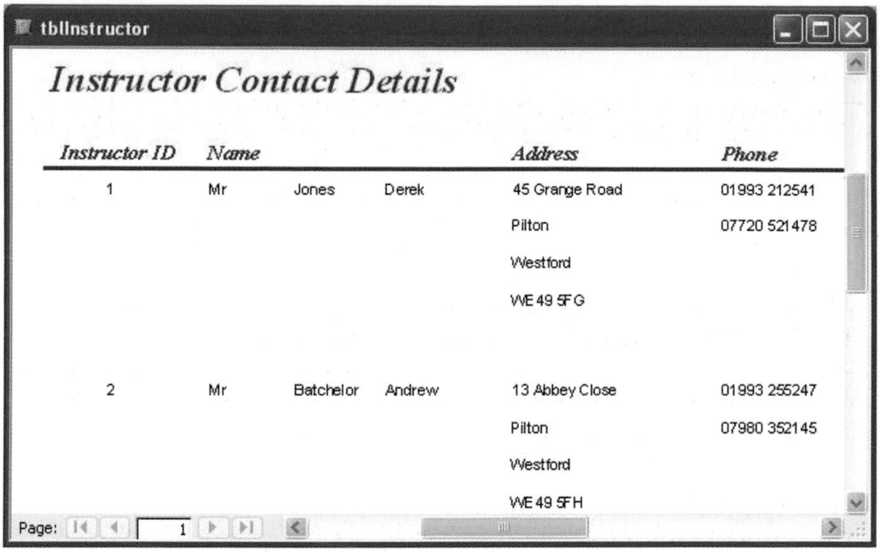

Professional looking reports

In this unit we have looked at methods of quickly developing a report using the Access wizards and customising the layout using simple formatting techniques. When planning and developing a system ideally the designer would agree on standard layouts and fonts so that all reports are consistent and have a professional look. Access offers a number of facilities to take report design further:

■ The Toolbox offers line, rectangle and image tools.
■ Colour fill options can be added to Header, Footer and Detail areas.
■ All objects on a report have properties giving you even greater control over the appearance of each.

With a little thought to design, the Instructor Report developed earlier in this unit can be presented as in Figure 1.12.21.

Figure 1.12.21 ▼

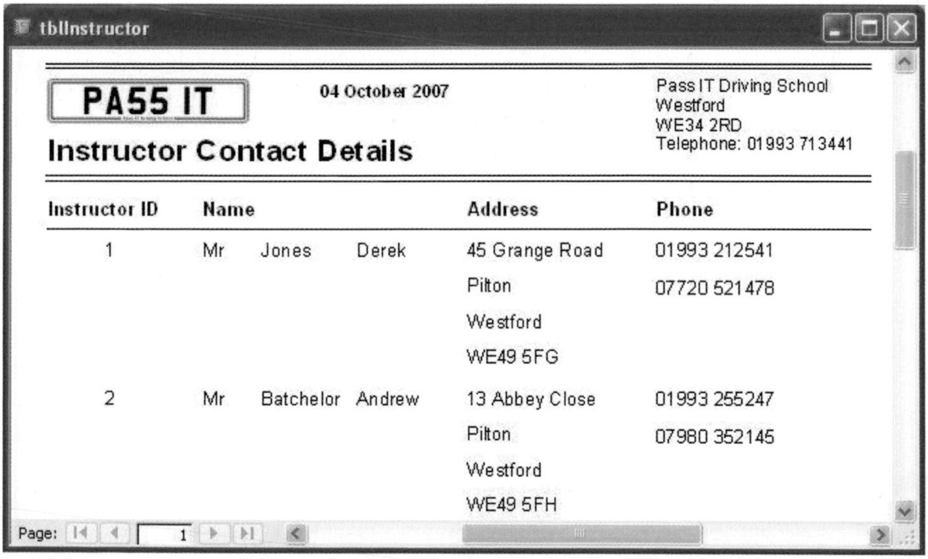

Load the Instructor report in Design View and experiment with the following instructions to achieve a more professional look:

1 Click on **File, Page Setup** and click on the **Page** tab to set the orientation of the report to **Portrait**. You will probably need to shorten the right margin to about 15–16 cm. To be able to do this you will have to drag across the lines and page numbering control inserted by Access until they sit inside the page limits. Click **Layout Preview** to view the page size.

In the Report Header:

2 You may have to drag the header down a little. Move the **Instructor Contact Details** title as shown in Figure 1.12.22. Press F4 to display its properties. Set its **Font Name** to **Arial**, **Font Size** to **16**, **Font Weight** to **Bold**, **Fore Colour** to **Black** and **Font Italic** to **No**.

Figure 1.12.22 ▼

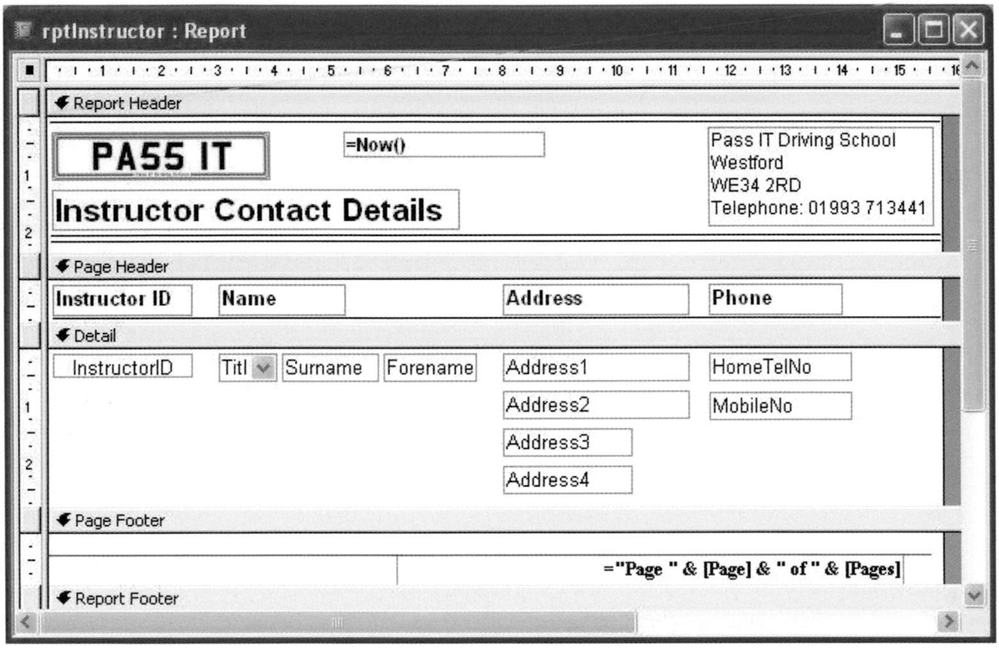

3 Click on the **Image** icon in the Toolbox and drag out a rectangle in the Report Header. Find the image you wish to insert as the logo and click on **OK**.
   If your image is too big for the rectangle you have drawn, either:

   ■ resize the rectangle or
   ■ right click on the image. Click on **Properties**. Click on the **Format** tab and in the **Size Mode** box click on **Zoom**.
   Alternatively you can use copy and paste to import an image from another application.
4 Drag the Date control in the Footer to the Report Header area and align with the logo. Click **View, Properties** and set its **Font Name** to **Arial**, **Font Size** to **9**, **Font Weight** to **Bold**, **Fore Colour** to **Black** and **Font Italic** to **No**.

Hint   There are many ways to view an object's properties on a report: the menus, right click or using F4. Choose whatever is the easiest. It is worth exploring some of the options.

5 From the Toolbox select the **Label** tool and drag out a Label to enter the details Pass IT Driving School, Westford, WE34 2RD, Telephone: 01993 713441. Use CTRL + ENTER to force a carriage return. Click on the Label to view its properties and set the **Font** to **Arial, 9pt, Black.**

6 From the Toolbox select the **Line** tool and drag out a line the width of the Report Header, this will be about 16 cm. View its properties and set its **Border Width** to **1 pt**. Use copy and paste to position two lines at the top of the header and two at the bottom.

Hint It is worth spending some time getting the Report Header area as you want it. It is then easy to copy and paste to all reports.

In the Page Header:

7 Select all the Heading controls and click **View, Properties**. Set the **Font Name** to **Arial**, **Font Size** to **10**, **Font Weight** to **Bold**, **Fore Colour** to **Black** and **Font Italic** to **No.**

8 Remove the blue line the Access wizard uses. From the Toolbox select the **Line** tool and drag out a line the width of the report. View its properties and set its **Border Width** to **1 pt** and **Border Colour** to **Black**. It may be easier to simply copy one of the lines used in the Report Header.

In the Page Footer:

9 Select the Page numbering control and set its **Font** properties to **Arial, 8pt, Bold**. Select the line and set its **Border Width** to **1 pt** and **Border Colour** to **Black.**

Your finished report should appear as in Figure 1.12.21.

Report 2: Setting up a report to display details of student lessons

In Units 6–8 you set up a number of queries to display information. All these queries can be used as a basis for a report.

We want to set up a report to show the lesson details for a particular student. This report will be based on the **qryStudentLesson**. You are asked to enter a Student ID and the query returns the lesson details for that student. You might like to run the query to remind yourself.

1 At the **Database Window** click on **Reports** and click on **New**.
2 Click on **Report Wizard** and in the drop-down list click on **qryStudentLesson**. Click on **OK**. (See Figure 1.12.23.)

Figure 1.12.23 ▶

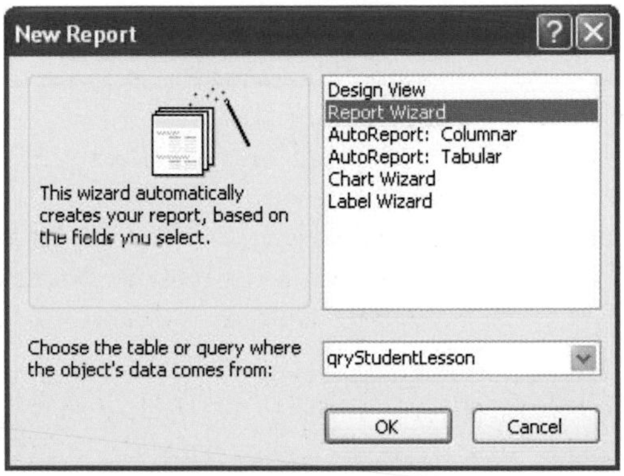

3 The next dialogue box asks you to select which fields are required on the report. Click on the double arrow to choose all the fields **StudentID**, **Date**, **StartTime**, **LengthOfLesson** and click on **Next**. (See Figure 1.12.24.)

Figure 1.12.24 ▶

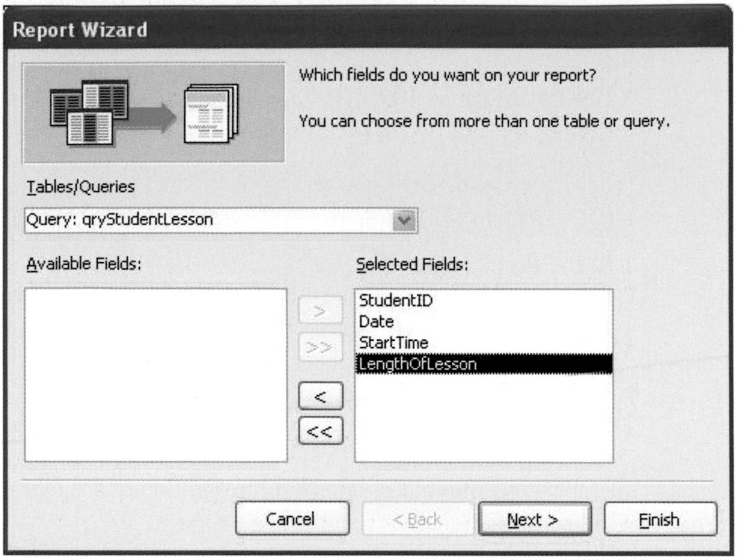

4 From the next dialogue box click on **Next** to ignore any grouping levels. Access will automatically set to group by **StudentID**. (See Figure 1.12.25.)

Figure 1.12.25 ▶

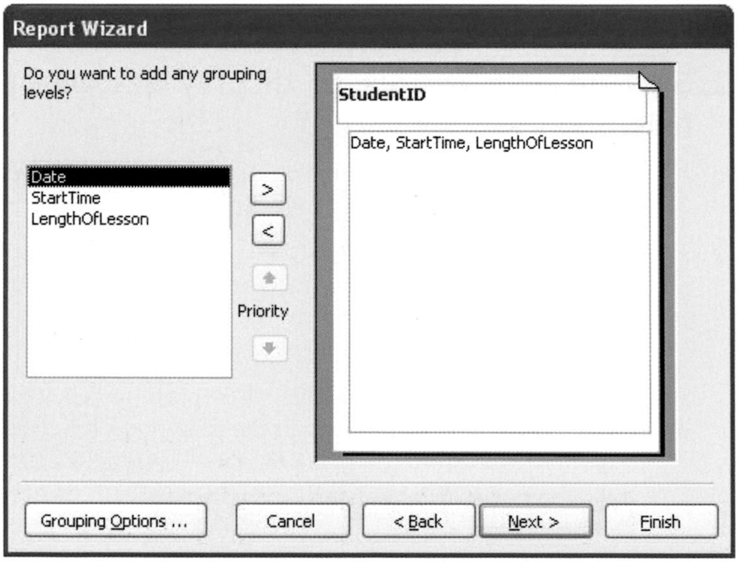

5 From the next dialogue box choose to **Sort** by **Date**. Click on **Next**. (See Figure 1.12.26.)

Figure 1.12.26 ▶

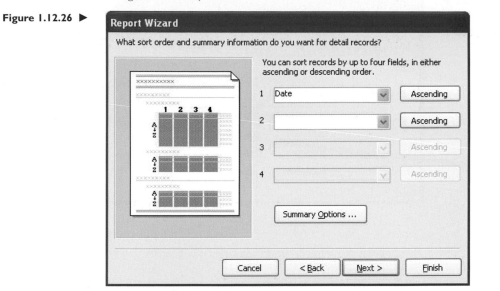

6 Select **Align Left 1** and **Portrait**. Click on **Next**. (See Figure 1.12.27.)

Figure 1.12.27 ▶

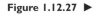

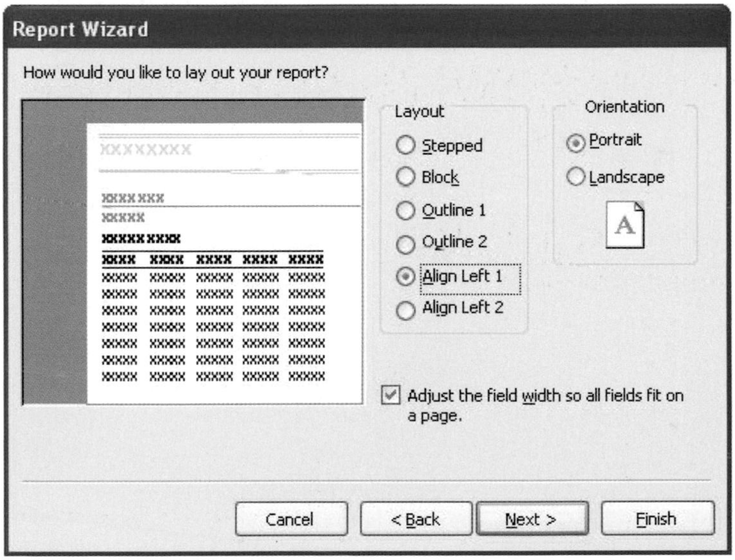

7 Select **Corporate** and click on **Next**. Call the report **rptStudentLesson** and click on **Finish**.
8 You will be prompted to enter a **StudentID**. Enter Student ID **1**.

The report will open in Report View as shown in Figure 1.12.28.

Figure 1.12.28 ▶

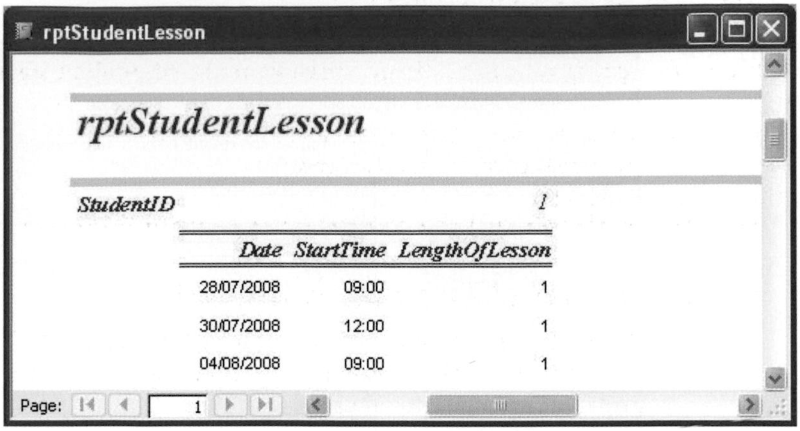

Note When designing reports it is important that the information is **meaningful**. In the **rptStudentLesson** above it clearly lacks details of the student's name, their instructor and collection point.

These details exist in other tables which means you would have to redesign the query to be able to display the correct information.

The following unit looks at ways of producing more complex reports based on multi-table queries.

Unit 13: Further reports

In this unit we are going to design three more reports. All will be based on multi-table queries.

■ A report to produce all the instructors' timetables for a particular date.
■ A report to produce details of all students' lessons.
■ A weekly timetable report.

Report 1: Instructors' Timetable Report

We are going to set up a report showing all the instructors' timetables for a particular date. We will base this report on the query called **qryFullDetailsByDate** set up in Unit 8.

This report introduces you to grouping data in reports and forcing page breaks. If you want to group data, it is easier to use the Report Wizard rather than AutoReport.

1 At the Database Window, click on **Reports** and click on **New**.
2 Click on **Report Wizard** and select **qryFullDetailsByDate** from the list. Click on **OK** (see Figure 1.13.1).

Figure 1.13.1 ▶

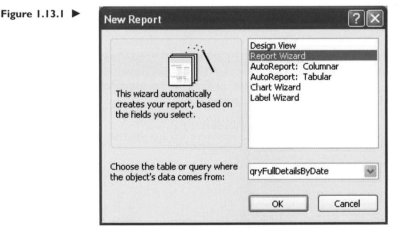

3 In the next dialogue box, click on the field **tblStudent_Forename**, then click on the single arrow (>) to add to the selected fields. In the same way add **tblStudent_Surname, InstructorID, StartTime, LengthOfLesson** and click on **Next**.

4 The next dialogue box asks how you want to view your data. Click on **tblLesson.** Click on **Next** (see Figure 1.13.2).

Figure 1.13.2 ▶

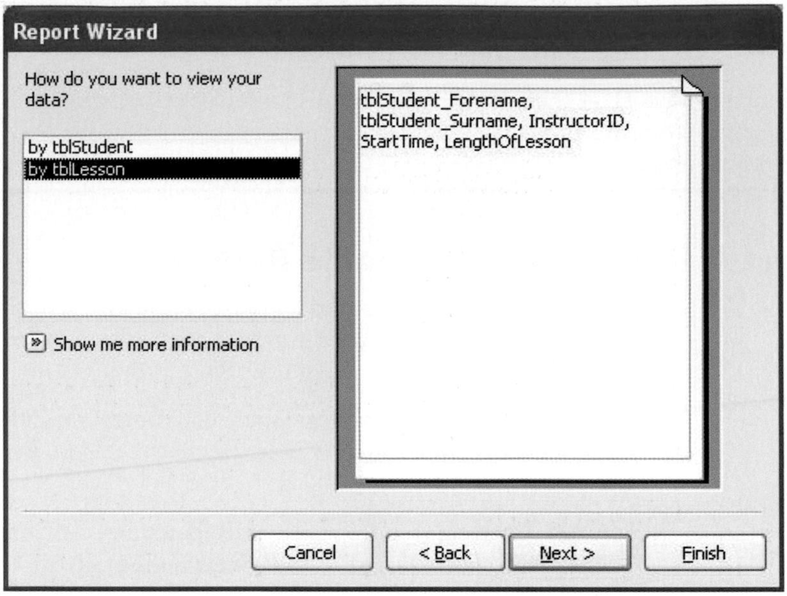

5 When asked do you want to add any grouping levels, click on **InstructorID** to group by Instructor and click on the arrow icon (**>**). Click on **Next** (see Figure 1.13.3).

Figure 1.13.3 ▶

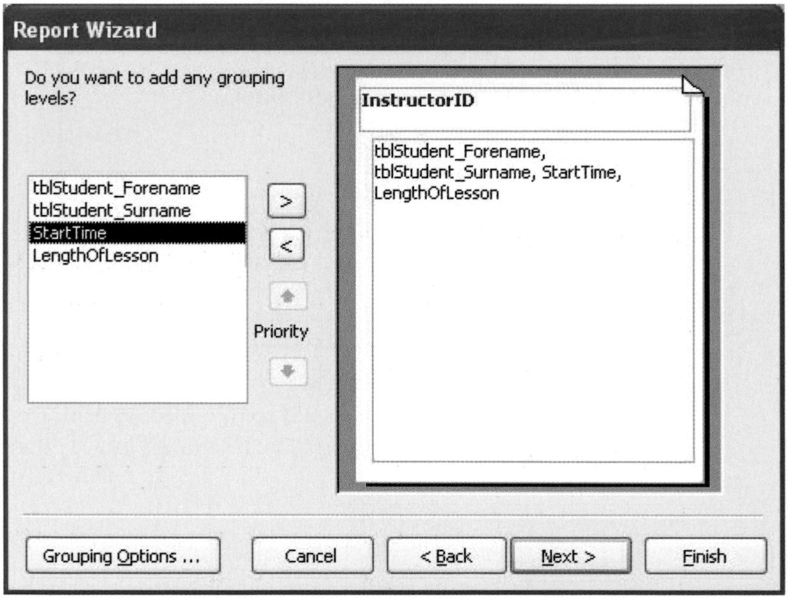

6 Sort by **StartTime**. Click on **Next**.
7 Click on **Align Left 1** and click on **Next**.
8 Click on **Corporate** and click on **Next**.
9 Call it **rptInstructorTimetable** and click on **Finish**.
10 Enter the date **31/07/08** when prompted.

The report should look like the one in Figure 1.13.4.

Figure 1.13.4 ▼

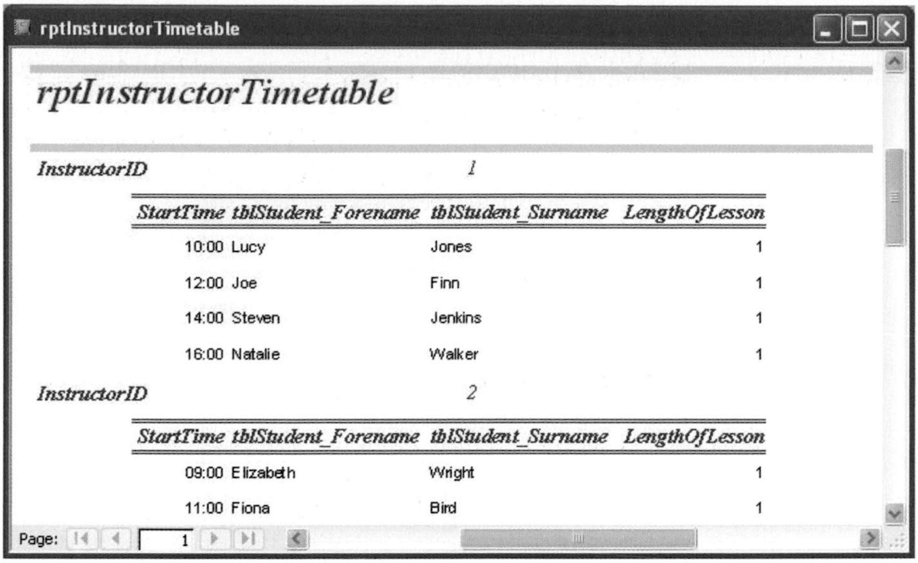

We can see that the output is grouped by instructor, but it is rather unsatisfactory because:

- the instructors' names are not on the report
- the date is not on the report
- the column headings are **tblStudent_Forename** and **tblStudent_Surname**

Switch to Design View and you will see that Access has inserted an InstructorID Header. This is because you chose to group by InstructorID. Controls placed here will head each section about each instructor.

1 Edit the **tblStudent_Forename** column heading in the **InstructorID Header** to read **Name** (see Figure 1.13.5).

Figure 1.13.5 ▼

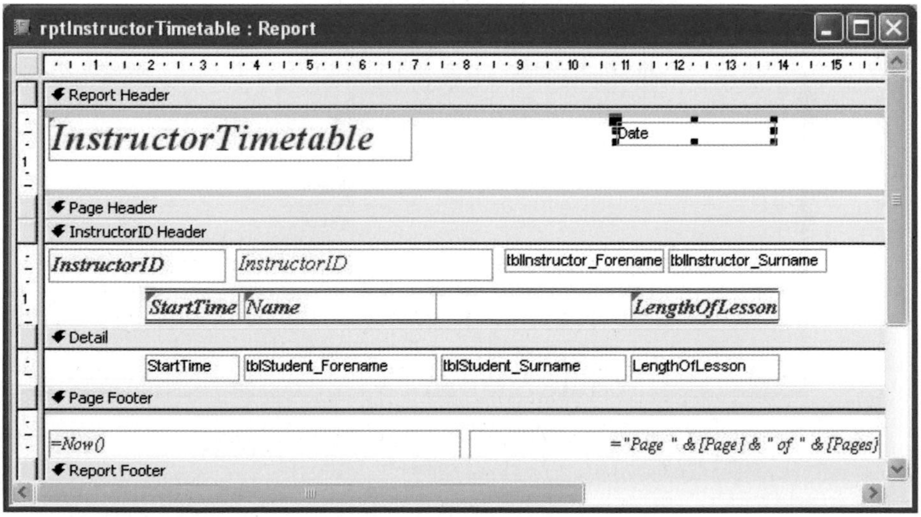

2 Delete the **tblStudent_Surname** column heading by selecting it and pressing the DELETE key.

3 If the Field List is not displayed, click on the **Field List** icon or click on **View, Field List**.

4 Drag **Date** from the Field List on to the Report Header.

5 Select the new **Date** control (not the label). Click on the **Properties** icon and click on the **Format** tab. Set the first (**Format**) property to **Long Date** (see Figure 1.13.6).

Figure 1.13.6 ▶

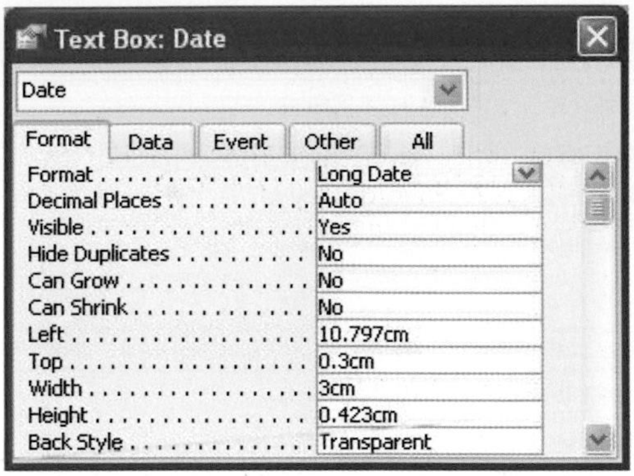

6 Select the label for the **Date** field and delete it by pressing the DELETE key.

7 Drag both the **tblInstructor_Forename** and **tblInstructor_Surname** from the Field List on to the **InstructorID Header**. Select the labels for these fields and delete them (see Figure 1.13.5).

8 Edit the title and align as shown in Figure 1.13.5.

9 Switch to Print Preview mode. Enter the date **31/07/08**. The report should look similar to Figure 1.13.7. Save your report as **rptInstructorTimetable.**

Figure 1.13.7 ▼

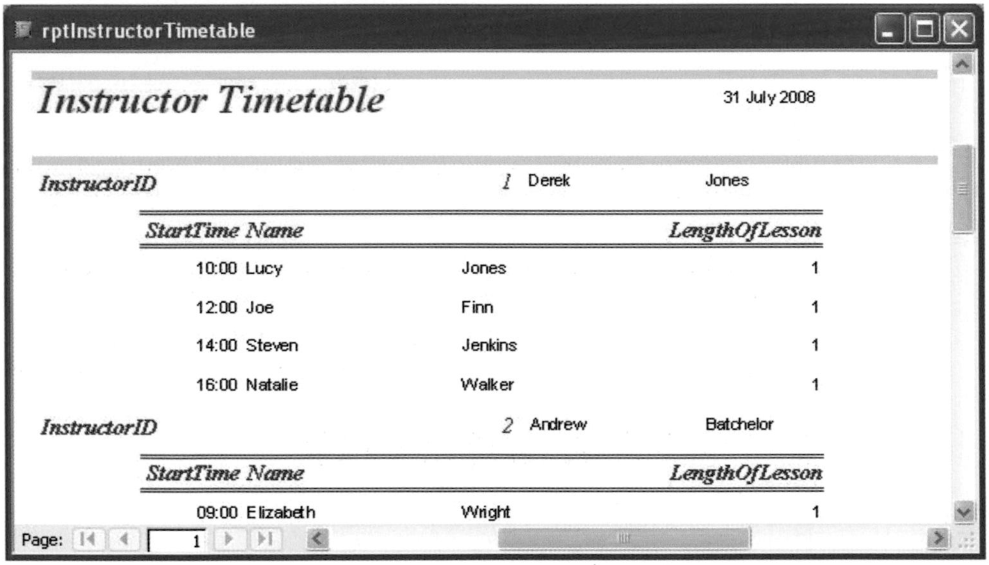

Putting each instructor on a new page

Sometimes you might want each section of a report on a new page. For example in the above report, you may want the timetable for each instructor printed on a separate page, one to give to each instructor.

To force a new page in a report:

1 Load the report in Design View. We need to set up an **InstructorID Footer**. Make sure the Report Design toolbar is showing (see Figure 1.13.8). Click on

Figure 1.13.8 ▼

the **Sorting and Grouping Icon** or click on **View, Sorting and Grouping**.

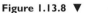

2 In the dialogue box that appears (see Figure 1.13.9), click on **InstructorID** and change **Group Footer** to **Yes**.

Figure 1.13.9 ►

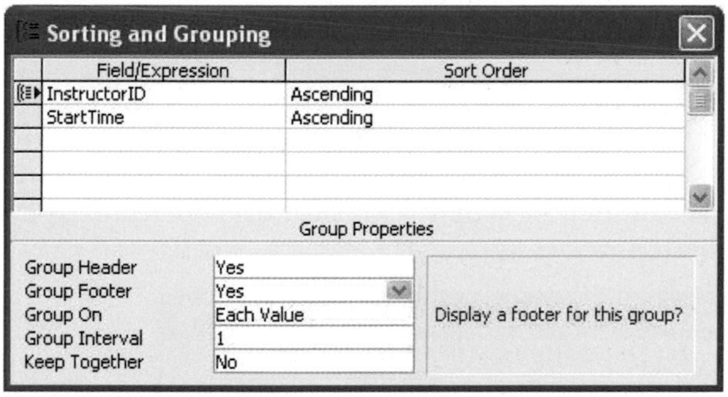

A blank **InstructorID Footer** has now appeared below the Detail section (see

Figure 1.13.10 ▼

Figure 1.13.10).

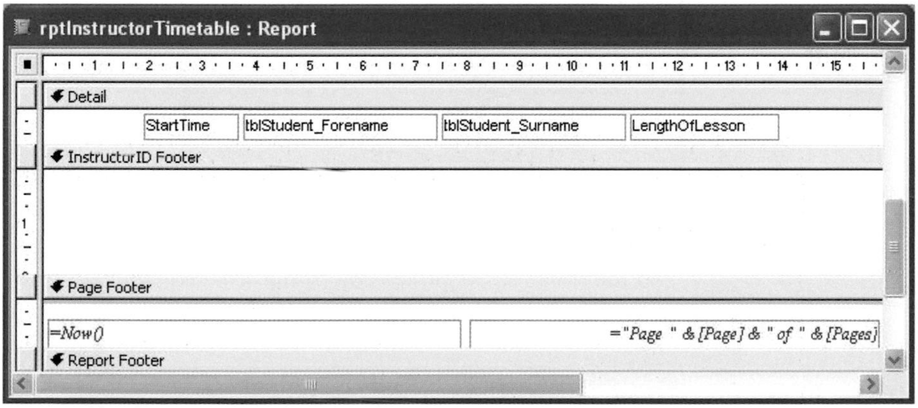

3 Click in the **InstructorID** Footer.
4 Click on the **Properties** icon or click on **View, Properties**.
5 Click on the **Format** tab and set **Force New Page** to **After Section** (see Figure 1.13.11).

Figure 1.13.11 ►

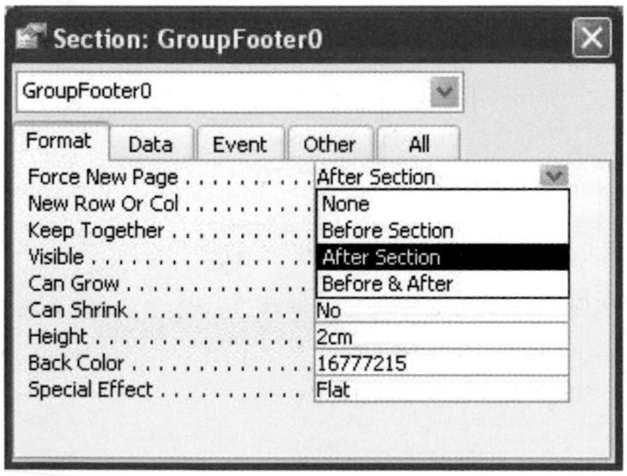

6 Switch to **Print Preview** mode to check that each instructor is on a new page. Save your report as **rptInstructorTimetable.**

Note You will notice that the title Instructor Timetable and date appear at the top of the report on page 1. These details should be in the Page Header and not the Report Header so that they appear on every page. Enlarge the Page Header, then select the contents of the Report Header and drag them into the Page Header.

You may wish to customise with the same report header style used in Unit 12.

Report 2: Student Lesson Details Report

We are now going to set up a report to display details of all student lessons. The report will be based on the query called **qryFullDetails** set up in Unit 8.

1 At the Database Window, click on **Reports** and click on **New**.
2 Click on **Report Wizard** and select **qryFullDetails** from the list. Click on **OK** (see Figure 1.13.12).

Figure 1.13.12 ▶

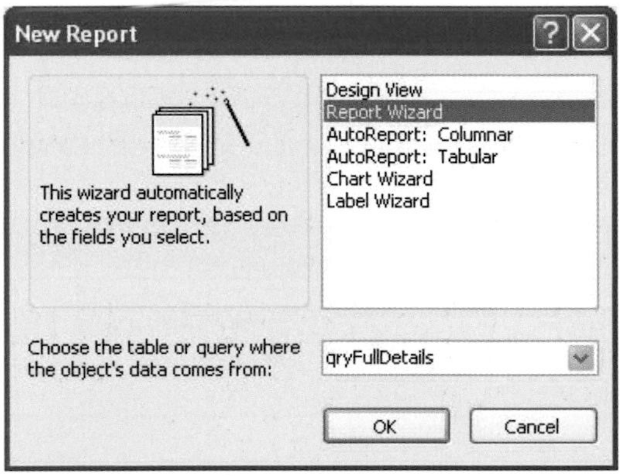

3 In the next dialogue box, click on the field **tblStudent_Forename**, then click on the single arrow (>) to add to the selected fields. In the same way add **tblStudent_Surname, tblInstructor_Forename, tblInstructor_Surname, Date, StartTime, LengthOfLesson, CollectionPoint** and click on **Next**.

Figure 1.13.13 ▶

4 The next dialogue box will ask you how to view the data. Click on
tblStudent (see Figure 1.13.14).

Figure 1.13.14 ▶

5 When asked do you want to add any grouping levels, Access will
automatically select **tblStudent_Forename** and **tblStudent_Surname**, click
on **Next** to accept (see Figure 1.13.15).

Figure 1.13.15 ▶

6 Sort by **Date** and **StartTime** and click on **Next** (see Figure 1.13.16).

Figure 1.13.16 ▶

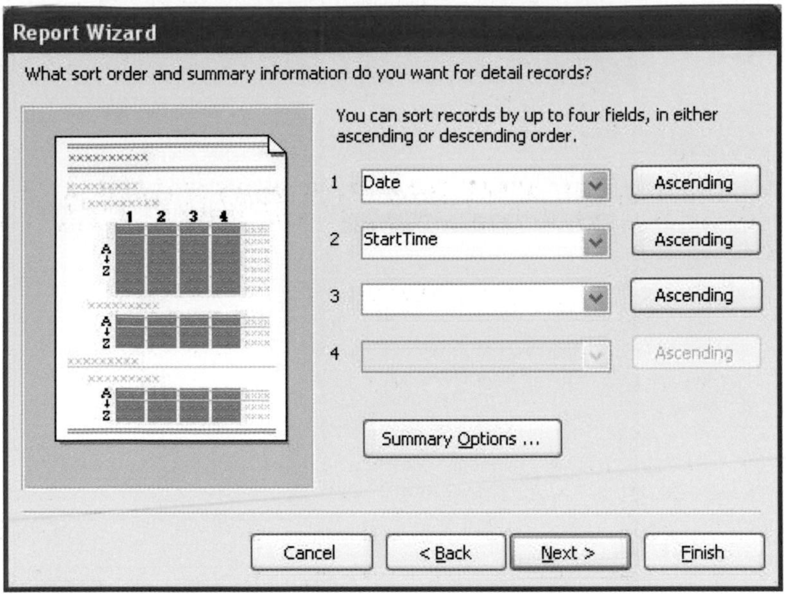

7 Select **Align Left 1** for layout and a **Corporate** style. Save your report as **rptStudentLessonDetails** and click on **Finish**. The report will open in Report View as shown below in Figure 1.13.17.

Figure 1.13.17 ▼

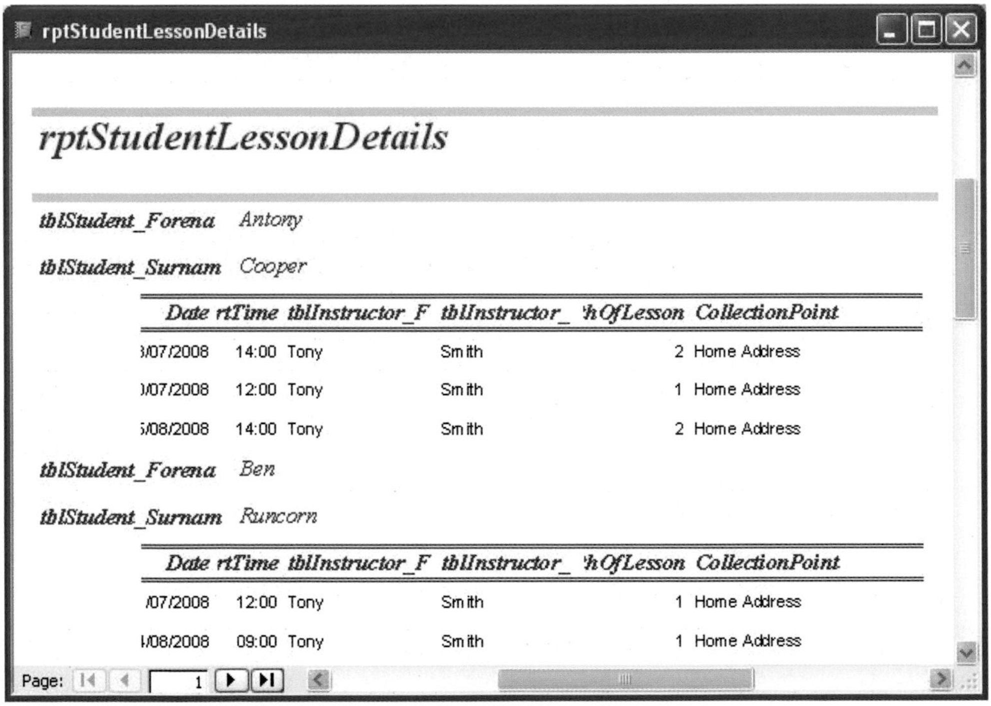

8 The report will need improving. Switch to Design View and edit the label **tblStudent_Forename** to read **Student Name**. Delete the label **tblStudent_Surname**. Align the **tblStudent_Forename** and **tblStudent_Surname** controls as shown in Figure 1.13.18.

9 Edit the Header labels to read **Date**, **Time**, **Instructor**, **Length Of Lesson** and **Collection Point** as shown in Figure 1.13.18. Format the **LengthOfLesson** control to centre from the formatting toolbar. You will need to spend some time aligning the data controls and Header labels.

10 Edit the title as shown in Figure 1.13.18.

Figure 1.13.18 ▼

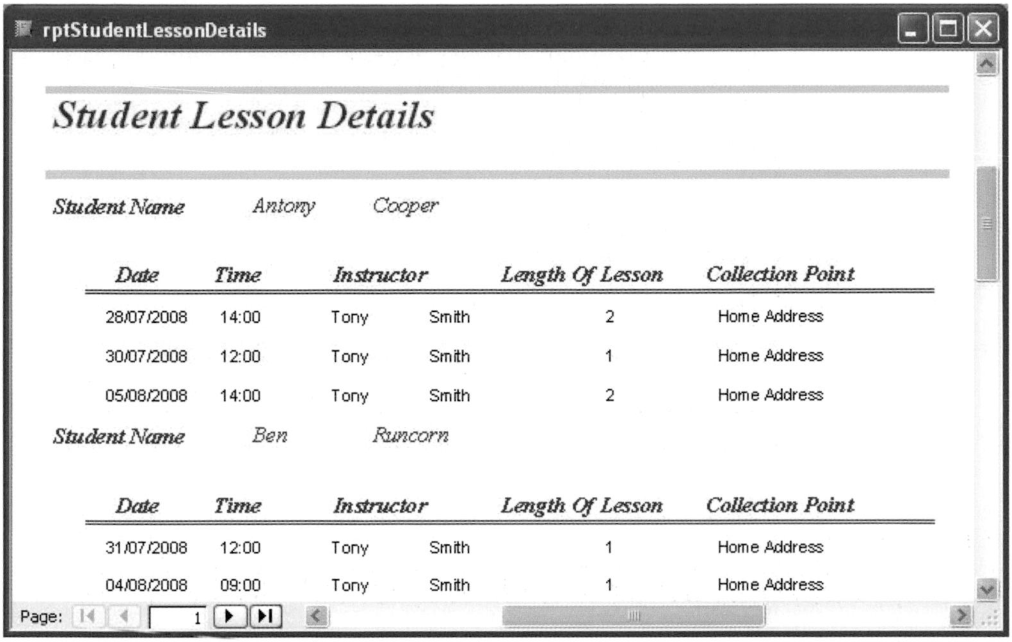

11 Switch to Design View. Drag out the Page Header and cut and paste the controls in the Report Header to the Page Header. Drag the Page Header up to close the Report Header gap. See Figure 1.13.19 below.

Figure 1.13.19 ▼

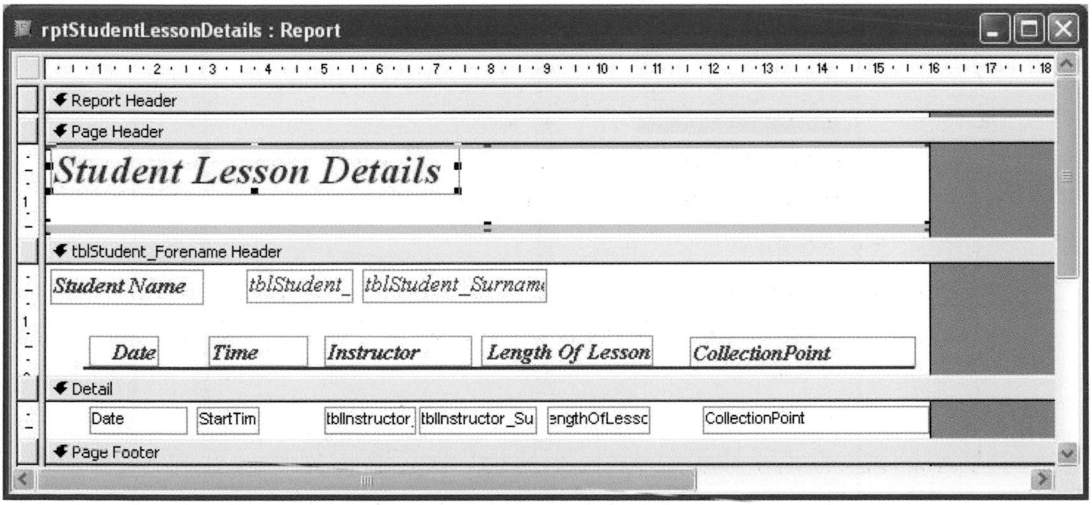

12 Use the techniques previously shown in the Instructor Timetable Report to force each Student to a new page and save your report as **rptStudentLessonDetails.**

Report 3: Producing a weekly timetable

The final report in this unit will produce a weekly timetable of lessons. The report will be based on the query called **qryNextWeeksLessons** set up in Unit 8.

1. At the Database Window, click on **Reports** and click on **New**.
2. Click on **Report Wizard** and select **qryNextWeeksLessons** from the list. Click on **OK.**
3. Select the following fields **Date, Start Time, tblStudent_Forename, tblStudent_Surname, tblInstructor_Surname, LengthOfLesson** and **CollectionPoint.** Click on **Next**.
4. The next dialogue box will ask you how to view the data. Click on **tblLesson** and click on **Next**.
5. When asked do you want to add any grouping levels, click on **Date** and click on the arrow icon (**>**). Do not click **Next** just yet.
6. **Date by Month** is displayed in the dialogue box. Click on the **Grouping Options** and select **Day** from the **Grouping Intervals** drop-down as shown in Figure 1.13.20. Click on **OK**.

Figure 1.13.20 ▶

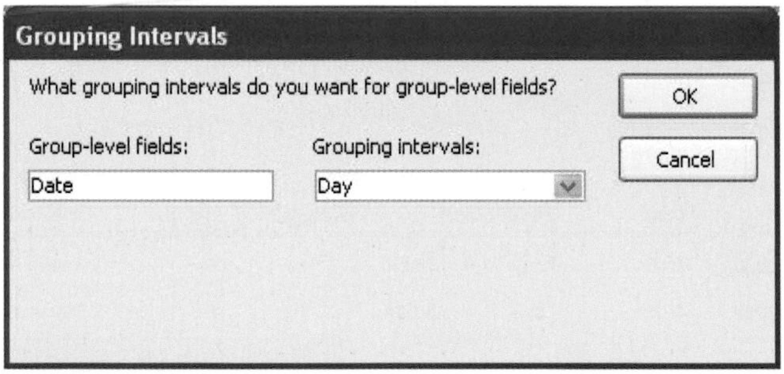

7. **Date by Day** is now displayed in the dialogue box as shown in Figure 1.13.21. Click on **Next**.

Figure 1.13.21 ▶

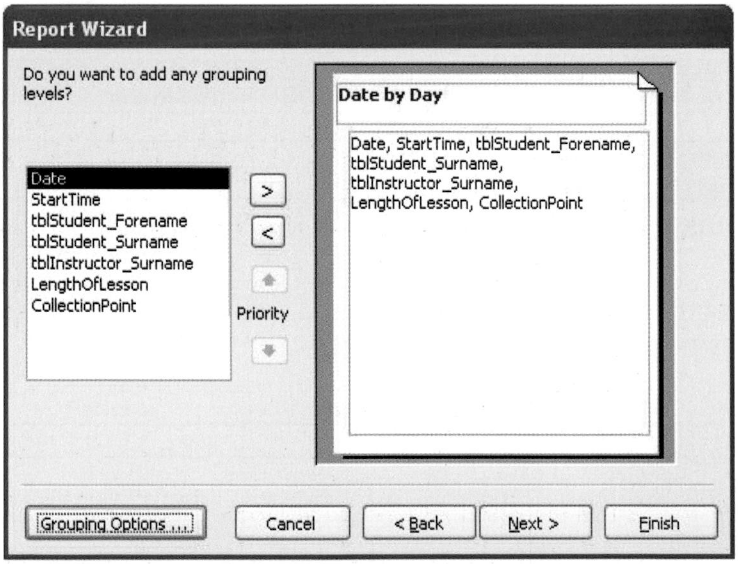

8. Sort by **Date**. Select **Align Left 1** for layout and a **Corporate** style. Save your report as **rptWeeklyTimetable** and click on **Finish**. Your report should appear as in Figure 1.13.22.

Note You will need to adjust the dates or change the time/date on your PC. In the example here the date has been set to 31/07/2008.

Figure 1.13.22 ▶

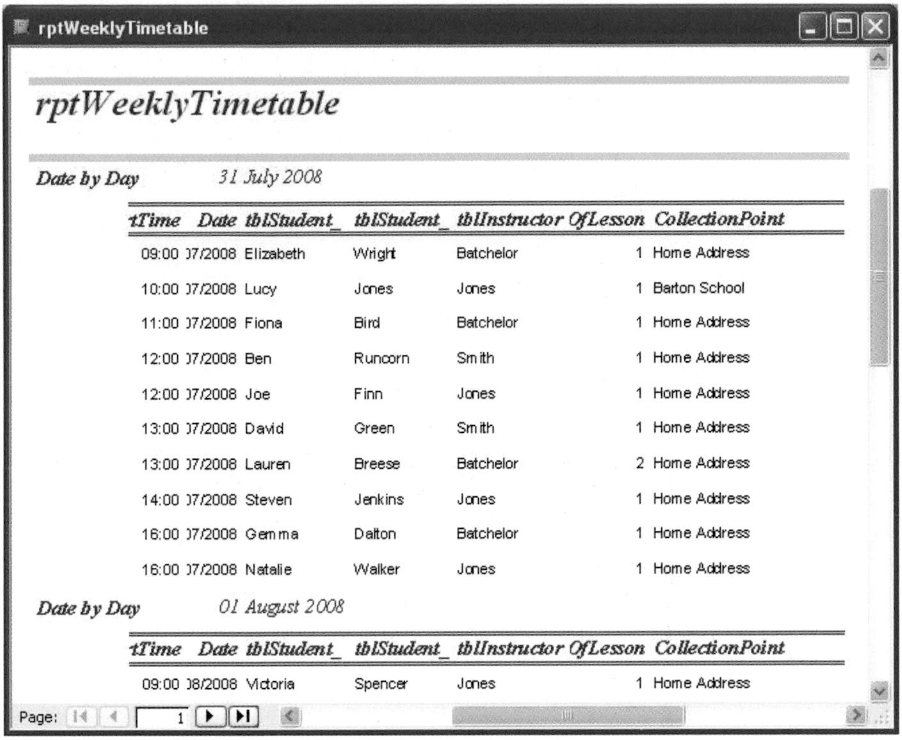

We are now going to develop the report using the in house style shown in Unit 12. Switch to Design View and take the following steps as shown in Figure 1.13.23.

9 Delete the controls in the Report Header and copy and paste the Report Header from the **rptInstructor** set up in Unit 12. Edit the title to **Weekly Timetable**.

Figure 1.13.23 ▼

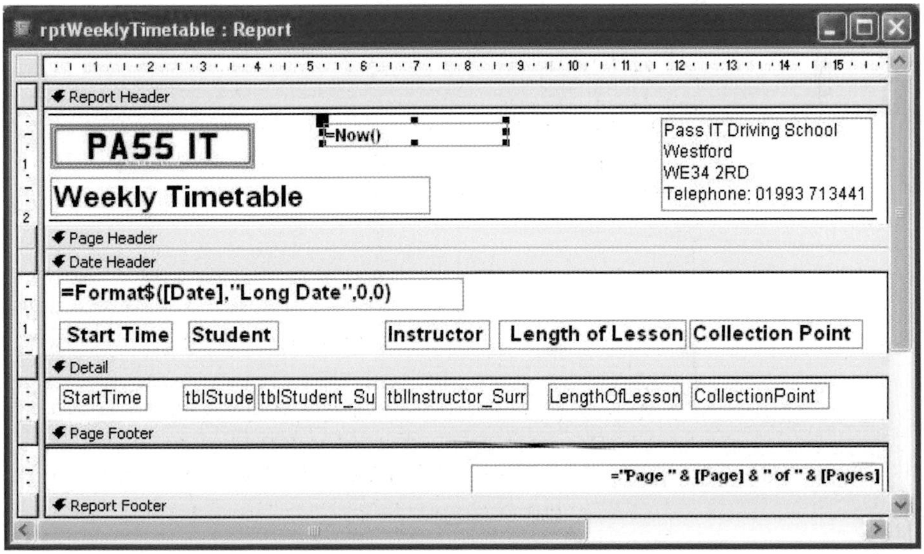

10 Leave the Page Header blank. This will be a continuous report with the heading at the top of the report on Page 1.

11 In the Date Header section remove the label **Date by Day**. Edit and align the header labels as shown. Set the **Font** of all controls in this section to **Arial, Bold, 9pt**.

12 In the Detail section change the font of the data controls to **Arial, 10pt**.

13 In the Page Footer remove the **Date** control. Select the Page numbering control and set its **Font** properties to **Arial, 8pt, Bold.** Select the line and set its **Border Width** to **1 pt** and **Border Color** to **Black.** Your report should appear as in Figure 1.13.24.

Figure 1.13.24 ▶

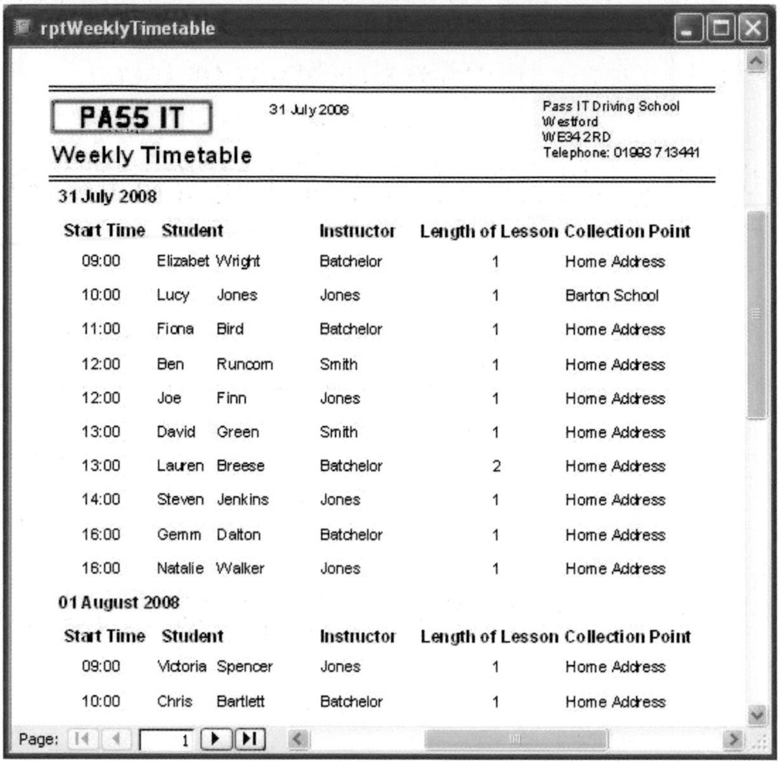

PA55 IT 31 July 2008   Pass IT Driving School
Westford
WE34 2RD
Telephone: 01993 713441

Weekly Timetable

31 July 2008

Start Time	Student		Instructor	Length of Lesson	Collection Point
09:00	Elizabet	Wright	Batchelor	1	Home Address
10:00	Lucy	Jones	Jones	1	Barton School
11:00	Fiona	Bird	Batchelor	1	Home Address
12:00	Ben	Runcom	Smith	1	Home Address
12:00	Joe	Finn	Jones	1	Home Address
13:00	David	Green	Smith	1	Home Address
13:00	Lauren	Breese	Batchelor	2	Home Address
14:00	Steven	Jenkins	Jones	1	Home Address
16:00	Gemm	Dalton	Batchelor	1	Home Address
16:00	Natalie	Walker	Jones	1	Home Address

01 August 2008

Start Time	Student		Instructor	Length of Lesson	Collection Point
09:00	Victoria	Spencer	Jones	1	Home Address
10:00	Chris	Bartlett	Batchelor	1	Home Address

Page: |◄ ◄ 1 ► ►|

Hint Use **Tricks and Tips** number 46 to set up Mailing Labels and/or Membership Cards.

Unit 14: Macros

A macro combines a series of Access instructions into a single command. Macros can be run by clicking a button, e.g. on a form or switchboard or can be triggered by an event, such as closing a form.

The Pass IT system consists so far of the three forms to manage information about the students, instructors and lesson bookings together with a number of reports.

In this unit you will learn how to use a few simple macros to begin to automate the system. Macros will be dealt with in more detail later.

Macro 1: A macro to open the Student form

1 At the Database Window click on **Macros** and click on **New**.

Figure 1.14.1 ▼

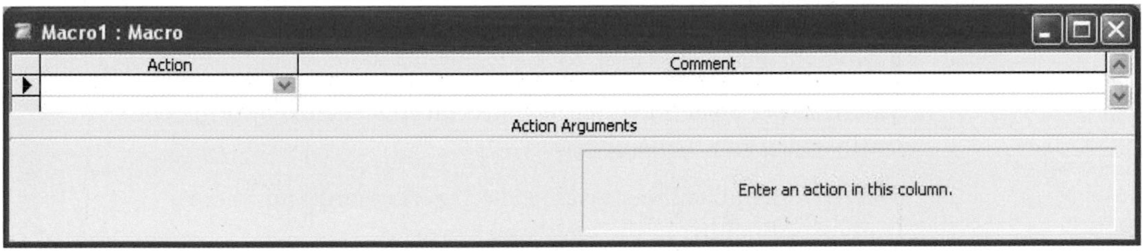

The Macro window opens as shown in Figure 1.14.1. It consists of an Action column from which you choose the actions and a Comment column where you can add comments to remind you of each function.

2 Click on the drop-down arrow in the **Action** column and click on **OpenForm** (see Figure 1.14.2).

Figure 1.14.2 ▼

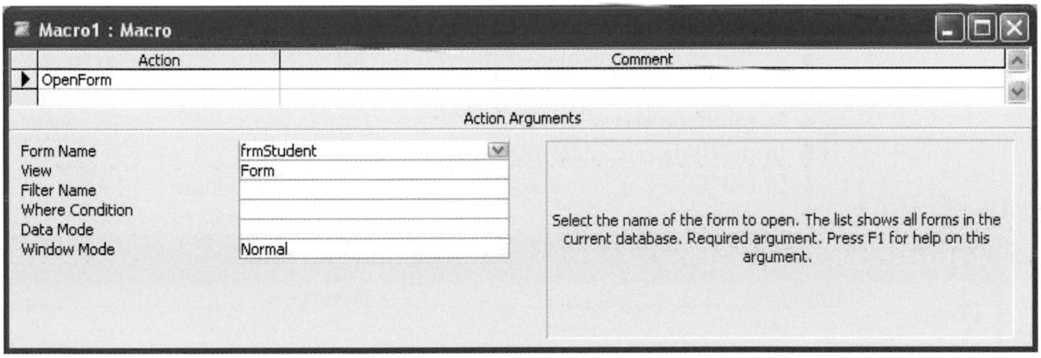

You now need to choose which form to open in the Action Arguments section.

3 Click on the **Form Name** box in the Action Arguments and click on **frmStudent** from the drop-down list as shown in Figure 1.14.2.
The **View** box will be set by default to **Form** and **Window Mode** to **Normal** as shown in Figure 1.14.2.

4 Close the Macro window and save as **mcrStudentForm**.

5 At the Database Window, test the macro by clicking on the Run icon.

Macros can have more than one action. When you open a form, you may want to add a new student. We can edit the macro to open the form with a new blank record.

6 Open the **mcrStudentForm** in Design View. In the second row of the Actions column select **GoToRecord** from the drop-down list (see Figure 1.14.3).

Figure 1.14.3 ▼

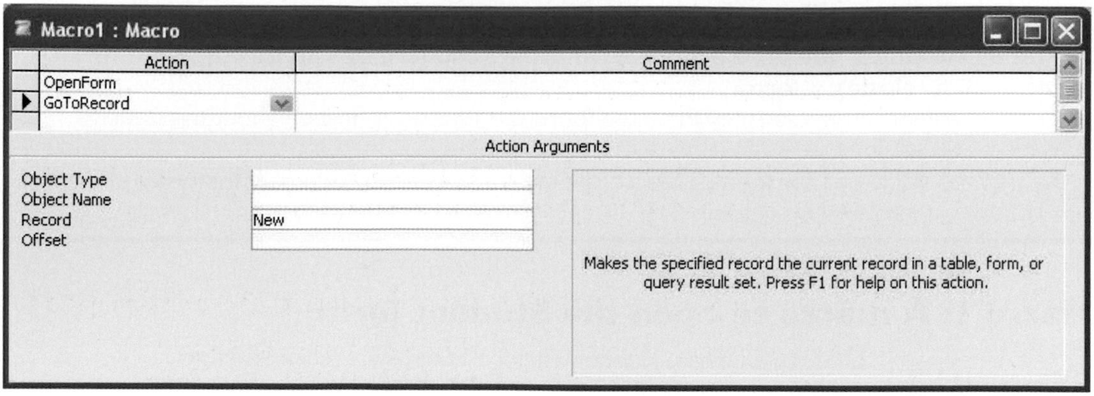

7 In the arguments section set **Record** to **New** (see Figure 1.14.3).
8 Save the macro. Go back to the Database Window and test it works.

Macro 2: Set up another macro called **mcrInstructorForm** to open **frmInstructor** in the same way.

Macro 3: Set up another macro called **mcrLessonForm** to open **frmLessonBooking** in the same way.

Macro 4: Setting up a message box

Most software packages have an About message box giving details of the company or developer. This can be set up using a macro.

1 At the Database Window click on **Macros** and click on **New**.
2 Select **MsgBox** in the Action column.
3 In the Action Arguments, click on the **Message** box and type **System by Ian Rendell © 2008**.
4 In the **Beep** box select **Yes**.
5 In the **Type** box select **Information**.
6 In the **Title** box type **Pass IT Driving School** (see Figure 1.14.4).

Figure 1.14.4 ▼

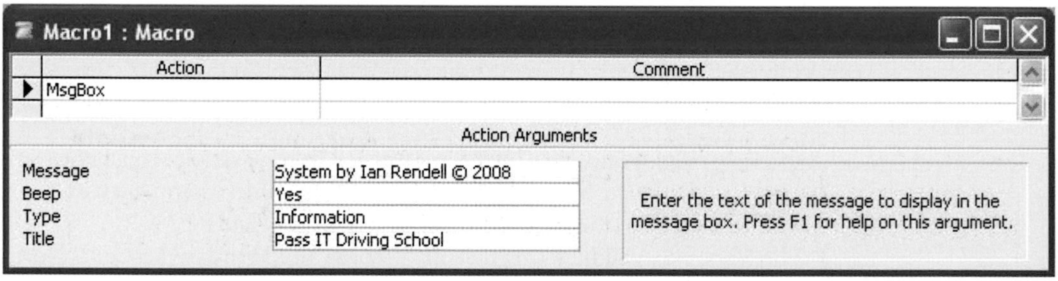

7 Save the macro as **mcrAbout** and test it (see Figure 1.14.5).

Figure 1.14.5 ▶

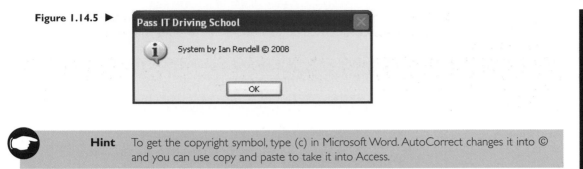

Pass IT Driving School

ⓘ System by Ian Rendell © 2008

OK

Hint To get the copyright symbol, type (c) in Microsoft Word. AutoCorrect changes it into ©
and you can use copy and paste to take it into Access.

Macro 5: A macro to print the Student Lesson Details report

1 At the Database Window click on **Macros** and click on **New**.
2 Click on the drop-down arrow in the **Action** column and click on
OpenReport (see Figure 1.14.6).

Figure 1.14.6 ▼

Action	Comment
▶ OpenReport	

Action Arguments

Report Name	rptStudentLessonDetails
View	Print Preview
Filter Name	
Where Condition	
Window Mode	Normal

Select the view in which to open the report: Print (to print the report immediately), Design view, or Print Preview. Press F1 for help on this argument.

3 Click on the **Report Name** box in the Action Arguments and click on
rptStudentLessonDetails from the drop-down list as shown in Figure 1.14.6.
4 In the **View** box select **Print Preview**.
5 Close the Macro window and save as **mcrStudentLessonReport.**
6 Using the **OpenReport** macro command set up 3 further macros to run the
following reports: **rptInstructor, rptInstructorTimetable**, and
rptWeeklyTimetable. Save your macros as **mcrInstructorReport,**
mcrInstructorTimetableReport, mcrWeeklyTimetableReport.

Using macros to customise a front end menu

You can use macros to link your system together and produce an automated
front end (see Figure 1.14.7).You may use this as an alternative to the
switchboard shown in Unit 15.

Figure 1.14.7 ▶

Main Menu

Pass IT Driving School   PA55 IT

Main Menu

Student Form	Lesson Booking Form	About Pass IT
Instructor Form	Report Menu	Exit

1 At the Database Window, click on **Forms**. Click on **New**. Click on **Design View** and click on **OK**. This produces a blank form. You will need to enlarge it.

2 Open **frmStudent** in Design View and copy and paste the Form Header controls on to the blank form as shown in Figure 1.14.8.

Figure 1.14.8 ▶

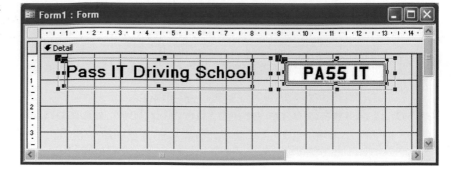

3 Use the **CommandButton** icon in the Toolbox to add command buttons to run the macros to open the **Student, Instructor** and **Lesson Booking** forms. You will have to click on **Miscellaneous** and select **Run Macro**. Set the text for the buttons as shown in Figure 1.14.7.

4 Add another button to run the **About** macro. Set the text to **About Pass IT**. Position and align the button as shown in Figure 1.14.7.

5 Set up another command button. Click on **Application.** Click on **Quit Application** and set the text to **Exit**. Position and align the button as shown in Figure 1.14.7. You will need to add the Report Menu option later.

6 Double click on the **Form Selector** to display the Form properties. Change the form caption using the **Caption** property to **Main Menu**. Make the form appear in the middle of the screen by setting the **Auto Center** property to **Yes**.

7 Remove the scroll bars, the navigation buttons, the record selector and the dividing lines.

8 Save the form as **frmMainMenu**.

The next stage is to create the Report Menu (see Figure 1.14.9) and link it to the Main Menu.

Figure 1.14.9 ▶

9 At the Database Window, click on **Forms**. Click on **New**. Click on **Design View** and click on **OK**. This produces a blank form. You will need to enlarge it.

10 Add Command Buttons to run the macros to open reports **rptInstructor, rptWeeklyTimetable, rptInstructorTimetable** and **rptStudentLessonDetails**. You will have to click on **Miscellaneous** and select **Run Macro**. Set the text for the buttons as shown in Figure 1.14.9.

11 Add another button to run the **About** macro and set the text as previously.

12 Double click on the **Form Selector** to display the Form properties. Change the form caption using the **Caption** property to **Report Menu**. Make the form appear in the middle of the screen by setting the **Auto Center** property to **Yes**.

13 Remove the scrollbars, the navigation buttons, the record selector and the dividing lines.

14 Save the form as **frmReportMenu**.

15 The next step is to link the two menus. Set up a new macro with two Actions. In the **Action** column click on **Close** and set the **Action Arguments** to **Close** the **Form** called **frmReportMenu** as shown in Figure 1.14.10.

16 Select the **OpenForm** Action and click on **frmMainMenu** in the Action Arguments. When run this macro will close the Report Menu and open the Main Menu. Save your macro as **mcrOpenMainMenu**.

Figure 1.14.10 ▼

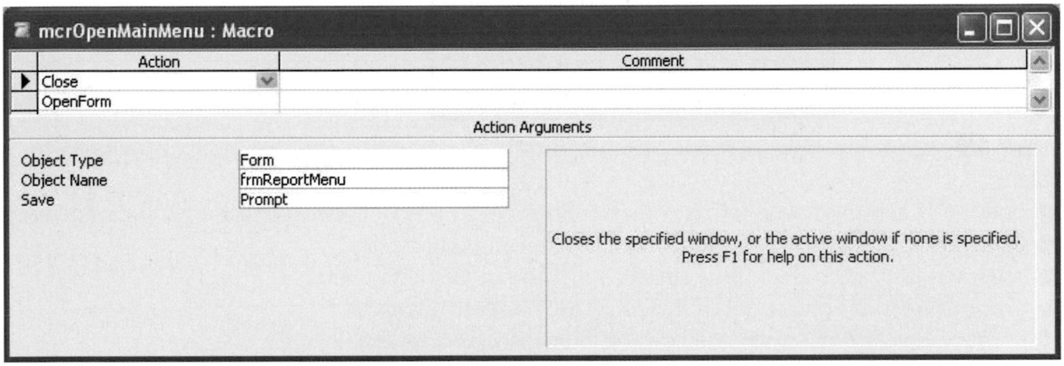

17 Open **frmReportMenu** in Design View and add a command button to run the macro **mcrOpenMainMenu** as shown in Figure 1.14.9.

18 In the same way set up a macro to close the Main Menu and open the Report Menu. Save your macro as **mcrOpenReportMenu** and add a command button to run the macro from the **frmMainMenu** as shown in Figure 1.14.7.

19 Refer to the **Tricks and Tips** number 49, to set up a macro called **autoexec** to load this form automatically when the file is opened.

Hint Use **Tricks and Tips** on Forms and Macros to further customise your solution.

Unit 15: Adding a switchboard

In the previous units you have designed the tables, queries, forms and reports that go to make up the Pass IT system.

All these options need to be available from a menu that loads when you start up your system. This is sometimes known as the front end or in Access as the switchboard (see Figure 1.15.1).

Figure 1.15.1 ▶

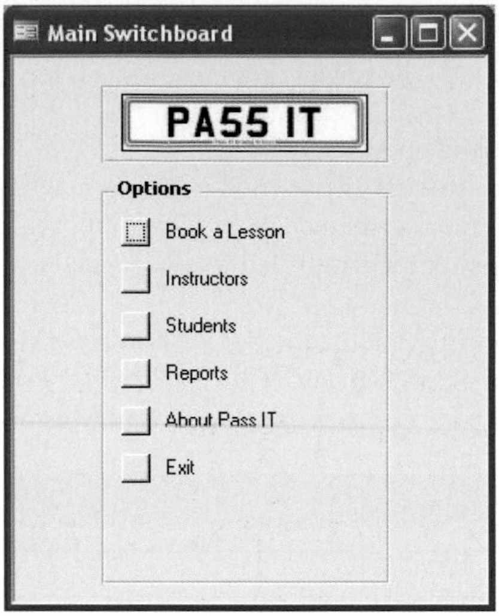

In this unit we look at how to create the switchboard shown above. The switchboard will need to be able to:

■ open the Lesson Booking form (frmLessonBooking) to find out lesson details or to book a lesson
■ open the Student form (frmStudent) to find out student details
■ open the Instructor form (frmInstructor) to find out instructor details
■ produce a list of contact details for instructors (rptInstructor)
■ produce details of all student lessons (rptStudentLessonDetails)
■ produce a timetable for an instructor (rptInstructorTimetable)
■ produce a weekly timetable of lessons (rptWeeklyTimetable)
■ run the About (message box) macro
■ exit from the system.

To include all these options, it is best to use two switchboards. One switchboard will link to the reports; the main switchboard will link to the other options.

Creating a switchboard with the Switchboard Manager

To set up a new switchboard go to the Database Window.

1 Click on **Tools, Database Utilities, Switchboard Manager**. It will ask if you want to create a switchboard (see Figure 1.15.2). Click on **Yes.**

Figure 1.15.2 ▶

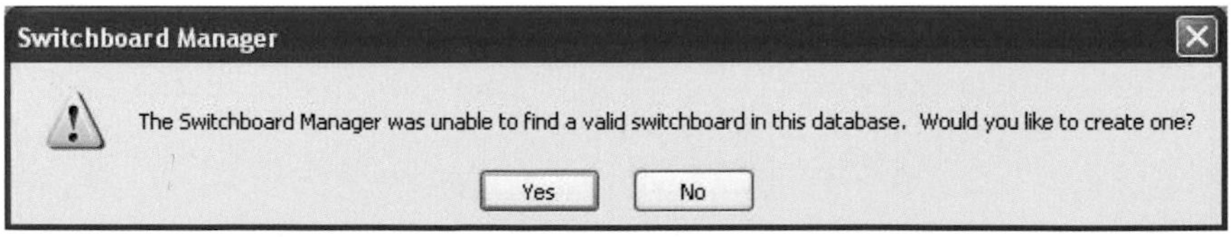

This sets up a default switchboard called the Main Switchboard (see Figure 1.15.3). From here we need to set up another switchboard for the reports.

Figure 1.15.3 ▶

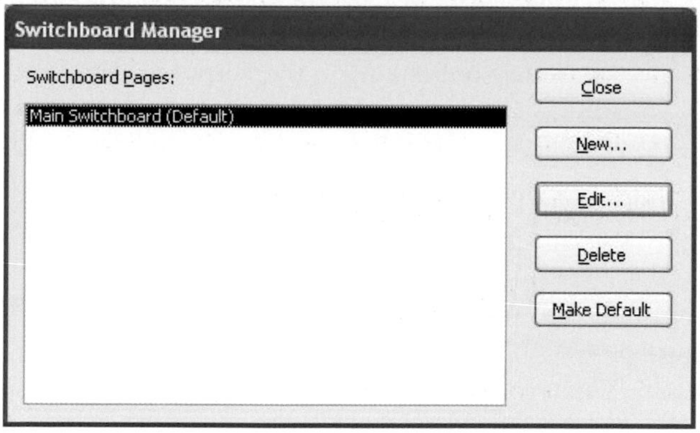

Switchboard Manager

Switchboard Pages:

Main Switchboard (Default)

Close

New...

Edit...

Delete

Make Default

2 At the **Switchboard Manager** dialogue box click on **New** (see Figure 1.15.3). Enter the name of the second switchboard: **Report Switchboard** and click on **OK** (see Figure 1.15.4).

Figure 1.15.4 ▶

Create New

Switchboard Page Name:

Report Switchboard

OK

Cancel

3 Select the **Main Switchboard** and click on **Edit** (see Figure 1.15.5).

Figure 1.15.5 ▶

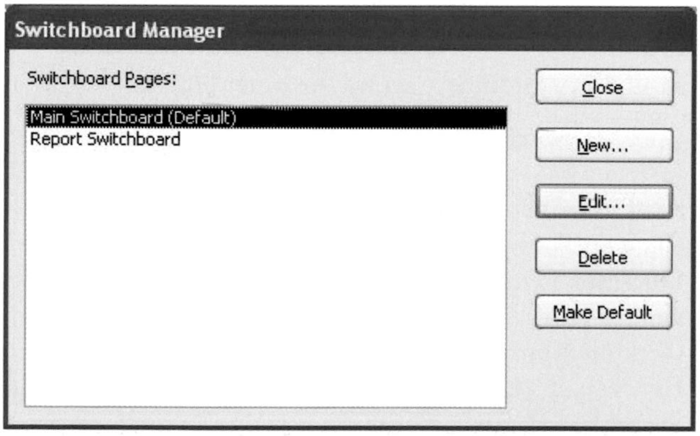

Switchboard Manager

Switchboard Pages:

Main Switchboard (Default)
Report Switchboard

Close

New...

Edit...

Delete

Make Default

4 At the **Edit Switchboard Page,** click on **New** (see Figure 1.15.6).

Figure 1.15.6 ▶

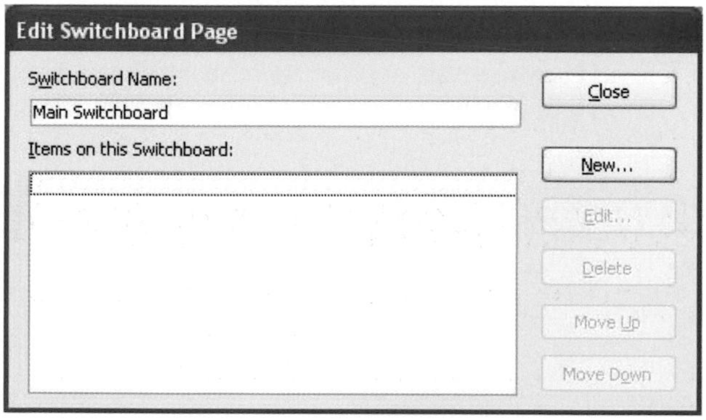

Edit Switchboard Page

Switchboard Name:

Main Switchboard

Items on this Switchboard:

Close

New...

Edit...

Delete

Move Up

Move Down

5 Edit the text in the **Edit Switchboard Item** dialogue box so that it reads **Book a Lesson** (see Figure 1.15.7).

6 Click on **Open Form in Edit Mode** from the drop-down in the **Command** box.

7 Click on **frmLessonBooking** in the **Form** box. Click on **OK**.

Figure 1.15.7 ▶

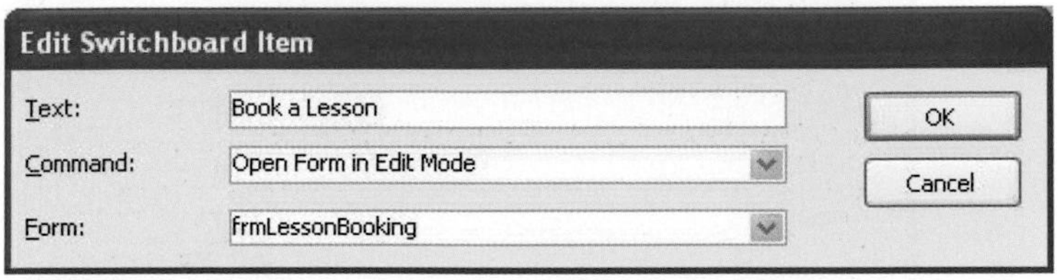

These steps set up the first button on our switchboard with the text Book a Lesson. When you click the button it will open the frmLessonBooking.

There are many options at this stage (see Figure 1.15.8). It is worth exploring the different options.

Figure 1.15.8 ▶

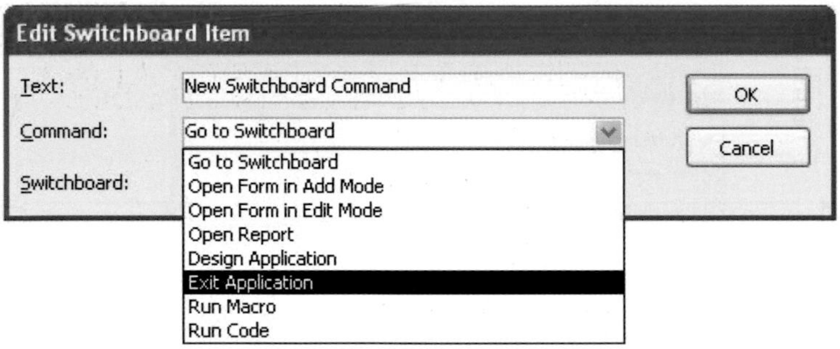

We will now continue to set up the other buttons on the switchboard.

1 Click on **New** to set up another Switchboard item. The text should be **Instructors**. Click on **Open Form in Edit Mode** in the **Command** box. Select **frmInstructor**. Click on **OK**.

2 Click on **New** to set up another Switchboard item. The text should be **Students**. Click on **Open Form in Edit Mode** in the **Command** box. Select **frmStudent**. Click on **OK**.

3 Click on **New** to set up another Switchboard item. The text should be **Reports**. Click on **Go to Switchboard** in the **Command** box. Select **Report Switchboard**. Click on **OK**.

4 Click on **New** to set up another Switchboard item. The text should be **About Pass IT**. Click on **Run Macro** in the **Command** box. Select **mcrAbout**. Click on **OK**.

5 Click on **New** to set up another Switchboard item. The text should be **Exit**. Click on **Exit Application** in the **Command** box (see Figure 1.15.9). Click on **OK**.

Figure 1.15.9 ▶

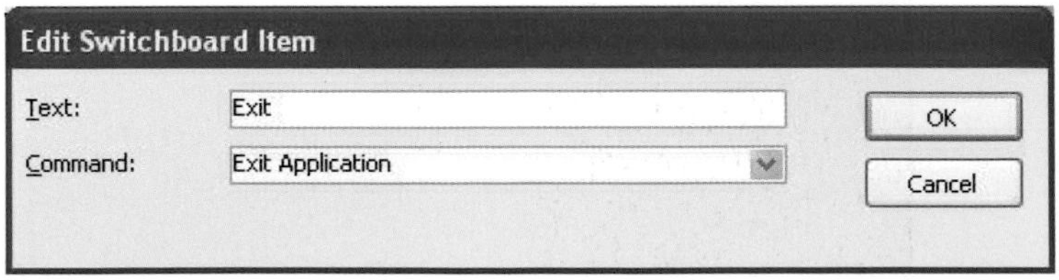

6 The **Edit Switchboard Page** will now appear as in Figure 1.15.10. You can use this page to edit the switchboard, delete or add new items. You can also move items up or down the switchboard list.

Figure 1.15.10 ▶

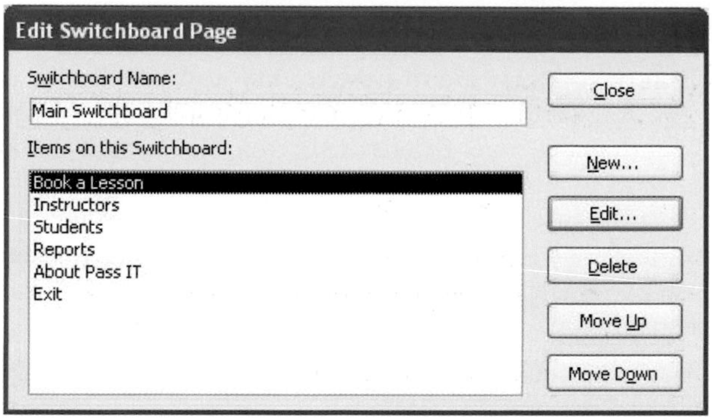

Edit Switchboard Page

Switchboard Name:

Main Switchboard

Close

Items on this Switchboard:

Book a Lesson
Instructors
Students
Reports
About Pass IT
Exit

New...

Edit...

Delete

Move Up

Move Down

7 You have now set up a switchboard with six options. Click on **Close** twice to go back to the Database Window. There will now be a new form listed called **Switchboard** (see Figure 1.15.11).

Figure 1.15.11 ▶

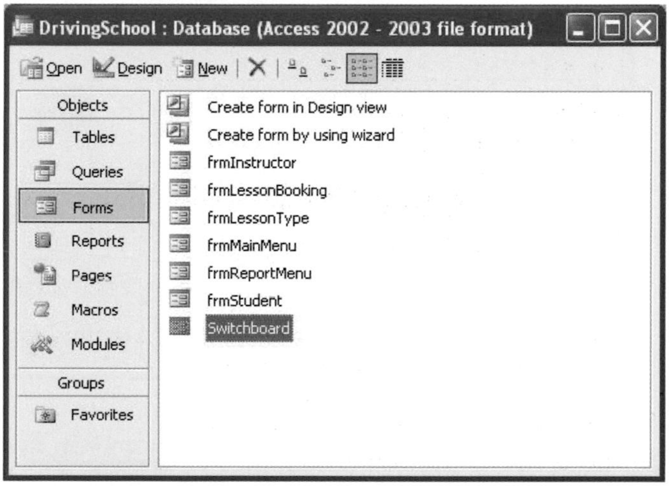

DrivingSchool : Database (Access 2002 - 2003 file format)

Open | Design | New | X | ᵃₒ | ᵗⁱ | 0-0-0- | ▦

Objects		Create form in Design view
Tables		Create form by using wizard
Queries		frmInstructor
Forms		frmLessonBooking
Reports		frmLessonType
Pages		frmMainMenu
Macros		frmReportMenu
Modules		frmStudent
		Switchboard

Groups

Favorites

8 Open the **Switchboard** form. It will look something like Figure 1.15.12.

Figure 1.15.12 ▶

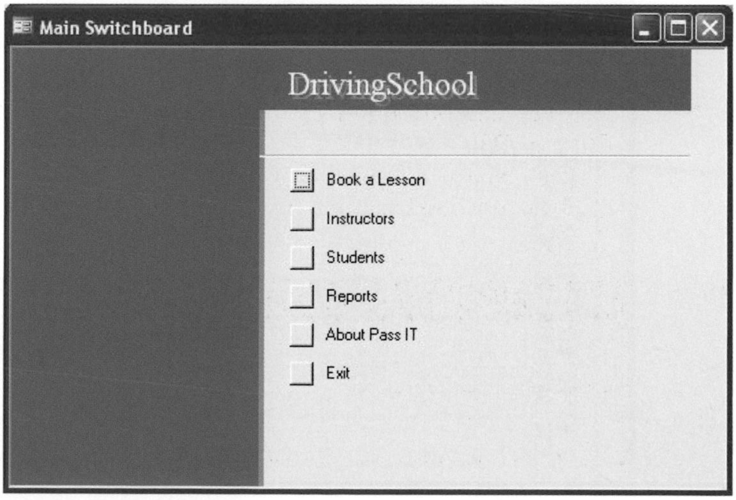

Main Switchboard

DrivingSchool

Book a Lesson

Instructors

Students

Reports

About Pass IT

Exit

Test that each of the buttons works. The Book a Lesson button will create a new record in the frmLessonBooking. The Report Switchboard will not yet be available.

Customising the switchboard

1 Open the switchboard in Design View so that it can be edited like any other form. You will notice that there are eight buttons even though we only set up six of them. (Do not delete the bottom two buttons.) You will also notice that the label for each button is not shown.
2 Select the title and delete it. There are two green rectangles, one dark grey rectangle and a sunken line. Select them and delete them.
3 Insert your logo near the top of the form in the usual way (see Figure 1.15.13) or simply copy and paste from **frmStudent**.

Figure 1.15.13 ▶

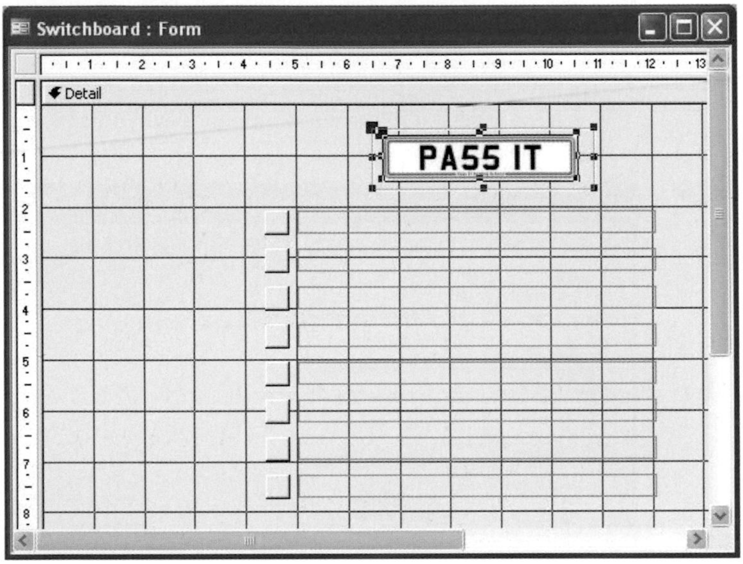

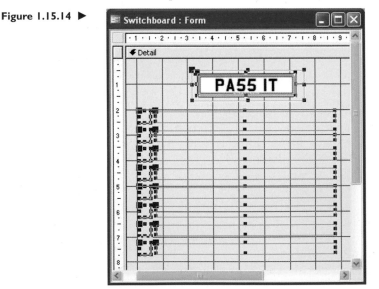

4 Highlight all the controls by pressing CTRL+A. Move all the controls to the left of the form and then make the form narrower as shown in Figure 1.15.14. It will help to reduce the size of the button labels.

Figure 1.15.14 ▶

5 From the Toolbox click on the Rectangle icon and draw a rectangle around the six options as shown in Figure 1.15.15. Add a label **Options**. You will need to set its **Back Style** property to **Normal** and its **Back Colour** to Access background (-2147483633). Position the label over the border of the rectangle.

The completed switchboard is shown in Figure 1.15.15.

Figure 1.15.15 ▶

Adding the Report Switchboard

1 At the Database Window, load the **Switchboard Manager** again. Click on **Report Switchboard** and click on **Edit**.

2 Click on **New** to set up another Switchboard item. The text should be **Instructor Contact Details**. Select **Open Report** in the **Command** box. Select **rptInstructor.** Click on **OK** (see Figure 1.15.16).

Figure 1.15.16 ▶

3 Click on **New** to set up another Switchboard item. The text should be **Instructor Timetable.** Select **Open Report** in the **Command** box. Select **rptInstructorTimetable.** Click on **OK**.

4 Click on **New** to set up another Switchboard item. The text should be **Weekly Timetable.** Select **Open Report** in the **Command** box. Select **rptWeeklyTimetable.** Click on **OK**.

5 Click on **New** to set up another Switchboard item. The text should be **Student Lesson Details.** Select **Open Report** in the **Command** box. Select **rptStudentLessonDetails.** Click on **OK**.

6 Click on **New** to set up the final Switchboard item. The text should be **Main Menu.** Click on **Go to Switchboard** in the **Command** box. Select **Main Switchboard**.

The Edit Switchboard Page is now shown in Figure 1.15.17.

Figure 1.15.17 ▶

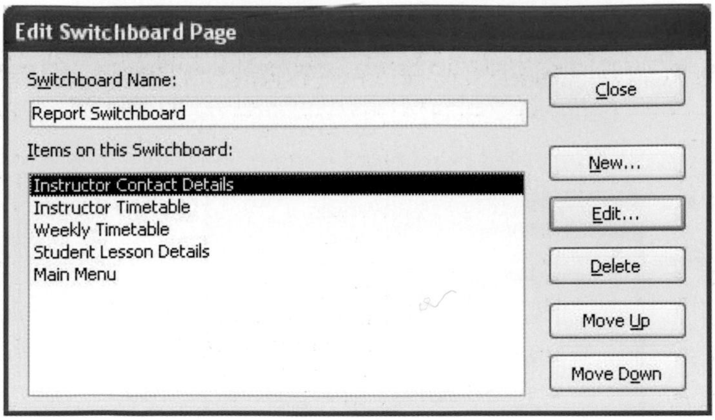

Edit Switchboard Page

Switchboard Name:

| Report Switchboard |

Items on this Switchboard:

| Instructor Contact Details |
| Instructor Timetable |
| Weekly Timetable |
| Student Lesson Details |
| Main Menu |

Close

New...

Edit...

Delete

Move Up

Move Down

7 Click on **Close** twice to exit from the Switchboard Manager.

8 At the Database Window, click on Forms to open the Switchboard and test that all the buttons on both switchboards work. The Report Switchboard will look like the one shown in Figure 1.15.18.

Figure 1.15.18 ▶

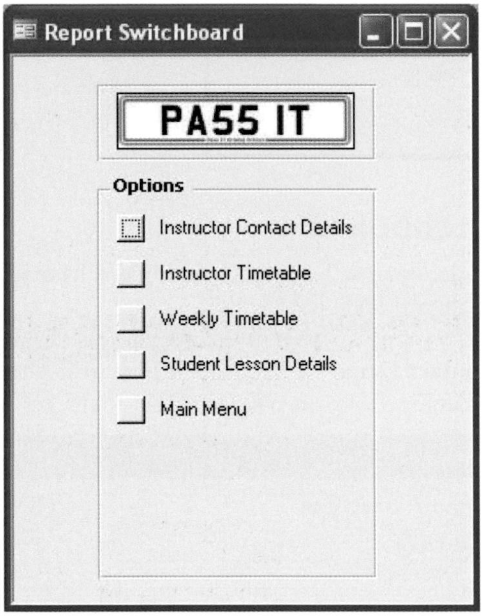

Report Switchboard

PA55 IT

Options

☐ Instructor Contact Details

☐ Instructor Timetable

☐ Weekly Timetable

☐ Student Lesson Details

☐ Main Menu

If you go back to the Database Window and click on **Tables**, you will see that an additional table called **Switchboard Items** has been set up. If you open the table (see Figure 1.15.19), you can see that it controls the switchboard.

Figure 1.15.19 ▼

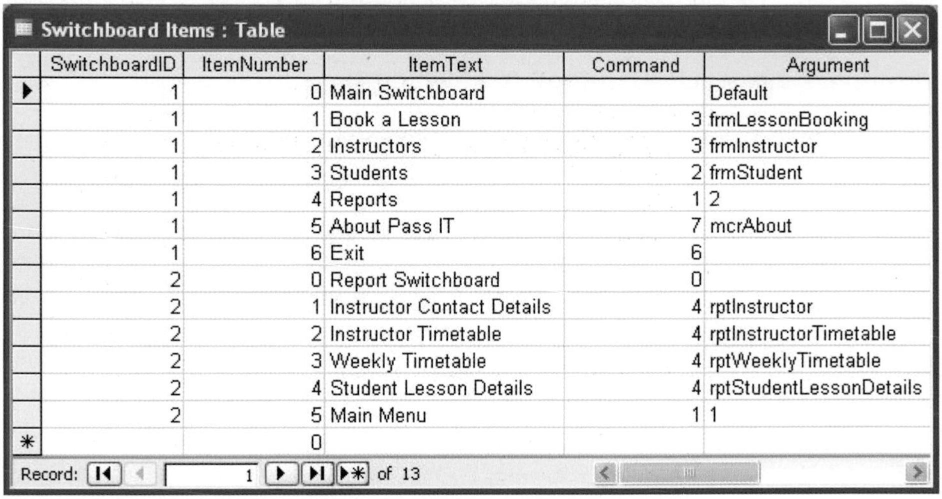

Switchboard Items : Table

SwitchboardID	ItemNumber	ItemText	Command	Argument
1	0	Main Switchboard		Default
1	1	Book a Lesson	3	frmLessonBooking
1	2	Instructors	3	frmInstructor
1	3	Students	2	frmStudent
1	4	Reports	1	2
1	5	About Pass IT	7	mcrAbout
1	6	Exit	6	
2	0	Report Switchboard	0	
2	1	Instructor Contact Details	4	rptInstructor
2	2	Instructor Timetable	4	rptInstructorTimetable
2	3	Weekly Timetable	4	rptWeeklyTimetable
2	4	Student Lesson Details	4	rptStudentLessonDetails
2	5	Main Menu	1	1
*	0			

Record: |◀ ◀ | 1 | ▶ ▶| ▶* | of 13

This table can be used to edit the switchboard text.

Setting the startup options

We want the switchboard to load automatically when the file is opened. One way of doing this is to use **Tools, Startup** from the main menu.

Set it up as follows:

1 At the Database Window, click on **Tools, Startup** to load the **Startup** dialogue box (see Figure 1.15.20).

Figure 1.15.20 ▶

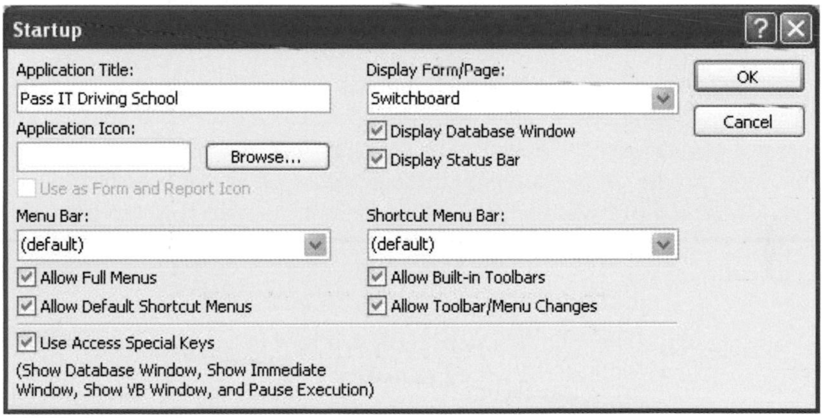

Startup

Application Title:
Pass IT Driving School

Application Icon:
[ ] Browse...

☐ Use as Form and Report Icon

Menu Bar:
(default)

☑ Allow Full Menus
☑ Allow Default Shortcut Menus

☑ Use Access Special Keys

(Show Database Window, Show Immediate Window, Show VB Window, and Pause Execution)

Display Form/Page:
Switchboard

☑ Display Database Window
☑ Display Status Bar

Shortcut Menu Bar:
(default)

☑ Allow Built-in Toolbars
☑ Allow Toolbar/Menu Changes

OK
Cancel

2 Click on the **Display Form/Page** drop-down arrow and select **Switchboard.** This is the name of the form you want to load on startup.

3 In the **Application Title** box enter **Pass IT Driving School.** This is the text that appears at the top of the Access screen.
This dialogue box can also be used to disable the right click, hide the Database Window and customise the menu bars. **Be careful.** While developing your system you need access to most of these options.

4 Close your system and reload it. Test that the switchboard opens when the system loads and that the application title is displayed.

Unit 16: Using SubForms

In this unit you will learn how to use SubForms.

In Access systems there will be many instances where it is necessary to see data from related tables on one screen. Using a SubForm is one of a number of ways of doing this.

For example:

In a video loans system you may wish to have membership details on screen alongside details of videos loaned to that member.

In a customer ordering system when a customer phones up with an order enquiry it would be useful to have the customer details and details of their orders on screen.

In the Pass IT Driving School you may wish to view instructor details alongside their lessons as shown in Figure 1.16.1. The Instructor Form is set just to show details of name and ID. A SubForm is added showing details of the lessons for that instructor.

Figure 1.16.1 ▶

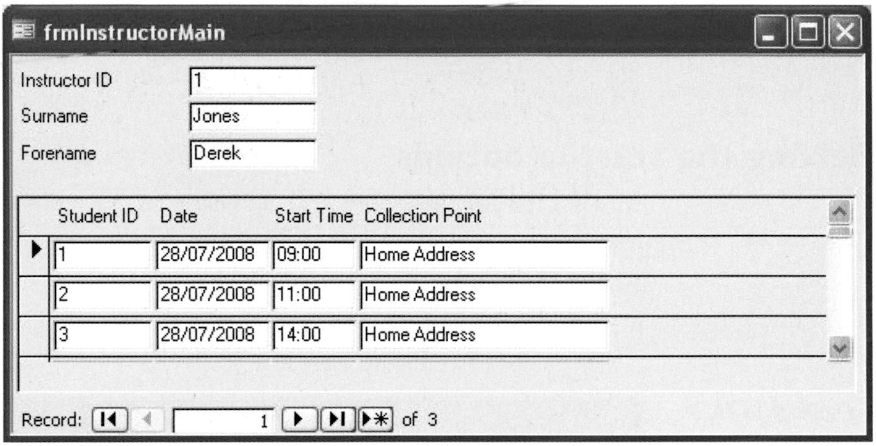

Typically in this sort of scenario a main form is set up based on the primary table Instructor with a SubForm based on the Lesson table. This is the simplest way forward but you will see later how to have greater control over the SubForm by basing it on a query.

The following three examples take you through setting up similar uses of SubForms but in slightly different ways. It is worthwhile practising the different methods to grasp the concepts involved here.

Example 1

The following steps show you how to set up the SubForm as shown above. We will use the wizard to make a start.

1 At the Database Window select **Forms** and click on **New** to bring up the New Form dialogue box.
2 Choose **Form Wizard** and select **tblInstructor** from the drop-down. Click **OK** (see Figure 1.16.2).

Figure 1.16.2 ▶

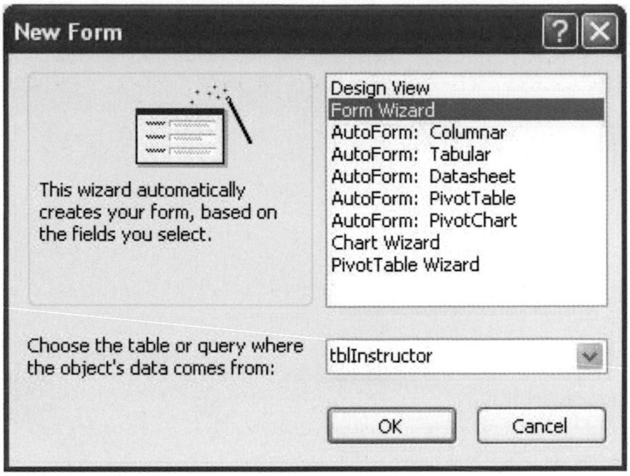

3 Select **tblInstructor** and choose the fields **InstructorID, Surname** and **Forename** from the available fields. Remember you can select the fields one by one by clicking the single arrow. Do not click **Next** yet.

Figure 1.16.3 ▶

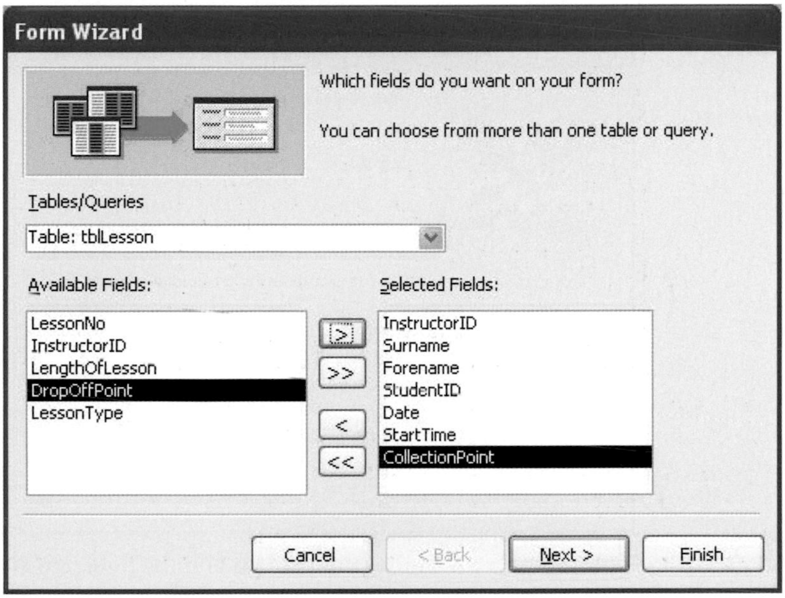

4 We now want to select the fields for the SubForm. Select **tblLesson** from the drop-down and add **StudentID, Date, StartTime** and **CollectionPoint** from the available fields. Click on **Next** (see Figure 1.16.3).

5 The Form Wizard then asks you "How do you want to view your data?" Make sure **by tblInstructor** is selected and **Form with subforms(s)** is checked. Click on **Next** (see Figure 1.16.4).

Figure 1.16.4 ▶

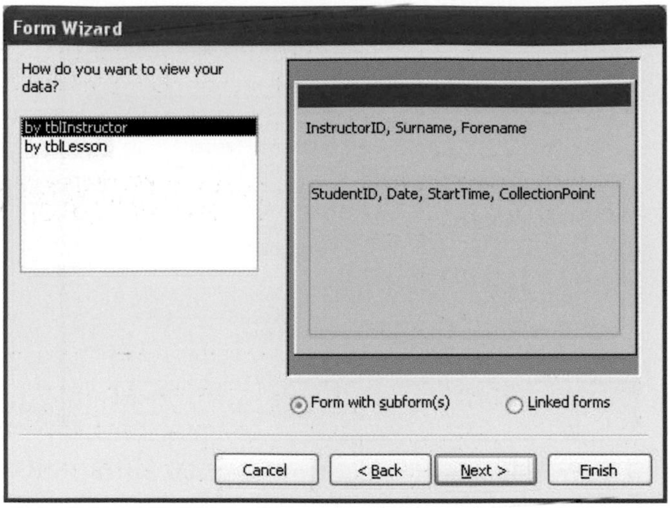

6 Select a **Tabular** layout and click on **Next**. Select a **Standard** style and click on **Next**.

Figure 1.16.5 ▶

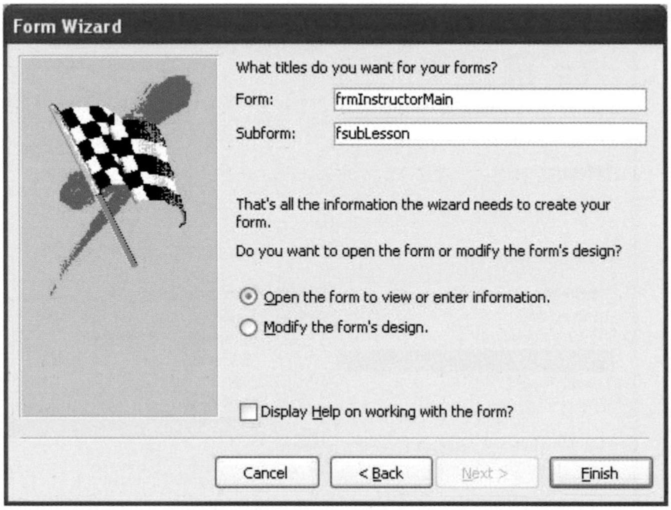

7 Name the form **frmInstructorMain** and the SubForm **fsubLesson.** Click on **Finish** (see Figure 1.16.5).

Your Main form/SubForm should appear a little like Figure 1.16.1 at the start of the unit. Its appearance will need a little fine-tuning.

8 Open **frmInstructorMain** in Design View and double click on the **Form Selector** to bring up the Properties. Remove the **Scroll Bars**, **Record Selectors** and **Dividing Lines**. Remove the label **fsubLesson**. Align and edit the controls on the Main Form as shown in Figure 1.16.1. Save your work.

Figure 1.16.6 ▶

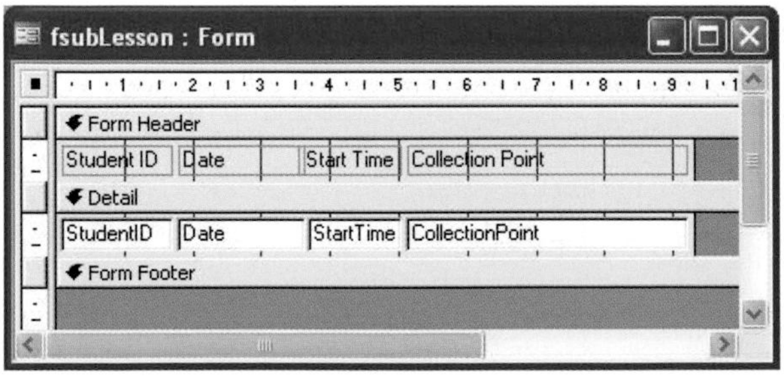

9 At the Database Window open **fsubLesson** in Design View as shown in Figure 1.16.6. From here you can edit the SubForm. Left align the controls in the Form Header and Detail section. Edit the label controls by inserting spaces. Double click on the **Form Selector** and remove the **Navigation buttons.** Save your work.

Figure 1.16.7 ▶

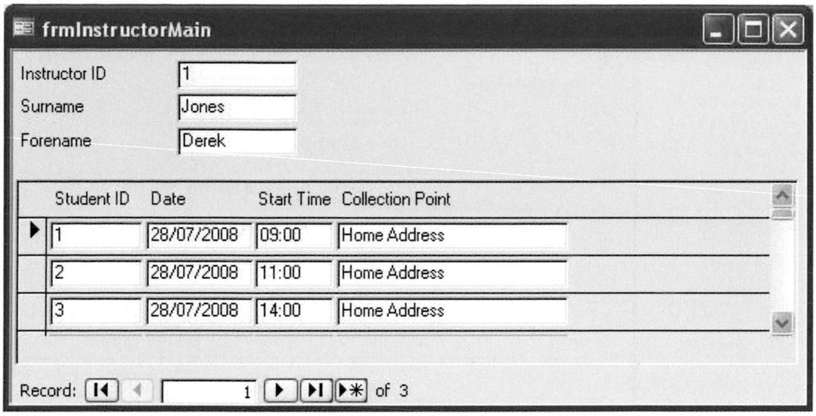

frmInstructorMain

Instructor ID	1
Surname	Jones
Forename	Derek

	Student ID	Date	Start Time	Collection Point
▶	1	28/07/2008	09:00	Home Address
	2	28/07/2008	11:00	Home Address
	3	28/07/2008	14:00	Home Address

Record: ◀◀ ◀ 1 ▶ ▶▶ ▶* of 3

10 With **frmInstructorMain** open scroll through the instructor details to view the details of their lessons in the SubForm (see Figure 1.16.7).

There are a number of ways of setting up SubForms in Access. As ever, you choose the method that suits you best. The next example will take you through setting up a SubForm in a slightly different way.

Example 2

We are going to set up a SubForm on the Student Form giving details of each student's lessons.

1 At the Database Window select **Forms** and click on **New**.
2 Set up a student form by choosing **AutoForm: Columnar** and selecting **tblStudent** from the drop down.
3 Go into Design View to remove the fields just leaving the StudentID, their name and address. Rearrange as shown in Figure 1.16.8.

Figure 1.16.8 ▼

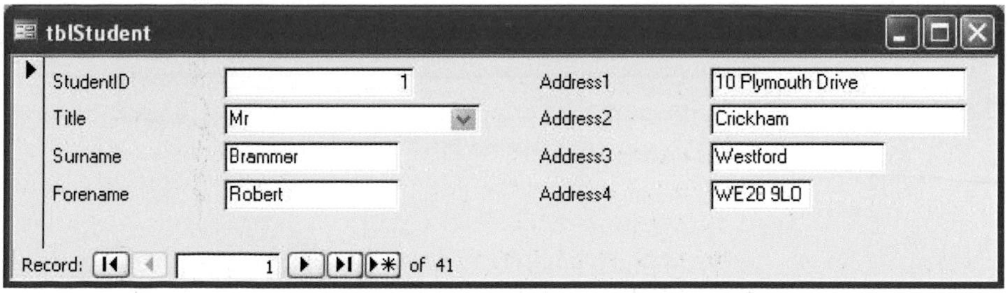

tblStudent

StudentID	1	Address1	10 Plymouth Drive
Title	Mr	Address2	Crickham
Surname	Brammer	Address3	Westford
Forename	Robert	Address4	WE20 9LO

Record: ◀◀ ◀ 1 ▶ ▶▶ ▶* of 41

4 Go into Design View and from the Toolbox click on the **Subform/Subreport** icon and drag out a rectangle about 13 cm by 2 cm across the foot of the form.

5 The SubForm Wizard is displayed. Check **Use existing Tables and Queries** click on **Next** (see Figure 1.16.9).

Figure 1.16.9 ▶

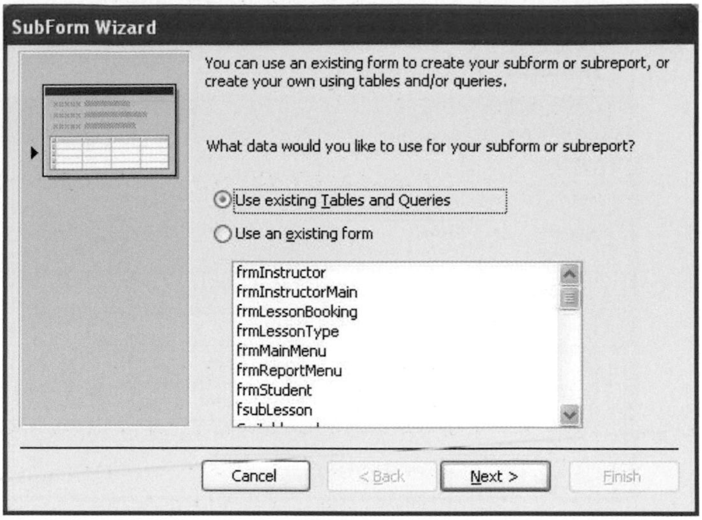

6 From the next SubForm Wizard dialogue box, select **tblLesson** from the drop-down and select the fields as shown in Figure 1.16.10. Click on **Next**.

Figure 1.16.10 ▶

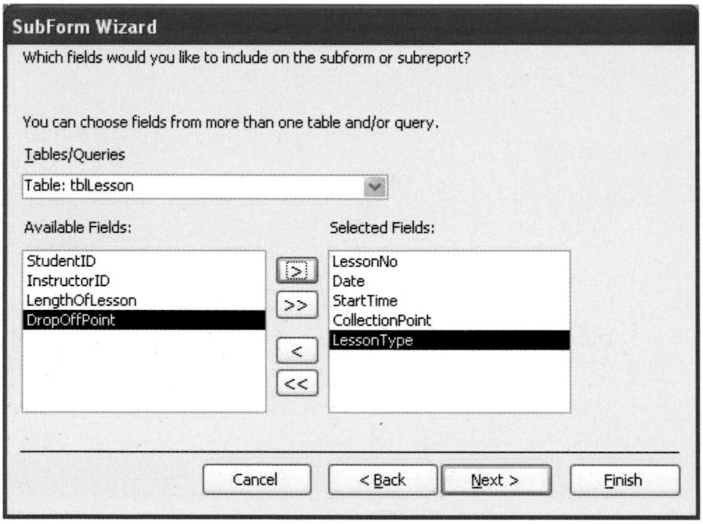

7 In the next SubForm Wizard dialogue box the wizard detects the linking fields for you so just click on **Next** (see Figure 1.16.11).

Figure 1.16.11 ▶

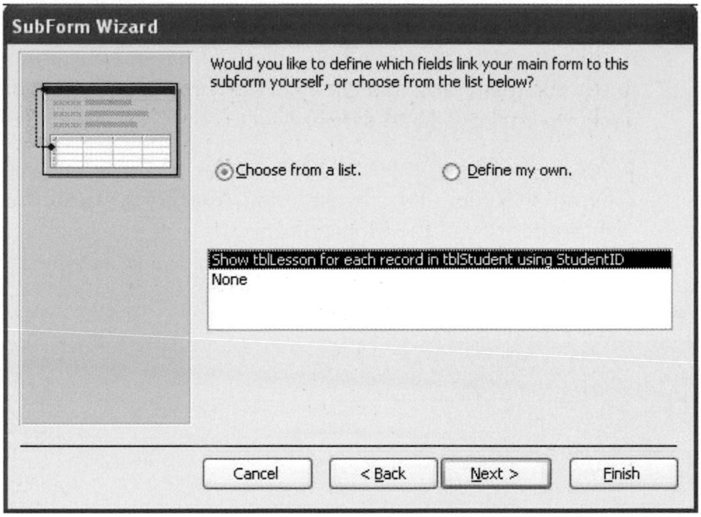

SubForm Wizard

Would you like to define which fields link your main form to this subform yourself, or choose from the list below?

◉ Choose from a list.   ○ Define my own.

Show tblLesson for each record in tblStudent using StudentID
None

| Cancel | < Back | Next > | Finish |

8 Call your SubForm **fsubLessonDetails** and click on **Finish**.
9 Save your form as **frmStudentLessonDetails**.
10 Open **frmStudentLessonDetails** in Form View. You will see that it needs some editing to improve its appearance.
11 Select Design View, double click on the Form Selector of the main form and remove the **Record Selector, Scroll Bars** and **Dividing Lines**. Insert spaces in the label controls. Remove the SubForm label and drag out the SubForm to fit the main form a little better.
12 Switch back to Form View. The SubForm appears by default in Datasheet View from which you can easily change the widths of the columns by dragging in/out the columns as required.
13 At the Database Window open **fsubLessonDetails** in Design View. Edit the labels and align the text as required.

Your form should look something like Figure 1.16.12.

Figure 1.16.12 ▶

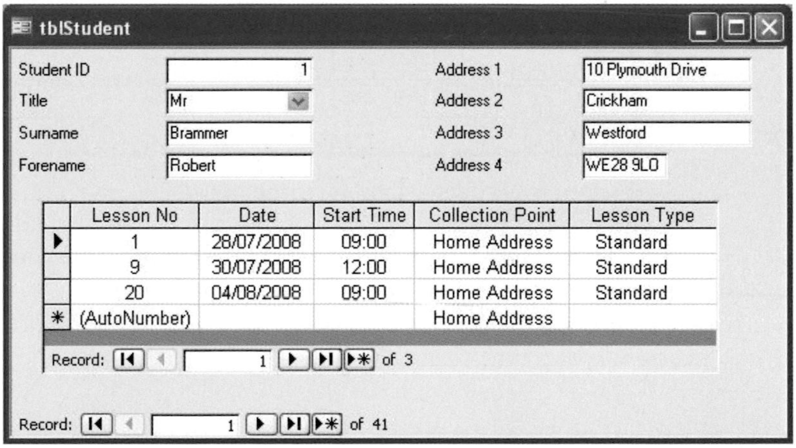

tblStudent

Student ID		1		Address 1	10 Plymouth Drive
Title	Mr			Address 2	Crickham
Surname	Brammer			Address 3	Westford
Forename	Robert			Address 4	WE28 9LO

	Lesson No	Date	Start Time	Collection Point	Lesson Type
▶	1	28/07/2008	09:00	Home Address	Standard
	9	30/07/2008	12:00	Home Address	Standard
	20	04/08/2008	09:00	Home Address	Standard
✱	(AutoNumber)			Home Address	

Record: |◀ ◀ | 1 | ▶ ▶| ▶✱ | of 3

Record: |◀ ◀ | 1 | ▶ ▶| ▶✱ | of 41

Note None of the forms developed in this unit so far are part of the Pass IT system. To avoid confusion it is recommended you go into the Database Window and delete the forms **frmInstructorMain**, **fsubLesson**, **fsubLessonDetails** and **frmStudentLessonDetails** by selecting each in turn and pressing DELETE.

Example 3

In the next example we will set up our forms without using the wizards. Very simply the main form and the SubForm are set up separately and then the SubForm is dragged and dropped on to the main form.

1 At the Database Window select **Forms** and click on **New**.
2 Set up a Student form by choosing **AutoForm: Columnar** and selecting **tblStudent** from the drop-down.
3 Go into Design View to remove the fields just leaving the name and address. Rearrange as shown in Figure 1.16.13.

Figure 1.16.13 ▼

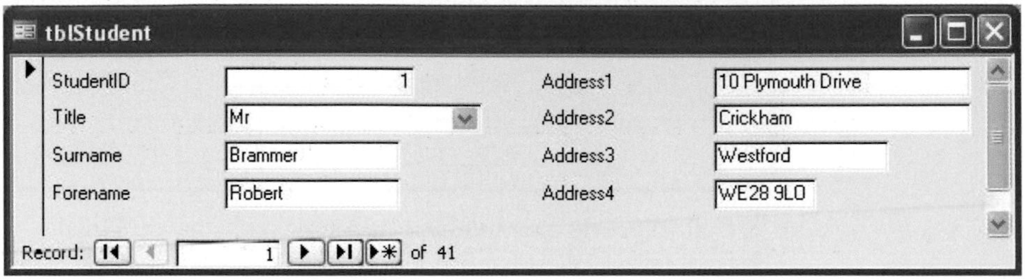

4 Save the form as **frmStudentMain**.
5 Use the Form Wizard to set up a form based on **tblLesson**. Select the fields **LessonNo, Date, StartTime, CollectionPoint** and **LessonType**.
6 Select a **Tabular** layout, **Standard** style and name the form **fsubLesson**. (You may decide to call it by a different name if you don't want to delete your previous work.) See Figure 1.16.14.

Figure 1.16.14 ►

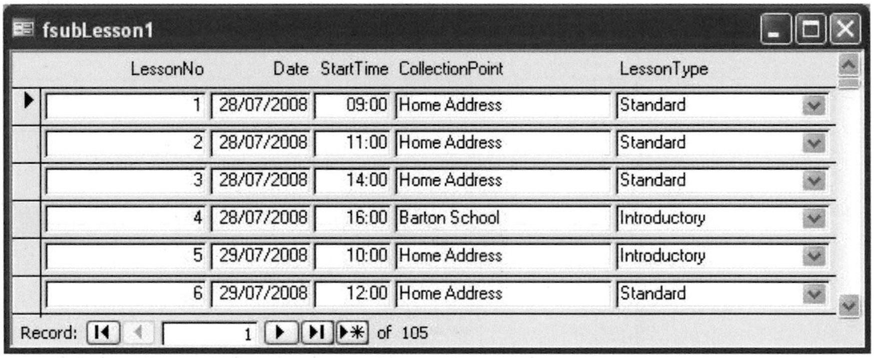

7 Open **frmStudentMain** in Design View.
8 Press F11 to view the Database Window and drag and drop the icon for **fsubLesson** onto the lower area of the **frmStudentMain** (see Figure 1.16.15).

Figure 1.16.15 ▼

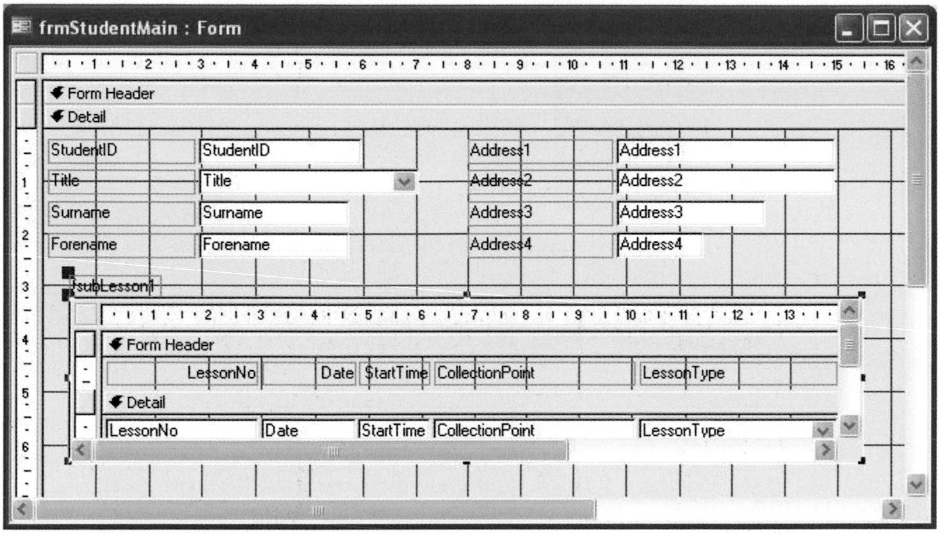

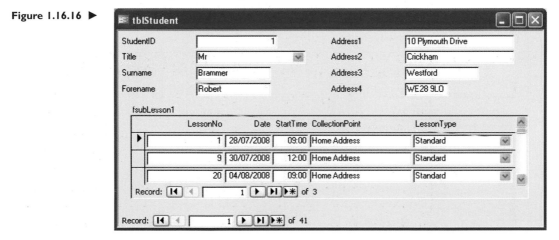

9 Click on Form Properties for **frmStudentMain** and remove the **Scroll Bars**, **Record Selectors** and **Dividing Lines**.

10 Position and resize the form as shown in Figure 1.16.16. There is no need to format, edit and align the controls.

Figure 1.16.16 ▶

Note Neither of these forms are needed in the Pass IT system and you may decide to delete them.

Setting up the SubForms in the Pass IT Driving School system

We are going to set up two SubForms in the Pass IT system. Both will be based on queries and both will be accessed and displayed from the main Lesson Booking Form at the heart of the system.

When a student rings up to book a lesson the driving school will want to be able to view quickly lesson availability for that day and perhaps for the week for their attached instructor.

This unit will also introduce you to using Tab Controls. The Tab Control is selected from the Toolbox as shown in Figure 1.16.17.

Figure 1.16.17 ▶

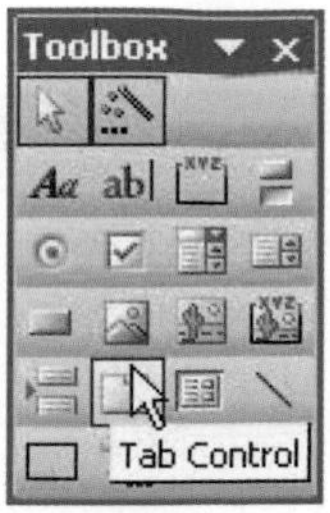

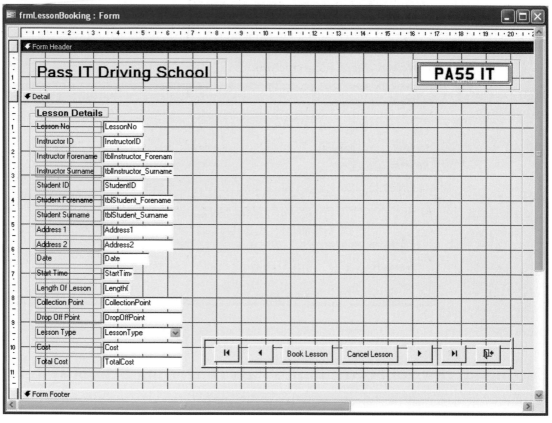

These are particularly useful when the information you wish to view is too much for one form.

1 Load the **frmLessonBooking** in Design View.
2 Drag out the right margin and Form Footer to fill the screen as shown in Figure 1.16.18.
3 Select the right hand controls and drag them to a position below the left hand controls. Move the control panel, logo and rectangle as shown in Figure 1.16.18. This creates room for our Tab Controls.

Figure 1.16.18 ▼

4 From the Toolbox choose the **Tab Control** and drag out a rectangle across the screen about 12 cm by 7 cm.

Figure 1.16.19 ▼

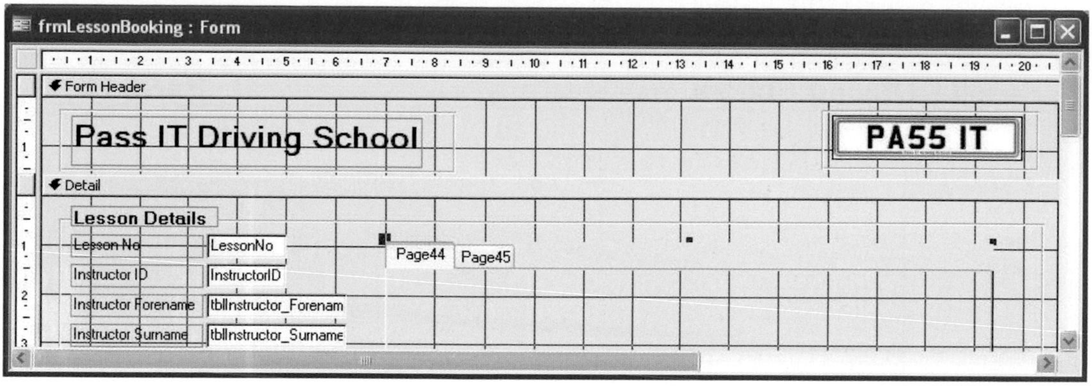

The Tab Control will be headed by some page numbers as shown in Figure 1.16.19. Double click on the left one and set its **Caption** property to **Daily Timetable** (see Figure 1.16.20).

Figure 1.16.20 ▶

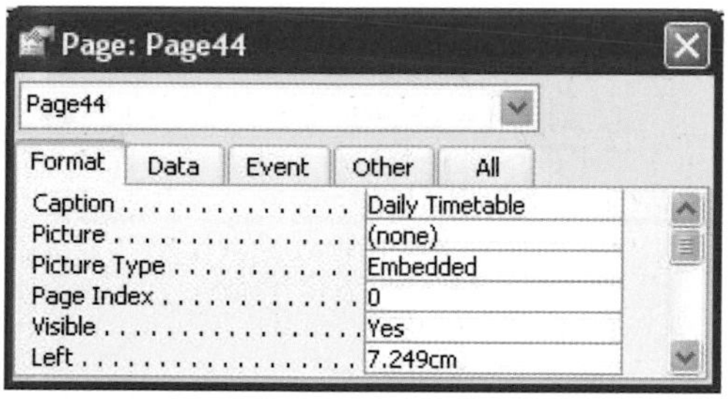

5 Double click on the other one and set its **Caption** property to **Weekly Timetable**.

6 We are now going to try and create a little more space. Delete the labels for **Instructor Surname** and **Student Surname**.

7 Move the text boxes for **Instructor Surname** and **Student Surname** as shown in Figure 1.16.21. Rename the labels **Instructor** and **Student** respectively.

8 You will need to align the controls, format the vertical spacing and edit the labels but your form should appear as below after a little tinkering.

Figure 1.16.21 ▼

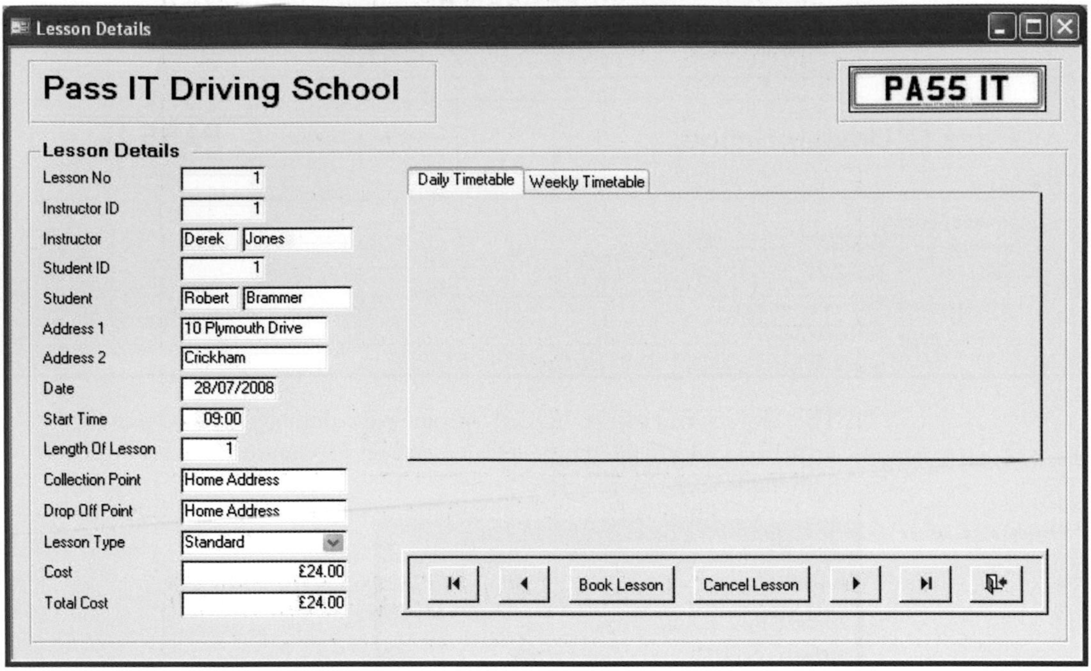

Lesson Details

Pass IT Driving School   PA55 IT

Lesson Details

Lesson No	1
Instructor ID	1
Instructor	Derek Jones
Student ID	1
Student	Robert Brammer
Address 1	10 Plymouth Drive
Address 2	Crickham
Date	28/07/2008
Start Time	09:00
Length Of Lesson	1
Collection Point	Home Address
Drop Off Point	Home Address
Lesson Type	Standard
Cost	£24.00
Total Cost	£24.00

Daily Timetable Weekly Timetable

|◄   ◄   Book Lesson   Cancel Lesson   ►   ►| ⬚▸

Adding the SubForm

1 Load the above form in Design View.
2 From the Toolbox click on the **SubForm/SubReport** icon and drag out a rectangle in the Tab Control area.
3 The SubForm Wizard opens. Click on **Use existing Tables and Queries** and click on **Next**.
4 In the next window choose the **qryFullDetails** and select the available fields as shown in Figure 1.16.22. Click on **Next.**

Figure 1.16.22 ►

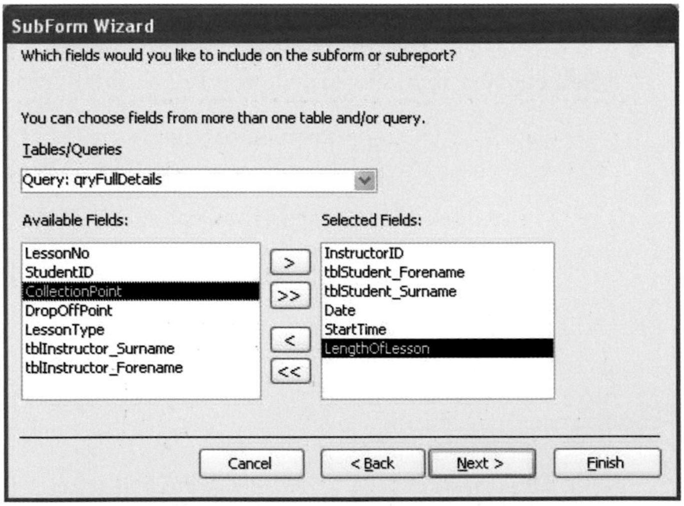

SubForm Wizard

Which fields would you like to include on the subform or subreport?

You can choose fields from more than one table and/or query.

Tables/Queries

Query: qryFullDetails

Available Fields:
LessonNo
StudentID
CollectionPoint
DropOffPoint
LessonType
tblInstructor_Surname
tblInstructor_Forename

Selected Fields:
InstructorID
tblStudent_Forename
tblStudent_Surname
Date
StartTime
LengthOfLesson

Cancel   < Back   Next >   Finish

5 You then have to define your linking fields. Check **Define my own** and select **InstructorID** and **Date** from the drop-down boxes as shown. Click on **Next** (see Figure 1.16.23).

Figure 1.16.23 ▶

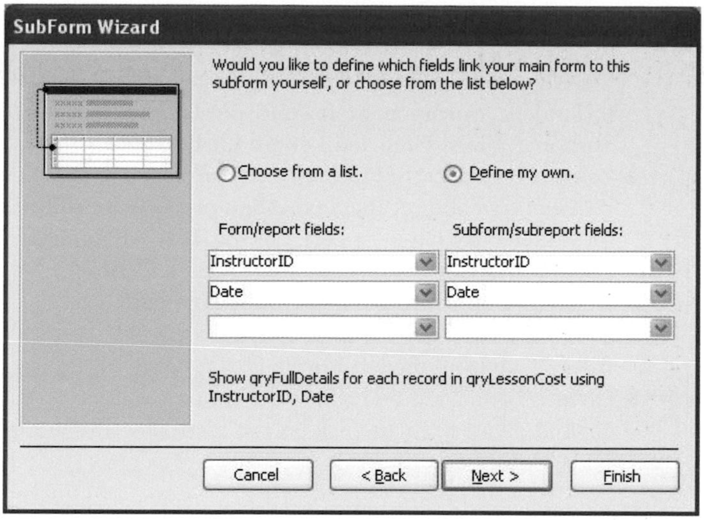

6 Call your SubForm **fsubDailyTimetable** (see Figure 1.16.24). Click on **Finish**.

Figure 1.16.24 ▶

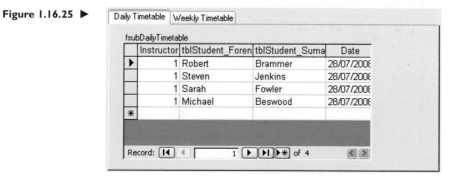

If you now open the Lesson Booking Form in Form View you will see it needs resizing and repositioning. This can be tricky and may require a lot of patience.

There are a number of general steps you can take.

Figure 1.16.25 ▶

	Instructor	tblStudent_Foren	tblStudent_Surna	Date
▶	1	Robert	Brammer	28/07/2008
	1	Steven	Jenkins	28/07/2008
	1	Sarah	Fowler	28/07/2008
	1	Michael	Beswood	28/07/2008
✳				

Daily Timetable | Weekly Timetable

fsubDailyTimetable

Record: I◀ ◀ 1 ▶ ▶I ▶✶ of 4

1 To change the column headings: In Design View select in turn each label in the **Detail** area of the SubForm. Right click and choose **Properties**. Click on the **All** tab and edit the **Caption**. Change tblStudent_Forename, **tblStudent_Surname, StartTime** and **LengthOfLesson** to **Forename, Surname, Start Time** and **Length Of Lesson**.

2 Using the same technique, select in turn each Text Box in the **Detail** area of the SubForm and set the **Text Align** property for **tblStudent_Forename** and **tblStudent_Surname** to **Left**. Set the **Text Align** property for **LengthOfLesson, StartTime** and **Date** to **Center**.

3 Delete the SubForm label **fsubDailyTimetable**.

4 In Design View, use the ruler to ensure the Tab Control does not go more than 19 cm from the left margin of the form.

5 Go into Form View and adjust the column widths by dragging out or in the column dividers. Right click on the InstructorID column header and select **Hide Columns**.

It will take a little time but your form should appear as shown in Figure 1.16.26 eventually!

Figure 1.16.26 ▼

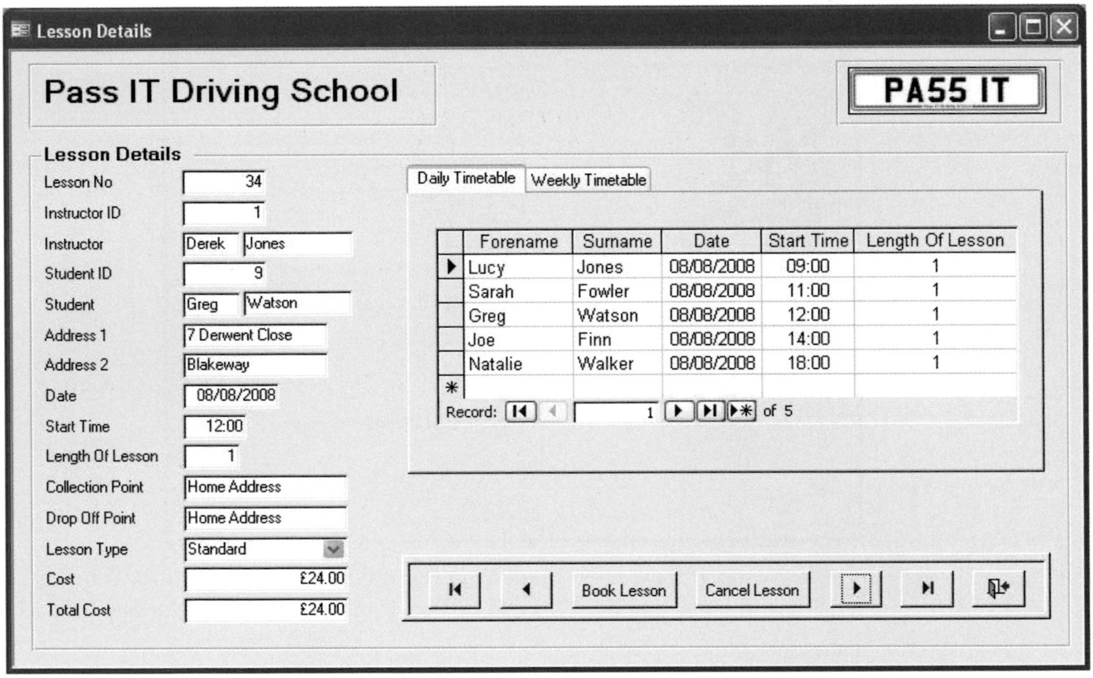

Using your SubForm

1 Open **frmLessonBooking** and ensure the **Daily Timetable** Tab is selected.

2 Click on the **Book Lesson** option and book a **Standard** lesson for **Instructor ID** 1 with **Student ID** 1 on the **28/07/08**.

3 The SubForm will display the available times on that date for that instructor. Press **Escape** to Undo the booking.

4 The next stage will allow us to view the available times over a week.

Adding the SubForm to display the Weekly Timetable

The process is nearly exactly the same as for the Daily Timetable but you need to base the form on a different query.

You will need to work on the second Tab Control called Weekly Timetable. Drag out a SubForm as before and base it on the query **qryNextWeeksLessons** set up in Unit 8.

Use the fields **InstructorID, tblStudent_Forename, tblStudent_Surname, Date, StartTime** and **LengthOfLesson** as before.

When you link the fields in the SubForm, only link the **InstructorID** and *not* the Date.

Again you will need to format, resize and reposition the SubForm (see Figure 1.16.27).

Figure 1.16.27 ▶

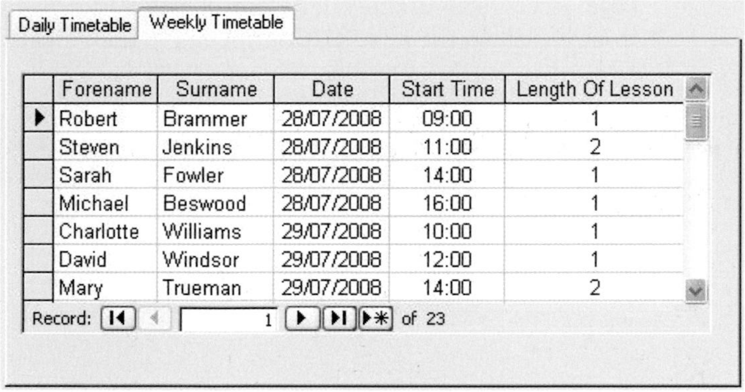

	Forename	Surname	Date	Start Time	Length Of Lesson
▶	Robert	Brammer	28/07/2008	09:00	1
	Steven	Jenkins	28/07/2008	11:00	2
	Sarah	Fowler	28/07/2008	14:00	1
	Michael	Beswood	28/07/2008	16:00	1
	Charlotte	Williams	29/07/2008	10:00	1
	David	Windsor	29/07/2008	12:00	1
	Mary	Trueman	29/07/2008	14:00	2

Daily Timetable | Weekly Timetable

Record: ◀◀ ◀ 1 ▶ ▶▶ ▶* of 23

To test the new SubForm you will need to adjust the dates in your table or adjust the time clock on your PC to 28/07/08.

Enter the data as above and now you will be able to toggle between the **Daily** and **Weekly Timetable** Tabs. Save your work.

Unit 17: Setting up search and sort options

The user of the Pass IT Driving School will often need to search and sort quickly through records of bookings, students and instructors.

In this unit we will add options to search, sort and enter data. The unit also includes an option to deal with the scenario when a student phones to book a lesson and cannot remember or does not know their ID.

To add these options we will need to add a further Tab Control.

Setting up a new Tab Control

1 Open **frmLessonBooking** in Design View.
2 Select the **Tab Control Page** and from the menu choose **Insert, Tab Control Page**. Access adds another Tab Control with a Page Number.
3 Double click on the new Tab Control and in the Property sheet set the **Name** property to **Further Options**. Save your new form as **frmLessonBooking**. It should appear as in Figure 1.17.1.

Figure 1.17.1 ▶

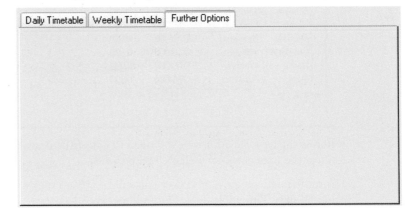

Adding filters

It is possible to filter data displayed in a form so that only the lessons with a particular student or only the lessons on a certain date are displayed.

We will set up a Command Button on the new Tab Control Page to run a macro which will run a filter.

1 Create a new query based on **tblLesson**. Add all the fields from the table.
2 Type **[Enter the ID number]** into the Criteria row of the StudentID column of the QBE grid.
3 Save the query as **qryFilterStudent**.
4 Create a new macro. In the action column select **ApplyFilter**. In the Action Arguments set the **Filter Name** to **qryFilterStudent**.
5 Save the macro as **mcrFilterStudent**.
6 Open **frmLessonBooking** in **Design View**. Click on the **Further Options** Tab. From the Toolbox add a Command Button to the Tab.
7 In the Command Button Wizard window choose the **Miscellaneous** category, select **Run Macro** and click on **Next**.

8 In the next window choose **mcrFilterStudent** and click on **Next**.

9 Select the Text option in the next window and set it to read **Search by Student**. Click on **Next** and click **Finish** (see Figure 1.17.2).

Figure 1.17.2 ▶

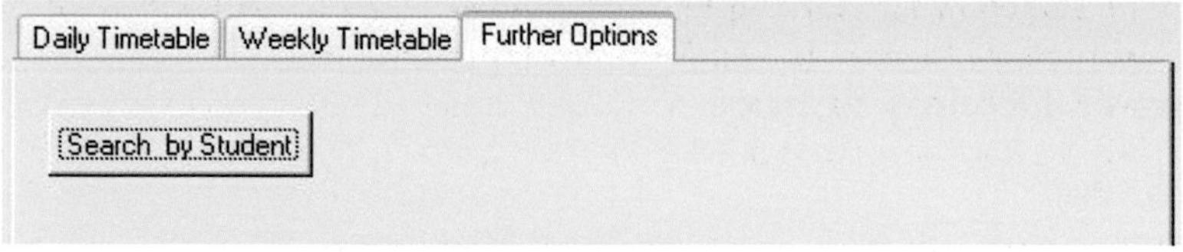

10 Go into **Form View** and test the button. You will be asked the Student ID. Scroll through the records to view this student's lessons.

11 Set up another Command Button to add a **Search by Date** option. You will first need to set up a macro as before using the **Apply Filter** action based on the qrySearchLessonDate. Call the macro **mcrSearchDate**.

When you use the option to filter data into a sub group of records it is important to restore all records before the next search. We will add a button to the Tab Control to remove the filter.

1 Create a new macro called **mcrShowAllRecords**. It has just one action **ShowAllRecords**.

2 Add a Command Button to the Tab Control Page to run this macro. The text on the button should read **Show All Records**. Your Tab Control Page should appear as in Figure 1.17.3. You will need to use the **Format, Align** and **Format, Size** menu options to position and size the buttons.

Figure 1.17.3 ▶

Adding sort options

You can sort the data displayed in a form into different orders. For example, you may want to cycle through the records in order of Student ID, Lesson Number or by Date.

We will set up a macro to sort the records and then use a Command Button to run the macro. The following steps take you through setting up the **Sort by Lesson** option.

1 Create a new macro. In the Action column select **GoToControl**. In the Action Arguments set the **Control Name** to **LessonNo**.

2 In the Action column select **RunCommand.** In the Action Arguments select **SortAscending** from the drop-down arrow.

3 Save the macro as **mcrSortLesson**.

4 Open **frmLessonBooking** in **Design View**. Click on the **Further Options** Tab. Use the Command Button Wizard to add a button to run **mcrSortLesson** and add the text **Sort by Lesson**.

5 Add further buttons to **Sort by Instructor** and **Sort by Student** (see Figure 1.17.4).

Figure 1.17.4 ▼

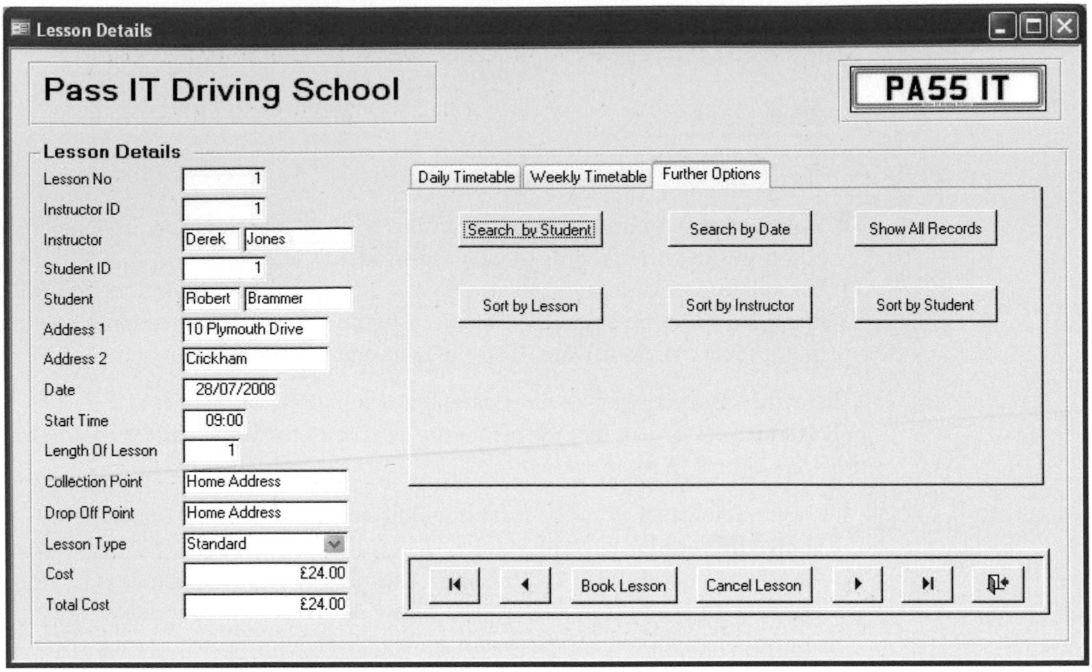

6 Go into Form View and test that the buttons work.

Adding further options

If you have tested your booking form during the course of these units you will appreciate that much is dependent on your knowing the StudentID or InstructorID. When a student phones the Pass IT Driving School to book a lesson they will quite often forget or don't know their Student ID.

The procedure is:

■ A student phones the school to book a lesson; the operator opens the booking form and clicks on Book a Lesson.
■ The student cannot remember their ID so the operator selects the student details from a drop-down box.

Adding a Combo Box to enter a student's details

1 Open **frmLessonBooking** in Design View. Click on the Combo Box tool in the Toolbox and drag out a Combo Box on the Further Options Tab Page.

2 The Combo Box Wizard dialogue box is displayed. Check **"I want the combo box to look up the values in a table or query"** and click on **Next** (see Figure 1.17.5).

Figure 1.17.5 ▶

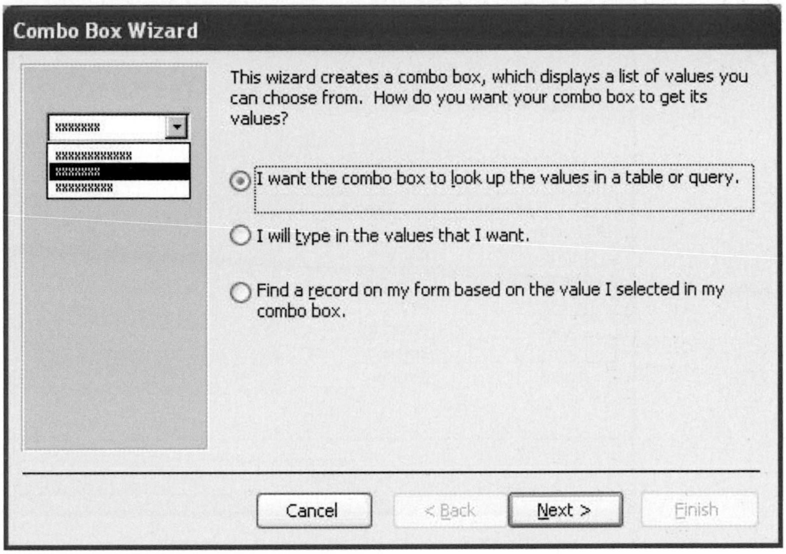

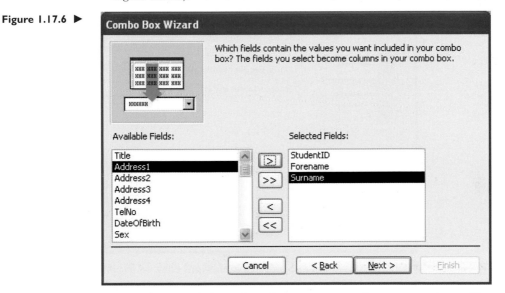

3 Select **tblStudent** from the next dialogue box and click on **Next**.
4 Select the fields **StudentID**, **Forename** and **Surname** and click on **Next** (see Figure 1.17.6).

Figure 1.17.6 ▶

5 From the next dialogue box choose to sort on **Surname**, in **Ascending** order and click on **Next**.

6 The next dialogue box shows you how the combo box will display the names. (See Figure 1.17.7). Click on **Next**.

Figure 1.17.7 ▶

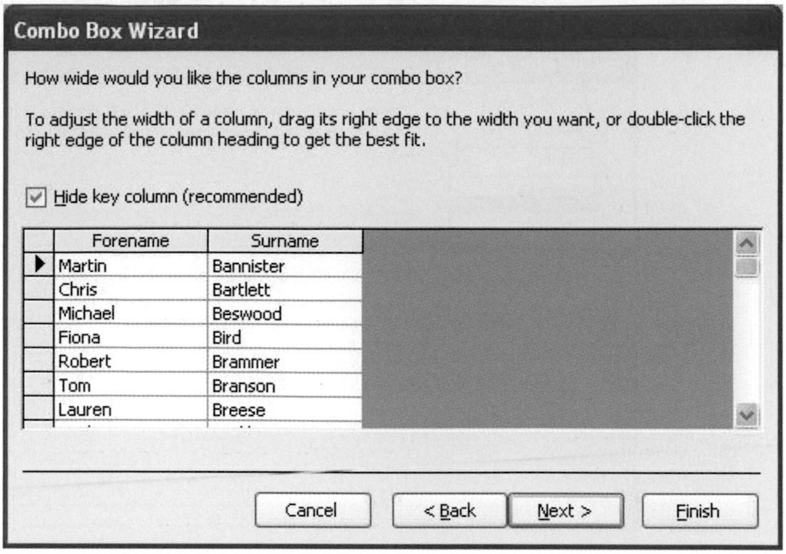

Combo Box Wizard

How wide would you like the columns in your combo box?

To adjust the width of a column, drag its right edge to the width you want, or double-click the right edge of the column heading to get the best fit.

☑ Hide key column (recommended)

Forename	Surname
▶ Martin	Bannister
Chris	Bartlett
Michael	Beswood
Fiona	Bird
Robert	Brammer
Tom	Branson
Lauren	Breese

| Cancel | < Back | Next > | Finish |

7 Check the **"Store that value in this field"** option and select **StudentID** from the drop down box. Click on **Next**. (see Figure 1.17.8).

Figure 1.17.8 ▶

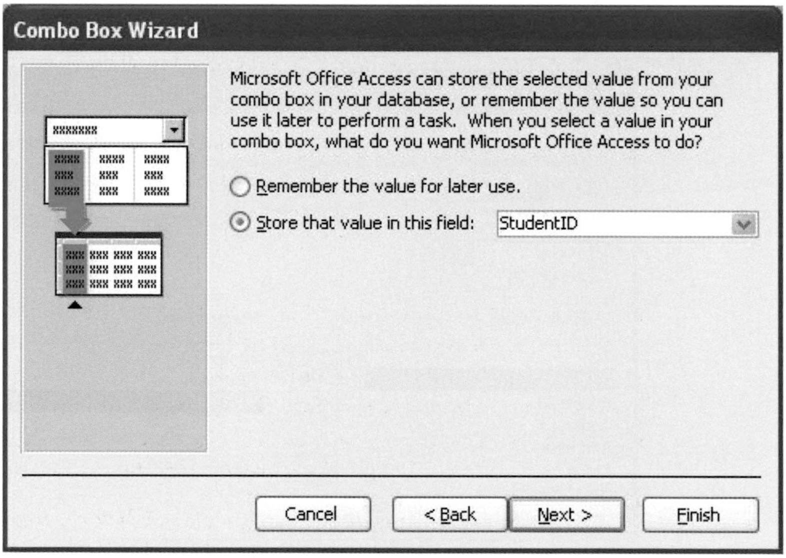

Combo Box Wizard

Microsoft Office Access can store the selected value from your combo box in your database, or remember the value so you can use it later to perform a task. When you select a value in your combo box, what do you want Microsoft Office Access to do?

○ Remember the value for later use.

◉ Store that value in this field: StudentID

| Cancel | < Back | Next > | Finish |

8 Change the Label to **Student Names** and click on **Finish**.
9 Repeat the above steps to set up another combo box to select an Instructor. Your finished form should appear as in Figure 1.17.9.

Figure 1.17.9 ▶

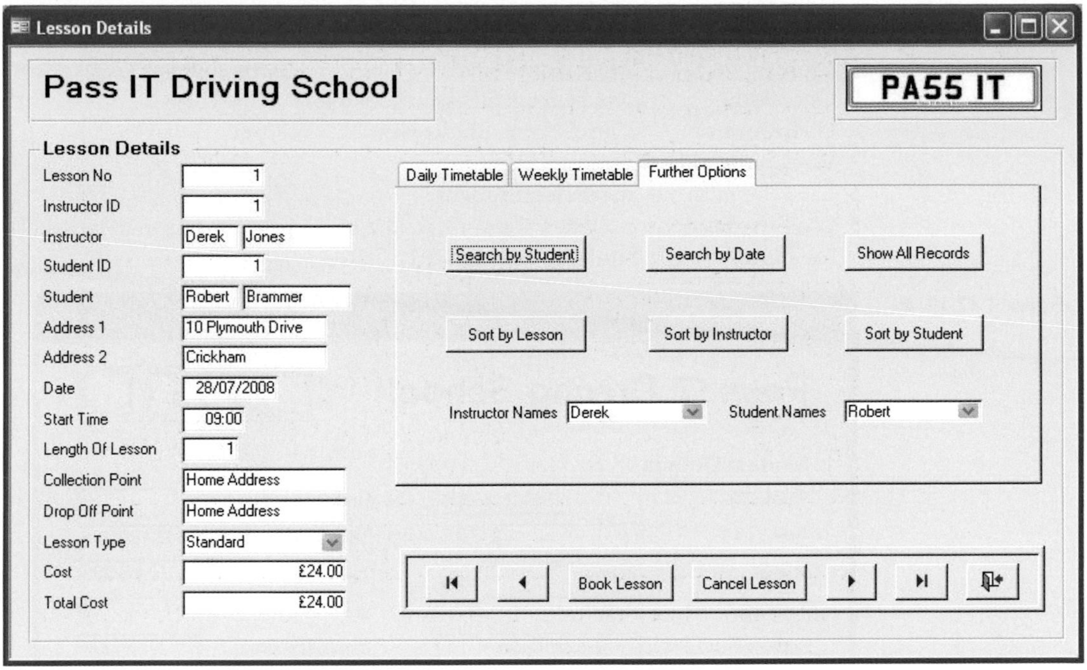

Using a copy and paste macro to look up and enter student details

In previous editions of this book the following technique has been used as an alternative to using a combo box. It is more complex but again gives the reader an opportunity to explore macros.

The procedure is:

■ A student phones the school to book a lesson; the operator opens the booking form and clicks on Book a Lesson.
■ The student cannot remember their ID so the operator opens the student form and uses the drop-down to find the student's surname and hence their ID.
■ The operator will then be able to click a button and Access will place the ID number into the Booking Form along with the student details.

1 Open **frmLessonBooking** in Design View. Click on the **Further Options** Tab and use the Command Button Wizard to add a button to open **frmStudent**. Set the text on the button to **Find Student**. You will need to reposition the combo boxes.
2 Save the form and test that the button opens **frmStudent**.
3 The Student Form is already set up with a combo box to select the student. We need to create a macro to paste these details into **frmLessonBooking**.

4 Create a new macro. The actions are as follows:

GoToControl.   Control Name **StudentID**
RunCommand   Command **Copy**
Close   Object Type **Form**   Object Name **frmStudent**
OpenForm   Form Name **frmLessonBooking**   View **Form**
GoToControl.   Control Name **StudentID**
RunCommand   Command **Paste**

5 Save the macro as **mcrSelectStudent**.
6 Load **frmStudent** in Design View and add a button to run this macro. Label the button **Select Student** (see Figure 1.17.10).

Figure 1.17.10 ▶

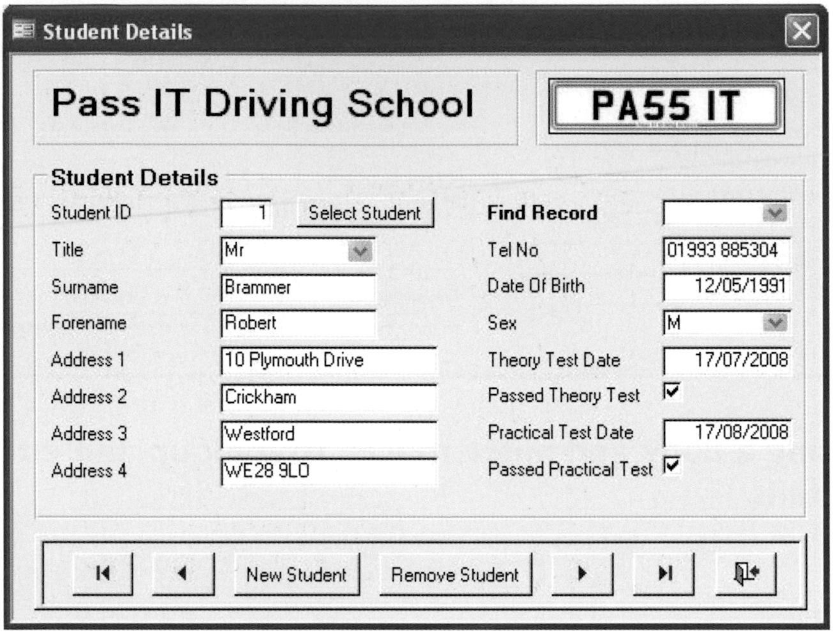

When you test this procedure you will find that the system places the ID into the Booking Form but you then have to press return to activate the form. This can be avoided by these simple steps.

1 Create a new macro called **mcrUpdate** with the single action **RunCommand** and argument **RefreshPage**.
2 Open **frmLessonBooking** in Design View and right click on the **StudentID** field to display its properties.
3 Click on the **Event Tab** and set its **On Change** property to run the macro called **mcrUpdate**.

Unit 18: Calculations in reports

The qryLessonCost in Unit 8 set up a calculated field to work out the cost of each lesson.

We are going to set up a report to add up the income from lessons for each instructor.

Calculating totals in a report

1 Create a new report based on the query **qryLessonCost** using the **Report Wizard.**

2 Use the arrow icon (>) to select these fields in this order: **InstructorID, tblInstructor_Forename, tblInstructor_Surname, tblStudent_Forename, tblStudent_Surname, Date** and **TotalCost** (see Figure 1.18.1). Click on **Next.**

Figure 1.18.1 ▶

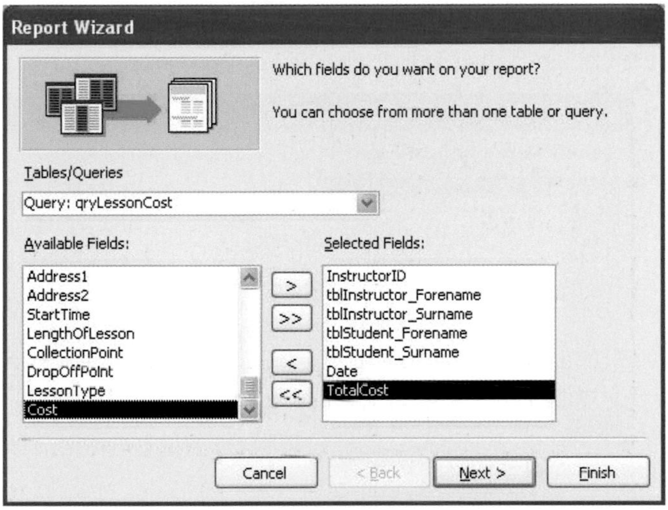

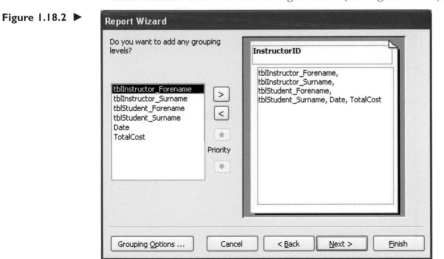

3 If the records are not grouped by InstructorID by default, click on **InstructorID** and click on the right arrow (see Figure 1.18.2). Click on **Next.**

Figure 1.18.2 ▶

4 Sort by **Date** and click on **Next** (see Figure 1.18.3).

Figure 1.18.3 ▶

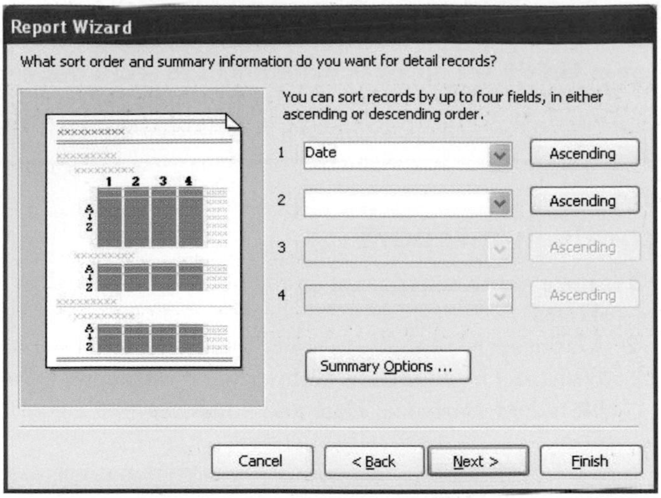

5 Click on **Align Left 1** and click on **Next** (see Figure 1.18.4).

Figure 1.18.4 ▶

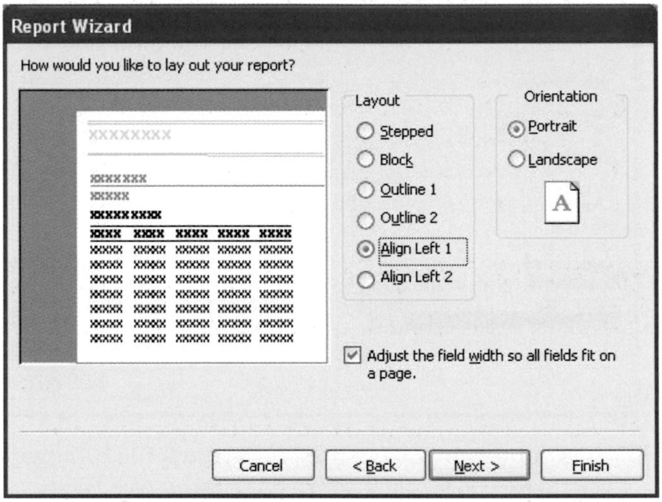

6 Click on **Corporate** and click on **Next** (see Figure 1.18.5).

Figure 1.18.5 ▶

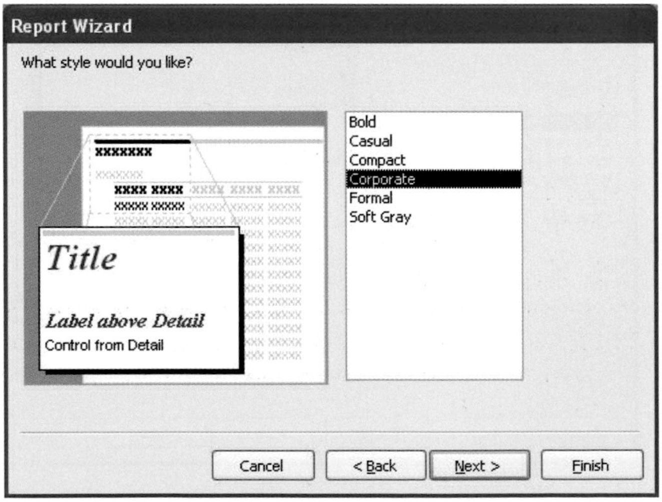

7 Name it **rptIncome** and click on **Finish**
The report opens and is shown in Figure 1.18.6. You will need to use the page navigation buttons to scroll through the instructors.

Figure 1.18.6 ▼

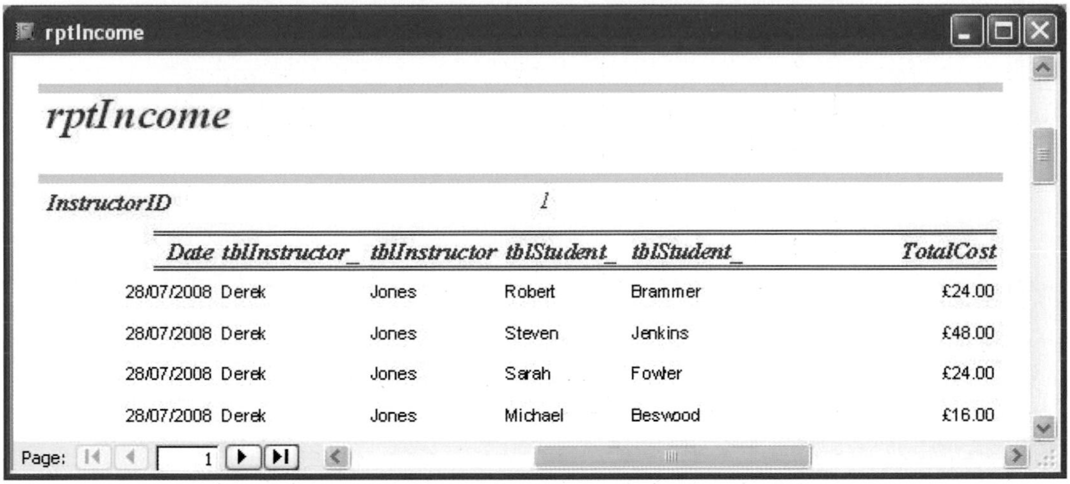

We are going to add up the total cost of lessons for each instructor to display the income.

8 Click on the **Design View** icon or click on **View, Design View** to switch to **Design View**.

9 Click on the **Sorting and Grouping** icon or click on **View, Sorting and Grouping** (see Figure 1.18.7).

Figure 1.18.7 ▼

10 Add an **InstructorID Group Footer** by selecting **InstructorID** and setting **Group Footer** to **Yes**. Close the dialogue box (see Figure 1.18.8).

Figure 1.18.8 ▶

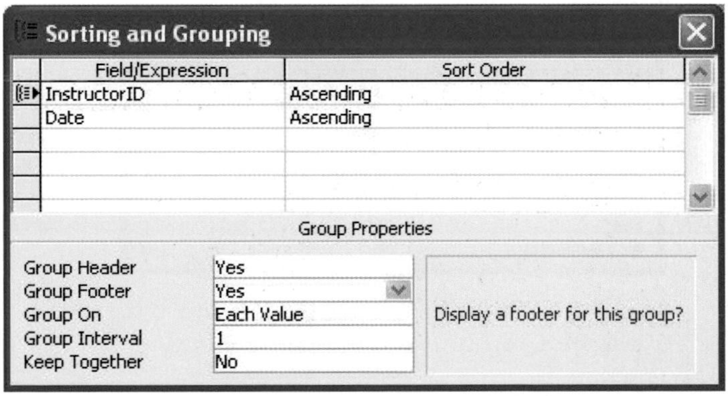

11 Click on the **Text Box** icon in the Toolbox and drag out a text box in the InstructorID Footer. It will say something like **Text27** and **Unbound** (see Figure 1.18.9).

Figure 1.18.9 ▼

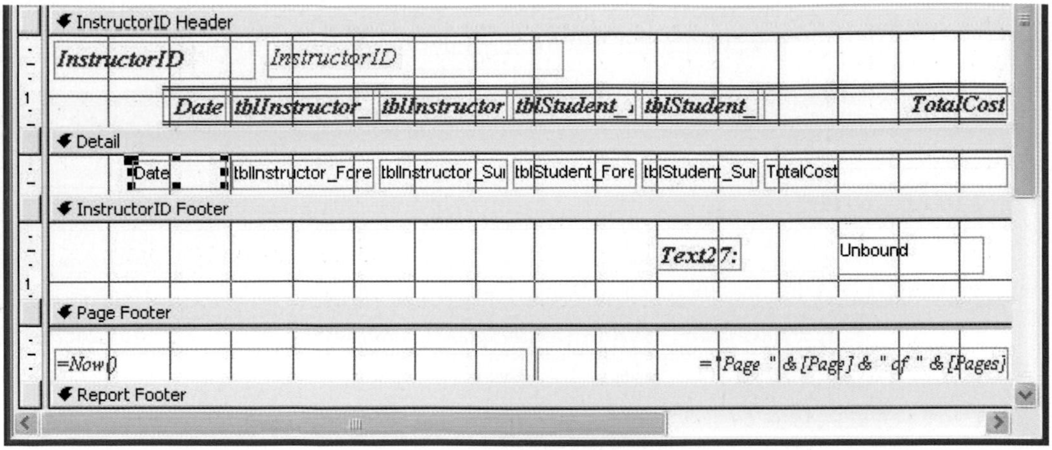

12 With the new text box selected, click on the **Properties** icon. Click on the **Data** tab. In the **Control Source** row type in **=Sum([TotalCost])**.

Note The field name in the square brackets must be exactly the same as the calculated field name set up in Unit 8. There is no space between Total and Cost (see Figure 1.18.10).

Figure 1.18.10 ▶

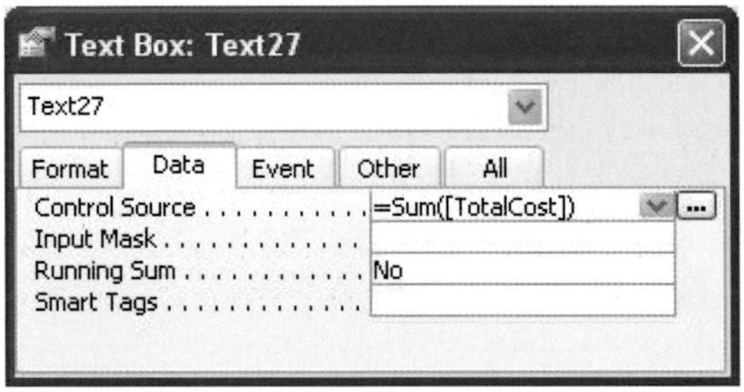

13 Still in the Properties window, click on the **Format** tab. In the Format row choose **Currency**. (See Figure 1.18.11.) Scroll down and set the **Font Weight** Property to **Bold**. Close the Properties window.

Figure 1.18.11 ▶

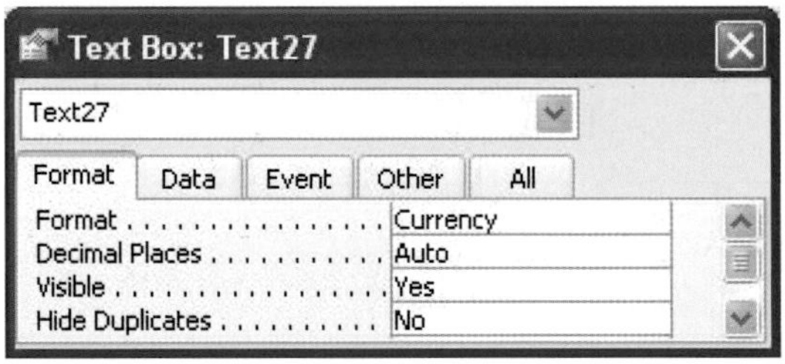

14 Edit the text in the label of the new text box (Text27) to read **Total** (see Figure 1.18.12).

Figure 1.18.12 ▼

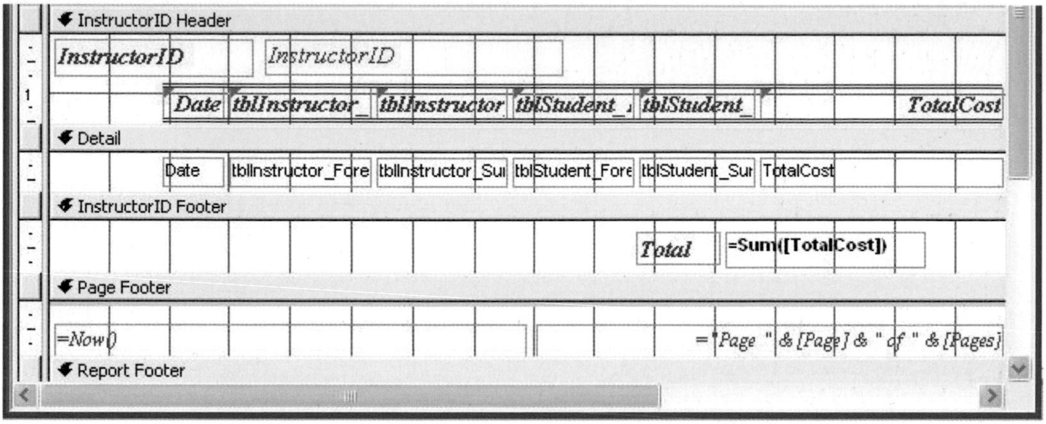

15 You will notice from Figure 1.18.6 that the instructor name repeats throughout the report. Drag **tblInstructor_Forename** and **tblInstructor_Surname** from the Detail area into the Instructor ID Header as shown in Figure 1.18.13.

16 Delete the **tblInstructor_Forename** and **tblInstructor_Surname** column headings.

17 Change the **tblStudent_Forename** column heading to **Name**. Delete the **tblStudent_Surname** column heading and change the title of the report to **Income Report**. See Figure 1.18.13.

Figure 1.18.13 ▼

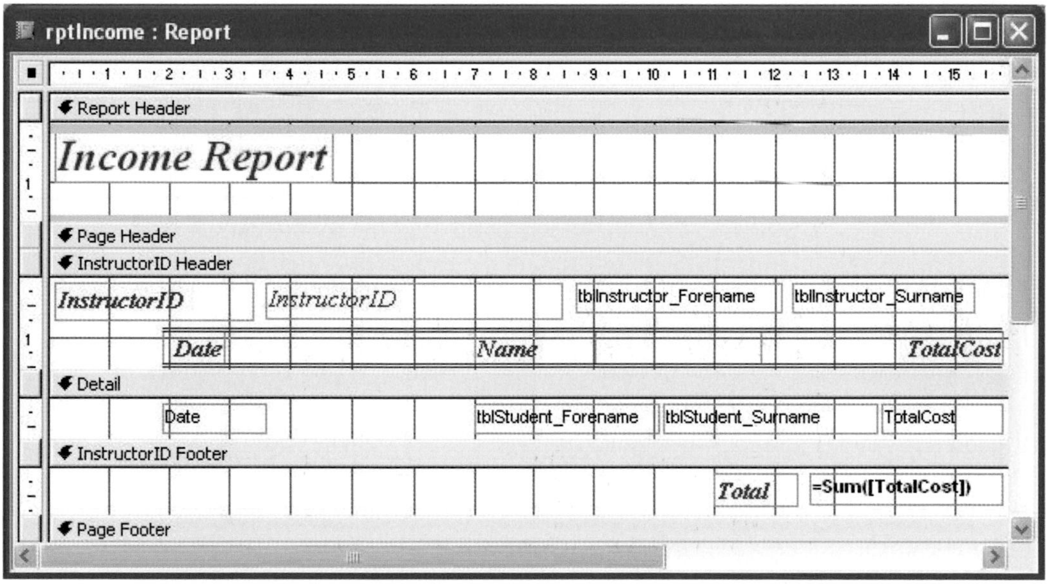

18 Go into Print Preview mode and test the report (see Figure 1.18.14). You may wish to format the layout of column headings and data further.

Figure 1.18.14 ▼

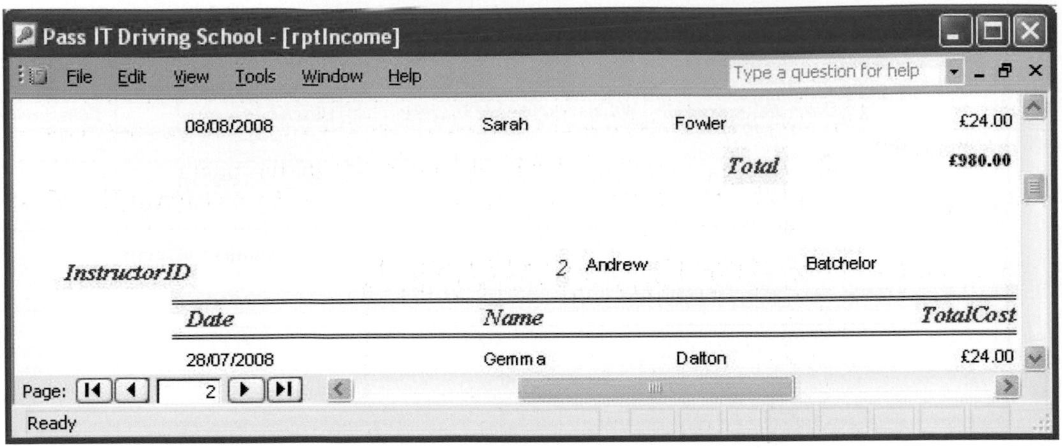

How to get an overall total in your report

1 Open the report in Design View. Drag out the Report Footer. Copy and paste the Total controls in the InstructorID Footer to the Report Footer and edit the Label as shown to **Grand Total**. (See Figure 1.18.15).

Figure 1.18.15 ►

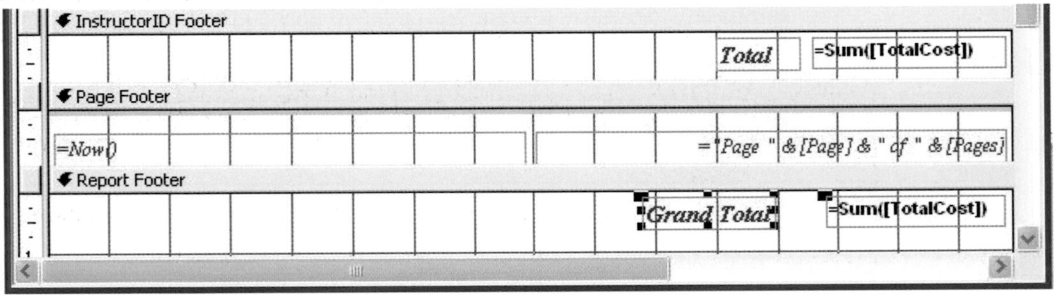

2 Switch to Print Preview to check that the total is correct (see Figure 1.18.16). Using the SUM function in the Report Footer gives overall totals.

Figure 1.18.16 ►

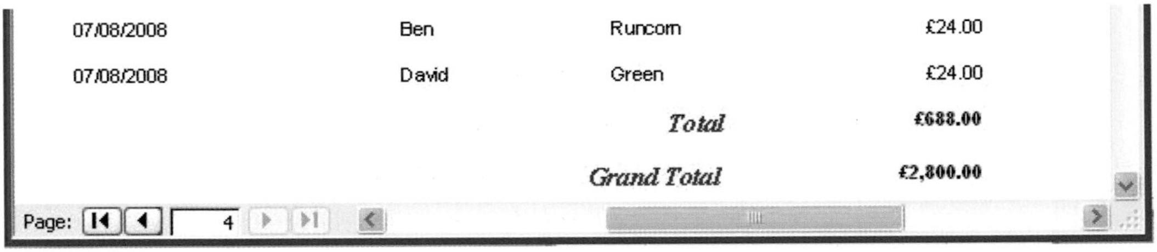

How to count records in a report

Sometimes you might want to count the number of records in a report. For example in the above report, you may want to know the number of lessons for each instructor.

1 Open the report in **Design View**.
2 Click on the **Text Box** icon and add a small text box to the InstructorID Footer section (see Figure 1.18.17).

Figure 1.18.17 ▼

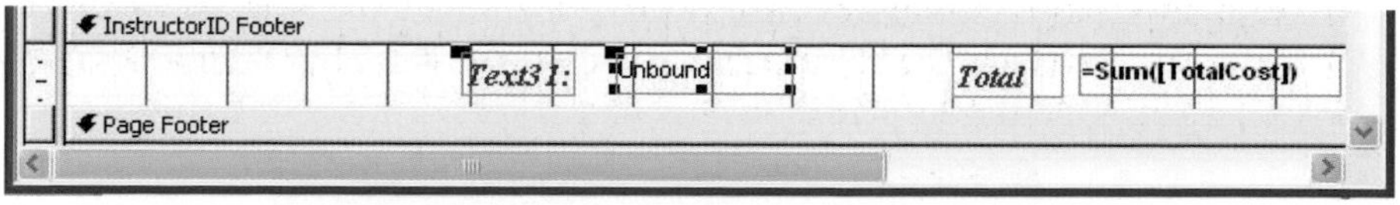

3 Select the new text box and click on the **Properties** icon.
4 Click on the **Data** tab and set the Control Source to **=Count([TotalCost])** (see Figure 1.18.18).

Figure 1.18.18 ▶

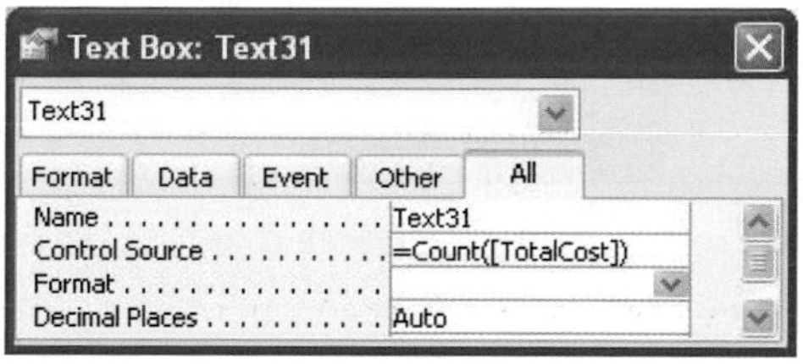

5 Edit the text box label so that it says **Number of Lessons** (see Figure 1.18.19).

Figure 1.18.19 ▼

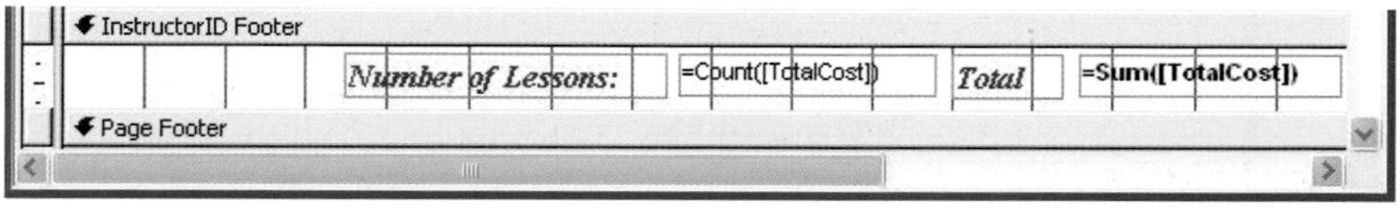

6 Switch to Print Preview to check that the count is correct (see Figure 1.18.20).

Figure 1.18.20 ▼

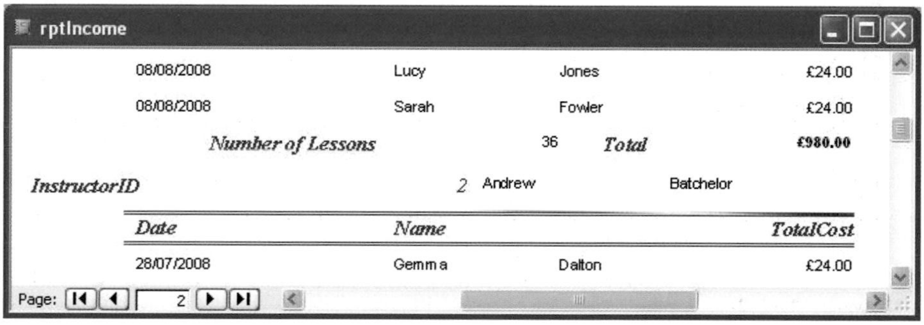

How to get a running total in a report

To set the total to be a running total:

1 Load the report **rptIncome** in **Design View**.
2 Copy the Total controls and paste below the existing control in the InstructorID Footer. Edit the **Label** to **Running Total** (see Figure 1.18.21).

Figure 1.18.21 ▼

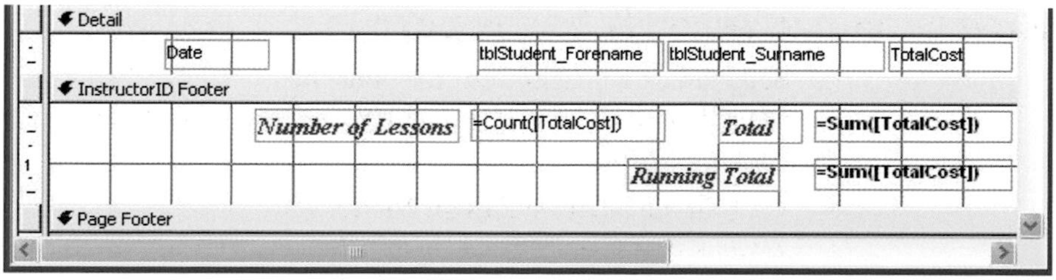

3 Select the **Running Total** control. Click on the **Properties** icon or click on **View, Properties**.

4 Click on the **Data** tab and set the **Running Sum** row to **Over All** (see Figure 1.18.22).

Figure 1.18.22 ▶

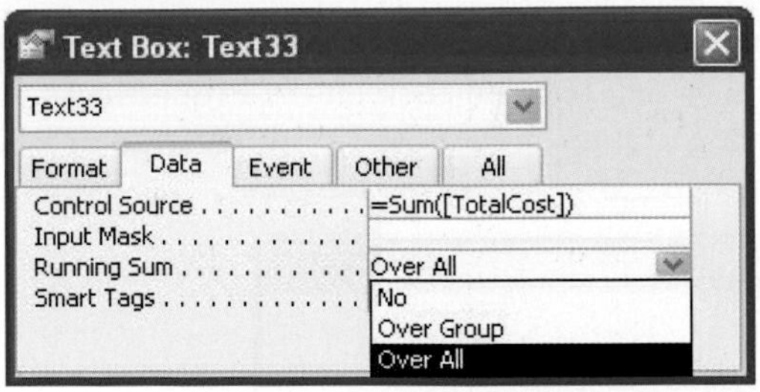

```
Text Box: Text33                          [X]

Text33                              [v]

Format  | Data | Event | Other | All

Control Source . . . . . . . . . .  =Sum([TotalCost])
Input Mask . . . . . . . . . . . .
Running Sum . . . . . . . . . . .  Over All          [v]
Smart Tags . . . . . . . . . . . .  No
                                    Over Group
                                    Over All
```

5 Switch to Print Preview mode and check that the running total is correct (see Figure 1.18.23).

Figure 1.18.23 ▼

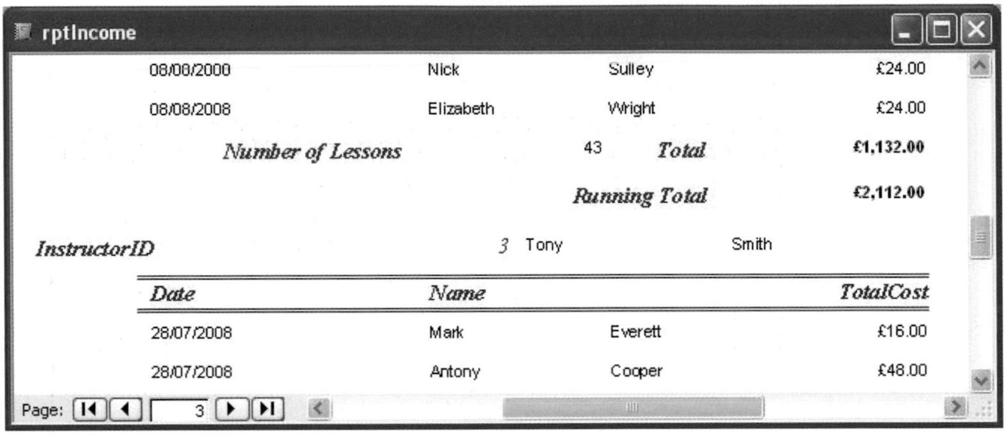

```
rptIncome                                        [_][□][X]

    08/08/2000          Nick          Sulley          £24.00
    08/08/2008          Elizabeth     Wright          £24.00

        Number of Lessons          43      Total      £1,132.00

                                Running Total          £2,112.00

InstructorID                    3   Tony          Smith

        Date              Name                    TotalCost

    28/07/2008          Mark          Everett         £16.00
    28/07/2008          Antony        Cooper          £48.00

Page: [|◀][◀]    3  [▶][▶|]  [◀]
```

Setting up a lesson analysis report

We are now going to set up a similar report to the previous one using a different method and an improved layout. The report will include two levels of grouping and make use of the Summary Options. In Unit 20 we will adjust the menus to include this report.

1 Create a new report based on **qryLessonCost** using the **Report Wizard**.

2 Use the arrow icon (>) to select these fields in this order: **InstructorID, tblInstructor_Forename, tblInstructor_Surname, StudentID, tblStudent_Forename, tblStudent_Surname, Date, LengthOfLesson, LessonType** and **TotalCost**. Click on **Next**.

3 If the records are not grouped by InstructorID by default, click on **InstructorID** and click on the right arrow (see Figure 1.18.24). Select **StudentID** also and click on the right arrow (see Figure 1.18.24). Click on **Next**.

Figure 1.18.24 ▶

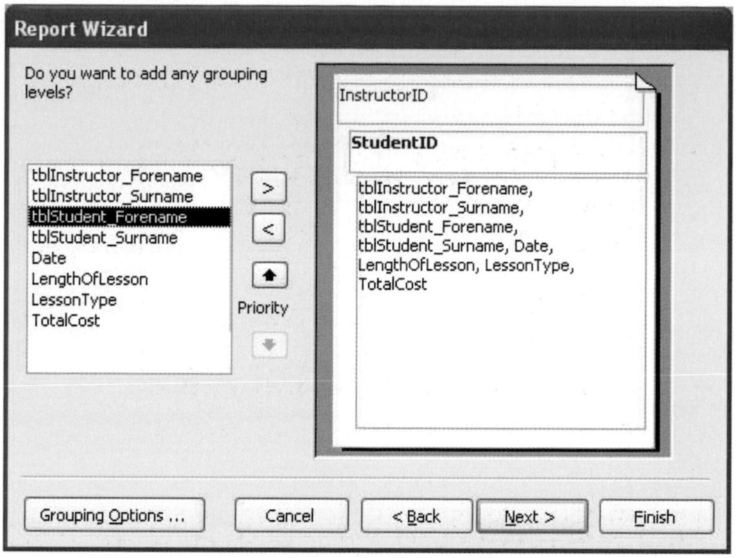

4 Sort by **Date** and click on **Summary Options**. (See Figure 1.18.25.)

Figure 1.18.25 ▶

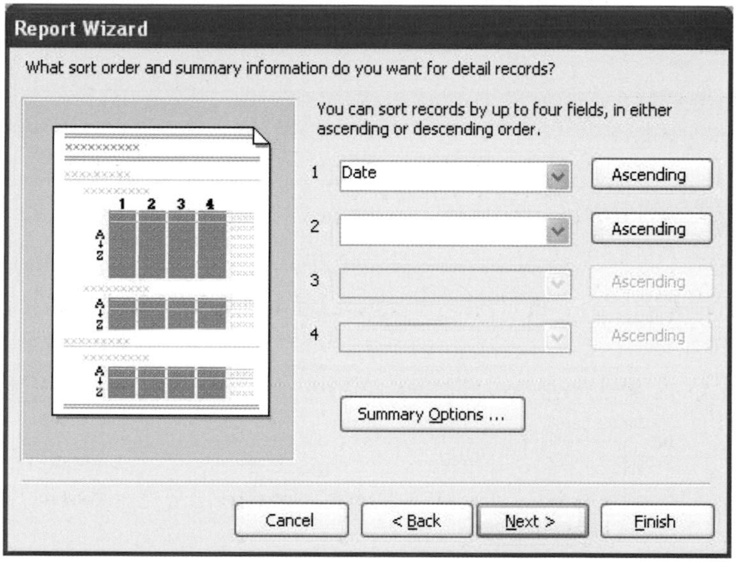

5 The Summary Options Wizard displays the fields it can carry out calculations on. Choose to sum **LengthOfLesson** and **TotalCost** as shown. (See Figure 1.18.26.) Click on **OK**. Click **Next**.

Figure 1.18.26 ▶

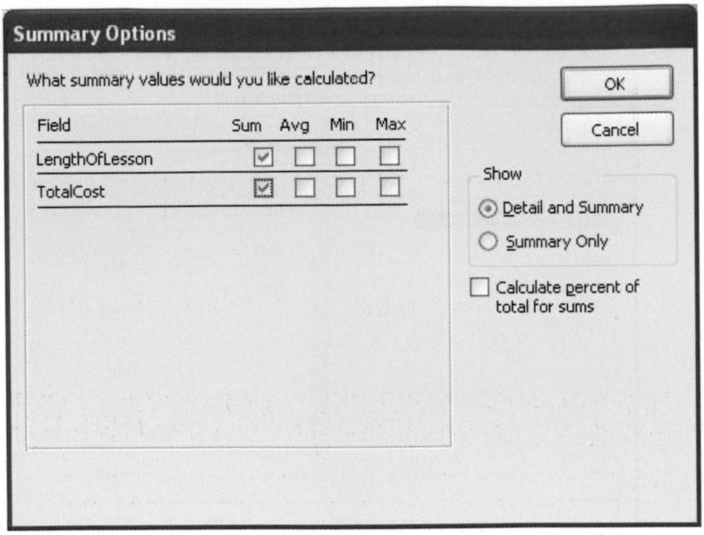

Summary Options

What summary values would you like calculated?

Field	Sum	Avg	Min	Max
LengthOfLesson	☑	☐	☐	☐
TotalCost	☑	☐	☐	☐

OK

Cancel

Show

◉ Detail and Summary

◯ Summary Only

☐ Calculate percent of total for sums

6 Click on **Align Left 1** and click on **Next**. Click on **Corporate** and click on **Next**.

7 Name it **rptLessonAnalysis** and click on **Finish**. Your report should look like Figure 1.18.27.

Figure 1.18.27 ▼

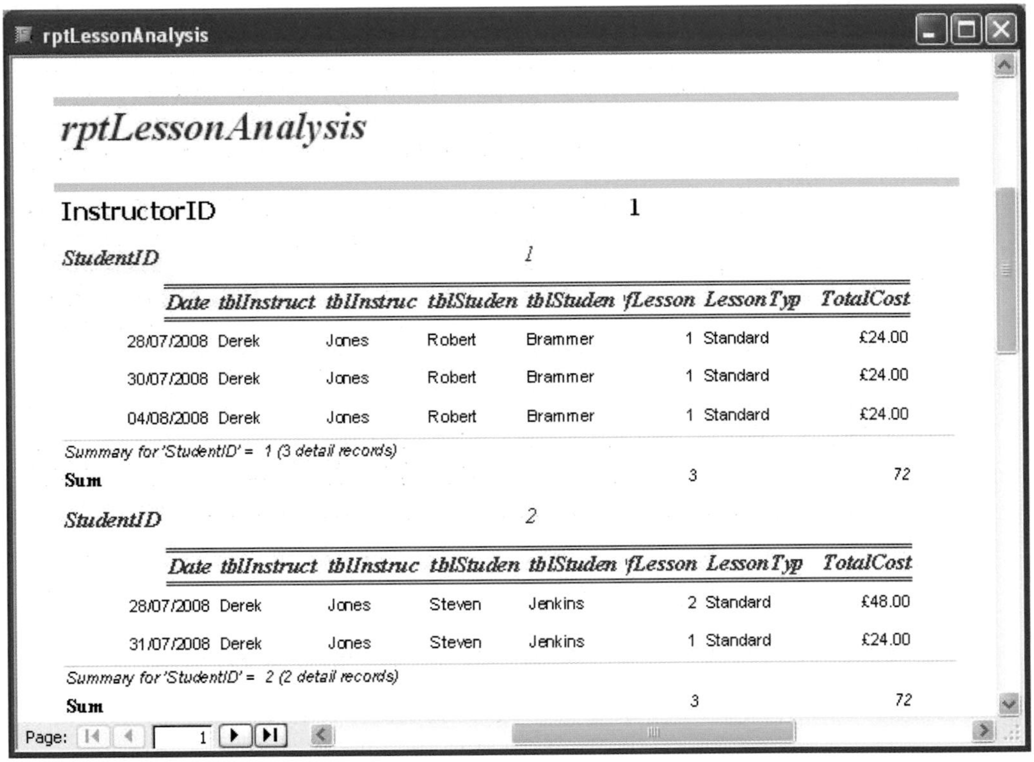

rptLessonAnalysis

rptLessonAnalysis

InstructorID   1

StudentID   1

Date	tblInstruct	tblInstruc	tblStuden	tblStuden	fLesson	LessonTyp	TotalCost
28/07/2008	Derek	Jones	Robert	Brammer	1	Standard	£24.00
30/07/2008	Derek	Jones	Robert	Brammer	1	Standard	£24.00
04/08/2008	Derek	Jones	Robert	Brammer	1	Standard	£24.00

Summary for 'StudentID' = 1 (3 detail records)

Sum   3   72

StudentID   2

Date	tblInstruct	tblInstruc	tblStuden	tblStuden	fLesson	LessonTyp	TotalCost
28/07/2008	Derek	Jones	Steven	Jenkins	2	Standard	£48.00
31/07/2008	Derek	Jones	Steven	Jenkins	1	Standard	£24.00

Summary for 'StudentID' = 2 (2 detail records)

Sum   3   72

Page: |◀ ◀ [1] ▶ ▶|

You will notice a number of things. The report is grouped by instructor. Within each instructor group the students for that instructor are also grouped.

The Summary Options has added the Sum of the LengthOfLesson and TotalCost fields. The number of records for each student is also displayed.

If you go to the end of the report you will see Summary Option has offered some Grand Totals.

If you go into Design View you will see the Sum formulae in the StudentID Footer, InstructorID Footer and Report Footer. (See Figure 1.18.28.)

The last stage is to give the report the in-house style developed in Unit 12.

I Copy and paste the Report Header from **rptInstructor** in Unit 12. Edit the title to read **Lesson Analysis**.

Figure 1.18.28 ▼

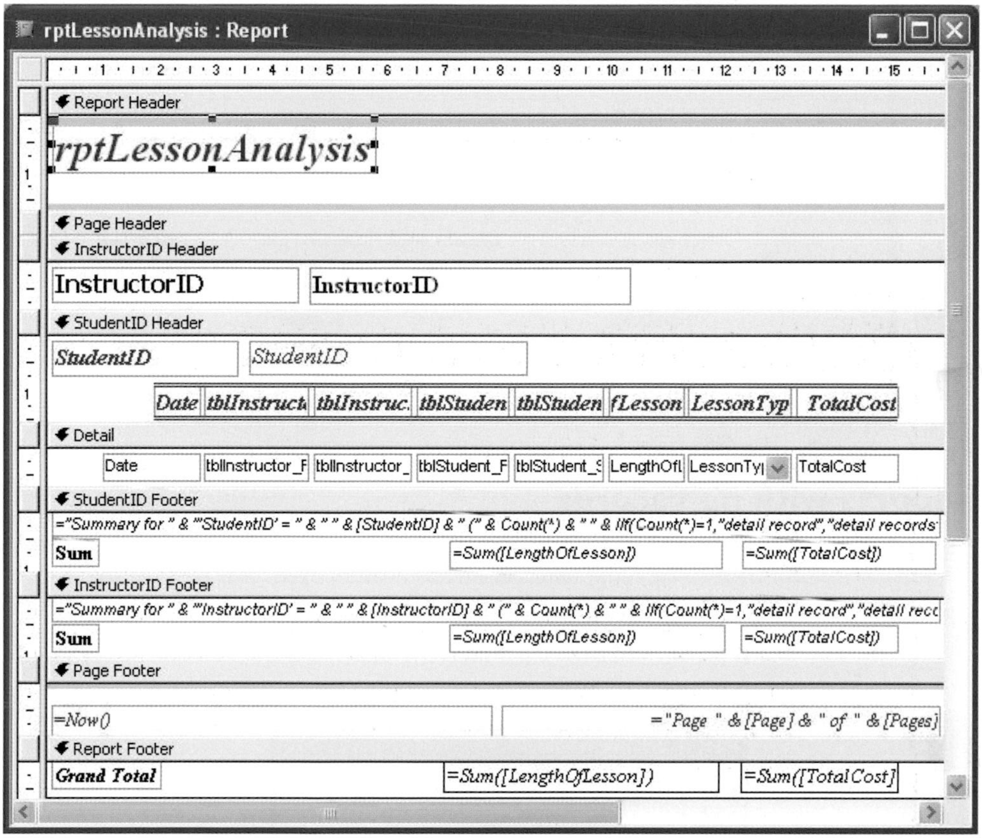

2 Drag the fields **tblInstructor_Forename, tblInstructor_Surname, tblStudent_Forename, tblStudent_Surname** to the InstructorID and StudentID Headers.

3 Rename the headings, change the fonts and align all the controls.

4 Add the labels **Hours Driven** and **Fees** to the StudentID Footer next to the Sum controls. Add also the labels **Hours Driven** and **Income** to the InstructorID Footer next to the Sum controls.

5 Delete the Summary controls inserted by Access (optional).

6 Add labels to the Report Footer as appropriate. Your finished report should appear as in Figure 1.18.29.

Figure 1.18.29 ▼

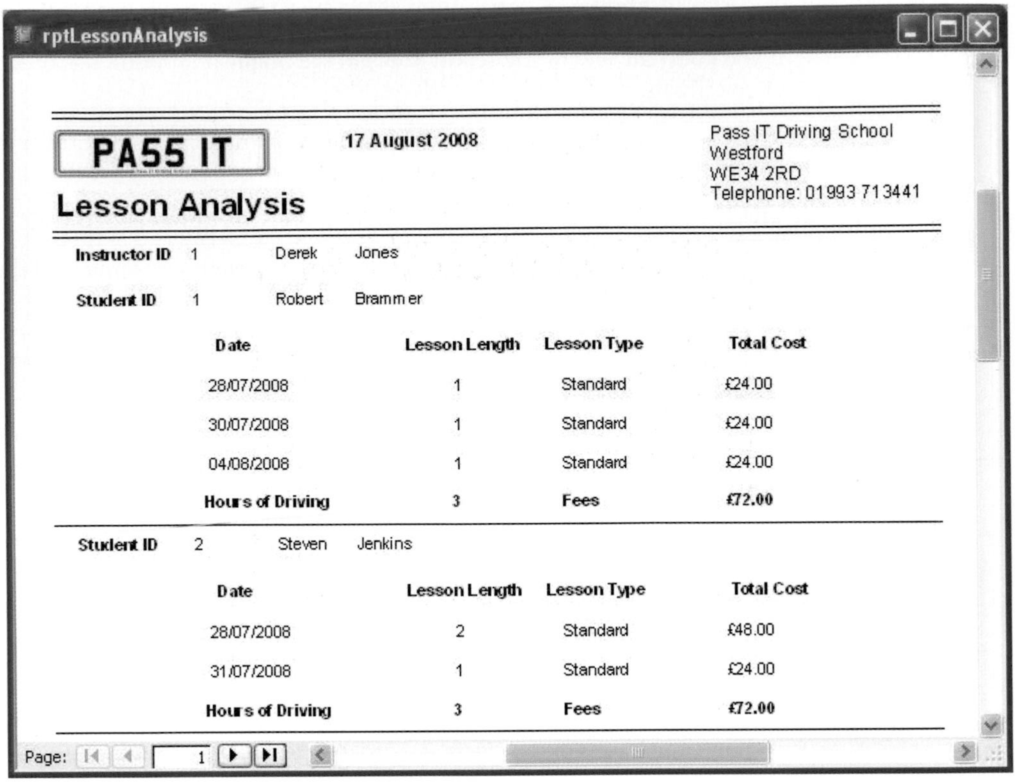

Reports with no records

Some reports have no data in them. For example you might be searching for lessons on a day when none has been booked. It is possible to check if there is no data in a report and give a warning to the user.

1 Set up a macro called **mcrNoData** that displays this message box (see Figure 1.18.30).

Figure 1.18.30 ▶

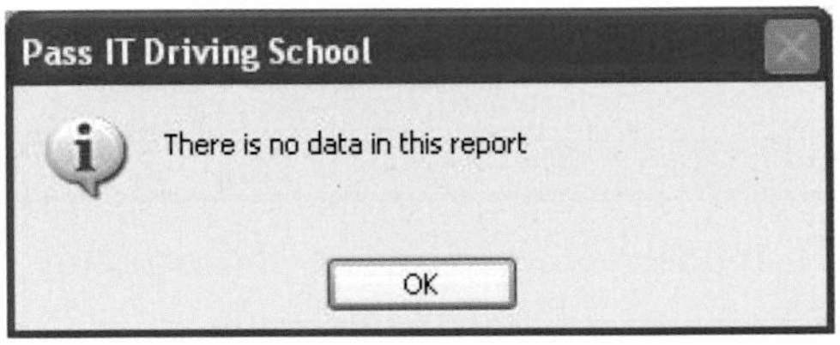

The action is **MsgBox.** The arguments are as shown (see Figure 1.18.31).

Figure 1.18.31 ▼

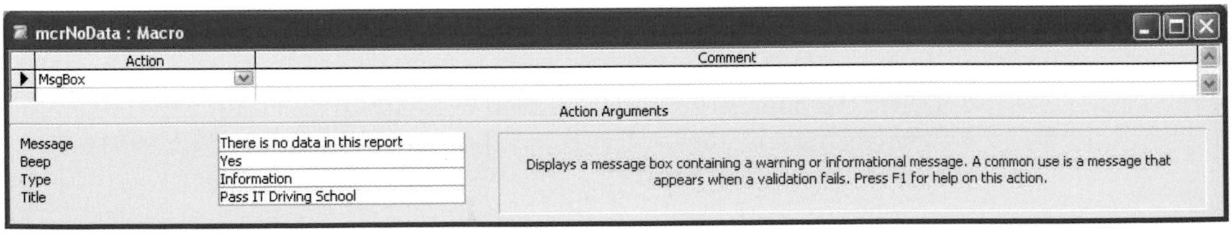

2 Save the macro and test it.

We want to run this macro when we open the Instructors' Timetable Report. We can set this up using the report properties.

3 At the Database Window, click on **Reports**.

4 Select **rptInstructorTimetable** and click on **Design**.

5 Click on the **Properties** icon or click on **View, Properties**.

The Report properties will be displayed.

6 Click on the **Event** tab (see Figure 1.18.32).

Figure 1.18.32 ▶

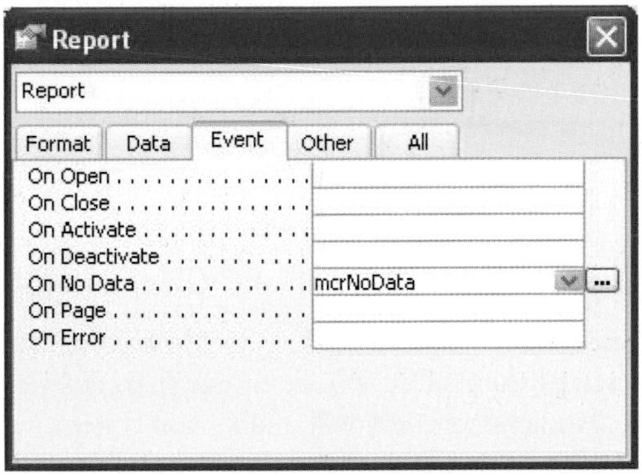

You can now select macros to run when the report:

On Open	When the report opens.
On Close	When the report closes.
On Activate	When the report becomes the active window.
On Deactivate	When the report stops being the active window.
On No Data	When the report has no data.
On Page	When a page of a report is formatted for printing.
On Error	When there is an error.

7 We want the **mcrNoData** macro to run when there is no data in the report so set the **On No Data** property to **mcrNoData** using the drop-down list as shown in Figure 1.18.32.

8 Save the report and test that the macro works when there is no data by opening the report and entering a date when you know that there are no lessons. (The message box actually will appear twice before the blank report loads.)

Hint Use **Tricks and Tips** numbers 15 and 16 to set up Weekday and Month queries. Set up appropriate reports based on these queries.

Unit 19: Using action queries

In Units 6, 7 and 8 you learned how to use a range of queries to view your data.
In this unit you will learn how to use action queries. Action queries actually do something to the data in your system by moving it, changing it or deleting it.
There are four types of action query.
■ Append query
■ Delete query
■ Update query
■ Make Table Query (not used in the Pass IT Driving School)

Append queries

An append query will take data from one table and add it to another.

In a club membership system you may decide to keep details of members who have not renewed their subscriptions rather than delete their records immediately. An append query will enable you to remove their details from the main membership table and transfer them to a table of, for example, expired memberships.

Similarly in a school or college. At the end of each year you could delete all leavers from the system but it is likely you will need to keep records for a period of time. An append query could be set up to transfer leaver details to a table of leavers.

Delete queries

A delete query will remove records from one or more tables according to set criteria.

In the school or college system above you may decide to keep records of ex-students for three years. At the end of each college year you would remove details of all students who left three or more years ago.

Similarly in a video hire / library loans system details of loans will build up. After a period of time you will need to clear old details from the system.

A delete query can be used to carry out these operations.

Update queries

An update query will make changes to data in one or more tables.

In an ordering system you may decide to reduce the prices of all products by 7.5%. At the end of each year in our school system all students will move up a year from Year 7 to Year 8 and so on.

Update queries allow you to make these changes to the data in your tables automatically.

Managing lesson details

In the Pass IT Driving School we need our system to handle information about old lessons. There follows a possible scenario.

- After a lesson has taken place, we will move details to a table of old lessons. (**Append query**)
- The details will also need removing from the current table of lessons. (**Delete query**)
- After a period of a year we will remove them from the table of old lessons. (**Delete query**)

Warning When working with action queries it is a good idea to make a copy of your lesson table because you are going to be moving and changing the data. Making a copy will save you re-entering data at a later stage.

1 At the Database Window, click on **Tables.** Click on **tblLesson** and click on **Edit, Copy** or click on the **Copy** icon.
2 At the Database Window, click on **Edit, Paste** or click on the **Paste** icon.
3 Call the new table **tblLessonCopy** and click on **Structure and Data.** Click on **OK** (see Figure 1.19.1). We will work on **tblLesson**.

Figure 1.19.1 ▶

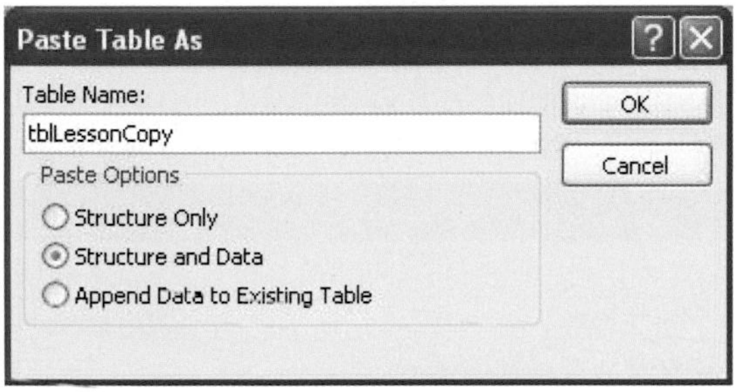

As action queries are often based on dates that clearly change you will have to edit the lesson dates before you start.

4 Open **tblLesson** and change the dates as follows. Use **Edit, Replace** to change all the lessons for one day at once.
- Change the 07/08/2008 lesson to today's date.
- Change the 08/08/2008 lesson to tomorrow's date.
- Change all the 06/08/2008 lessons to yesterday's date.
- Change all the 05/08/2008 lessons to the date exactly one year ago today.

Remove all other lessons by highlighting the rows and pressing **Delete.** To make this easier **Right Click** on the **Date** column and select **Sort Descending**. It will leave you with 37 records to work with.

Append query to transfer lesson details

We are going to move details of all old lessons from the Lesson table to a table called Old Lesson.

1 At the Database Window, click on **Tables.** Click on **tblLesson** and click on **Edit, Copy** or click on the **Copy** icon.
2 At the Database Window, click on **Edit, Paste** or click on the **Paste** icon.
3 Name the new table **tblOldLesson** and click on **Structure Only.** Click on **OK**.

4 This has created a new empty table called **tblOldLesson.** Open this table in **Design View.**

5 Set the **Data Type** of the **LessonNo** to **Number.** (This is vital. It will not work if you don't do this.)

6 Save the table and close it.

7 At the Database Window, click on **Queries** and double click on **Create query by using wizard.**

8 Select **tblLesson** from the drop-down. Click on the double arrow to choose all the fields and then click on **Next.**

9 In the Simple Query Wizard window click on **Next** again.

10 Name the query **qryOldLessonAppend** and click on **Finish.**

11 Open the query in **Design View** and set the Criteria row in the **Date** column to **<Date().**

12 If the Query design toolbar is showing click on the **Query Type** icon and click on **Append Query** or click on **Query, Append Query** (see Figure 1.19.2).

Figure 1.19.2 ▼

13 The Append dialogue box is displayed. Choose **tblOldLesson** from the drop down and click on **OK** (see Figure 1.19.3).

Figure 1.19.3 ►

Append [?][X]

Append To
Table Name: tblOldLesson ▼

OK
Cancel

◉ Current Database
◯ Another Database:
File Name:

Browse...

Figure 1.19.4 ▼

Details of the query are then displayed as shown in Figure 1.19.4.

qryOldLessonAppend : Append Query [_][□][X]

tblLesson
*
LessonNo
StudentID
InstructorID
Date

Field:	LessonNo	StudentID	InstructorID	Date	StartTime	LengthOfLesson
Table:	tblLesson	tblLesson	tblLesson	tblLesson	tblLesson	tblLesson
Sort:						
Append To:	LessonNo	StudentID	InstructorID	Date	StartTime	LengthOfLesson
Criteria:				<Date()		
or:						

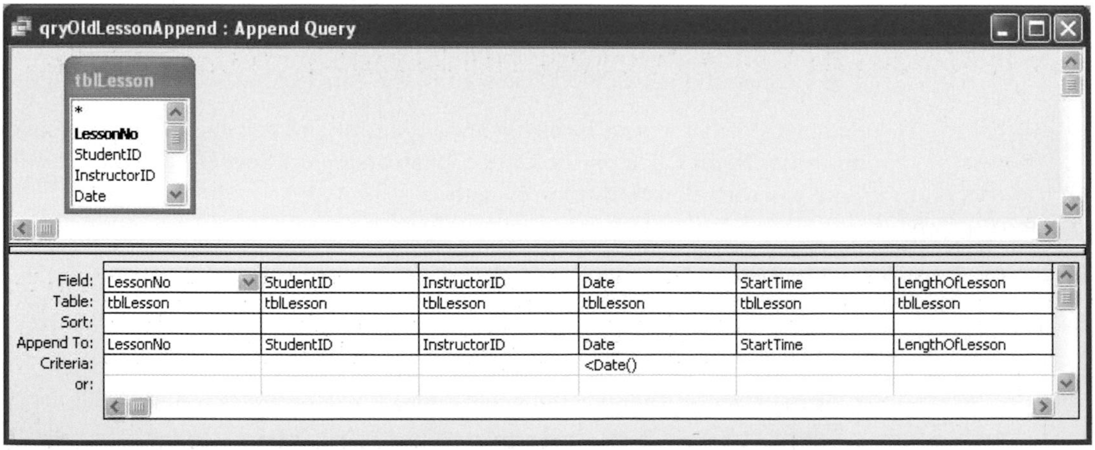

14 Save the query and close it.

15 At the Database Window, click on **Open** to run **qryOldLessonAppend.**

16 You will be prompted with two warning messages. Click on **Yes** (see Figure 1.19.5).

Figure 1.19.5 ►

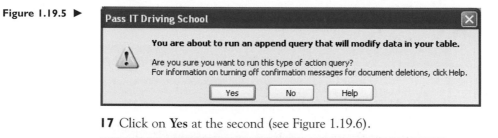

17 Click on **Yes** at the second (see Figure 1.19.6).

Figure 1.19.6 ►

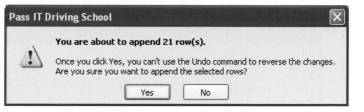

18 At the Database Window, open **tblOldLesson**. 21 records should have been added.

Delete query to remove lesson details from the Lesson table

We now need to clear out the details of all the old lessons which are still stored in the Lesson table. These should be the same 21 records.

1 At the Database Window, click on **Queries** and double click on **Create query by using wizard**.

2 Select **tblLesson** from the drop down. Click on the double arrow to choose all the fields and then click on **Next**.

3 In the Simple Query Wizard window click on **Next** again.

4 Name the query **qryOldLessonDelete** and click **Finish**.

5 Open the query in **Design View**. If the Query design toolbar is showing click on the **Query Type** icon and click on **Delete Query** or click on **Query, Delete Query**.

Figure 1.19.7 ▼

6 Set the Criteria row in the **Date** column to **<Date()** (see Figure 1.19.7).

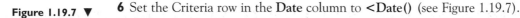

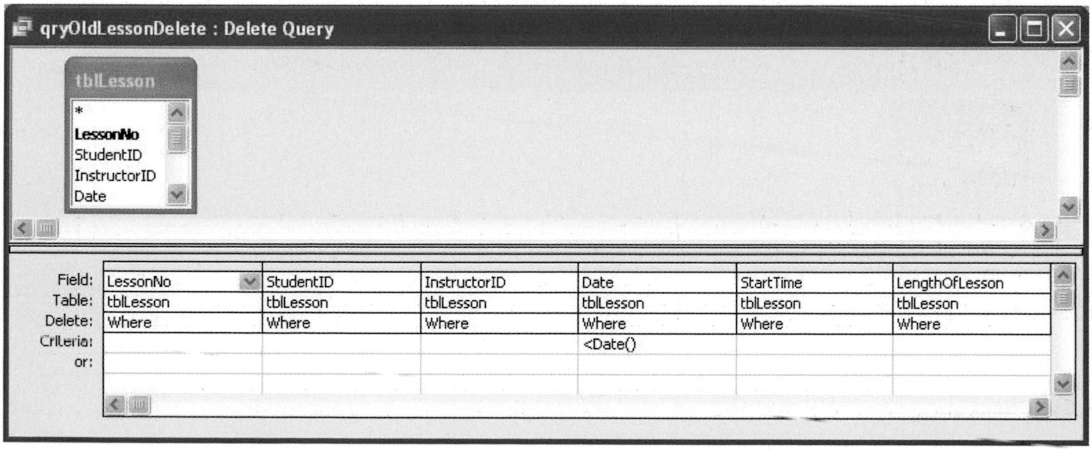

7 Save the query and close it.

8 At the Database Window, click on **Open** to run the query **qryOldLessonDelete**.

9 On running the query you will get the following warning prompts. Just click on **Yes** (see Figure 1.19.8 and Figure 1.19.9).

Figure 1.19.8 ▼

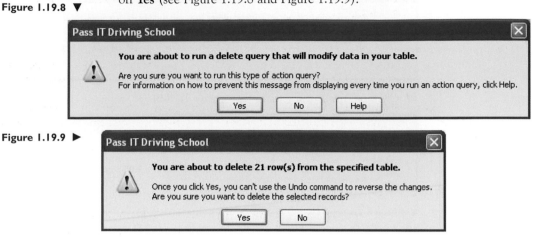

10 At the Database Window, click on **Tables**. Open **tblLesson** and see that the lessons have been deleted. 16 lessons should remain for today and tomorrow.

Delete query to clear out lesson details after a year

We wish to delete details of all lessons over a year old.

1 At the Database Window, click on **Queries** and double click **Create query by using wizard**.

2 Select **tblOldLesson** from the drop down. Click on the double arrow to choose all the fields and then click on **Next**.

3 In the Simple Query Wizard window click on **Next** again.

4 Name the query **qryOverOneYearDelete** and click **Finish**.

5 Open the query in **Design View.** If the Query design toolbar is showing click on the **Query Type** icon and click on **Delete Query** or click on **Query, Delete Query.**

6 Set the Criteria row in the **Date** column to **<=Date()-365** (see Figure 1.19.10).

Figure 1.19.10 ▼

qryOverOneYearDelete : Delete Query

tblOldLesson

*
LessonNo
StudentID
InstructorID
Date

Field:	LessonNo	StudentID	InstructorID	Date	StartTime	LengthOfLesson
Table:	tblOldLesson	tblOldLesson	tblOldLesson	tblOldLesson	tblOldLesson	tblOldLesson
Delete:	Where	Where	Where	Where	Where	Where
Criteria:				<=Date()-365		
or:						

7 Save the query and close it.

8 At the Database Window, click on **Open** to run **qryOverOneYearDelete**.

9 Click on **Yes** to accept the warning prompts.

10 Open **tblOldLesson** to check that the year old lessons have been deleted. 12 should be removed.

Note It is absolutely vital you think carefully about how and when you clear data from your system. We have employed a daily cycle here. Lessons are moved daily to another table and kept on file for a year. It is particularly important to think about your reports and where the data is in the system and at what point it is cleared from the system.

If you go back to Unit 5 you will see that we decided not to set Cascade Delete when deleting a Student or Instructor because it would clear lessons from the system that would be needed in reports. This also has to be taken into account.

Setting a macro to automate this task

To have to do this every day or every week is an awkward job. We want the user to be able to do it at the click of a button. We will design a macro to do this task and later attach it to a button on the menu.

1 In the Database Window click on **Macros** and select **New**.

2 Click on the drop-down arrow in the Action column and click on **SetWarnings**. When you do this the Action Arguments section appears in the lower half of the screen. Set the argument to **No**. (This will turn off the warning prompts when running the macro.)

3 In the Action Column select **OpenQuery** and in the arguments section choose **qryOldLessonAppend** from the drop-down box.

4 In the Action Column select **OpenQuery** and in the arguments section choose **qryOldLessonDelete** from the drop-down box.

5 In the Action Column select **OpenQuery** and in the arguments section choose **qryOverOneYearDelete** from the drop-down box. (The queries must be run in this order.) (See Figure 1.19.11.)

6 In the Action Column select **MsgBox** and in the arguments section enter the details as shown in Figure 1.19.11.

Figure 1.19.11 ▼

7 Save the macro as **mcrLessonArchive**.

8 Set your data back to the original state and test the macro moves all the data correctly.

Managing lesson prices

The driving school might occasionally want to increase or decrease its prices. We will use an update query to automate this process.

1 At the Database Window, click on **Queries** and double click on **Create query by using wizard**.
2 Select **tblLessonType** from the drop-down. Choose **Cost** from the available fields by clicking on the single arrow and clicking on **Next**.
3 In the next Simple Query Wizard window, ensure that **Detail** is checked and click on **Next** again.
4 Call the query **qryPriceUpdate** and click **Finish**.
5 Open the query in Design View and click on **Query, Update Query**. In the **Update To** row of the **Cost** column of the QBE grid, enter **[Cost]*1.05**.
This increases the value by 5 per cent (see Figure 1.19.12).
To increase by 25 per cent, use the formula **[Cost]*1.25**
To increase by £1, use the formula **[Cost]+1**, etc.

Figure 1.19.12 ▼

6 Click on the **Run** icon on the Query Design toolbar or from the menu select **Query, Run** to update the records.
7 You will get a warning message. Click on **Yes** (see Figure 1.19.13).

Figure 1.19.13 ▶

> **Pass IT Driving School**
>
> ⚠ **You are about to update 4 row(s).**
> Once you click Yes, you can't use the Undo command to reverse the changes. Are you sure you want to update these records?
>
> [Yes] [No]

8 The original prices were £16.00, £17.00, £24.00 and £22.00. Click on the **View** icon to check that the prices have been updated to £16.80, £17.85, £25.20 and £23.10 respectively.
9 Set up a macro called **mcrAdjustPrices** to remove the warnings and run this query.

Unit 20: Finishing touches

In this unit we will put the finishing touches to our system including updating the switchboard, tidying up our forms, adding a splashscreen, adding a clock to the switchboard and customising the menu.

Updating the switchboard

After completing the additions to the system in Units 16–19, it is necessary to edit the switchboard to include the new options.

1 Open the **Switchboard Manager** and click on **New**. Enter the name of the third switchboard, **System Switchboard** and click on **OK** (see Figure 1.20.1).

Figure 1.20.1 ▶

2 Select the Main Switchboard and click on **Edit**. Click on **New**. Enter the text **System Functions**. Select the command **Go to Switchboard**. Select the **System Switchboard** (see Figure 1.20.2).

Figure 1.20.2 ▶

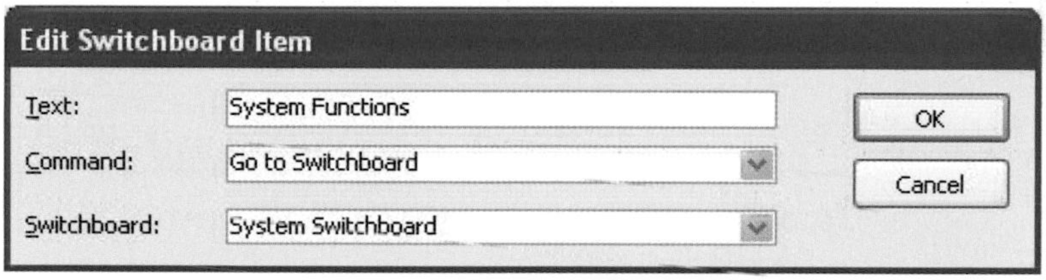

3 Use the **Move Up** button so that this option is below the Reports option (see Figure 1.20.3).

Figure 1.20.3 ▶

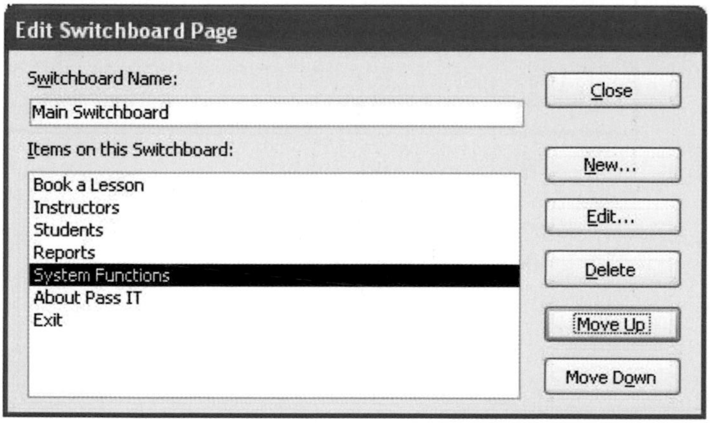

4 Click on **Close** and then select the **Report Switchboard**. Click on **Edit**.
5 Add a new option to open the report **rptLessonAnalysis** (see Figure 1.20.4).

Figure 1.20.4 ▶

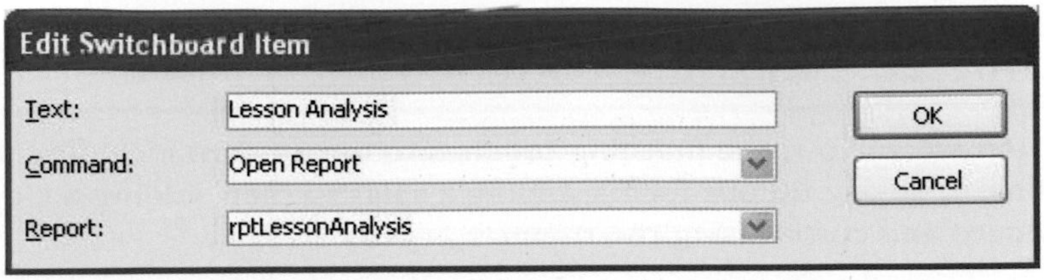

Edit Switchboard Item

Text:	Lesson Analysis	OK
Command:	Open Report	Cancel
Report:	rptLessonAnalysis	

6 Use the **Move Up** and **Move Down** button so that the **rptLessonAnalysis** option is above the Main Menu option.

7 Click on **Close** and then select the **System Switchboard**. Click on **Edit**.

8 Add a new option called **Archive Lessons** to run **mcrLessonArchive** (see Figure 1.20.5).

Figure 1.20.5 ▶

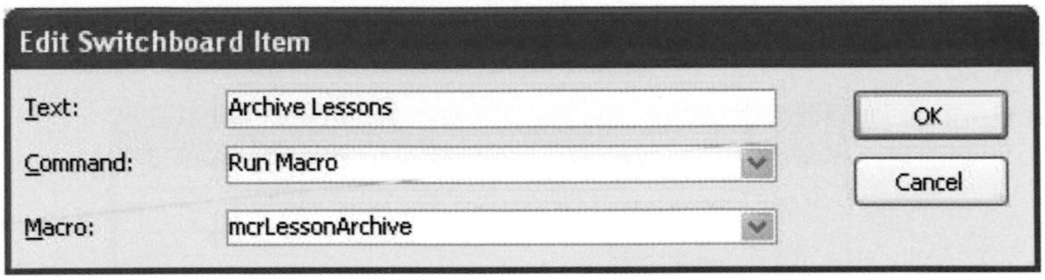

Edit Switchboard Item

Text:	Archive Lessons	OK
Command:	Run Macro	Cancel
Macro:	mcrLessonArchive	

9 Add a new option called **Update Prices** to run **mcrAdjustPrices** (see Figure 1.20.6).

Figure 1.20.6 ▶

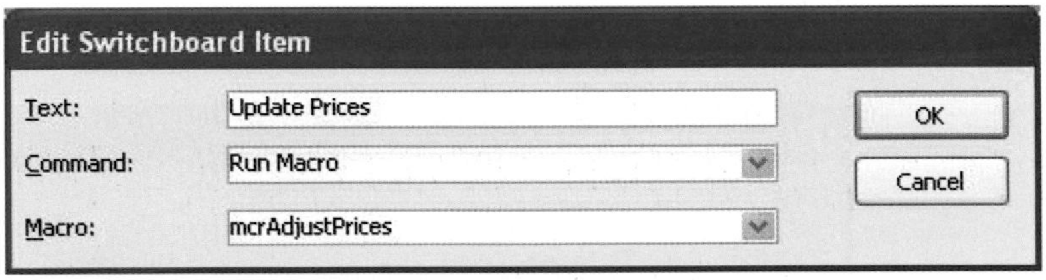

Edit Switchboard Item

Text:	Update Prices	OK
Command:	Run Macro	Cancel
Macro:	mcrAdjustPrices	

10 Add a new option named **Main Menu** to return to the **Main Switchboard** (see Figure 1.20.7).

Figure 1.20.7 ▶

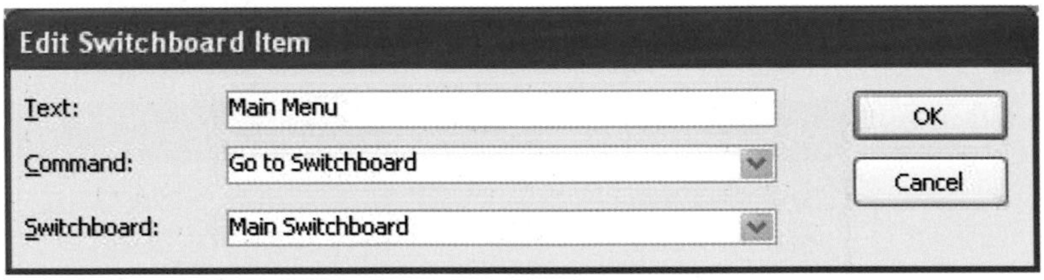

Edit Switchboard Item

Text:	Main Menu	OK
Command:	Go to Switchboard	Cancel
Switchboard:	Main Switchboard	

11 Close the Switchboard Manager.

12 At the Database Window click on **Forms** and open the **Switchboard**. The new Main Switchboard should now look like that shown in Figure 1.20.8. Test all the buttons to see that they work.

Figure 1.20.8 ▶

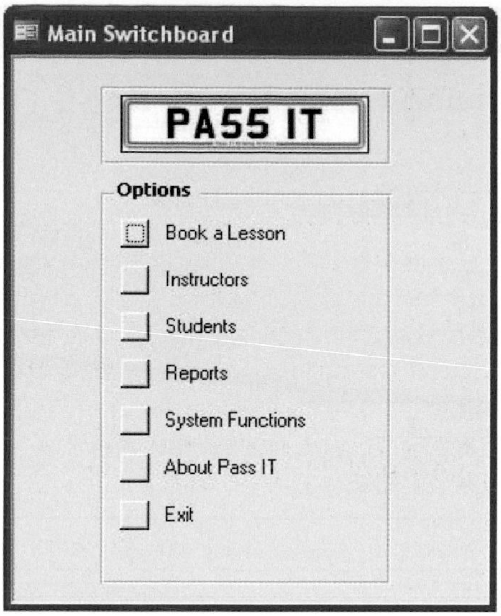

Tidying up forms

The form in Figure 1.20.9 works as expected but is a little untidy. The Student ID control is much too long for a small number. The title control is much too big for a title that is only a few letters long. The dates are right aligned. You can probably see other improvements that could be made.

Figure 1.20.9 ▶

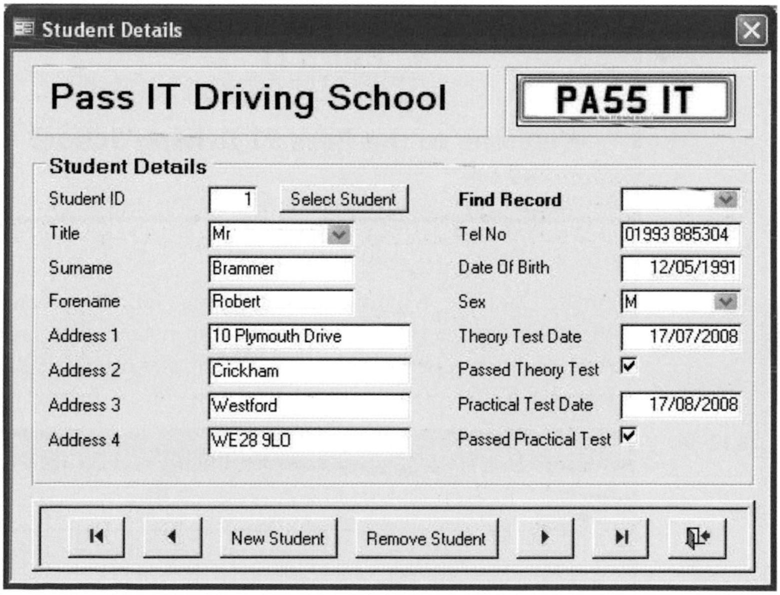

Open all your forms in turn and edit them so that controls are aligned, evenly spaced and the right size as shown in Figure 1.20.10.

Figure 1.20.10 ▶

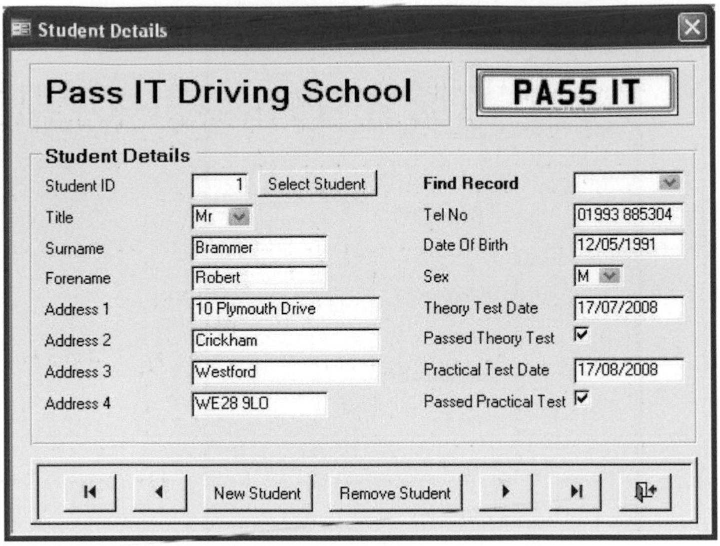

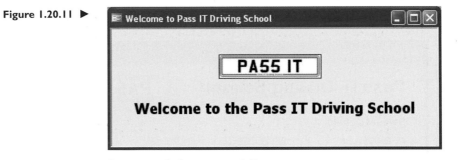

Student Details

Pass IT Driving School		PA55 IT

Student Details

Student ID	1	Select Student		**Find Record**	▼
Title	Mr ▼			Tel No	01993 885304
Surname	Brammer			Date Of Birth	12/05/1991
Forename	Robert			Sex	M ▼
Address 1	10 Plymouth Drive			Theory Test Date	17/07/2008
Address 2	Crickham			Passed Theory Test	☑
Address 3	Westford			Practical Test Date	17/08/2008
Address 4	WE28 9LO			Passed Practical Test	☑

| ◄◄ | ◄ | New Student | Remove Student | ► | ►► | ◻← |

Setting up a splashscreen

A 'splashscreen' like the one shown in Figure 1.20.11, usually loads when the system loads. It appears for a few seconds before the main switchboard loads.

Figure 1.20.11 ▶

Welcome to Pass IT Driving School

PA55 IT

Welcome to the Pass IT Driving School

Set up a splashscreen as follows:

1 At the Database Window click on **Forms**. Click on **New**. Click on **Design View**. Do *not* select a table or query but instead click on **OK**.
2 A blank form appears. Enlarge it so that it is roughly 12 cm by 5 cm (see Figure 1.20.12).

Figure 1.20.12 ▶

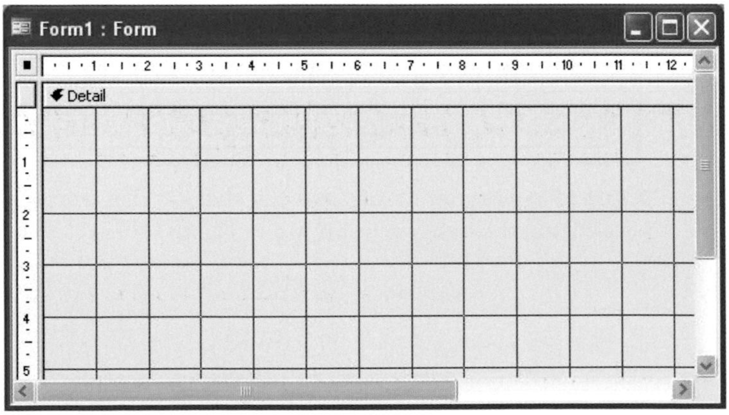

Form1 : Form

◀ Detail

3 Use the Toolbox to add the image and display the text as shown in Figure 1.20.13.

Figure 1.20.13 ▶

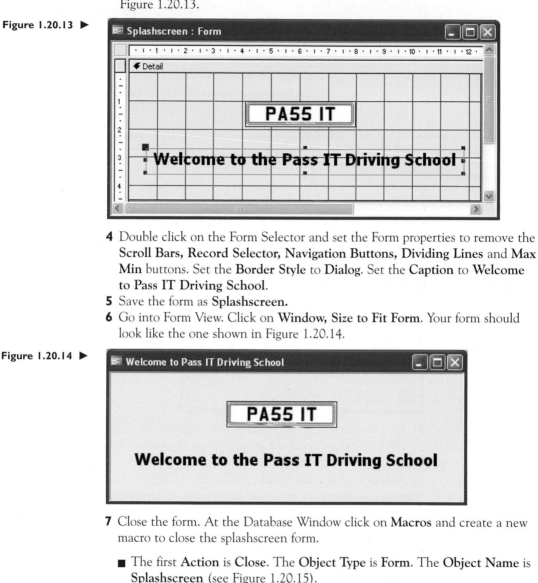

4 Double click on the Form Selector and set the Form properties to remove the **Scroll Bars, Record Selector, Navigation Buttons, Dividing Lines** and **Max Min** buttons. Set the **Border Style** to **Dialog**. Set the **Caption** to **Welcome to Pass IT Driving School**.

5 Save the form as **Splashscreen**.

6 Go into Form View. Click on **Window, Size to Fit Form**. Your form should look like the one shown in Figure 1.20.14.

Figure 1.20.14 ▶

7 Close the form. At the Database Window click on **Macros** and create a new macro to close the splashscreen form.

- The first **Action** is **Close**. The **Object Type** is **Form**. The **Object Name** is **Splashscreen** (see Figure 1.20.15).
- The second action is to open another form – the **Switchboard** (see Figure 1.20.16).

Figure 1.20.15 ▼

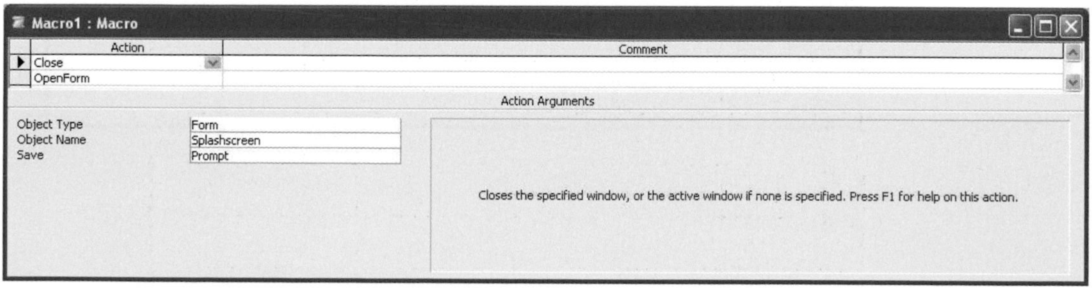

Figure 1.20.16 ▼

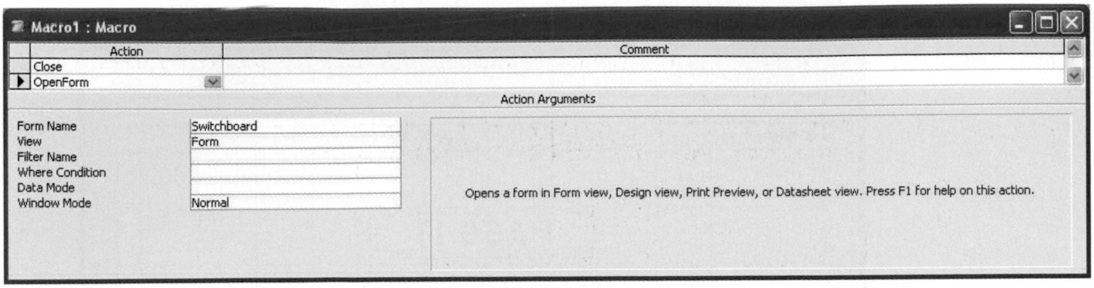

8 Save the macro as **mcrSplash**.

9 Load the splashscreen form in Design View and double-click on the Form Selector to view the Form properties. Click on the **Event** tab and set the **Timer Interval** property to **3000**. This is in milliseconds, so this would mean 3 seconds.

10 Click on the **OnTimer** property and select **mcrSplash**. You may need to go back to the Timer Interval property to adjust your timing a little to get it just right (see Figure 1.20.17).

Figure 1.20.17 ▶

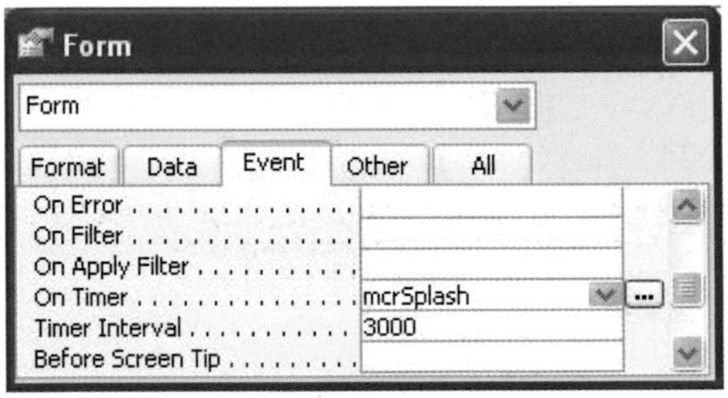

11 Save the form. Load the form in Form View mode and test that it stays on the screen for three seconds before switching to the Switchboard.

12 Click on **Tools, Startup** to set the startup options to load the splashscreen form when the system loads (see Figure 1.20.18).

Figure 1.20.18 ▶

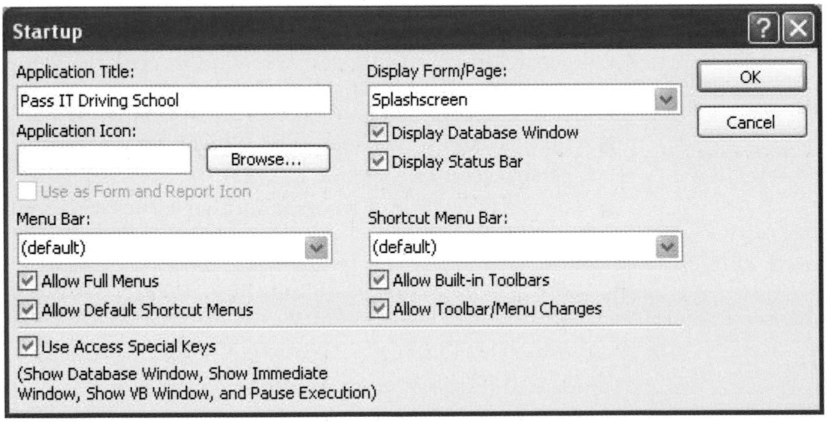

Are you sure?

This is an option on the switchboard to exit from the application. It is a good idea to have an 'Are you sure' box in case this button is pressed by mistake (see Figure 1.20.19).

Figure 1.20.19 ▶

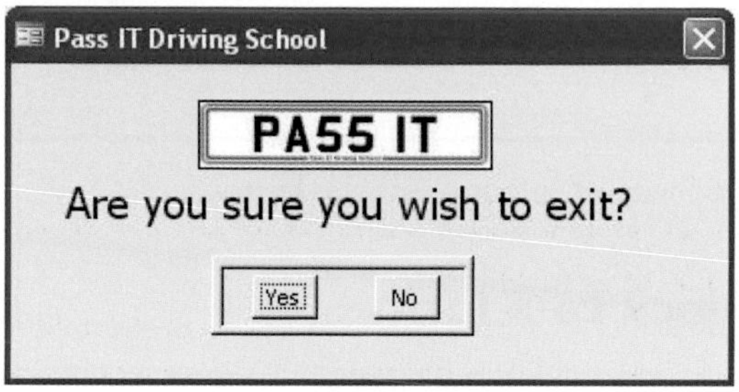

To set this up:

1 Open another blank form in Design View.
2 Set the Form properties to remove the **Scroll Bars, Record Selector, Navigation Buttons, Dividing Lines** and **Max Min buttons.** Set the **Border Style** to **Dialog.** Set the **Caption** to **Pass IT Driving School.**
3 Save the form as **Finish.**
4 Create a macro called **Exit.** The only Action is **Quit** with Arguments set to **Exit** (see Figure 1.20.20).

Figure 1.20.20 ▼

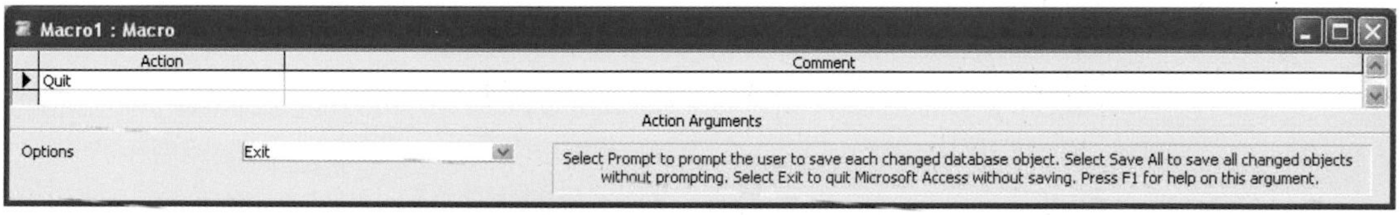

5 Create another macro called **NoExit** to close the **Finish** form (see Figure 1.20.21).

Figure 1.20.21 ▼

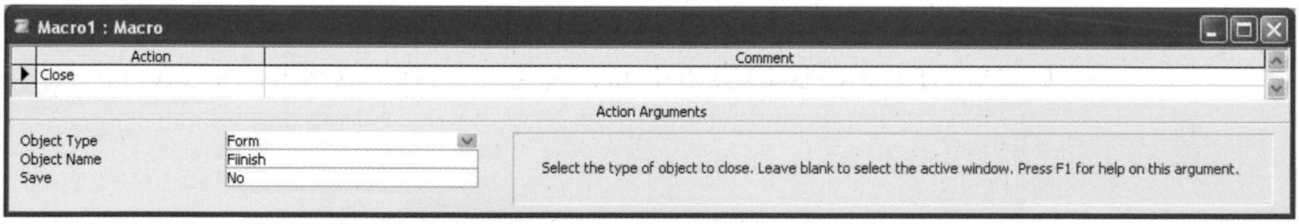

6 Open the **Finish** form in Design View. Use the Label icon in the Toolbox to add text similar to the form shown above.
7 Add an image as shown.
8 Add a command button to run the **Exit** macro. Set the text on this button to **Yes.**
9 Add a command button to run the **NoExit** macro. Set the text on this button to **No.**
10 Save the form and close it.

11 Use the Switchboard Manager to edit the Exit Application button so that it opens the Finish form in edit mode (see Figure 1.20.22).

Figure 1.20.22 ▶

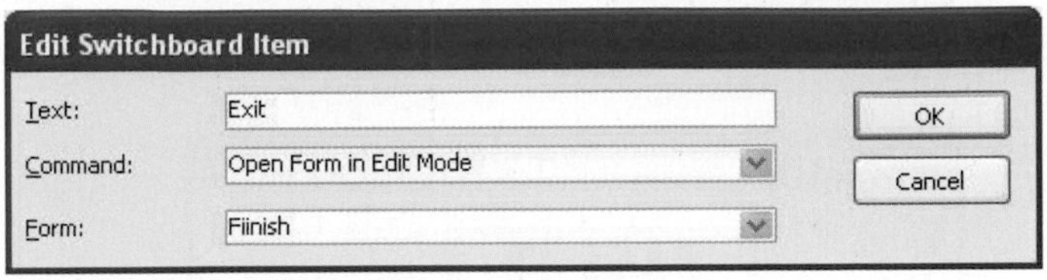

Edit Switchboard Item		
Text:	Exit	OK
Command:	Open Form in Edit Mode	Cancel
Form:	Fiinish	

12 Open the Switchboard and test the buttons.

Adding a real time clock to a form

It is possible to add a clock, which updates every second, to an Access form such as the switchboard.

1 Open the switchboard in **Design View** mode.
2 Choose the **Text Box** icon in the Toolbox and drag out a text box at the bottom of the switchboard. The text box will be called something like Text26 (see Figure 1.20.23).

Figure 1.20.23 ▶

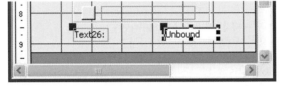

3 Click on the label that says the name (Text26) and delete it (see Figure 1.20.24).

Figure 1.20.24 ▶

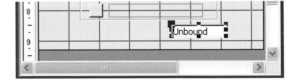

4 Click on the text box and click on the **Properties** icon or right click on the text box and choose **Properties**. Click on the **All** tab and edit the name to **Timer1** (see Figure 1.20.25).

Figure 1.20.25 ▶

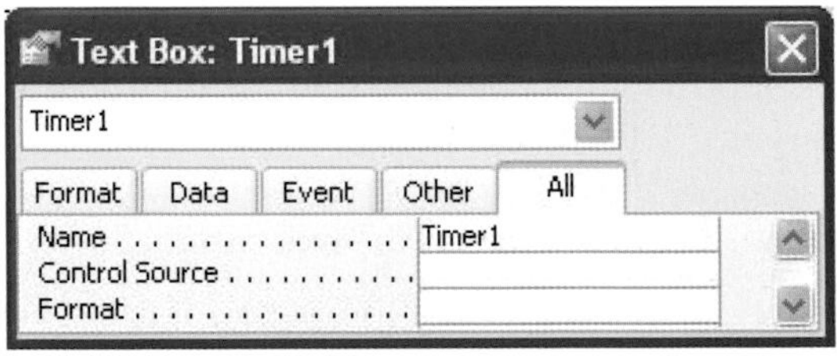

Text Box: Timer1	✕
Timer1	
Format	Data	Event	Other	All
Name Timer1
Control Source . . . .
Format . . . .

5 Click on the **Format** tab and choose the format, **Long Time**.
6 Set the **Font Weight** to **Bold** and **Text Align** to **Center**.
7 With the properties window still displayed, click on the Form Selector.

8 This will display the properties for the form. Click on the **Event** tab and set the **Timer Interval** to 1000 (this is one second). (See Figure 1.20.26.)

Figure 1.20.26 ▶

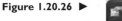

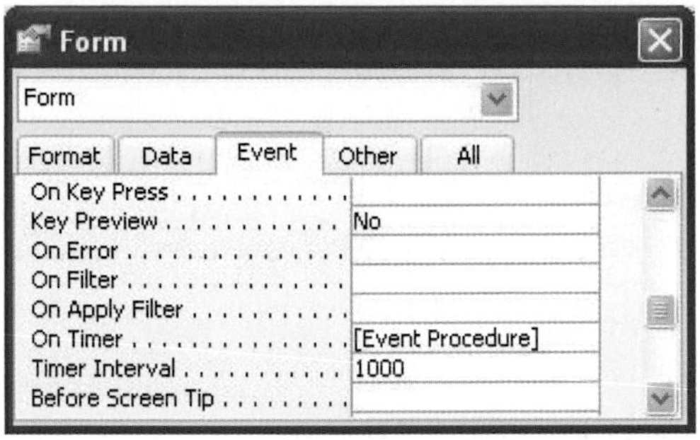

9 Choose the **On Timer** property above Timer Interval. Click on the three dots icon and choose **Code Builder**. The Visual Basic Editor loads displaying:

```
Private Sub Form_Timer()

End Sub
```

In the middle line type in: `[Timer1]=Now`

10 Close the Visual Basic Editor and go into Form View mode to test it (see Figure 1.20.27).

Figure 1.20.27 ▶

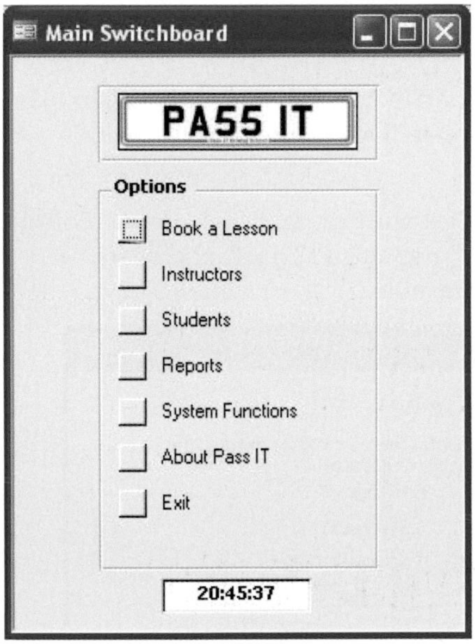

Customising menus and toolbars

A fully customised Access system is likely to have customised menus and toolbars. In this section you will learn how to set up a macro to remove or display toolbars, add icons to and remove icons from a toolbar and set up your own toolbar.

Customising toolbars

You can set up the Autoexec macro to remove all toolbars. The Autoexec macro runs automatically when a system loads. For more on the Autoexec macro see Tip no. 49.

Removing toolbars means that you can then devote more of the screen to the forms and reports you have set up.

Use the **ShowToolbar** action. Select the toolbar from the list and set Show to **No**. You need to use this action several times to remove all the toolbars (see Figure 1.20.28).

Figure 1.20.28 ▼

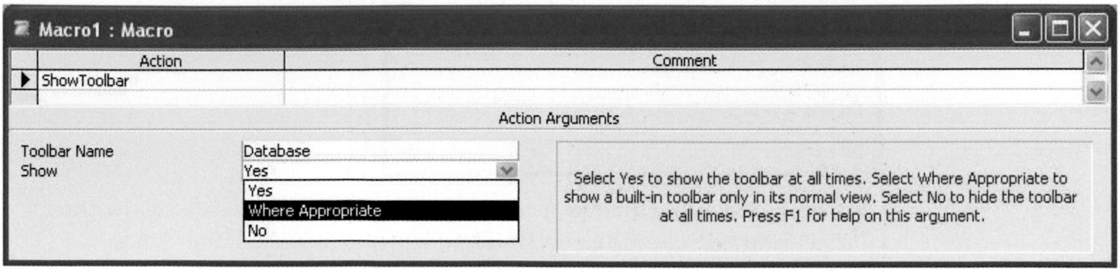

However before you remove all the toolbars, make sure that your system is fully working. It is very annoying to have to edit the system without any icons.

Note   You can set up a macro to show toolbars only where they are appropriate as shown in Figure 1.20.28.

Removing or adding single icons

It is possible to add or remove icons from the toolbars. The method is exactly the same as in Microsoft Word and Microsoft Excel, so you may have seen it before.

1 Click on **Tools, Customize** or right click on the toolbars and click on **Customize**. The Customize dialogue box appears.
2 Click on the **Commands** tab (see Figure 1.20.29).

Figure 1.20.29 ▶

3 To remove an icon from a toolbar simply drag it on to the dialogue box.
4 To add an icon, select the menu in the **Categories** box. Find the icon in the **Commands** box and drag it on to the toolbar.

For example, to add an icon to run the **mcrAbout**:

1 Click on the **Commands** tab and scroll down in the **Categories** box until you find **All Macros**.

2 Find **mcrAbout** in the **Commands** box (see Figure 1.20.30).

Figure 1.20.30 ▶

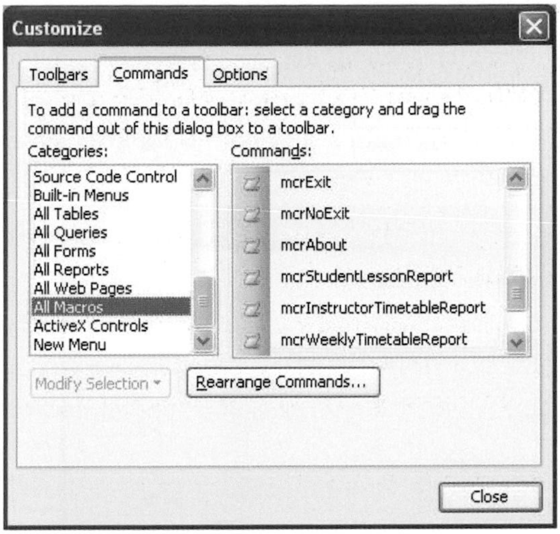

3 Drag the **mcrAbout** icon on to the toolbar (see Figure 1.20.31). Close the dialogue box.

Figure 1.20.31 ▶

4 You can edit this icon by clicking on **Tools, Customize** and then right clicking on the icon (see Figure 1.20.32).

Figure 1.20.32 ▼

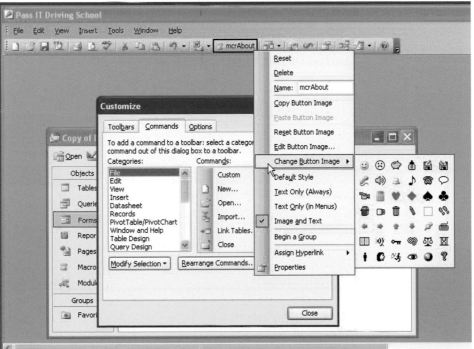

5 Select **Edit Button Image** to load a simple painting program to edit the icon or click on **Change Button Image** to show a menu of alternative icons. You can remove the icon by simply dragging it off the toolbar.

Customising menus

Customised menus create finishing touches to a system, bringing a professional feel to it.

1 Click on **Tools, Customize**. Click on the **Toolbars** tab and click on **New** (see Figure 1.20.33).

Figure 1.20.33 ▶

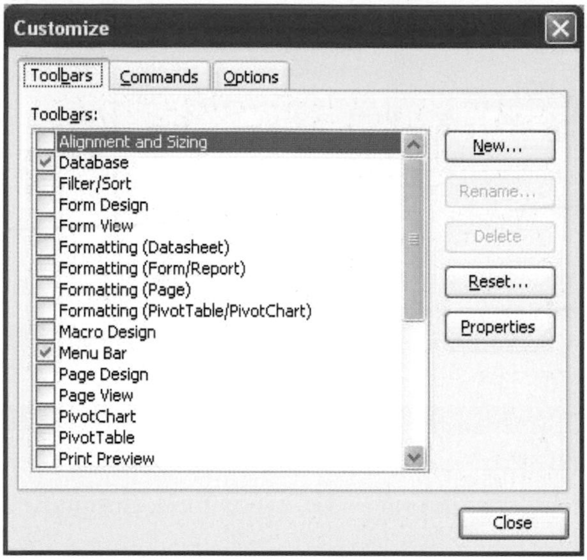

2 Call the new toolbar **Pass IT Driving School** (see Figure 1.20.34) and click **OK**.

Figure 1.20.34 ▶

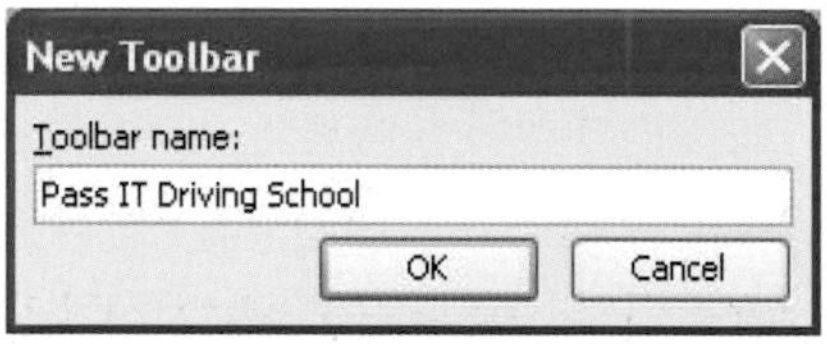

A small new blank toolbar has appeared on the screen (see Figure 1.20.35).

Figure 1.20.35 ▼

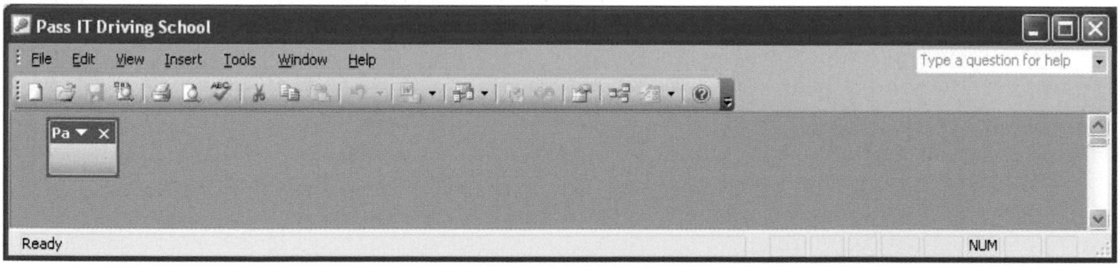

3 Drag the toolbar to the toolbar area at the top of the screen (see Figure 1.20.36).

Figure 1.20.36 ▼

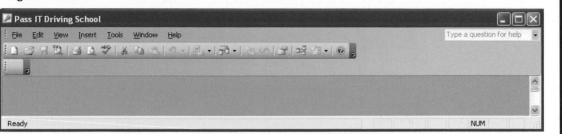

4 Scroll down in the **Categories** box until you find **New Menu**. (It is the last one in the list, see Figure 1.20.37.)

Figure 1.20.37 ►

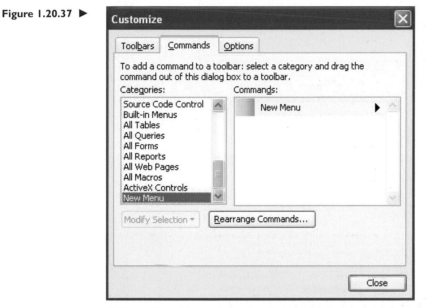

5 Drag **New Menu** from the Commands box on to the new toolbar (see Figure 1.20.38).

Figure 1.20.38 ▼

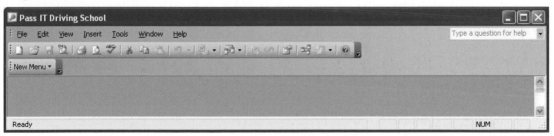

6 Right click on the words **New Menu** and change the name to **Navigate**.

7 Click on the word **Navigate** and a small blank menu drops down (see Figure 1.20.39).

Figure 1.20.39 ▼

Figure 1.20.39 ▼

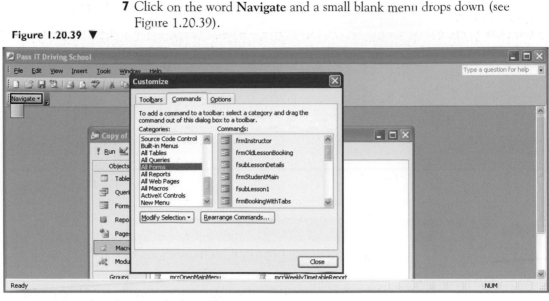

8 Click on **All Forms** in the **Categories** list in the dialogue box.
9 Find **frmLessonBooking** in the Commands list and drag it on to the blank menu (see Figure 1.20.40).

Figure 1.20.40 ▼

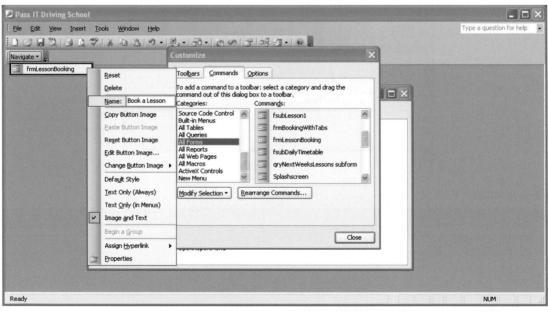

10 Click on **Navigate** to make the menu drop down. Right click on **frmLessonBooking**.

11 Change the name to **Book a Lesson** as shown in Figure 1.20.41.

Figure 1.20.41 ▼

12 Close the dialogue box and test that the new menu loads **frmLessonBooking**.

You can add more items to your menu and more menus to your toolbar. Include links to your forms and reports. It is a good idea to include links to the Database Window and have online help in your customised menu.

When your new menu bar is complete, click on **Tools, Startup** and change the startup menu bar as shown in Figure 1.20.42.

Figure 1.20.42 ▶

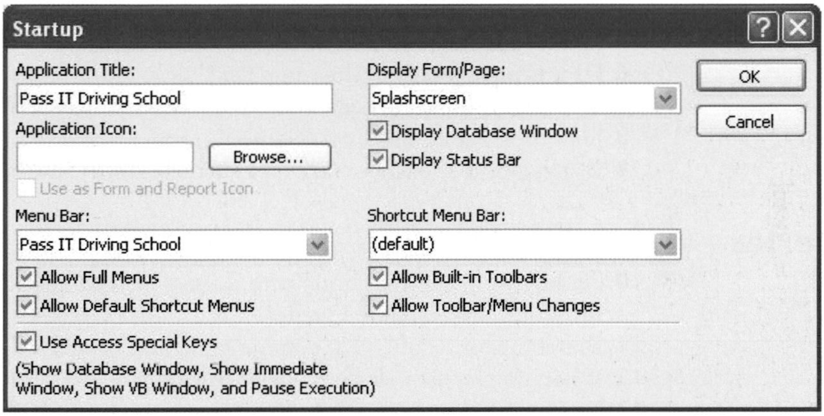

Don't forget that to disable the startup options, hold down the SHIFT key as you load the file.

Hint   Use **Tricks and Tips** numbers 57–60 to customise your solution further.

2 Access tricks and tips

Here are 70 tricks and tips that have been found to be more than useful when implementing Access projects. CD-ROM support files are shown in brackets.

Tables

1 Error messages that may occur when setting relationships between tables (Errors)
2 Using the Default Value property to enter a date
3 Adding a Code Prefix to an AutoNumber Field (StationeryCodes)
4 Shortcuts for entering data using the CTRL key
5 Making an AutoNumber field start from 1 again
6 Preventing duplicate values in a field
7 Preventing duplicate combinations of data (DoubleBooking)
8 Importing data from Excel (Names)
9 Using copy and paste to take an Excel worksheet into Access (Names)

Queries

10 Finding surnames that begin with a letter or combination of letters (qryWildCardSearch in Queries)
11 Searching for records that contain no values (qryIsNull in Queries)
12 When do you use calculated fields in a query? (qryLessonCost in Queries)
13 Using a query to combine (concatenate) two fields, e.g. Forename and Surname (qryConcatenateFullName in Queries)
14 Using a query to calculate initials from a person's forename (qryCalculateInitial in Queries)
15 Calculating the weekday (or month) from the Date using Format Properties (qryCalculateWeekday in Queries)
16 Calculating the month name from the Date using the Month function (qyCalculateMonthName in Queries)
17 Using a query to calculate the difference between dates – DateDiff function (DateDiffQuery)
18 Using a query to calculate the future dates – DateAdd function (DateAddQuery)
19 Make-Table queries (Queries)
20 Making decisions using the IIf Function in a query (IIfQuery)

Forms

21 Adding a calculated field to a form (frmLesson in Forms)
22 Using the Expression Builder
23 Formatting dates on forms and reports
24 Making a command button the default button (frmLessonBooking in Forms)

25 Changing the properties of a group of controls

26 Preventing users from adding records to a form

27 Creating read-only fields on a form (frmLessonBooking in Forms)

28 Moving the focus to another control on a form (frmLessonBooking in Forms)

29 Putting a border around a control (frmLessonBooking in Forms)

30 Designing your own button images

31 Creating a command button from a graphic image (frmLessonBooking in Forms)

32 Customising a Quit or Exit button (frmMainMenu in Forms)

33 Positioning and sizing your form automatically (frmLessonBooking in Forms)

34 Using option buttons or radio controls (frmStudent in Forms)

35 Using option groups (frmInstructor in Forms)

36 Printing a form without the buttons

37 Adding customised tool tips (Screen Tips) to your controls (frmInstructor in Forms)

38 Pop Up and Modal forms

39 Removing the Menu Bar from a form

40 Starting a form from scratch

Reports

41 Forcing a page break on a report

42 Concatenating text strings on reports (ConcatenateStrings)

43 Replacing check boxes and coded fields with text (Reports)

44 Using Switch to change a coded field

45 Formatting Invoice Numbers

46 Mailing labels, business and membership cards

Macros

47 Formatting text to bold in a Message Box (mcrNoData in Macros)

48 Putting hard returns in a Message Box (mcrAbout and mcrAbout1 in Macros)

49 The AutoExec macro (mcrAutoexec in Macros)

50 Hiding and Unhiding the Database Window from your AutoExec macro

51 Running your system from customised keys (mcrAutoKeys in Macros)

52 Copy (Cut) and Paste macro (mcrFileAway in Macros)

53 Using Conditions in macros (mcrTestDateCheck in Macros)

54 Using a Conditional macro for cross field validation (ConditionalMacro)

55 Control printing multiple copies from a macro (mcrMultipleCopies in Macros)

Others

56 Changing the caption text

57 Changing the application icon

58 Password protecting files

59 Adding a loading progress meter to the Status Bar (LoadingMeter)

60 Customising information displayed in the Status Bar

61 My Access Database is getting very large in size – what do I do?

62 Setting up a Calendar Control to enter dates (CalendarSpinner)

63 Using a Spinner Control to enter dates/numbers (CalendarSpinner)

64 Using SetValue to enter dates easily

65 Displaying SubForm Totals on the Main Form (No65)

66 Customising a Parameter Query dialogue box (ParameterQuery)

67 Printing a report from an Option Group control (No67–68)

68 Printing the current record displayed on a form as a report (No67–68)

69 Using a macro to email a report

70 Using Tab Controls

Tables

1. Error messages that may occur when setting relationships between tables

Error message 1

Figure 2.1.1 ▶

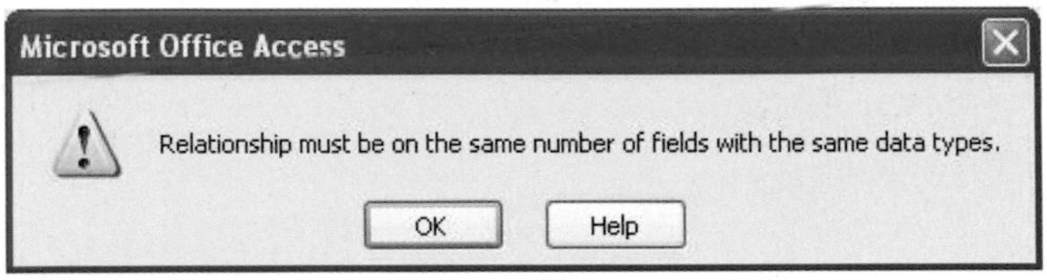

Microsoft Office Access

⚠ Relationship must be on the same number of fields with the same data types.

[OK] [Help]

Relationships join a field in one table to another field in a second table. These fields should be of the same data type. If one field is set to text then so should the other in the related table. Note that if the primary key field in one table is set to **AutoNumber** and **Long Integer**, e.g. StudentID, then the corresponding field in the other table, e.g. tblLesson, should be set to **Number** and **Long Integer**.

Error message 2

Figure 2.1.2 ▶

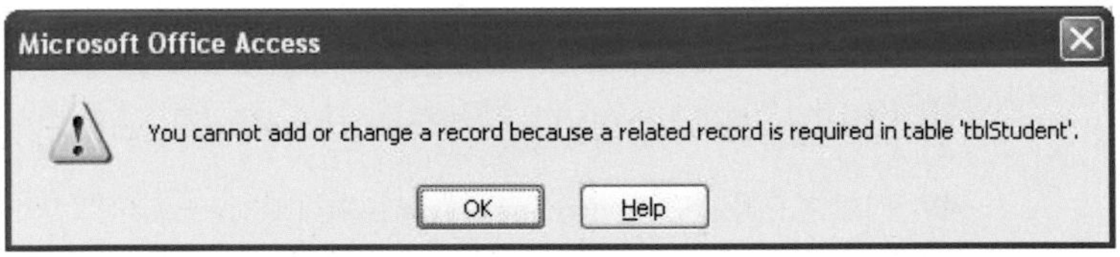

Microsoft Office Access

⚠ You cannot add or change a record because a related record is required in table 'tblStudent'.

[OK] [Help]

In the Pass IT solution you have worked through, you will get this error message if you try to enter a StudentID (or InstructorID) into the Lesson table when the StudentID does not exist in the related Student table. Referential integrity requires data to be present in both tables. The solution is to enter details of the Student (or Instructor) in the respective table.

Error message 3

Figure 2.1.3 ▶

Microsoft Office Access

Microsoft Office Access can't create this relationship and enforce referential integrity.

Data in the table 'tblLesson' violates referential integrity rules.
For example, there may be records relating to an employee in the related table, but no record for the employee in the primary table.

Edit the data so that records in the primary table exist for all related records.
If you want to create the relationship without following the rules of referential integrity, clear the Enforce Referential Integrity check box.

[OK]

You will get this error message when you enforce referential integrity and already have data in your tables which violates the integrity rule. In other words in the Pass IT solution you will have StudentIDs (or InstructorIDs) in the Lesson table which are not present in the linked Student (or Instructor) table.

Error message 4

Figure 2.1.4 ▶

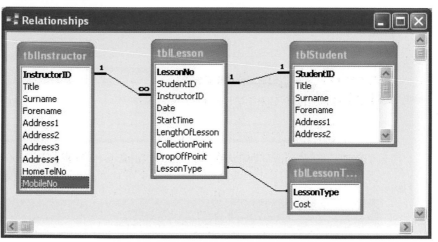

If when you set your relationships they just appear as a line without the '1' and '∞', it is probably because you have not checked **Referential Integrity**. Delete the relationship and set it up again.

If when you set your relationships it appears as 1:1 when you were expecting '1' and '∞', it is because you are trying to join a Primary Key (StudentID) to a Foreign Key (StudentID in the Lesson table) with the **Index** property of the latter set to **No Duplicates**. The property should be set to **Duplicates OK**.

2. Using the Default Value property to enter a date

In systems such as book or video loaning you invariably will be issuing a loan on today's date and if there is a fixed period of hire, you will know the date of return. In a library for example the book will be issued on that day, with a return due in 7 days. You can use the Default Value property in Table Design view to do this automatically.

For the field **DateOut** set the default value to **=Date()** as shown in Figure 2.1.5 and for **DateOfReturn** set it to **=Date()+7**.

Figure 2.1.5 ▶

General	Lookup	
Format	Short Date	
Input Mask		
Caption		
Default Value	=Date()	...
Validation Rule		
Validation Text		
Required	No	
Indexed	No	
IME Mode	No Control	
IME Sentence Mode	None	
Smart Tags		

3. Adding a Code Prefix to an AutoNumber Field

When dealing with systems involving sales and stock, products are often coded. For example stationery products might be coded STA001, STA002 etc.

Figure 2.1.6 ▼

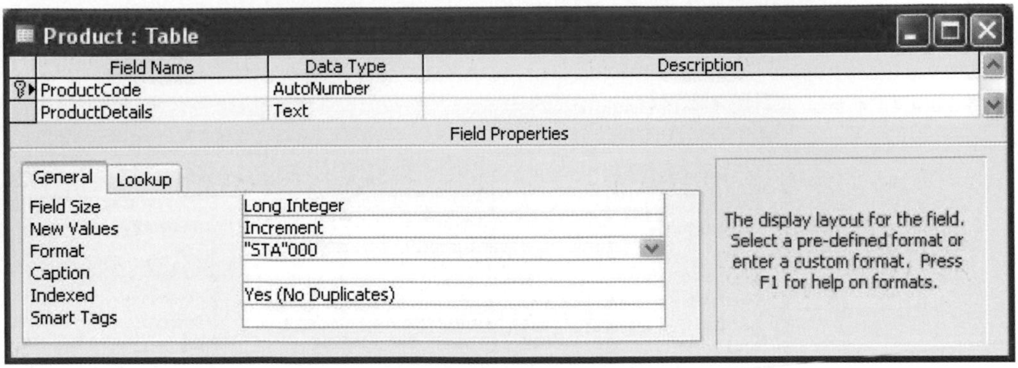

Setting the **Format** of the **AutoNumber** field to "STA"000 as shown above will automatically increment the value of the field by one STA001, STA002 etc.

Figure 2.1.7 ▼

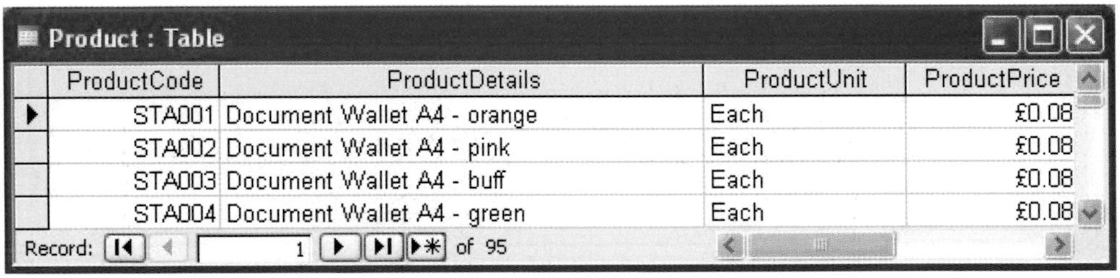

4. Shortcuts for entering data using the CTRL key

- When entering data in a table, you may often want to copy the data from the previous record. Do this by simply pressing CTRL and '(apostrophe).
- You can enter the current time into a table by simply pressing CTRL and : (colon).
- Similarly you can enter the current date into a table by simply pressing CTRL and ; (semi-colon).

5. Making an AutoNumber field start from 1 again

When you first set up the tables in your database the AutoNumber field will automatically increment. While entering data or testing the solution you will make mistakes and may need to delete rows in the table. You will find you may want to start the numbering from 1 again. To do this:

a) Remove the relationships between all tables.

b) If the AutoNumber field is a primary key, click on the primary key icon to unset it.

c) Delete the row for this field.

d) Insert the row again and recreate the field as an AutoNumber field.

e) Reset it as a primary key, if appropriate.

f) Set up the table relationships again.

6. Preventing duplicate values in a field

Data in a key field cannot be repeated; for example, you could not have two cars with the same Reg. No. You can prevent two records in another field having the same value as follows:

a) At the Database Window, select the table and click on **Design**.

b) Select the Field Name and set the Field Property **Indexed** to **Yes (No Duplicates)**.

7. Preventing duplicate combinations of data

A theatre uses an Access database to store details of seats sold. A seat such as A1 may be sold many times. Many seats may be sold for a performance on 12 October. But any seat must only be sold once for each performance. How can we prevent seats being sold twice?

The theatre has a booking table. The key field is the **BookingNo**. Among the other fields in this table are **SeatNo** and **Date**. Once a seat number and date has been entered this combination cannot be entered again.

a) In the **Design View** for the **tblBooking** click on the **Indexes** icon or click on **View, Indexes**.

The Indexes dialogue box is displayed as in Figure 2.1.8

Figure 2.1.8 ▶

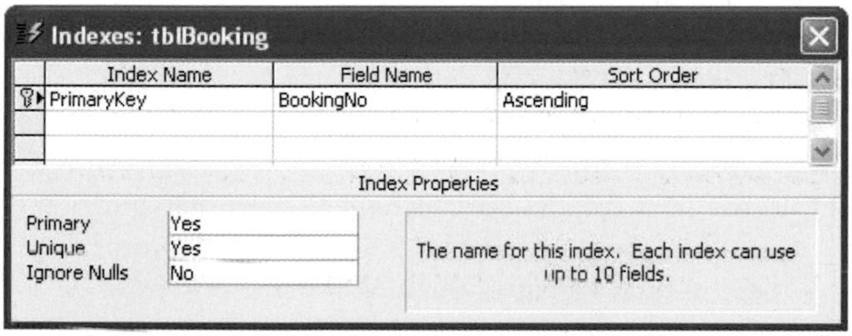

b) Add an Index Name such as **DoubleBooking** underneath the Primary Key as in Figure 2.1.9. The name you choose does not matter.

Figure 2.1.9 ▶

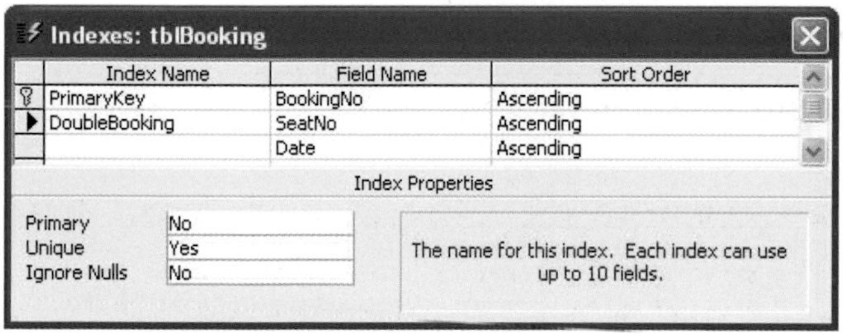

c) In the next column select the first of the two fields which must not be duplicated. Below it select the second field. See Figure 2.1.9.

d) Click on **DoubleBooking** and set the **Unique** property to **Yes** as in Figure 2.1.9.

e) Test it to make sure you get the error message in Figure 2.1.10.

Figure 2.1.10 ▶

8. Importing data from Excel

Importing data from Excel is easily done in Access using the **Import Spreadsheet Wizard**.

Suppose we wish to import into Access the Excel file of **Names** shown in Figure 2.1.11.

Note Row 1 contains the **Field Names** for each column and the names are stored in **Sheet1**.

Figure 2.1.11 ▶

	A	B	C	D	E	F	G
1	Title	Surname	Forename	Address 1	Address 2	Address 3	Address 4
2	Mr	Brammer	Robert	10 Plymouth Drive	Stenson Fields	Derby	DE28 9LO
3	Mr	Jenkins	Steven	7 Woodfield Close	Etwall	Derby	DE49 5PQ
4	Miss	Fowler	Sarah	19 Sea View Road	Mickleover	Derby	DE34 8NT
5	Mr	Beswood	Michael	25 Lundie Close	Allestree	Derby	DE45 5AF
6	Miss	Williams	Charlotte	21 Church Street	Littleover	Derby	DE33 8RD
7	Mr	Windsor	David	86 Milford Road	Allenton	Derby	DE57 4PT
8	Miss	Trueman	Mary	156 Station Road	Allestree	Derby	DE45 9HS
9	Miss	Spencer	Victoria	73 Mayfield Road	Stenson Fields	Derby	DE28 9VB
10	Mr	Watson	Greg	7 Derwent Close	Etwall	Derby	DE49 8HU
11	Miss	Jones	Lucy	183 Uttoxeter Road	Allenton	Derby	DE57 2GN

Names.xls — Sheet1 / Sheet2 / Sheet3

a) Open the database into which you wish to import the file called **Names**. Click on **File, Get External Data** and select **Import**. The **Import** dialogue box appears. Select the file **Names** from the **Look in** and click on **Import**.

b) The **Import Spreadsheet Wizard** loads. Click on **Sheet1** (if it is not already highlighted) to tell the wizard where the data is stored. Click on **Next**.

c) In the next **Import Spreadsheet Wizard** dialogue box check **First Row Contains Column Headings** as shown in Figure 2.1.12 . (Access will use these as field names in the table). Click on **Next**.

Figure 2.1.12 ▶

Import Spreadsheet Wizard

Microsoft Access can use your column headings as field names for your table. Does the first row specified contain column headings?

☑ First Row Contains Column Headings

	Title	Surname	Forename	Address 1	Address
1	Mr	Brammer	Robert	10 Plymouth Drive	Stenson
2	Mr	Jenkins	Steven	7 Woodfield Close	Etwall
3	Miss	Fowler	Sarah	19 Sea View Road	Mickleov
4	Mr	Beswood	Michael	25 Lundie Close	Allestre
5	Miss	Williams	Charlotte	21 Church Street	Littleov
6	Mr	Windsor	David	86 Milford Road	Allenton

[Cancel] [< Back] [Next >] [Finish]

d) Select the **New Table** option. Click on **Next**.

e) The next **Import Spreadsheet Wizard** dialogue box gives you the option to specify information about the data or skip import. Click on **Next**.

f) In the next dialogue box you are given some **Primary key** options. Select **Let Access add primary key** (see Figure 2.1.13). You will notice Access inserts a Primary Key ID. Click on **Next**.

Figure 2.1.13 ▶

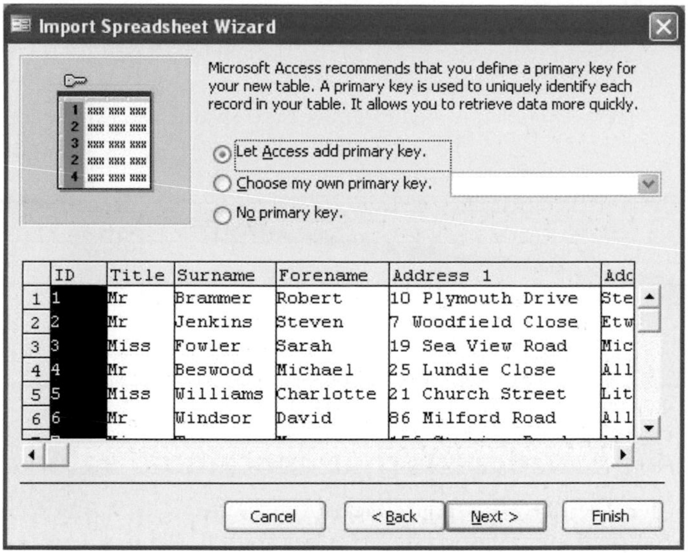

g) In the final dialogue box click in the **Import to Table** box and type **tblNames**. Click on **Finish**. At the Database Window open **tblNames** to check the import has been successful.

9. Using copy and paste to take an Excel worksheet into Access

This method gives you less control than Tip 8 but is quick and easy. It helps to include the field names in the first data row of the Excel worksheet. To try it you will need the Excel file called Names used in Tip 8.

a) Open the Excel file **Names** and select the data (including column headings) that you want to paste into Access. Click on **Edit, Copy**.
b) At the Database Window in Access, select the **Tables** tab and click **Edit, Paste**.
c) Access will ask you if the first row of data contains column headings. Answer **Yes**.
d) Open the table to view your data. Access calls the table **Sheet1**. Switch to Design View and edit as you need.

Queries

10. Finding surnames that begin with a letter or combination of letters

You can use the asterisk (*) as a wildcard in searches and queries.

For example: a query searching on a postcode equal to **WE34*** will find all the postcodes beginning with WE34.

We want to set up a query so that when we enter a letter or combination of letters, the query will return all surnames beginning with those letters. For example, if we enter **Ste** the query would return Stebbins, Stephenson and Stevens etc.

Create a parameter query in the normal way based on **tblStudent** using the **LIKE** operator and the wildcard symbol (*).Use this statement in the query, as shown in Figure 2.2.1. **Like [Enter the first letter of the surname:] & "*"**

Figure 2.2.1 ▼

Field:	StudentID	Title	Surname		Forename	Address1	
Table:	tblStudent	tblStudent	tblStudent		tblStudent	tblStudent	
Sort:							
Show:	✓	✓	✓		✓	✓	
Criteria:			Like [Enter first letter of surname:] & "*"				
or:							

11. Searching for records that contain no values

In the Pass IT system, suppose you wanted a list of students who hadn't arranged a Theory Test Date. You need to set up a query using the **Is Null** operator which returns missing or unknown data.

Set up a query based on **tblStudent** and in the Criteria cell for the **Field: TheoryTestDate** enter **Is Null**.

Figure 2.2.2 ▼

Field:	StudentID	Forename	Surname	TelNo	TheoryTestDate	
Table:	tblStudent	tblStudent	tblStudent	tblStudent	tblStudent	
Sort:						
Show:	✓	✓	✓	✓	✓	
Criteria:					Is Null	
or:						

The operator **Is Not Null** would return all records containing any value.

12. When do you use calculated fields in a query?

In Unit 8 you added a calculated field to a query. The query created a new field based on the data from two other fields. In this case the new field **TotalCost** which was the result of **[Length of Lesson] * [Cost]**.

Figure 2.2.3 ▼

Field:	LengthOfLesson	CollectionPoint	DropOffPoint	LessonType	Cost	TotalCost: [LengthOfLesson]*[Cost]	
Table:	tblLesson	tblLesson	tblLesson	tblLesson	tblLessonType		
Sort:							
Show:	✓	✓	✓	✓	✓	✓	
Criteria:							
or:							

This query forms the basis of forms and reports. Calculated fields are created by using a blank column of the QBE grid and entering the formula in the Field row as shown above. Other examples are:

Purpose	Example
Multiply a field by a number	VAT: [Cost]*17.5/100
Add one field to another	Total: [Cost]+[VAT]
Adding 7 days to a date	ReturnDate: [Date]+7
Calculating the number of years since a date	Age:DateDiff("yyyy",[DateOfBirth],Now())

13. Using a query to combine (concatenate) two fields, e.g. Forename and Surname

You can join together the text from two fields by using a calculated field in a query.

Set up a query based on **tblStudent** with the fields as shown. Add a new column to the QBE grid and set up the new field: **Full Name: [Forename] & " " & [Surname]**

Figure 2.2.4 ▼

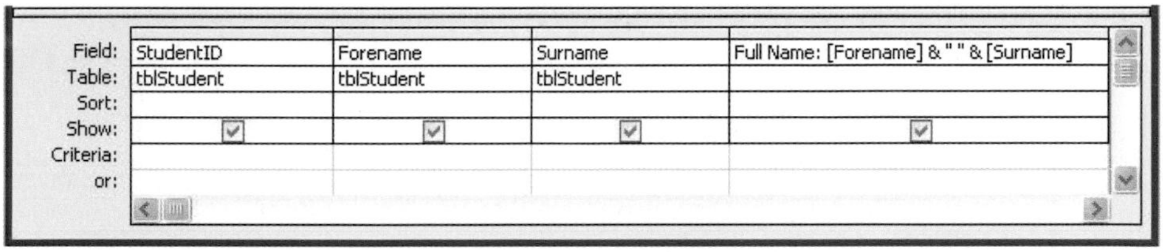

When you run the query it concatenates Surname and Forename to give the field Full Name as shown in Figure 2.2.5.

Figure 2.2.5 ►

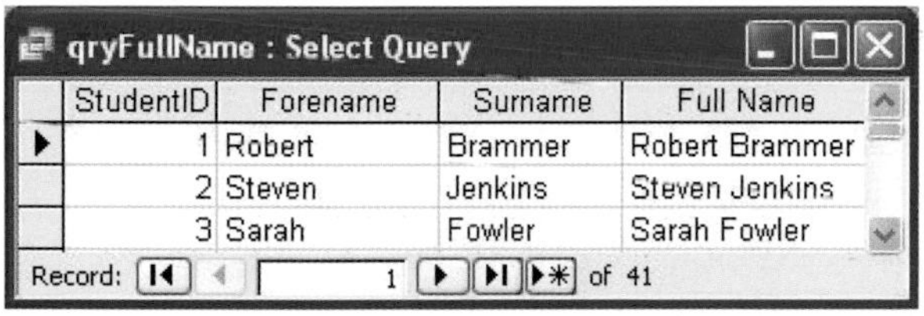

14. Using a query to calculate initials from a person's forename

Using the principles in the tip above, set up a query based on **tblStudent** with the fields as shown. Add a new column to the QBE grid and set up the new field:

Initial:Left([Forename],1)

This will return 1 character from the left of the field **Forename** i.e. the initial. Add another column to the QBE grid and set up the new field:

Full Name: [Title] & " "& [Initial] & " " & [Surname]

Figure 2.2.6 ▼

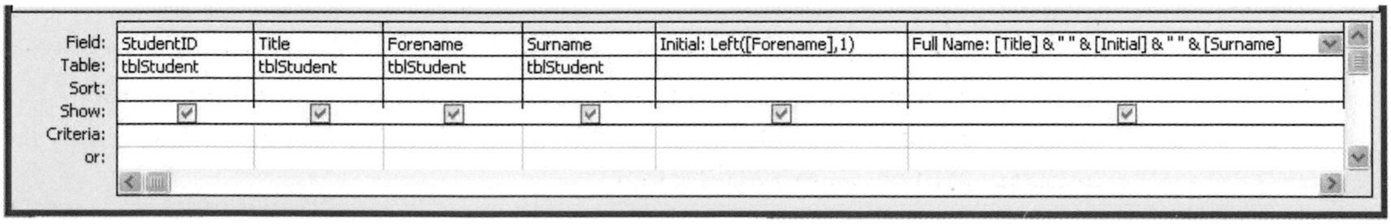

When you run the query it concatenates the fields **Title** and **Surname** with the calculated field **Initial** to give the field **Full Name** as shown in Figure 2.2.7.

Figure 2.2.7 ▶

	StudentID	Title	Forename	Surname	Initial	Full Name
▶	1	Mr	Robert	Brammer	R	Mr R Brammer
	2	Mr	Steven	Jenkins	S	Mr S Jenkins
	3	Miss	Sarah	Fowler	S	Miss S Fowler
	4	Mr	Michael	Beswood	M	Mr M Beswood

qryCalculateInitial : Select Query

Record: ◀◀ ◀ 1 ▶ ▶▶ ▶* of 41

15. Calculating the weekday (or month) from the Date using Format Properties

The following method is a simple way of giving the name of the weekday from a date. It can easily be adapted to give the month name.

a) Set up a query based on **tblLesson** with the fields as shown. Add a new column to the QBE grid and set up the new field: **DayOfTheWeek: Date**.

Figure 2.2.8 ▼

Field:	LessonNo	StudentID	InstructorID	Date	DayOfTheWeek: Date
Table:	tblLesson	tblLesson	tblLesson	tblLesson	tblLesson
Sort:					
Show:	☑	☑	☑	☑	☑
Criteria:					
or:					

b) Right click on this field and select **Properties**.
c) In the **Format** box type **dddd** as in Figure 2.2.9.

Figure 2.2.9 ▶

Field Properties

General | Lookup

Description . . . .
Format . . . . dddd
Input Mask . . . .
Caption . . . .
Smart Tags . . . .

d) Run the query to test it. You should get the results in Figure 2.2.10.

Figure 2.2.10 ▶

qrySimpleDayOfWeek : Select Query

LessonNo	StudentID	InstructorID	Date	DayOfTheWeek
4	4	1	28/07/2008	Monday
5	5	1	29/07/2008	Tuesday
6	6	1	29/07/2008	Tuesday
7	7	1	29/07/2008	Tuesday
8	8	1	30/07/2008	Wednesday

Record: ◀◀ ◀ 1 ▶ ▶▶ ▶* of 105

In the same way a field **MonthName** could be set up with **Properties** set to **mmmm**.

16. Calculating the month name from the Date using the Month function

Set up a query based on **tblLesson** with the fields as shown. Add a new column to the QBE grid and set up the new field:

Month:MonthName(Month([Date]))

Figure 2.2.11 ▼

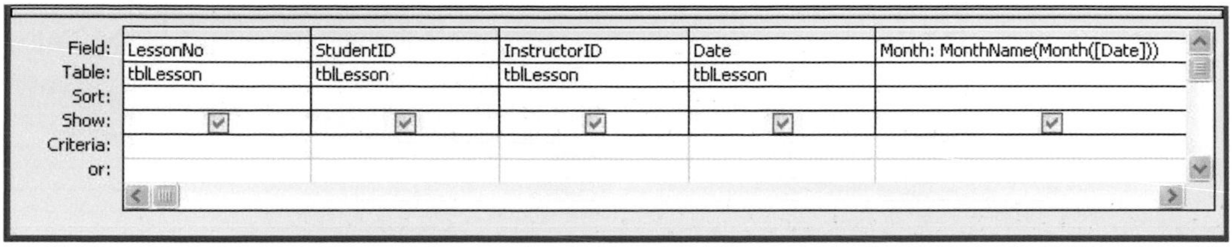

Field:	LessonNo	StudentID	InstructorID	Date	Month: MonthName(Month([Date]))
Table:	tblLesson	tblLesson	tblLesson	tblLesson	
Sort:					
Show:	☑	☑	☑	☑	☑
Criteria:					
or:					

The function **Month** returns a month number from the Date. The function **MonthName** returns the name of the month from the month number as shown in Figure 2.2.12.

Figure 2.2.12 ▶

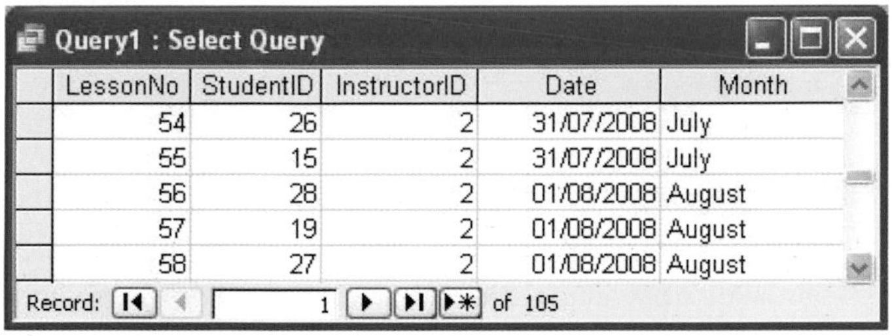

	LessonNo	StudentID	InstructorID	Date	Month
	54	26	2	31/07/2008	July
	55	15	2	31/07/2008	July
	56	28	2	01/08/2008	August
	57	19	2	01/08/2008	August
	58	27	2	01/08/2008	August

Query1 : Select Query

Record: 1 of 105

In the same way the built-in Access functions **Weekday** and **WeekdayName** can be used to return the day name.

17. Using a query to calculate the difference between dates – DateDiff function

If you have two date fields you may need to calculate the time between them. This can be done by adding a calculated field to the query.

In the example shown in Figure 2.2.13 the calculated field **DaysOnLoan** is added which returns the value from the calculation **[DateBack] – [DateOut]**.

Figure 2.2.13 ▼

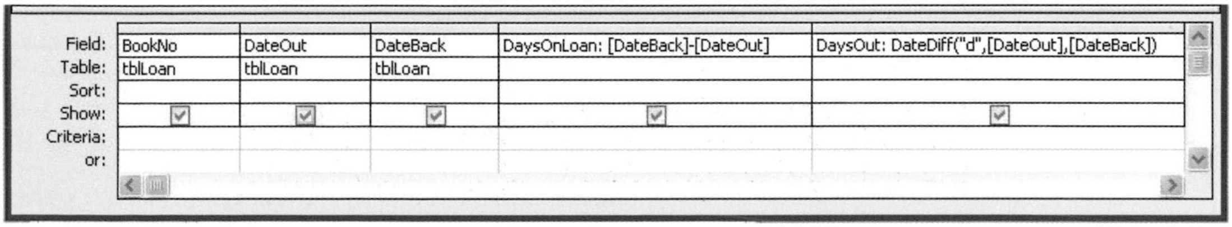

Field:	BookNo	DateOut	DateBack	DaysOnLoan: [DateBack]-[DateOut]	DaysOut: DateDiff("d",[DateOut],[DateBack])
Table:	tblLoan	tblLoan	tblLoan		
Sort:					
Show:	☑	☑	☑	☑	☑
Criteria:					
or:					

There is also a DateDiff() function which uses an argument to determine how the time interval is measured. Use "m" to calculate date differences in months, "ww" to calculate in weeks, "yyyy" for years and "d" to calculate in days.

Figure 2.2.13 also shows the calculated field **DaysOut** using the **DateDiff** function to return the difference between fields **DateOut** and **DateBack**.

18. Using a query to calculate the future dates – DateAdd function

If you have a date field and a period of time, you may need to calculate the future date, e.g. date of return from number of days on hire. This can be done by adding a calculated field to the query.

In the example shown in Figure 2.2.14 the calculated field **DateOfReturn** is added which returns the value from the calculation **[DateOut] + [NoOfDays]**

Figure 2.2.14 ▼

Field:	BookNo	DateOut	NoOfDays	DateOfReturn: [DateOut]+[NoOfDays]	DateDueBack: DateAdd("d",[NoOfDays],[DateOut])	
Table:	tblDaysOut	tblDaysOut	tblDaysOut			
Sort:						
Show:	✓	✓	✓	✓	✓	
Criteria:						
or:						

There is also a **DateAdd** function which is used in much the same way as the **DateDiff** function. Figure 2.2.14 also shows the calculated field **DateDueBack** using the **DateAdd** function to return the sum of the fields **NoOfDays** and **DateOut**.

19. Make-Table queries

In Unit 19 you were introduced to Action Queries and shown how to move data with Append and Delete Queries. A **Make-Table** query does just that: it creates a new table from the results of a query.

The following example searches the student table and makes a table of students who have passed their Practical Test.

a) Set up a query in the usual way based on **tblStudent**. Select the fields **StudentID, Forename, Surname, Address1, Address2, Address3, Address4** and **PassedPracticalTest**.

Figure 2.2.15 ▼

Field:	StudentID	Forename	Surname	Address1	Address2	Address3	Address4	PassedPracticalTest	
Table:	tblStudent	tblStudent	tblStudent	tblStudent	tblStudent	tblStudent	tblStudent	tblStudent	
Sort:									
Show:	✓	✓	✓	✓	✓	✓	✓	✓	
Criteria:								Yes	
or:									

b) In the Field **PassedPracticalTest** set the Criteria to **Yes**.
c) Click on **Query, Make-Table Query**.
d) You will be prompted for a Table Name. Type **tblPassedPracticalTest**.
e) Run the Query. You will receive the warning that a number of rows are to be pasted into a new table. Click on **OK**.
f) In the Database Window open your new **tblPassedPracticalTest** and check the data has transferred correctly.

Figure 2.2.16 ▼

```
tblPassedTest : Table
    StudentID  Forename  Surname   Address1           Address2   Address3   Address4    PassedPracticalTest
         1     Robert    Brammer   10 Plymouth Drive  Crickham   Westford   WE28 9LO              -1
         6     David     Windsor   86 Milford Road    Pilton     Westford   WE49 4PT              -1
         7     Mary      Trueman   156 Station Road   Pilton     Westford   WE49 9HS              -1
         8     Victoria  Spencer   73 Mayfield Road   Crickham   Westford   WE28 9VB              -1
        35     Tom       Heaney    6 Cavendish Way    Blakeway   Westford   WE44 3W               -1
        37     Lee       Giles     4 Devonshire Drive Crickham   Westford   WE28 6YR              -1
Record: [14] [◄] [      1 ] [►] [►I] [►*] of 6
```

Note You will notice that the new table does not inherit the field properties or primary key settings from the original table. Go into table Design View and set the Format for the PassedPracticalTest field to Yes/No.

20. Making decisions using the IIf Function in a query

You can use the IIf function in a query when you want to do a calculation on some records in one way and in another for others. The syntax is IIf (condition,true,false).

For example in the Pass IT Driving School, students with a valid NUS card can get 10% discount off the usual cost of lessons. We want to be able to click a Check Box if Student Discount applies and automatically recalculate the Cost with Discount as shown below.

Figure 2.2.17 ►

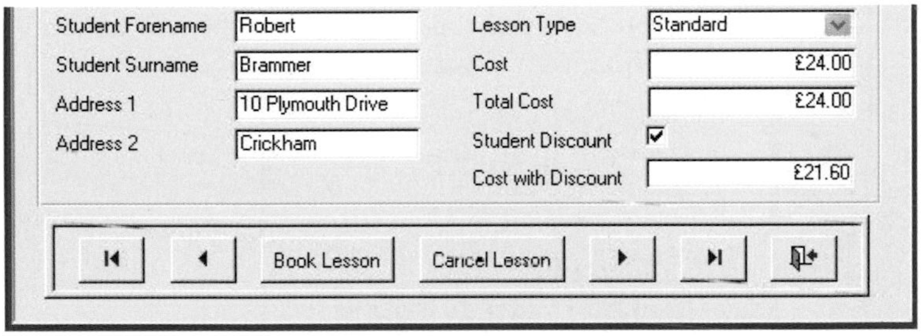

A Yes/No field called **Discount** is added to **tblLesson** and the **qryLessonCost** set up in Unit 8 as shown below. A calculated field:

DiscountedCost:IIf([Discount]=True,[TotalCost]*0.9,[TotalCost])

is added as shown below.

Figure 2.2.18 ▼

The IIf function looks to see if the **Discount** field is checked (True). If it is, it sets the **DiscountedCost** to **90%** of the **TotalCost** else it leaves the **DiscountedCost** at the value of **TotalCost**.

The same technique can be used for adding where applicable: VAT, Delivery Charges, Postage etc. N.B. The label on the form has been edited to read Student Discount.

Forms

21. Adding a calculated field to a form

In Unit 8 you set up a calculated field in a query to work out the cost of a lesson. Calculated fields can also be added to forms.

a) Load the **qryLessonCost** from Unit 8 in Design View and delete fields to leave those shown in Figure 2.3.1.

Figure 2.3.1 ▼

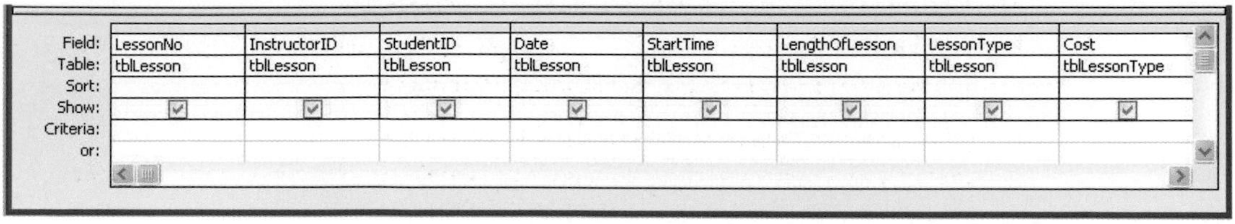

Field:	LessonNo	InstructorID	StudentID	Date	StartTime	LengthOfLesson	LessonType	Cost
Table:	tblLesson	tblLesson	tblLesson	tblLesson	tblLesson	tblLesson	tblLesson	tblLessonType
Sort:								
Show:	☑	☑	☑	☑	☑	☑	☑	☑
Criteria:								
or:								

b) Use the Form Wizard to set up a form based on the above query.

c) Switch to Design View and from the Toolbox add a text box at the foot of the form. Edit the label to read **TotalCost.** In the Text Box type **=[LengthOfLesson]*[Cost]**. See Figure 2.3.2.

Figure 2.3.2 ▶

Cost	Cost
TotalCost	=[LengthOfLesson]*[Cost]

d) Display the **Properties** for the Text Box, click the **Format** tab and set the **Format** to **Currency** and **Right Align**. Switch to Form View to see the form as shown. Save your form as **frmLesson.**

Figure 2.3.3 ▶

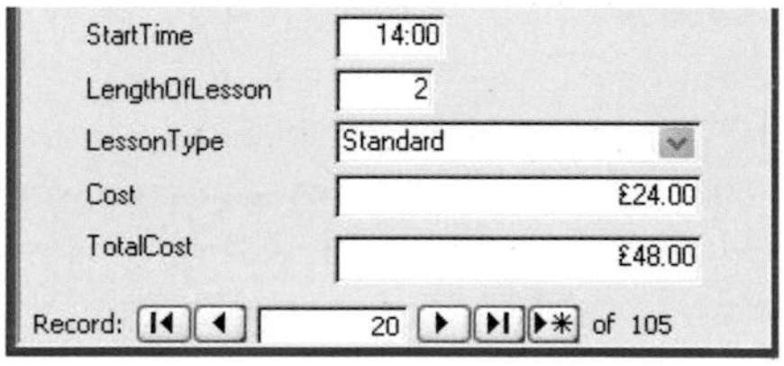

StartTime	14:00
LengthOfLesson	2
LessonType	Standard
Cost	£24.00
TotalCost	£48.00

Record: |◄ ◄ 20 ► ►| ►✱ of 105

22. Using the Expression Builder

The Expression Builder shown in Figure 2.3.4 helps you easily set up expressions in Access, for example when setting up calculated fields in a query or calculated controls on a form.

Figure 2.3.4 ▶

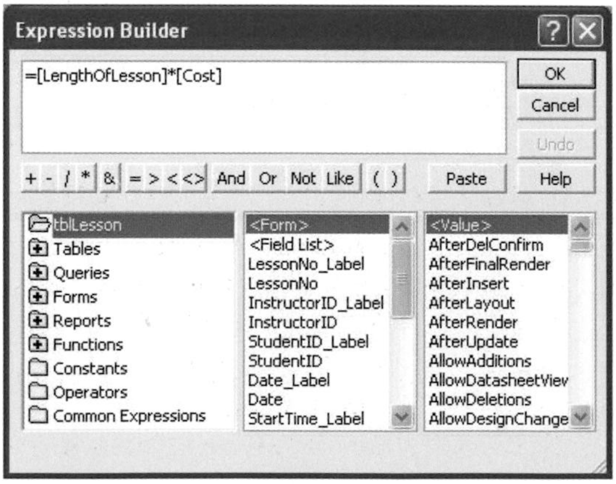

Expression Builder ? ✕

=[LengthOfLesson]*[Cost]   OK
                                  Cancel
                                  Undo

+ - / * & = > < <> And Or Not Like ( )   Paste   Help

📁 tblLesson	<Form>	<Value>
⊞ Tables	<Field List>	AfterDelConfirm
⊞ Queries	LessonNo_Label	AfterFinalRender
⊞ Forms	LessonNo	AfterInsert
⊞ Reports	InstructorID_Label	AfterLayout
⊞ Functions	InstructorID	AfterRender
▢ Constants	StudentID_Label	AfterUpdate
▢ Operators	StudentID	AllowAdditions
▢ Common Expressions	Date_Label	AllowDatasheetView
	Date	AllowDeletions
	StartTime_Label	AllowDesignChange

a) Load the form from the previous tip called **frmLesson** in Design View.
b) Highlight the **TotalCost** text box and delete the formula.
c) Right click to call up its properties, select the **Data** tab and in the Control Source click the three dots to load the Expression Builder.
d) Build your expression by pasting the symbols and field names from the dialogue box.

23. Formatting dates on forms and reports

You can use the Format function to display different dates in different formats or different date components on a form or a report.

For example, suppose you have a field called Date.
Set up a new text box called **Day of the Week** and set the Control Source property to: **=Format([Date],"dddd")**

Figure 2.3.5 ▶

```
Text Box: Day of the Week                    [X]

Day of the Week                          [v]

Format   Data   Event   Other    All
Name . . . . . . . . . . . . . . . Day of the Week
Control Source . . . . . . . . . . =Format([Date],"dddd")
Format . . . . . . . . . . . . . .
Decimal Places . . . . . . . . . . Auto
Input Mask . . . . . . . . . . . .
Default Value . . . . . . . . . .                    [...]
IME Hold . . . . . . . . . . . . . No
IME Mode . . . . . . . . . . . . . No Control
```

This will display the date's day, e.g. Monday if the date was 28/07/08.

=Format([Date],"m") displays the month number, e.g. 12.
=Format([Date],"yy") displays the abbreviated year number, e.g. 01.
=Format([Date],"mmm") displays the abbreviated month name, e.g. Dec.
=Format([Date],"mmmm") displays the full month name, e.g. December.
=Format([Date],"yyyy") displays the full year number, e.g. 2008.

You can also combine the formats to create your own format, e.g.

=Format([Date],"dmmmyy")

which would display the day, the abbreviated month, and a two-digit year value, with no spaces in between each component.

You can also display a literal character, such as a comma and space in a date to make it 17 June, 2008. Just use this format:

=Format([Date], "d mmmm" "," "yyyy")

24. Making a command button the default button

When you open a form you can make a command button the default and respond by just hitting enter. Typically this might be the most commonly used operation e.g. Book a Lesson on the Lesson Booking form.

a) Open the form in Design View, right click on the button you want to respond to ENTER and choose **Properties**.
b) Click the **Other** tab and set the **Default** property to **Yes**.

Figure 2.3.6 ▶

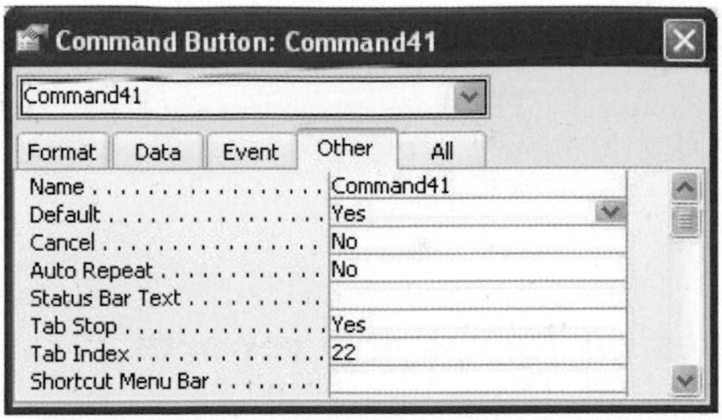

When you open the form pressing ENTER will run the command button action.

25. Changing the properties of a group of controls

    a) Open the form in Design View.
    b) Select the first control whose property you wish to change. Hold down SHIFT and select the other controls you wish to change.
    c) Right click on any of the controls and choose **Properties**.
    d) The Properties window opens with the title **Multiple selection**. From here any property you select will be applied to all selected controls.

Figure 2.3.7 ▶

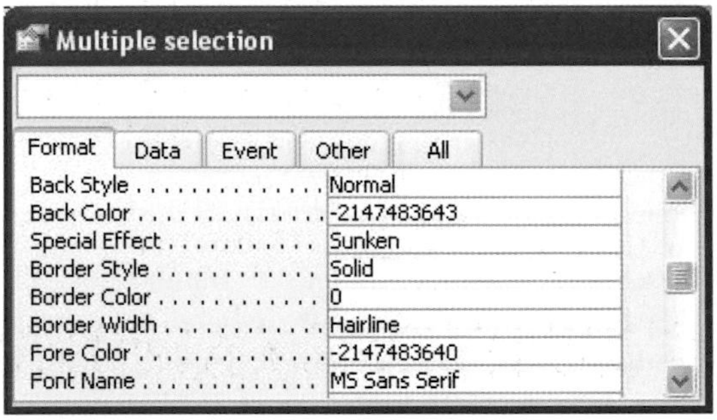

26. Preventing users from adding records to a form

    a) Load the form in Design View and choose the **Form Properties**.
    b) Click on the **Data** tab and set the **Allow Additions** property to **No**. When the form is opened the New Record icon is greyed out.
    c) To control access further, also set the **AllowDeletions** and **AllowEdits** properties to **No**.

27. Creating read-only fields on a form

Sometimes you may wish to make a field available but not allow it to be changed by the user.

    a) In Design View, select the field and click on the Properties icon. Click on the **Data** tab.
    b) Set the **Enabled** property to **No** and the **Locked** property to **Yes**. The field will not receive the focus and the user will not be able to change it.
    c) If you set the **Enabled** property to **No** and the **Locked** property to **No** the field will not receive the focus and will appear dimmed as shown in Figure 2.3.8.

Figure 2.3.8 ▶

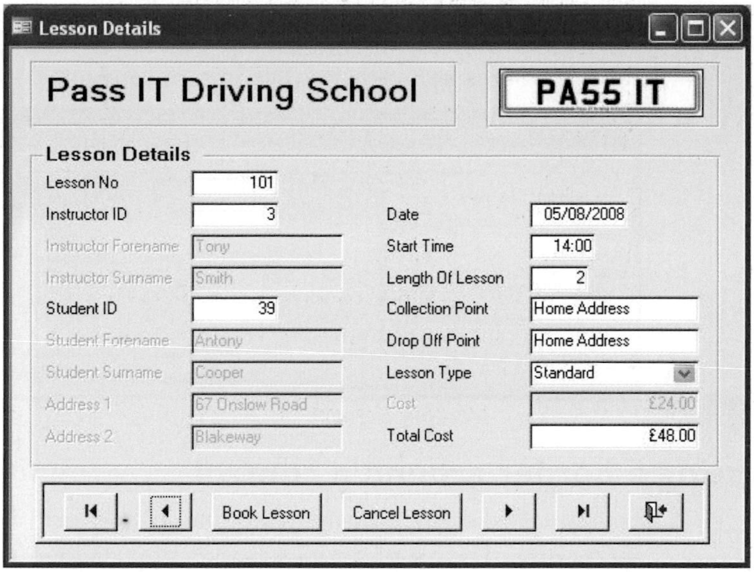

Lesson Details

Pass IT Driving School · PA55 IT

Lesson Details

Lesson No	101		
Instructor ID	3	Date	05/08/2008
Instructor Forename	Tony	Start Time	14:00
Instructor Surname	Smith	Length Of Lesson	2
Student ID	39	Collection Point	Home Address
Student Forename	Antony	Drop Off Point	Home Address
Student Surname	Cooper	Lesson Type	Standard
Address 1	67 Onslow Road	Cost	£24.00
Address 2	Blakeway	Total Cost	£48.00

Book Lesson   Cancel Lesson

28. Moving the focus to another control on a form

Often when entering data into a form you need to move the cursor to another control. For example, when booking a lesson in the Driving School, you need to automatically move the cursor to the StudentID field after entering the InstructorID. You can do this with a macro.

a) In the **Action** column select **GoToControl** and set the **Control Name** to **StudentID**.

Figure 2.3.9 ▶

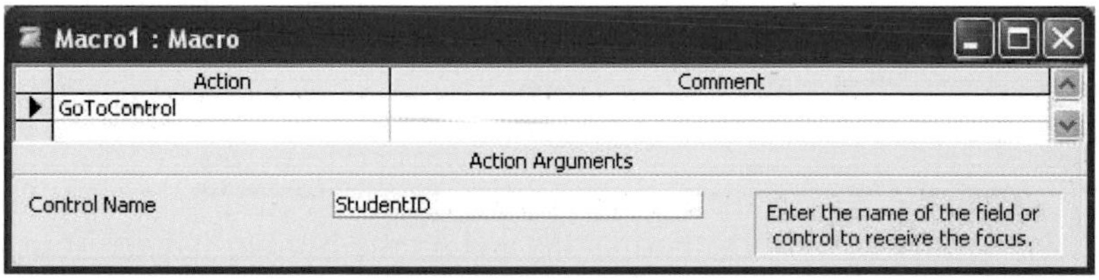

Macro1 : Macro

Action	Comment
GoToControl	

Action Arguments

Control Name	StudentID	Enter the name of the field or control to receive the focus.

b) Name the macro **mcrGoToStudent** and attach it to the **After Update** property of the **InstructorID** control.

Figure 2.3.10 ▶

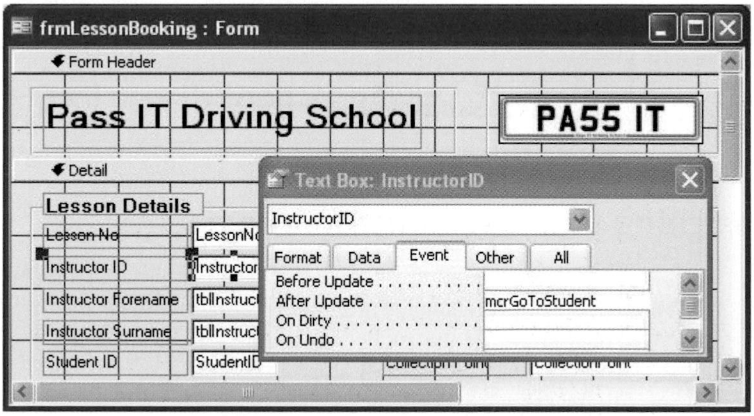

frmLessonBooking : Form

Form Header

Pass IT Driving School · PA55 IT

Detail

Lesson Details

Lesson No	LessonN...
Instructor ID	Instructor
Instructor Forename	tblInstruc...
Instructor Surname	tblInstruc...
Student ID	StudentID

Text Box: InstructorID

InstructorID

Format | Data | Event | Other | All

Before Update . . . .
After Update . . . . mcrGoToStudent
On Dirty . . . .
On Undo . . . .

Another way of achieving this is using the **Tab Stop** property. Simply group the controls you wish the cursor to skip e.g. **InstructorForename** and **InstructorSurname** and set the **Tab Stop** property to No.

Figure 2.3.11 ▶

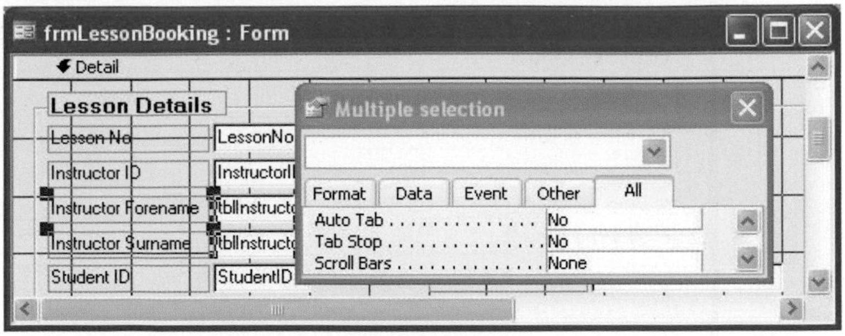

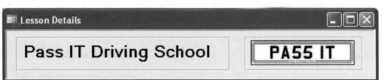

29. Putting a border around a control

Borders and other effects can be attached to controls using the control's properties.

Figure 2.3.12 ▶

a) Right click the Logo in Design View and select **Properties**.

Figure 2.3.13 ▶

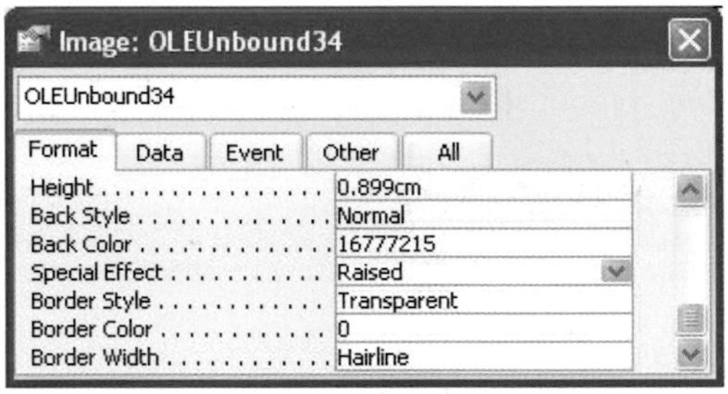

b) Click the **Format** tab and set the **Border Style** to **Transparent** instead of **Solid**.
c) Set the **Special Effect** property to **Raised** (see Figure 2.3.14).
d) Select the other controls and set their **Special Effect** property to **Raised**.

Figure 2.3.14 ▶

30. Designing your own button images

You can use images as buttons on a form. There are two ways to get started:

■ Use Paint or a similar program to design your image or
■ Find an image via a Clip Art Library or the Internet.

Figure 2.3.15 ▶

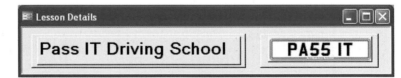

It is important to resize your image to the size of an Access button (about 39 x 39 pixels). This is easily done in an image editor such as Paint, Photoshop or Paint Shop Pro.

a) Open a form in Design View and use the Command Button Wizard to set up a button, choosing picture when asked if you want text or a picture on your button.
b) Select the button and right click on it to display its properties.
c) Click on the **Format** tab.
d) In the **Picture** property click on the three dots to display the **Picture Builder** window.
e) Click on **Browse** to find the image.
f) Resize and position the image as required.

31. Creating a command button from a graphic image

You can create buttons from graphic images with just a little VB. In Unit 14 you added the simple Pass IT graphic to the menu. You can turn any graphic into a command button. This example shows you how to make the graphic run a macro.

Figure 2.3.16 ▶

a) In Design View, click on the graphic and display its Properties.
b) Change the **Name** property to **Logo**; it will be something like Figure 2.3.17. Set the **OnClick** property to run the macro **mcrAbout**.

Figure 2.3.17 ▶

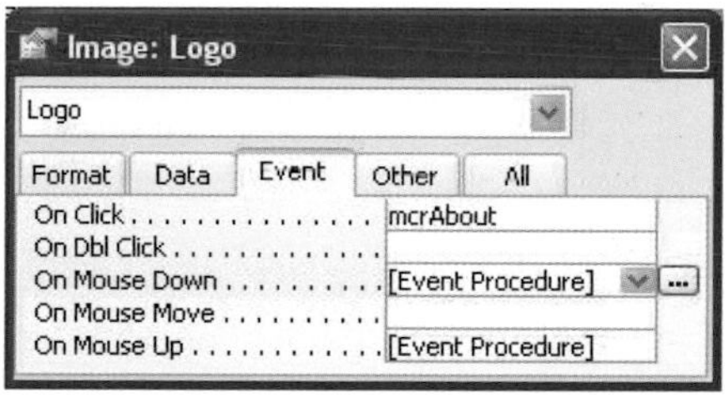

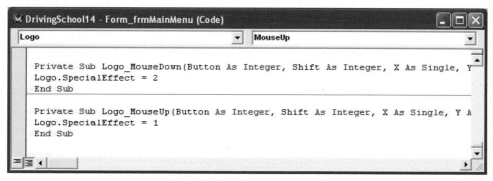

c) Go to the **On Mouse Down** property, choose **Code Builder** and add the line of code: **Logo.SpecialEffect = 2**
d) Repeat for the **On Mouse Up** property as shown below.

Figure 2.3.18 ▼

e) Test the button runs the macro **mcrAbout**.

32. Customising a Quit or Exit button

If you design a button to Quit Application using the wizards it doesn't give you an "Are you sure?" option. This can easily be achieved with a simple few lines of VB.

Figure 2.3.19 ▶

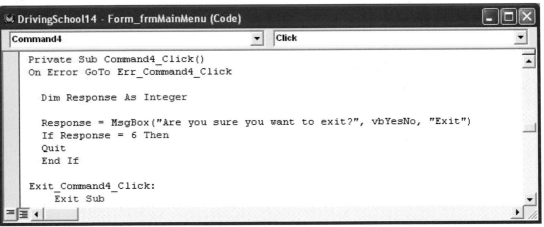

a) Go into **Design View** and display the properties of the **Quit/Exit** command button.

b) If you view the **Event Procedure** attached to the **OnClick** property you will see the code for the quit procedure. Remove the line of code **DoCmd. Quit** and replace with the 5 lines of code shown below.

Figure 2.3.20 ▼

```
DrivingSchool14 - Form_frmMainMenu (Code)

Command4                              Click

  Private Sub Command4_Click()
  On Error GoTo Err_Command4_Click

     Dim Response As Integer

     Response = MsgBox("Are you sure you want to exit?", vbYesNo, "Exit")
     If Response = 6 Then
     Quit
     End If

  Exit_Command4_Click:
       Exit Sub
```

c) On clicking the **Exit** button you will be given the message box shown with **Yes** and **No** buttons. If you press **No** nothing happens. If **Yes** is pressed then the quit procedure takes place.

33. Positioning and sizing your form automatically

It is easy to position your form using its Form properties. Set the properties as follows. Your form will open centred and sized to display a complete record.

a) Open the form in Design View.
b) From the menu choose **View, Properties**.
c) Click the **Format** tab in the Properties Window.
d) Set the **Auto Center** property to **Yes**.
e) Set the **Auto Resize** property to **Yes**.

Figure 2.3.21 ▶

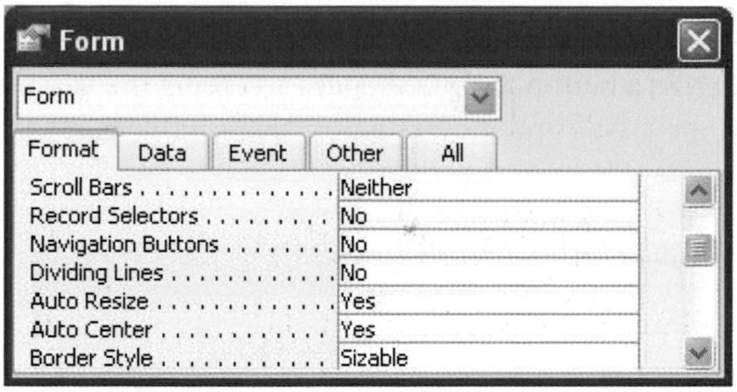

34. Using option buttons or radio controls

Option buttons are frequently used to represent Yes/No fields. For example, on the Student form shown in Figure 2.3.22, an option button could be used for the Passed Practical Test field.

Figure 2.3.22 ▶

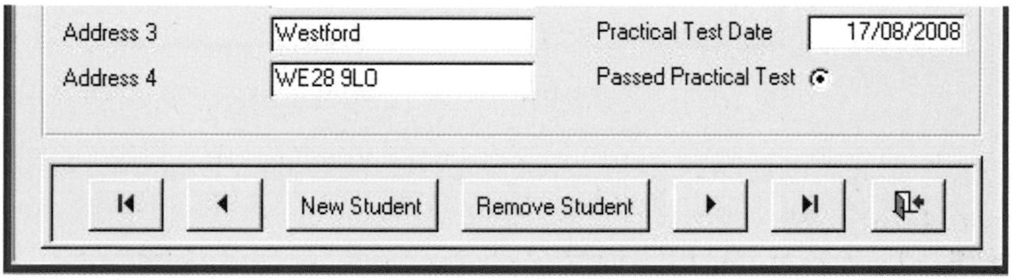

a) Open **frmStudent** in Design View and delete the PassedPracticalTest field check box.

Figure 2.3.23 ▶

b) From the Toolbox, click on the **Option Button** icon and drag out a button on the form. Set the label to **Passed Practical Test**.

c) Select the control and right click to view its properties. Click on the **Data** tab and set the **Control Source** to the **PassedPracticalTest** field as shown in Figure 2.3.24.

Figure 2.3.24 ▶

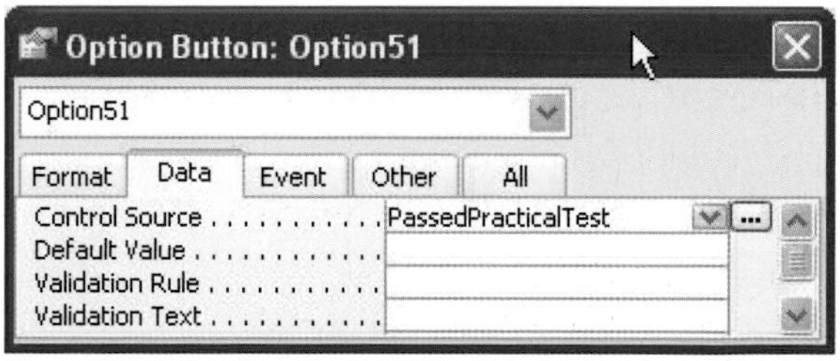

Toggle Buttons and Check Boxes can be set up in the same way but it is important when designing forms to be consistent.

35. Using option groups

Option groups let the user choose one option from a list of alternative values. For example, the title field on the Instructor form shown below could be entered using option buttons in a group. It is important to note Access stores the data as a number e.g. 1 = Mr, 2 = Mrs, etc.

Figure 2.3.25 ▶

a) Open the **frmInstructor** in Design view, delete the **Title** field and create some room for the Option Group.

b) From the Toolbox, click on the **Option Group** icon and drag out a rectangle. In the **Option Group** dialogue box set the labels as shown in 2.3.26 and click on **Next**.

Figure 2.3.26 ▶

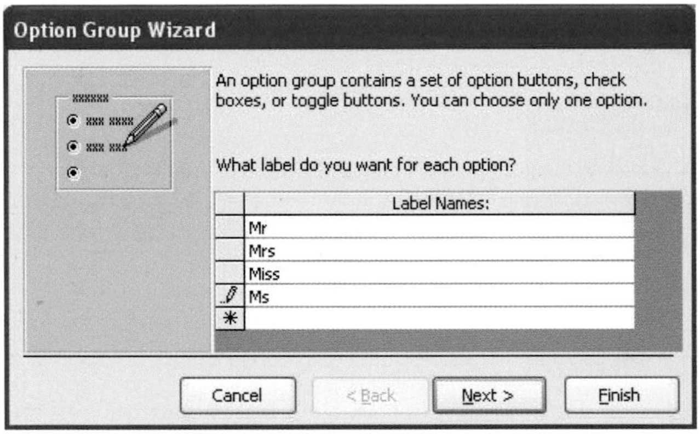

c) Select the default value required and click on **Next**. Click on **Next** again to accept the values as shown in Figure 2.3.27.

Figure 2.3.27 ▶

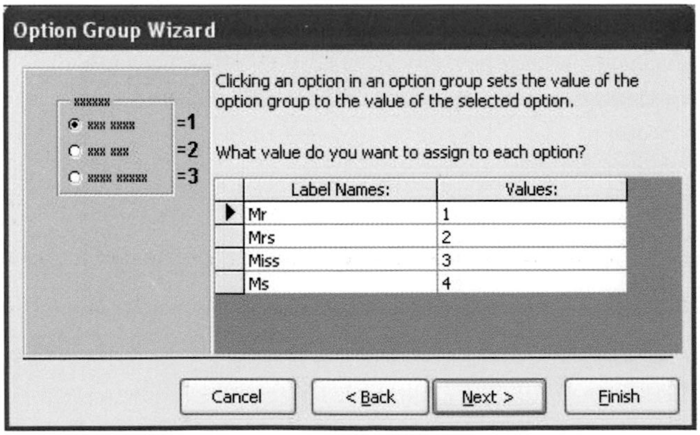

d) Click on **Store the value in this field** and select **Title** from the drop-down. Click on **Next**.

e) Choose your control style, click on **Next** and set the **Caption** to **Title**. Click on **Finish**.

36. Printing a form without the buttons

You may wish to print an on-screen form without printing the buttons and other objects such as images. We will use the Instructor Form set up in the Driving School as an example.

a) Open the **frmInstructor** in Design View. Highlight the objects you don't want to print, in this case the Control Panel.

Figure 2.3.28 ▶

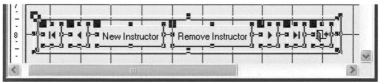

b) Click on **View, Properties** and set the **Display When** property to **Screen Only**. Save the form and return to Form View.

Figure 2.3.29 ▶

```
┌─────────────────────────────────────────────┐
│ 📋 Multiple selection                     ✕ │
├─────────────────────────────────────────────┤
│  ┌──────────────────────────────┐ ▼         │
│  └──────────────────────────────┘           │
│  Format │ Data │ Event │ Other │ All         │
│  Visible . . . . . . . . . . . . . Yes       │
│  Display When . . . . . . . . . . Screen Only│
│  Left . . . . . . . . . . . . . .            │
│  Top . . . . . . . . . . . . . .             │
└─────────────────────────────────────────────┘
```

If you chose to Print now you would get all the forms printing without the objects. We only want the currently displayed record to print.

c) At the Database Window, select **Macros** and click on **New**.

d) In the **Action** column select the **PrintOut** command. In the **Action Arguments**, click in the **Print Range** box and choose **Selection**. Name the macro **Print Form**.

Figure 2.3.30 ▼

```
┌───────────────────────────────────────────────────────────────────┐
│ 📄 mcrPrintForm : Macro                              _ □ ✕         │
├───────────────────────────────────────────────────────────────────┤
│        Action              │              Comment                  │
│ ▶ PrintOut                 │                                       │
│                            │                                       │
├───────────────────────────────────────────────────────────────────┤
│                        Action Arguments                            │
│  Print Range      Selection          │                            │
│  Page From                           │  Select Yes to collate     │
│  Page To                             │  printed copies. Select    │
│  Print Quality    High               │  No to print multiple      │
│  Copies           1                  │  copies of each page       │
│  Collate Copies   Yes                │  together. Multiple copies │
│                                      │  may print faster if this  │
│                                      │  is set to No.             │
│                                      │  Press F1 for help on this │
└───────────────────────────────────────────────────────────────────┘
```

e) Set up a command button on the Instructor Form to run the **mcrPrintForm**.

37. Adding customised tool tips (Screen Tips) to your controls

When you move the mouse pointer over a button you get a screen tip explaining what the button does as shown in Figure 2.3.31.

Figure 2.3.31 ▶

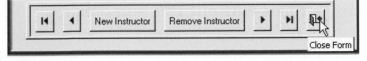

In Access it is easy to customise these tips and make them more user-friendly.

a) Open a form in Design View; we have chosen the **frmInstructor** in the Driving School.

b) Right click on the button to view its properties. Click on the **Other** tab. Set the **ControlTip Text** property to **Add a New Instructor** or whatever you choose. See Figure 2.3.32.

Figure 2.3.32 ▶

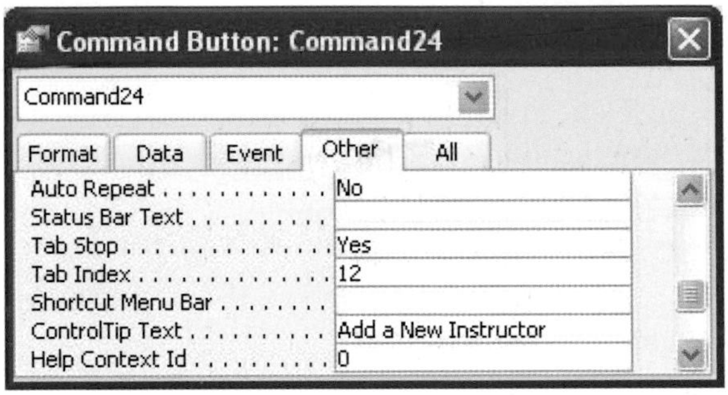

```
Command Button: Command24                [X]

Command24                          [v]

Format   Data   Event   Other   All

Auto Repeat . . . . . . . . . . . . No
Status Bar Text . . . . . . . . . .
Tab Stop . . . . . . . . . . . . . . Yes
Tab Index . . . . . . . . . . . . . 12
Shortcut Menu Bar . . . . . . .
ControlTip Text . . . . . . . . . . Add a New Instructor
Help Context Id . . . . . . . . . . 0
```

c) Save the form and move the pointer over the button to view your tip.

Figure 2.3.33 ▶

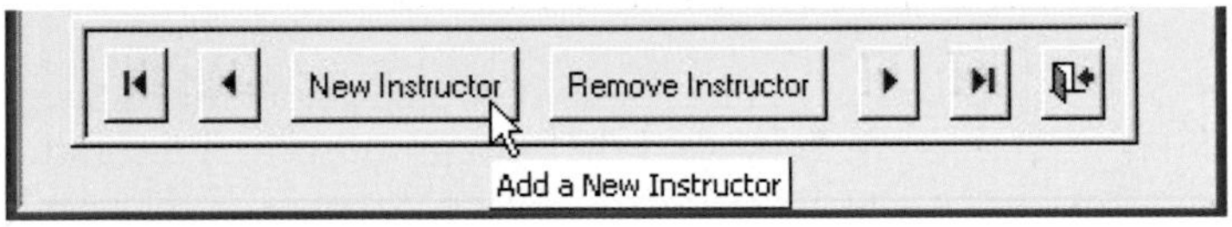

```
|◀   ◀   New Instructor   Remove Instructor   ▶   ▶|   ↵|
                    ⟍
          Add a New Instructor
```

38. Pop Up and Modal forms

When a **Modal** form is open, you cannot move to another object such as another form. This is important if you want data to be entered into the form before moving on.

A **Pop Up** form always remains on top of other Microsoft Access windows when it is open.

When we open the Student Form or the Instructor Form to paste in details, we may want these forms to remain on top and do not want the user to choose any other object. In other words, these forms will be pop-up modal forms.

We can set this up in Form Design View.

a) Load each form in turn in **Design View**.

b) Double-click on the **Form Selector** to show the **Form Properties**.

c) Click on the **Other** tab and set the **Modal** and **Pop Up** properties to **Yes**.

Figure 2.3.34 ►

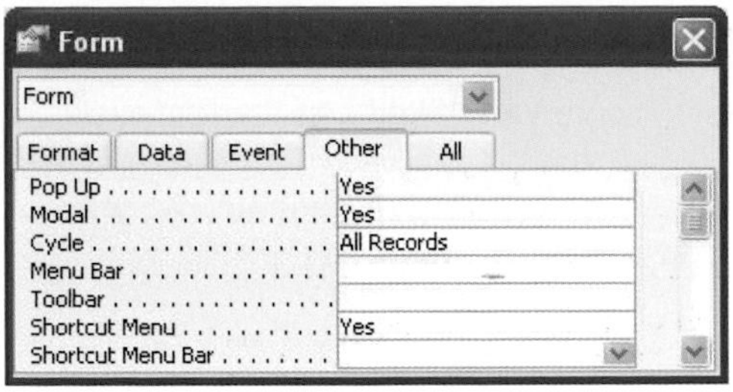

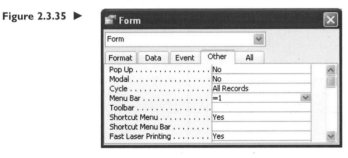

d) Switch to **Form View** and test that you cannot click on objects outside the Form window.

39. Removing the Menu Bar from a form

The Menu Bar is the area across the screen that says File, Edit, View, etc. To remove the Menu Bar when a form is loaded:

a) Load the form in Design View and choose the **Form Properties**.
b) Click on the **Other** tab and set the **MenuBar** property to =1 as shown in Figure 2.3.35.

Figure 2.3.35 ►

40. Starting a form from scratch

Throughout the study units we used the wizards to set up our forms. Of course, as ever, you could choose to ignore the wizards and set up the form manually.

a) In the Database Window, select **Forms** and then click on **New**.
b) Select Design View and base the form on **tblStudent**.
c) The blank form will open in Design View with the **Field List** for the Student table as shown in Figure 2.3.36.

Figure 2.3.36 ►

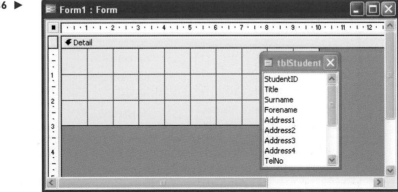

d) Drag and drop the fields needed as required.

Note If the Field List is not displayed then choose **View**, **Field List** from the menu.

If you accidentally delete a control during the customisation of your form, display the Field List and drag and drop the field from the Field List on to the form.

Reports

41. Forcing a page break on a report

Typically at setup a report would be grouped by customer, supplier or order number. This produces a header section on the report.

Ensure the section has a footer by clicking on the **Sorting and Grouping** icon and setting **Group Footer** to **Yes**. In the properties of the **Group Footer** set **Force New Page** to **After Section**.

Figure 2.4.1 ▶

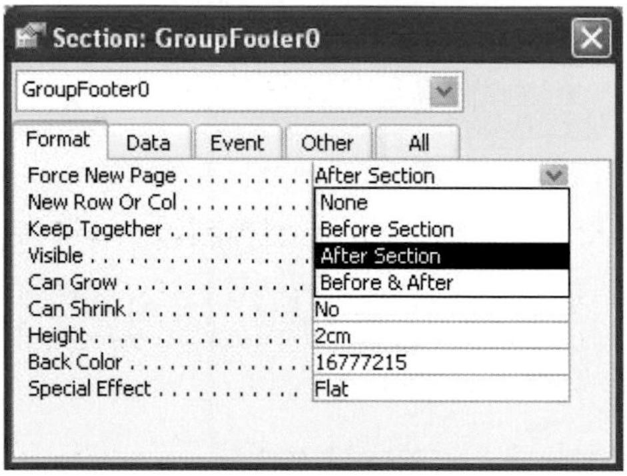

42. Concatenating text strings on reports

It can often be difficult on reports to align text properly, as shown below. It can be easier to combine data fields using & or what is known as concatenate strings.

Figure 2.4.2 ▶

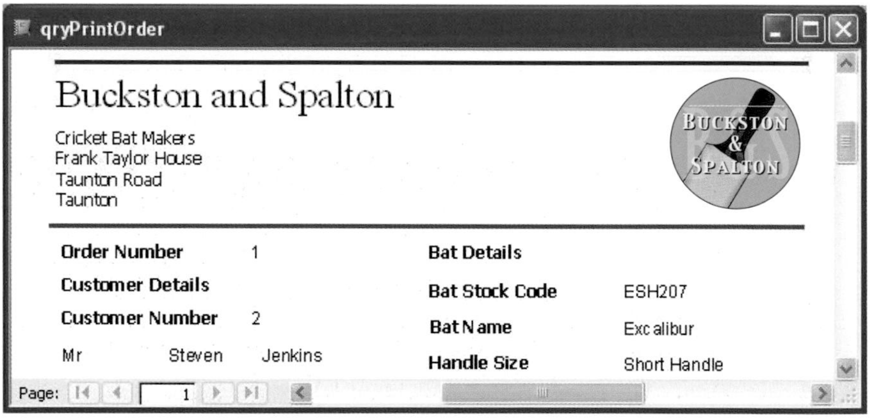

For example remove the fields Title, Surname and Forename from your report and replace with an unbound text box. Enter into the text box or set its control source as shown: = [Title] & " " & [Forename] & " " & [Surname]

Figure 2.4.3 ▶

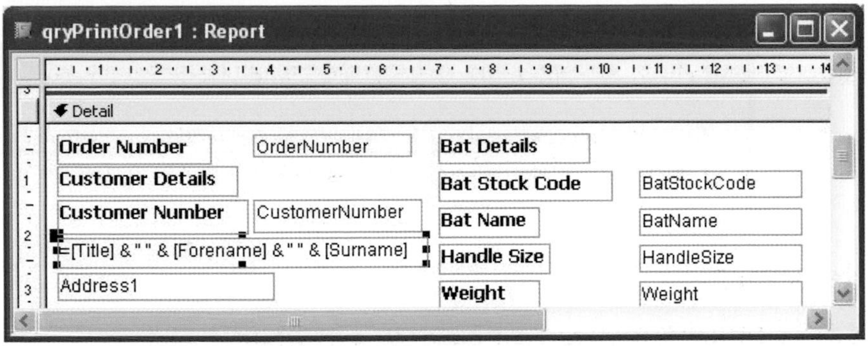

qryPrintOrder1 : Report

Order Number	OrderNumber	Bat Details	
Customer Details		Bat Stock Code	BatStockCode
Customer Number	CustomerNumber	Bat Name	BatName
=[Title] & " " & [Forename] & " " & [Surname]		Handle Size	HandleSize
Address1		Weight	Weight

This will join the three fields and insert a space between them. You might need to display the initial only. Using **Left([Forename],1)** will do just that.

You can add text in much the same way on a report. In the Footer of an order/invoice to be completed on **[CompletionDate]**, simply add a text box and again enter the following:

=**"Order to be completed by " & " " & [CompletionDate]**

=**"Payable within 28 days from completion of order" & " " & [CompletionDate]+28**

43. Replacing check boxes and coded fields with text

Using a check box for a Yes/No field returns a –1 for Yes. The check box itself can look a little meaningless on reports. Remove the check box field and replace with an unbound text box.

The IIf statement can be used as shown. Enter the statement into the text box or via its Control Source to change the check box or code as shown. If the check box field is called Status:

=**IIf([status]=–1,"Yes","No")**
=**IIf([status]=–1,"Order Paid ","Order Unpaid")**

or for a field called Gender
=**IIf([Gender]= "M","Male","Female")**

or the field PassedPracticalTest in the Pass IT Driving School
=**IIf([PassedPracticalTest]=–1,"Passed","Not yet taken")**

Figure 2.4.4 ▼

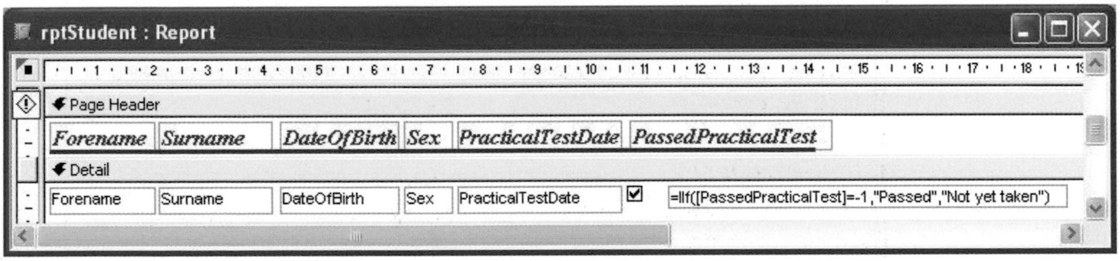

rptStudent : Report

Page Header

| Forename | Surname | DateOfBirth | Sex | PracticalTestDate | PassedPracticalTest |

Detail

| Forename | Surname | DateOfBirth | Sex | PracticalTestDate | ☑ | =IIf([PassedPracticalTest]=-1,"Passed","Not yet taken") |

In this example we have left the check box but added an unbound text box to display the meaning of the check box as shown in Figure 2.4.4. The output is shown in Figure 2.4.5.

Figure 2.4.5 ▼

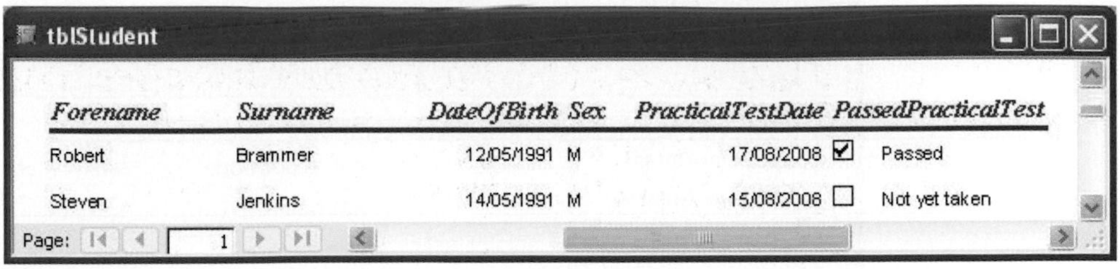

44. Using Switch to change a coded field

If a field is coded then the Switch command can be used in the same way. In this example a field called Status is coded A, Pd and P. Switch is used to convert to Active, Paid or Pending. The statement is:

=Switch([Status]="A","Active",[Status]="Pd","Paid",[Status]="P", "Pending")

45. Formatting Invoice Numbers

If you are using Autonumber or Numeric for an OrderNumber field you might want the report to display preceding zeros e.g. for OrderNumber 1 to be displayed as OrderNumber 000001 simply use the code below:

=Format([OrderNumber]),"000000"

46. Mailing labels, business and membership cards

If you have a list of names and addresses as in the Student table of the Driving School, you can easily customise and print mailing labels for them as follows:

a) At the Database Window, click on **Reports** and click on **New**.
b) Select the **Label Wizard** and select **tblStudent**. Click on **OK**.
c) Select your label manufacturer, label size and other options as shown in Figure 2.4.6.

Figure 2.4.6 ►

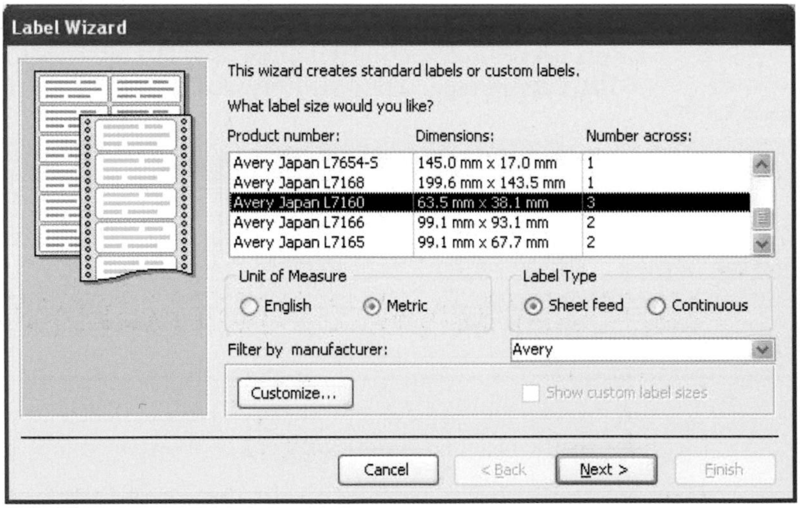

d) Choose the **Font Name**, **Font Weight**, **Font Size** and **Text colour** as shown in Figure 2.4.7 and click on **Next**.

Figure 2.4.7 ▶

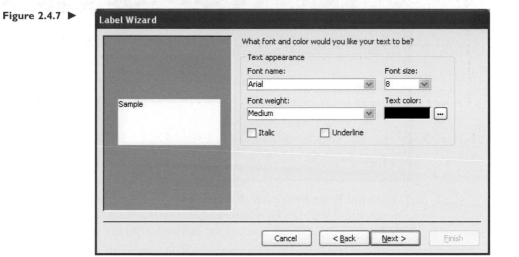

The next stage is to position the text and fields on the Prototype label.

Figure 2.4.8 ▶

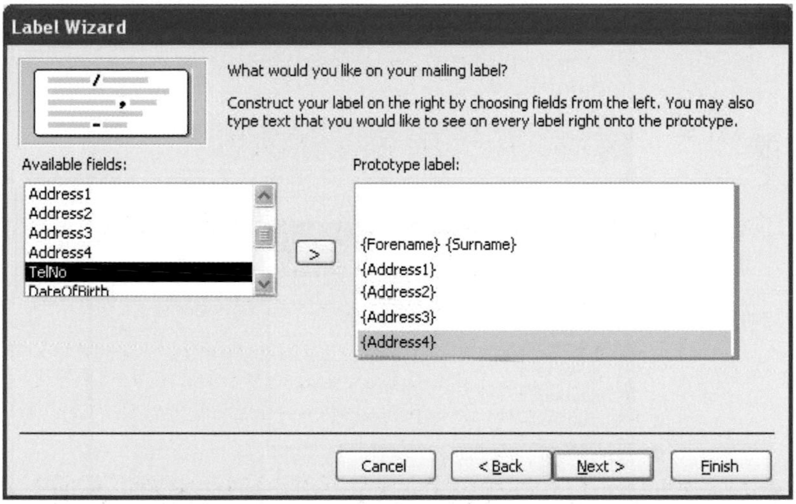

e) Press RETURN twice. Transfer across the fields **Forename** and **Surname** remembering to press the space bar in between them. Press RETURN.
f) Continue to transfer the fields **Address1**, **Address2**, **Address3** and **Address4**. Click on **Next**.
g) Choose to sort by **Surname**. Click on **Next**.
h) Name the report **rptLabels** and click on **Finish**. The labels should appear as in Figure 2.4.9.

Figure 2.4.9 ▼

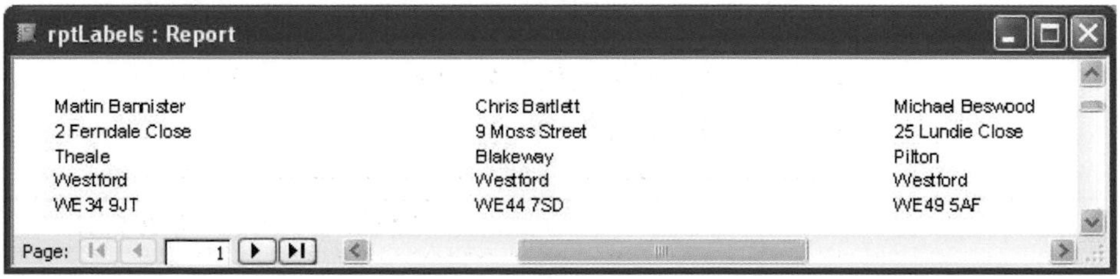

i) With the report open, switch to Design View as shown in Figure 2.4.10.

Figure 2.4.10 ▶

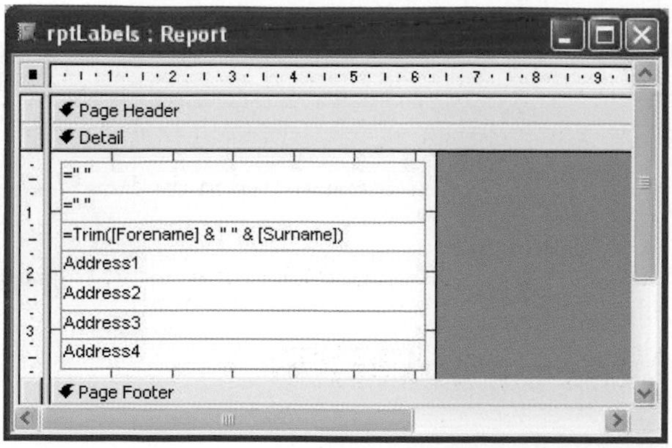

j) From the Toolbox select the **Rectangle** tool and carefully position a rectangle around the label. Click on **Format, Send to the Back**.

k) With the rectangle still selected, set its **Border Width** property to **2pt**. Figure 2.4.11.

l) From the Toolbox select the **Image** icon and import the Pass IT logo (or use Copy, Paste). Position the logo as shown. You will have to set its **Size Mode** property to **Zoom**.

m) Add a Label with the text Driving School. Set the **Font Weight** property to **Semi-Bold**.

Figure 2.4.11 ▶

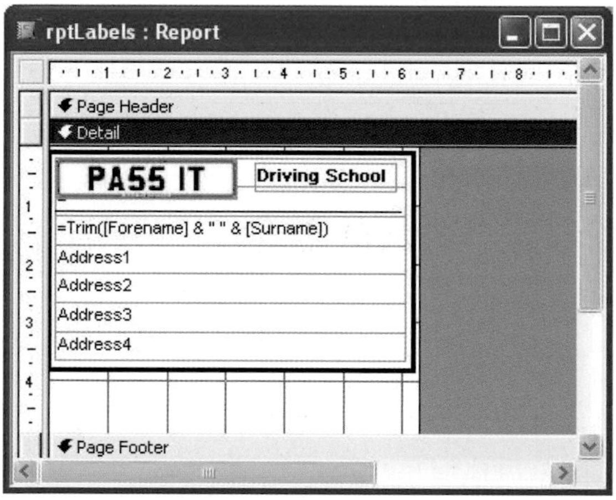

n) Switch to Print Preview to view the Mailing Labels as shown in Figure 2.4.12. Save the report as **rptLabels**.

Figure 2.4.12 ▼

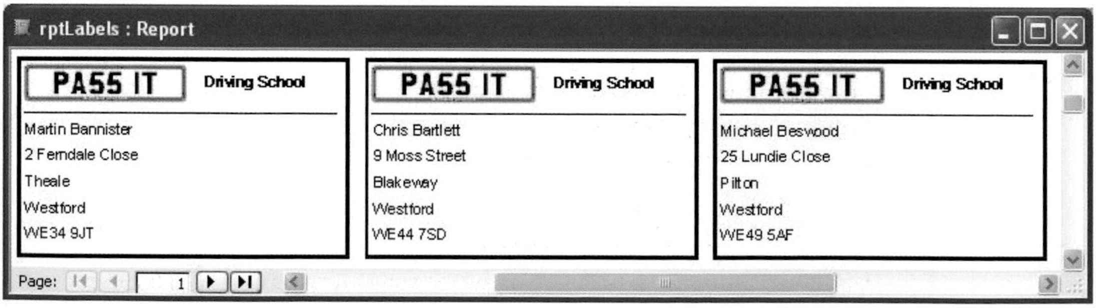

Macros

47. Formatting text to bold in a Message Box

You can set text to bold in a message box using the @ symbol. Access allows 3 sections in a message box separated by @. The first is displayed in bold.

For example, in the No Data macro used in the Pass IT system set the message as follows:

There is no data in this report@Close the report now@Check with your System Administrator

Figure 2.5.1 ▶

Run the macro and the message box is displayed as in Figure 2..5.1.

48. Putting hard returns in a Message Box

You can force Access to put text on the next line in a message box by using the ASCII code for a carriage return: Chr(13).

a) Set up a new macro and choose the **Action: MsgBox**.
b) In the **Action Arguments**, click in the **Message** box and copy and paste:
   ="The Pass IT Driving School"& Chr(13) & "by" & Chr(13) & "Ian Rendell"

Figure 2.5.2 ▶

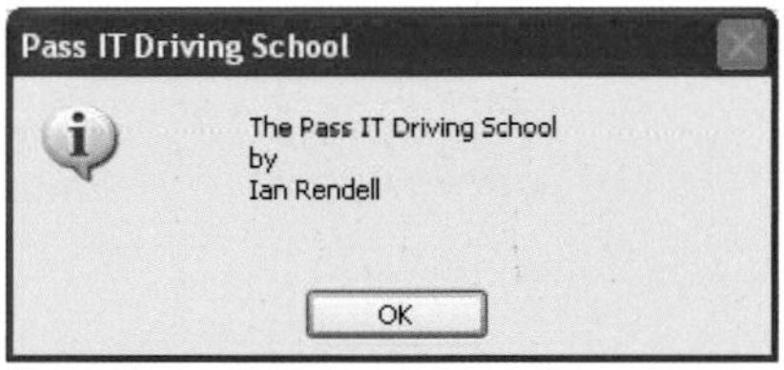

You can improve the presentation of your message box further by using the code Chr(9) for a tab space and Chr(32) for a space.

The message box shown in Figure 2.5.3 uses this statement:
=Chr(9) & "The Pass IT Driving School" & Chr(13) & Chr(9) & Chr(9) & "by" & Chr(13) & Chr(9) & Chr(32) & Chr(32) & Chr(32) & Chr(32) & Chr(32) & "Ian Rendell"

Figure 2.5.3 ▶

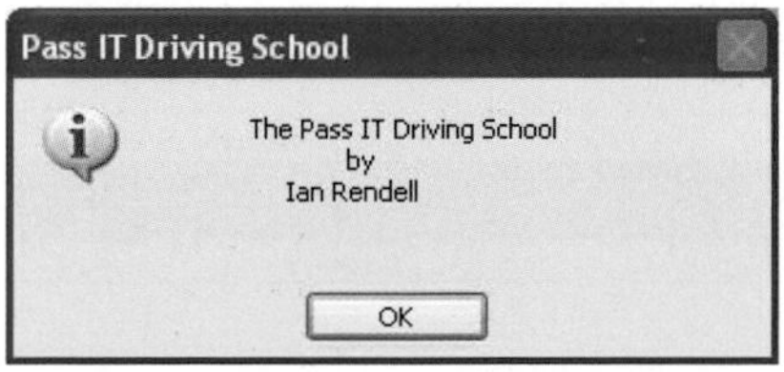

Don't forget that by pressing SHIFT and F2 you can zoom and see all the text in a message box.

49. The AutoExec macro

A macro saved as **AutoExec** automatically runs when the database is opened. You can control start-up options from this macro.

Create a new macro as shown in Figure 2.5.4 with the following Actions and Arguments. Save the macro as **mcrAutoExec**. To run automatically rename as **AutoExec**.

Action	Argument	Comment
Echo	No	Hides events
Hourglass	Yes	Pointer displayed as hourglass
RunCommand	WindowHide	Hides the Database Window
OpenForm	Switchboard	Opens the Switchboard or Main Menu

Figure 2.5.4 ▼

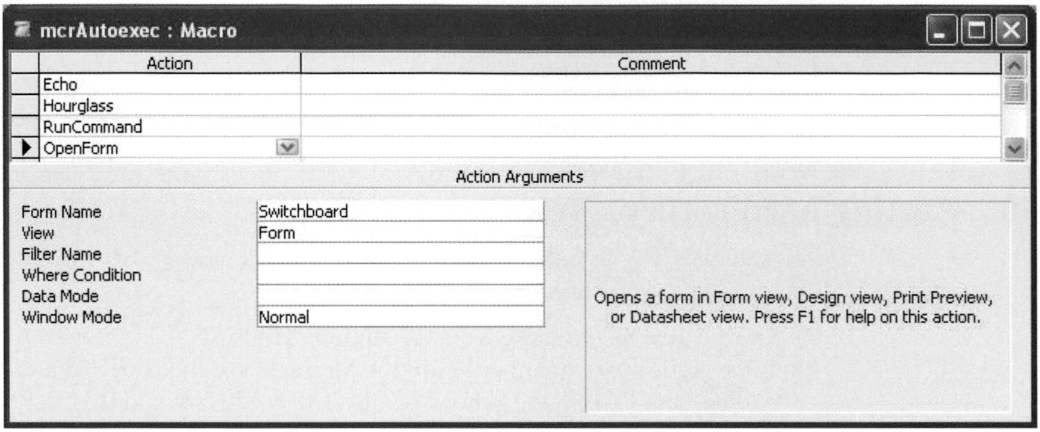

Note Use F11 to display the Database Window again.

Note If you don't want the AutoExec macro or the Start-up options to run, hold down the SHIFT key when you open the database.

50. Hiding and Unhiding the Database Window from your AutoExec macro

On startup you may wish to hide the **Database Window** as part of your **AutoExec** macro.

Simply use the **RunCommand** action with its argument set to **WindowHide** as shown below. Then use the **OpenForm** action to open your switchboard or front end menu.

Figure 2.5.5 ▼

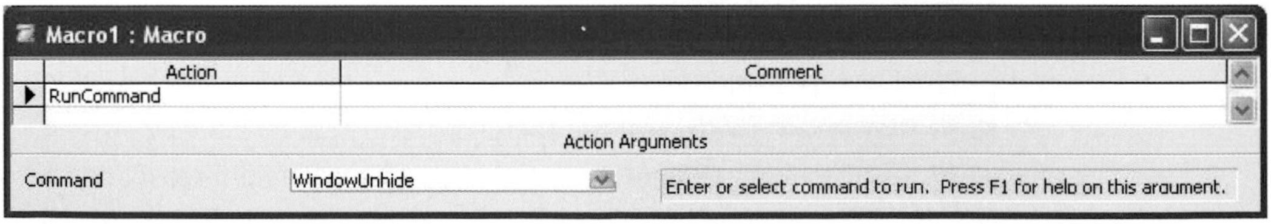

If you have fully customised your solution to hide Access from the user you might offer a System Design or Maintenance option from your switchboard. This would be a command button that ran the reverse of the above macro and allowed the user access to the Database Window.

Use the **RunCommand** action with its argument set to **WindowUnhide**.

51. Running your system from customised keys

An **Autokeys** macro allows you to customise keys, typically to run frequently used actions.

In Unit 14 we set up macros to open the **Student, Instructor, Lesson Booking Forms** and the **About** message box. Suppose we want to set up hot-keys such as:

- CTRL + S to run **mcrStudentForm**
- CTRL + I to run the **mcrInstructorForm**
- CTRL + L to run the **mcrLessonBookingForm** and
- CTRL + A to run the **mcrAbout**

(Choose your hot-keys carefully as CTRL + A is already used for **Select All** and CTRL + S for **Save**. You may wish to use another combination of keys. The key combination you choose replaces that used by Access.)

a) At the Database Window click on **Macros** and click on **New**.
b) In the **Action** column select **RunMacro**.
c) In the **Macro Name** box at the bottom select **mcrStudentForm**.
d) Click on the **Macro Names** icon or click on **View, Macro Names**.
e) A new column appears headed **Macro Name**. In the first row of this new column enter the key combination ^S (press CTRL + S).
f) Set up the other key combinations as shown below. The macro design window should appear as in Figure 2.5.6.

Figure 2.5.6 ▼

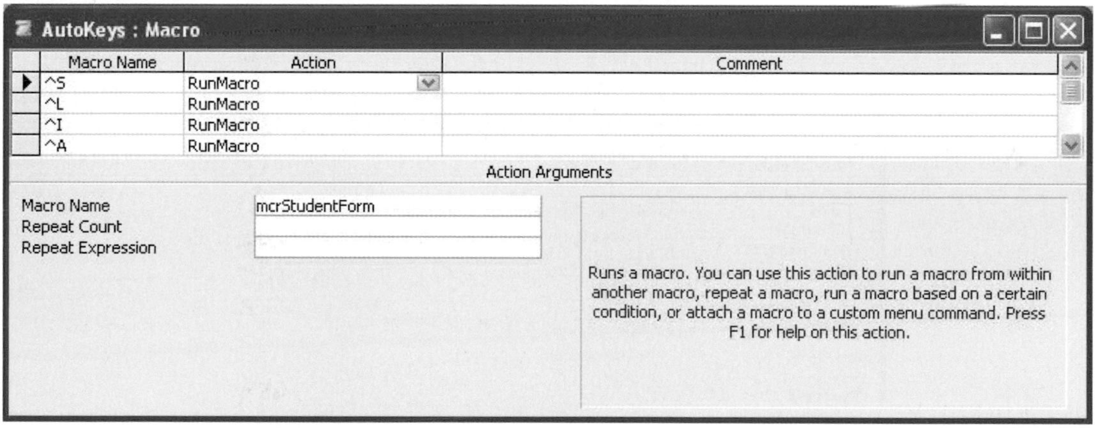

g) Save the macro as **mcrAutokeys**. To run automatically rename as **Autokeys**.

The new keys are in effect as soon as you save the macro and each time you open the database. Search Microsoft Access Help for more on key combinations.

52. Copy (Cut) and Paste macro

A macro can be used to cut or copy a record from one table and paste it into another.

Imagine the scenario in the Driving School system when a driving instructor leaves the school. You don't want to delete the record entirely from the Driving School system but just move it into a table of Ex instructors so that you have a record of their details.

a) Load the **Driving School** database and at the Database Window highlight **tblInstructor** and click on **Copy**.

Figure 2.5.7 ▶

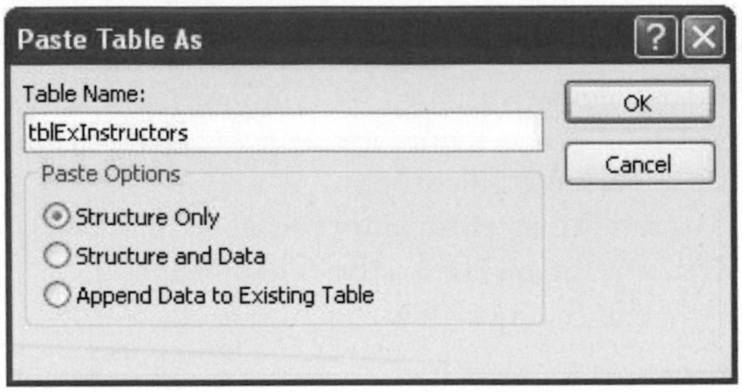

Paste Table As

Table Name:

tblExInstructors

Paste Options
- ⦿ Structure Only
- ◯ Structure and Data
- ◯ Append Data to Existing Table

OK   Cancel

b) Click on **Paste** and in the **Paste Table As** dialogue box name the table **tblExInstructors** and select **Structure Only**. Ensure the InsructorID field has data type **Number**.

c) Create a new macro using the following commands:

Action	**RunCommand**	Command	**Select Record**		
Action	**RunCommand**	Command	**Cut**		
Action	**Close**	Object Type	**Form**	Object Name	**frmInstructor**
Action	**Open Table**	Table Name	**tblExInstructors**		
Action	**RunCommand**	Command	**Paste Append**		
Action	**Close**	Object Type	**Table**	Object Name	**tblExInstructors**
Action	**OpenForm**	Form Name	**Instructor Form**	View	**Form**

Figure 2.5.8 ▶

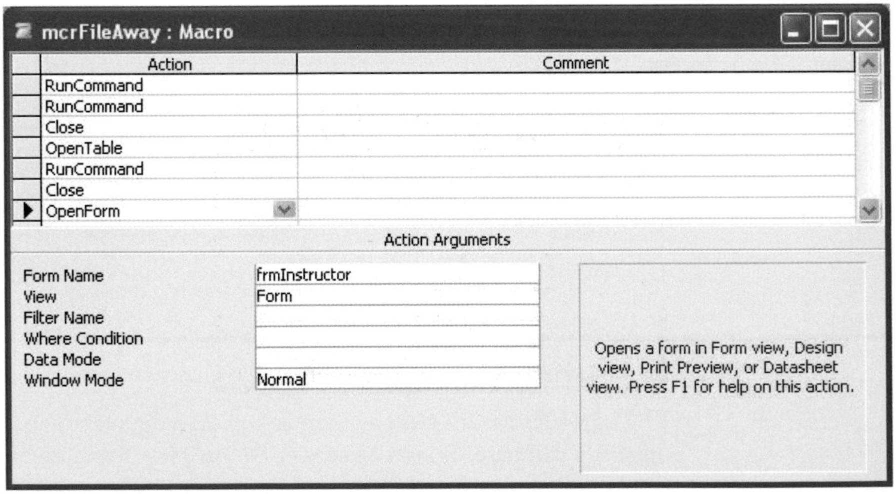

mcrFileAway : Macro

Action	Comment
RunCommand	
RunCommand	
Close	
OpenTable	
RunCommand	
Close	
OpenForm	

Action Arguments

Form Name	frmInstructor
View	Form
Filter Name	
Where Condition	
Data Mode	
Window Mode	Normal

Opens a form in Form view, Design view, Print Preview, or Datasheet view. Press F1 for help on this action.

d) Name the macro **mcrFileAway**. Open **frmInstructor** in Design View and place a command button on the form to run the macro.

e) Open **frmInstructor** in Form View and test the macro. You will need to ensure also that Cascade Delete Related Records is checked between **tblInstructor** and **tblLesson**.

53. Using Conditions in macros

a) In the Database Window select the **Macro** tab and click on **New**.

b) In the Macro window click on **View, Conditions** to insert the **Conditions** column.

It is possible to enter expressions in the **Conditions** column. When the value in the **Conditions** column is true, the action to its right in the **Action** column is performed.

In the example shown in Figure 2.5.9, the macro will look to see if a student's practical test is today's date. If it is it will display a message box reminding them. Open **frmStudent** in the Driving School system in Design View and attach the macro to the **On Current** event of the Form.

Figure 2.5.9 ▼

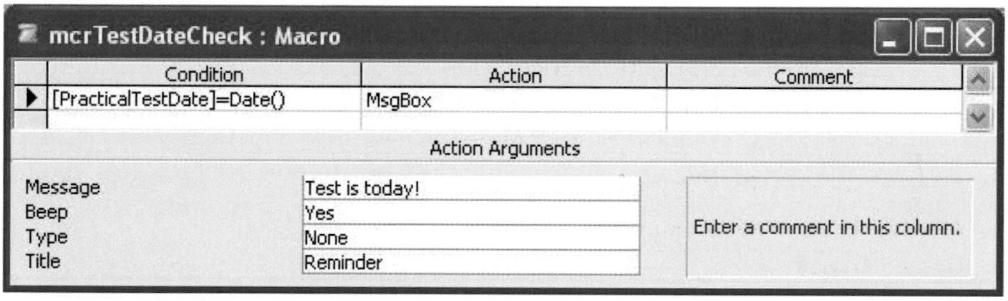

Using conditions in macros is an immensely powerful tool. Use Microsoft Help to explore further possibilities.

54. Using a Conditional macro for cross field validation

A conditional macro can be used to ensure that if Mr is chosen, Male is stored in the Sex field. If Ms, Mrs or Miss is chosen, Female is stored in the Sex field.

Figure 2.5.10 ▶

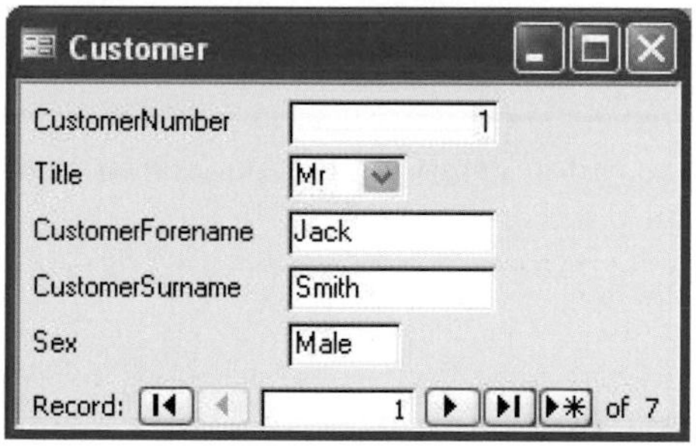

When you run the macro Access evaluates the first condition and if True, uses the **SetValue** Action to set **[Sex]** to **Male**.

Figure 2.5.11 ▶

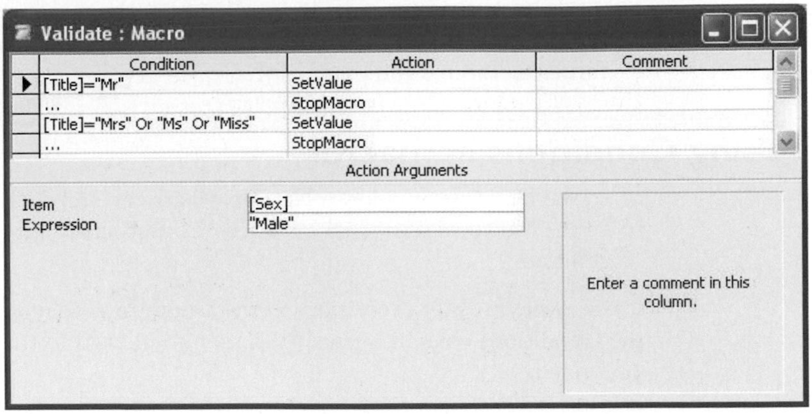

Validate : Macro

Condition	Action	Comment
▶ [Title]="Mr"	SetValue	
...	StopMacro	
[Title]="Mrs" Or "Ms" Or "Miss"	SetValue	
...	StopMacro	

Action Arguments

Item	[Sex]
Expression	"Male"

Enter a comment in this column.

If the condition is False, Access ignores the action and any following actions preceded by an ellipsis. The macro is attached to the **AfterUpdate** property of the field **Title**.

55. Control printing multiple copies from a macro

It is easy to use the wizards to set up a command button to run a report. Using a macro, however, will always give you greater control over how the report prints.

Setting up a macro using the **OpenReport** action allows you to **Print** directly or open the report in **Print Preview** mode. It is sometimes better to offer both options to the user.

Figure 2.5.12 ▼

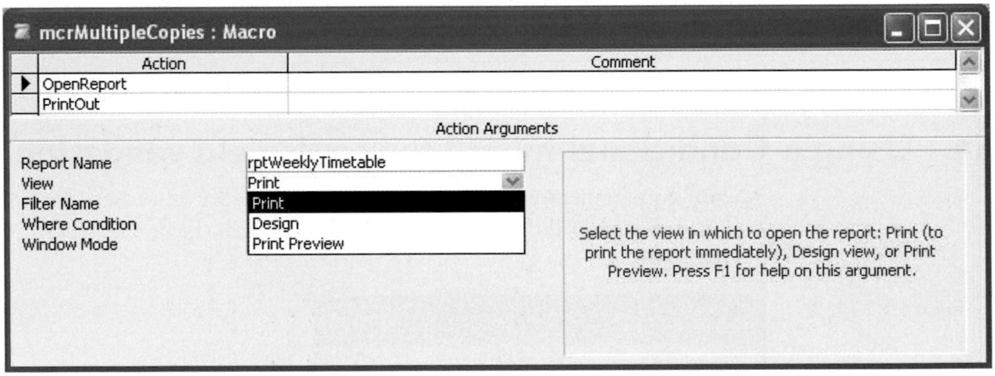

mcrMultipleCopies : Macro

Action	Comment
▶ OpenReport	
PrintOut	

Action Arguments

Report Name	rptWeeklyTimetable
View	Print
Filter Name	Print
Where Condition	Design
Window Mode	Print Preview

Select the view in which to open the report: Print (to print the report immediately), Design view, or Print Preview. Press F1 for help on this argument.

By adding the macro action **PrintOut**, it is possible to control the number of copies and the pages printed.

Others

56. Changing the caption text

The caption appears at the top of the screen. It normally says Microsoft Access.

Figure 2.6.1 ▶

Microsoft Access

| File | Edit | View | Insert | Tools | Window | Help |

You can customise the caption to include your own text by clicking on **Tools, Startup…** and entering the text in the Application Title box.

Figure 2.6.2 ▶

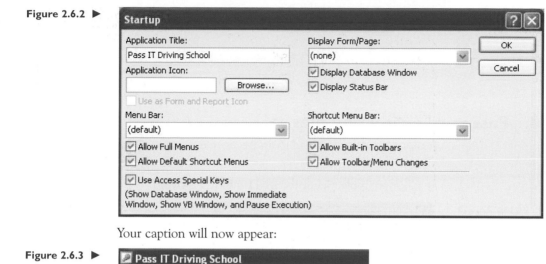

Your caption will now appear:

Figure 2.6.3 ▶

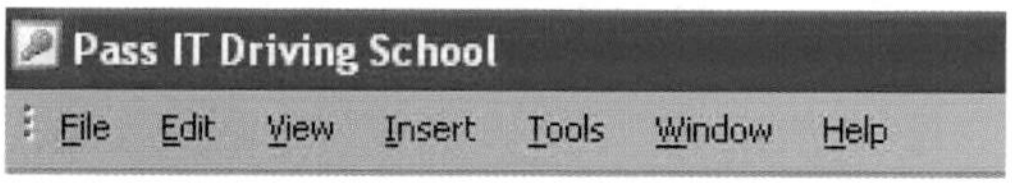

57. Changing the application icon

The Microsoft Access icon is normally displayed in the top left of the Access window as shown below.

Figure 2.6.4 ▶

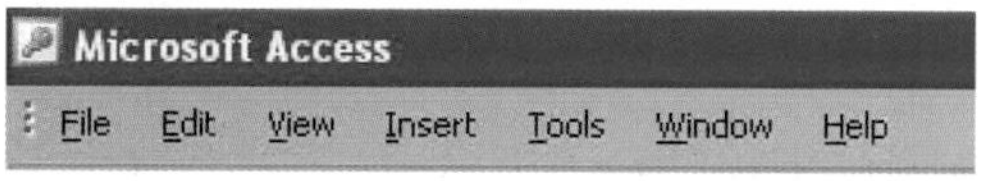

The first stage in replacing this icon is to create your own Icon (*.ico) file.

a) Open **Paint**, and create a new file by clicking **File, New**.
b) Set the attributes of the file by clicking on **Image, Attributes**. Set the **width** to **32 pixels** and the **height** to **32 pixels**, as shown in Figure 2.6.5.

Figure 2.6.5 ▶

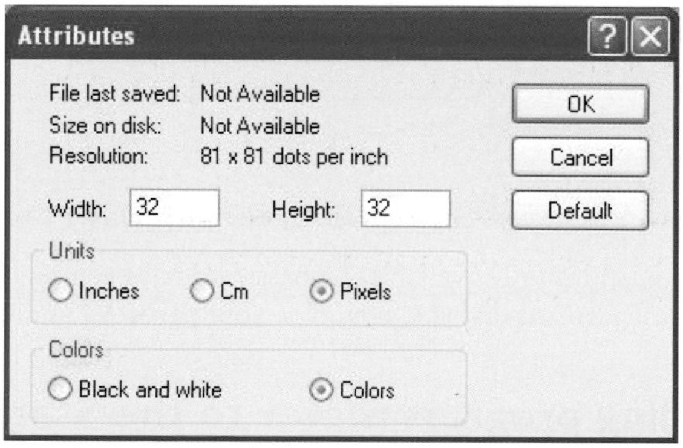

c) You can now create the icon from scratch or cut and paste an image from another source.
d) When you are happy with the picture click on **File, Save As…** and save the file as **logo.ico**, in the same folder as your Access project.

e) To change the logo to your own icon file, go to **Tools, Startup** and click the three dots to the right of 'Application icon:' Find the icon file that you have just created and click **OK**.

f) Click **OK** again and your icon will be displayed instead of the Access logo.

Note It is important that you save the picture as a 256 Color Bitmap, with an 'ico' file extension and that it is in the same directory as your Access file.

58. Password protecting files

It is easy to add a password to an Access file to prevent unauthorised access, but be careful.

a) Click on **Tools, Security, Set Database Password**.

Figure 2.6.6 ▶

b) In the **Password** box, type your password.

c) In the **Verify** box, confirm your password by typing the password again, and then click **OK**.

The password is now set. Passwords are case-sensitive. The next time you open the database, a dialogue box will be displayed requesting the password.

Figure 2.6.7 ▶

Note You won't be able to set a password in Access unless you have opened the database using Open Exclusive. Click on File, Open and choose Open Exclusive.

To remove a password, click on **Tools, Security, Unset Database Password**.

This command is only available if a password has been set. In the **Unset Database Password** dialogue box, type your password and click on **OK**.

59. Adding a loading progress meter to the Status Bar

Figure 2.6.8 ▶

a) At the Database Window click on **Modules** and select **New**.

b) Type in (or copy and paste) this function called **meter**.

```
Function meter()
Dim counter1, counter2
Action = SysCmd(acSysCmdInitMeter, "Loading the Pass IT Driving
School", 1000)
For counter1 = 1 To 1000
For counter2 = 1 To 20000
Next counter2
Action = SysCmd(acSysCmdUpdateMeter, counter1)
Next counter1
Action = SysCmd(acSysCmdSetStatus, "Ready")
End Function
```

Figure 2.6.9 ▼

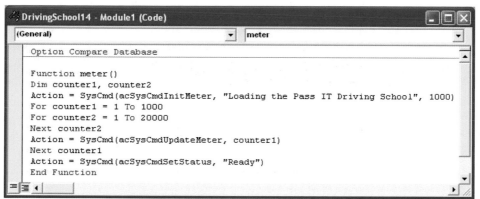

a) Save and close Visual Basic.
b) Set up a new macro. The only command is **Run Code** and the function is **Meter()**.
c) Run the macro when loading the switchboard or attach the command to an AutoExec macro.

Note It is easy to edit the displayed text or timing of the loading bar by editing the above code.

60. Customising information displayed in the Status Bar

If you want to display information in the status bar, then you can use SysCmd to do so:

```
Dim varStatus As Variant
varStatus=SysCmd(acSyscmdSetStatus,"The Pass IT Driving
School")
```

Figure 2.6.10 ▼   Simply attach the code to the **On Load** property of the switchboard.

And you can clear the status bar by using a different Access constant:

```
Dim varStatus As Variant
varStatus=SysCmd(acSyscmdClearStatus)
```

However, there are several problems with using the status bar. The user might have used the Startup Options to turn off the status bar. As Access also uses the status bar to display information, you might find that your text is overwritten.

61. My Access Database is getting very large in size – what do I do?

Figure 2.6.11 ▶

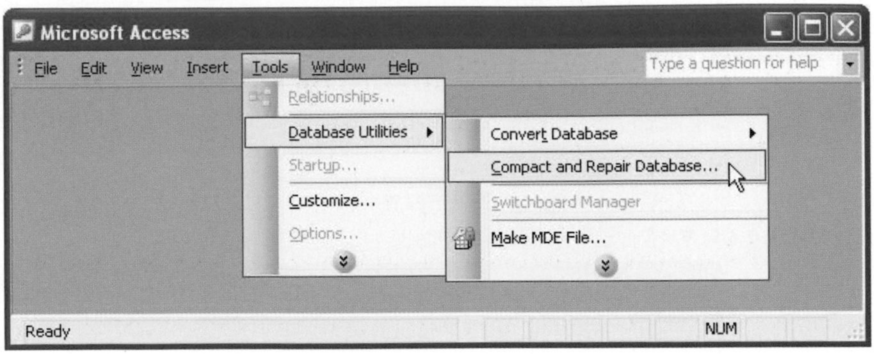

As you work on your database, the file size will get bigger. As you add, edit and delete objects particularly graphics then the file can become fragmented and use disk space inefficiently.

From time to time you should ensure that you run the **Compact and Repair** option. Compacting your database can reduce the size of the file by up to a third.

Open the database you would like to perform the Compact and Repair on and click on **Tools, Database Utilities, Compact and Repair Database**.

62. Setting up a Calendar Control to enter dates

a) Open your form in Design View. From the Toolbox select **More Controls**, **Calendar Control 11.0** (depending on the version of Access you are using).

Figure 2.6.12 ▶

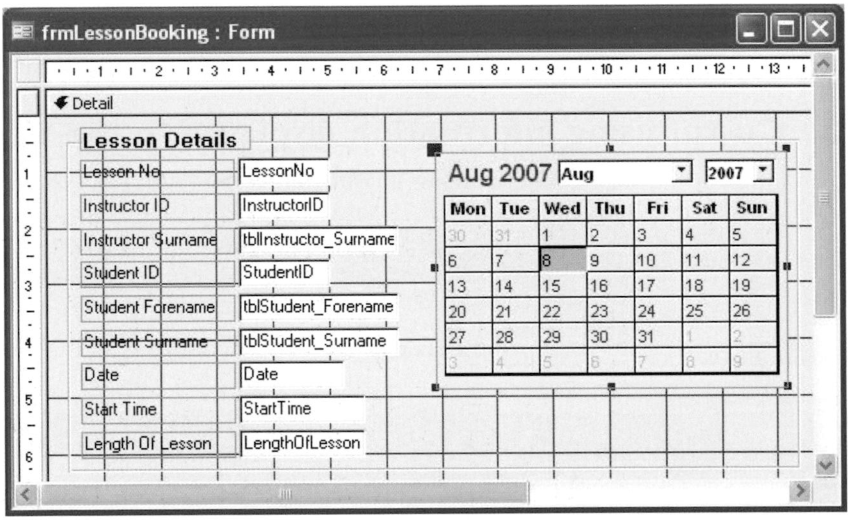

b) Drag out the calendar on the form, select the control and click on **Properties**. Note the name of the calendar control. It will probably be something like **Calendar3**.

c) Select the **On Updated** property and click on the three dots icon. Select **Code Builder**.

d) The Visual Basic editor screen will load. In the top right is a drop-down box labeled **Updated**. Click on it and choose **Click**.

e) Type in **Me.Date = Calendar3.Value**.

Figure 2.6.13 ▼

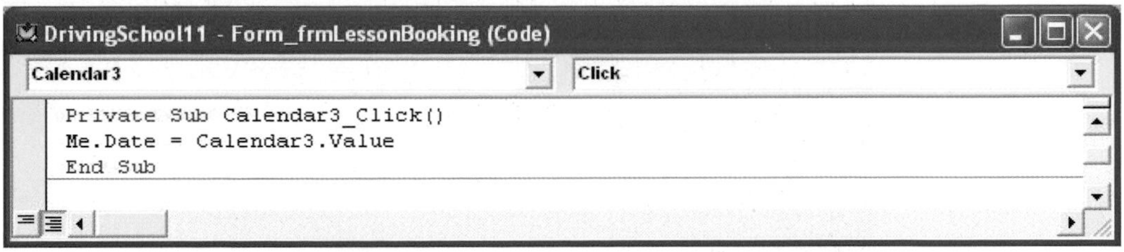

```
DrivingSchool11 - Form_frmLessonBooking (Code)

Calendar3                          ▼   Click                          ▼

    Private Sub Calendar3_Click()
    Me.Date = Calendar3.Value
    End Sub
```

f) Save and close the Visual Basic Editor. Go into Form View and test that when you click on a date, it appears in the Date text box as shown below.

Figure 2.6.14 ▶

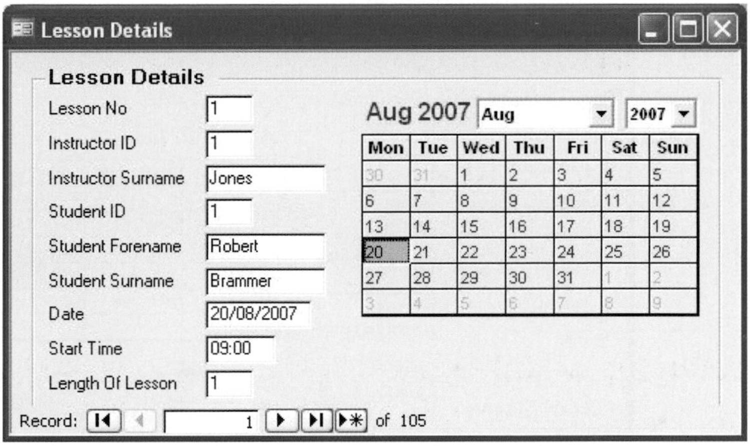

Lesson Details

Lesson No	1
Instructor ID	1
Instructor Surname	Jones
Student ID	1
Student Forename	Robert
Student Surname	Brammer
Date	20/08/2007
Start Time	09:00
Length Of Lesson	1

Aug 2007 Aug ▼ 2007 ▼

Mon	Tue	Wed	Thu	Fri	Sat	Sun
30	31	1	2	3	4	5
6	7	8	9	10	11	12
13	14	15	16	17	18	19
20	21	22	23	24	25	26
27	28	29	30	31	1	2
3	4	5	6	7	8	9

Record: ◀◀ ◀ [1] ▶ ▶◀ ▶* of 105

63. Using a Spinner Control to enter dates/numbers

a) Open your form in Design View and from the Toolbox select **More Controls** and scroll down to choose **Microsoft Forms 2.0 SpinButton**.

b) Drag out the spinner on the form, select the control and click on Properties. Select **On Updated**, click on the three dots icon and choose **Code Builder**.

Figure 2.6.15 ▶

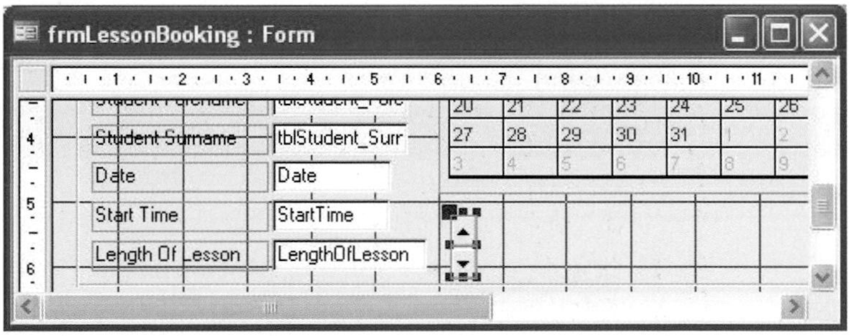

```
frmLessonBooking : Form

  · 1 · 1 · 2 · 1 · 3 · 1 · 4 · 1 · 5 · 1 · 6 · 1 · 7 · 1 · 8 · 1 · 9 · 1 · 10 · 1 · 11 · 1

                                          20   21   22   23   24   25   26
 4   Student Surname    tblStudent_Surr   27   28   29   30   31   1    2
                                          3    4    5    6    7    8    9
     Date               Date
 5   Start Time         StartTime
     Length Of Lesson   LengthOfLesson
 6
```

c) The Visual Basic Editor screen will load. In the top right corner is a drop-down box labelled Updated. Click on it and choose **SpinDown**.

d) The coding for a field called **LengthOfLesson** will be **Me.LengthOfLesson.Value = Me.LengthOfLesson.Value − 1**.

e) Repeat for **SpinUp** as shown below.

Figure 2.6.16 ▶

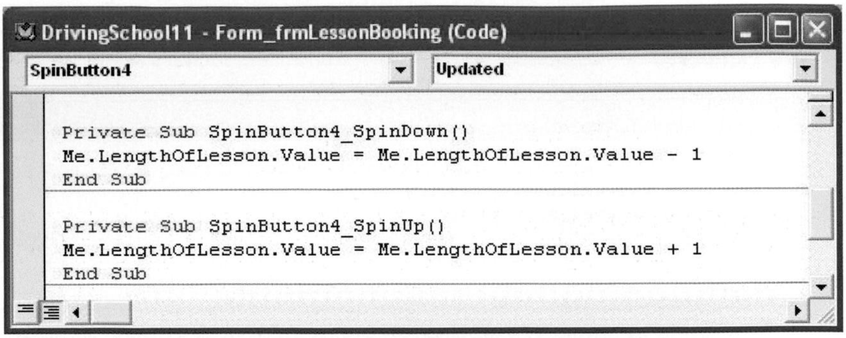

```
DrivingSchool11 - Form_frmLessonBooking (Code)

SpinButton4                          ▼    Updated                ▼

    Private Sub SpinButton4_SpinDown()
    Me.LengthOfLesson.Value = Me.LengthOfLesson.Value - 1
    End Sub

    Private Sub SpinButton4_SpinUp()
    Me.LengthOfLesson.Value = Me.LengthOfLesson.Value + 1
    End Sub
```

f) Save and close the VB Editor. Test your spin control increases or decreases the Length of Lesson.

Figure 2.6.17 ▶

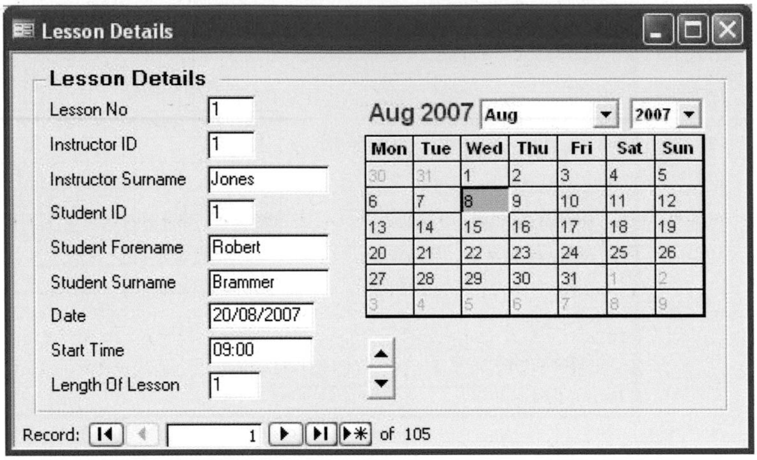

64. Using SetValue to enter dates easily

The SetValue Action can be used in a macro to enter a date easily.

Assuming you have a field called for example **[DateOfLoan]**:

Set up a macro using the Action **SetValue** with **Item** set to **[DateOfLoan]** and **Expression** set to **Date()**.

Figure 2.6.18 ▼

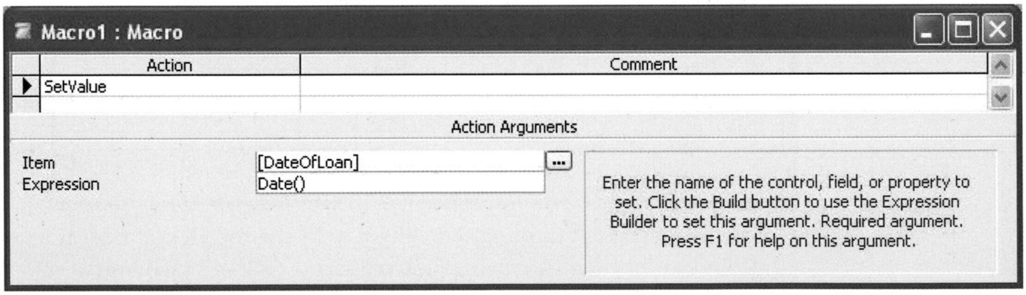

Call the macro **mcrSetDate** and attach to a Command Button.

Another button could be set using Date()+1, Date()+3 etc. for Date of Return.

65. Displaying SubForm Totals on the Main Form

It is not possible in Access to add a control to the main form which directly totals data in a subform. You have to create a control in the subForm which totals the data and then reference the control on the main form.

In the Stationery Store example we added a text box to the Form Footer of the subForm and set its **Control Source** property to **=Sum([Cost])**.

Figure 2.6.19 ▼

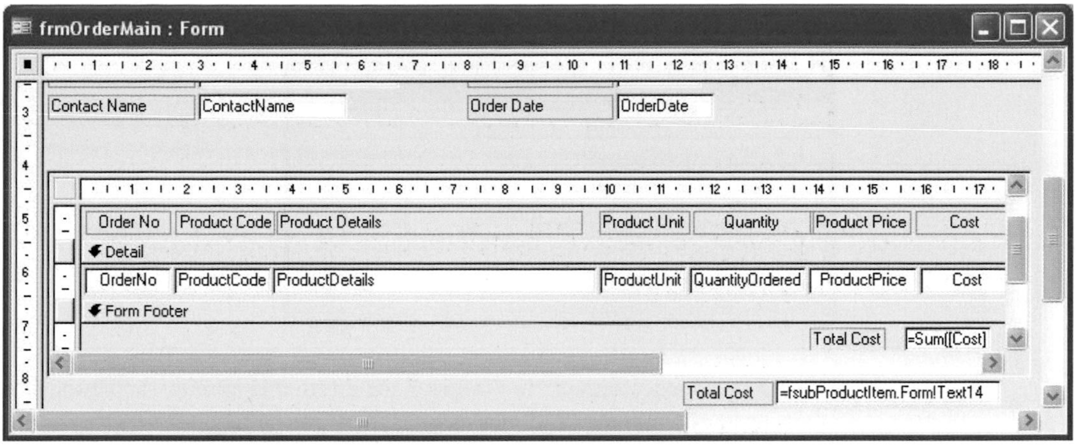

This gives us the Total Cost of the Products. You need to make a note of the **Text Box** name, it will be something like **Text14**.

In the Detail area of the Main Form add a **Text Box** control and set its **Control Source** property to **=fsubProductItem.Form!Text14** where fsubProductItem is the subForm name.

Set the **Format** property to **Currency** and **Text Align** to **Left**. Click on the **Text Box** control in the subForm and set its **Visible** property to **No**.

The finished Main Form will appear as below.

Figure 2.6.20 ▼

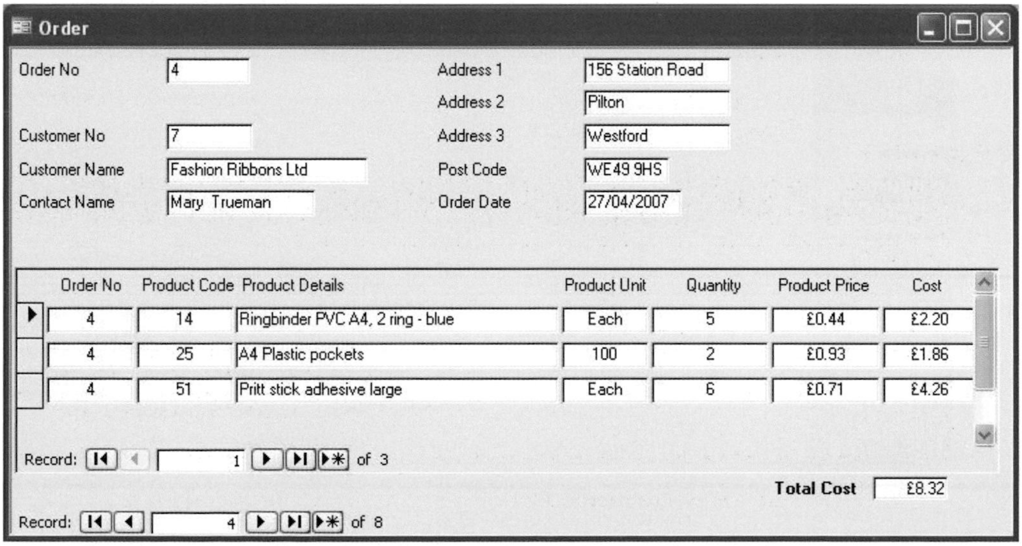

66. Customising a Parameter Query dialogue box

In Unit 7 of the Driving School you set up a number of simple parameter queries including **qrySearchLessonDate**. When you run the query it produces a dialogue box.

You can set up your own dialogue box by designing a blank form and using Form Referencing. Open a **New Form** in **Design View** and add an unbound **Text Box** to receive the date. Note the name of the control; it will be something like Text0.

Figure 2.6.21 ▶

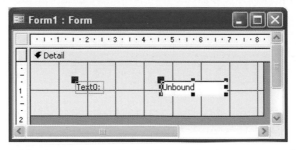

Add a logo, change the background colour, remove the Scroll Bars, Dividing Lines, Record Selector and Navigation Buttons etc and change the **Properties** of the form as required. Save your form as **frmEnterDate**.

Figure 2.6.22 ▶

Form referencing allows you to identify an object on the form in the format **Forms![Form Name]![Name of Field]**. In this case the date will be stored as the value **Forms![frmEnterDate]![Text0]**.

Figure 2.6.23 ▼

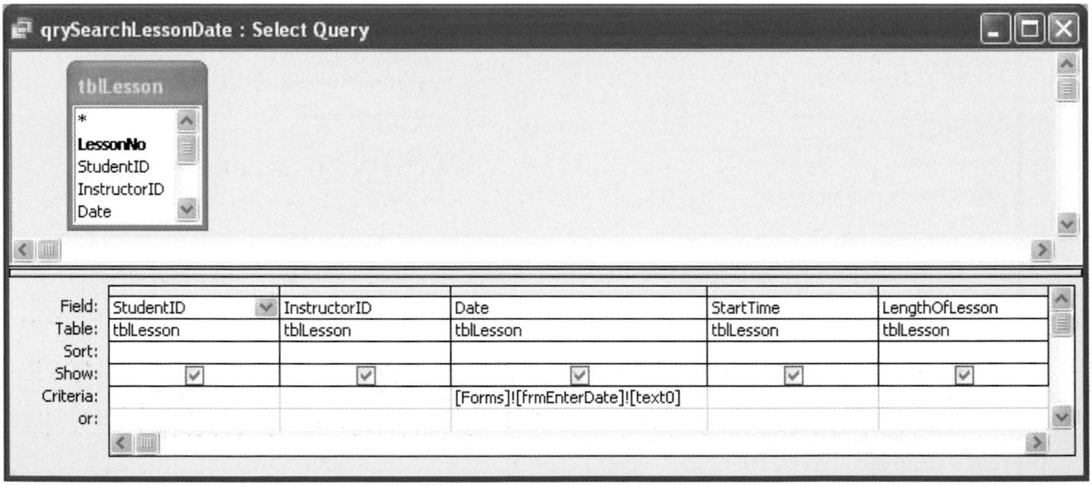

You can now use this expression in the query criteria as shown. You will need to set up a macro to first run the form and then open the query.

67. Printing a report from an Option Group control

On a new form or existing form add an Option Group. Use the Form Wizard to list the reports you want to display as options, as shown below.

Figure 2.6.24 ▶

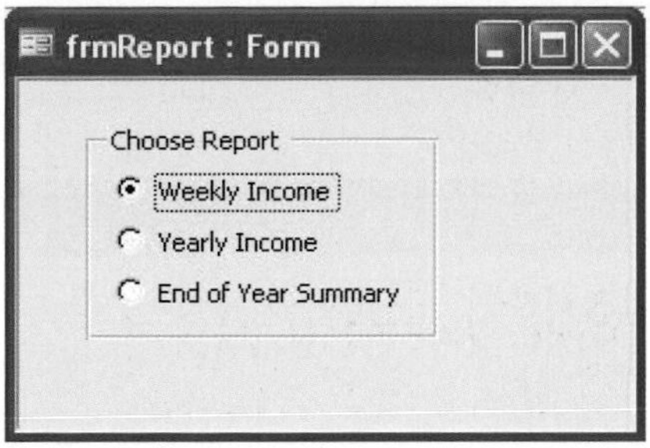

Make a note of the Option Group name. It will be something like **Frame0**. The name of the form in this case is called **frmReport**.

Set up a macro as shown below which references the option chosen on the named form and prints the report selected depending on the condition met.

Figure 2.6.25 ▼

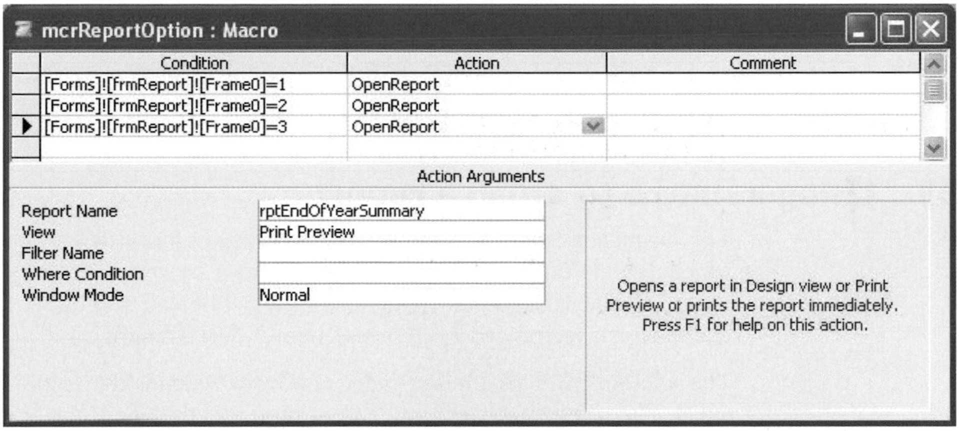

Attach the macro to the After Update property of the OptionGroup control.

68. Printing the current record displayed on a form as a report

Normally in systems there will be a form through which orders, sales, quotes, bookings or appointments are made. The form will be based on a multi-table query.

In the Pass IT Driving School the Lesson Booking Form is based on the **qryLessonCost**. Make a copy of the query and call it **qryLessonConfirmation**.

Figure 2.6.26 ▼

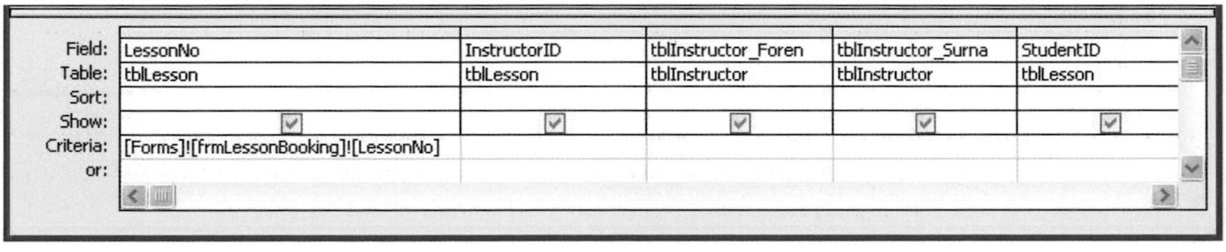

Field:	LessonNo		InstructorID	tblInstructor_Foren	tblInstructor_Surna	StudentID
Table:	tblLesson		tblLesson	tblInstructor	tblInstructor	tblLesson
Sort:						
Show:	☑		☑	☑	☑	☑
Criteria:	[Forms]![frmLessonBooking]![LessonNo]					
or:						

Add the criteria **[Forms]![frmLessonBooking]![LessonNo]** as shown, referencing the control **LessonNo** on **frmLessonBooking**. Base a report on this query and call it **rptBookingConfirmation**.

Use the Form Wizard to add a command button to the Lesson Booking Form to run **rptBookingConfirmation**. Select the **Report Operations** category and the action **Preview Report**.

Figure 2.6.27 ▼

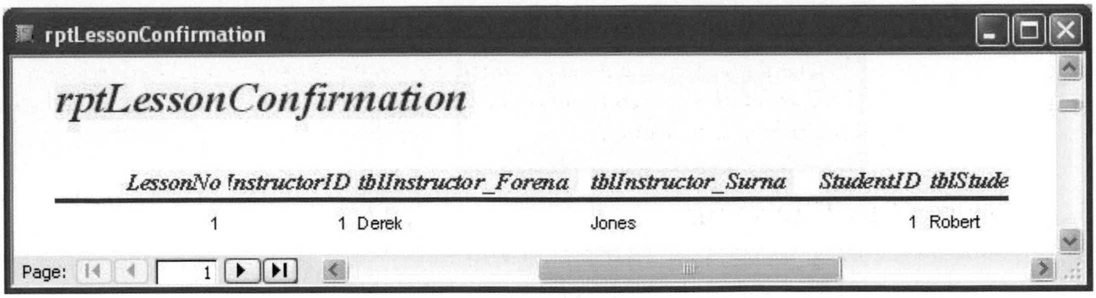

The report will need a lot of customising but will always show the current record displayed on the form.

Note Turning the query into an append and/or delete query enables you to file away the current booking shown on the screen.

69. Using a macro to email a report

This example assumes you are working on an open form such as an order form which displays the email address of the customer to whom you wish to send the order. The email address is contained in the field Email and using form referencing is referenced by: **[Forms]![frmOrder]![Email]**.

The solution contains a report called **rptOrder** which is the report we wish to email. The macro is set up using a Condition and the **SendObject** Action as shown below.

Figure 2.6.28 ▼

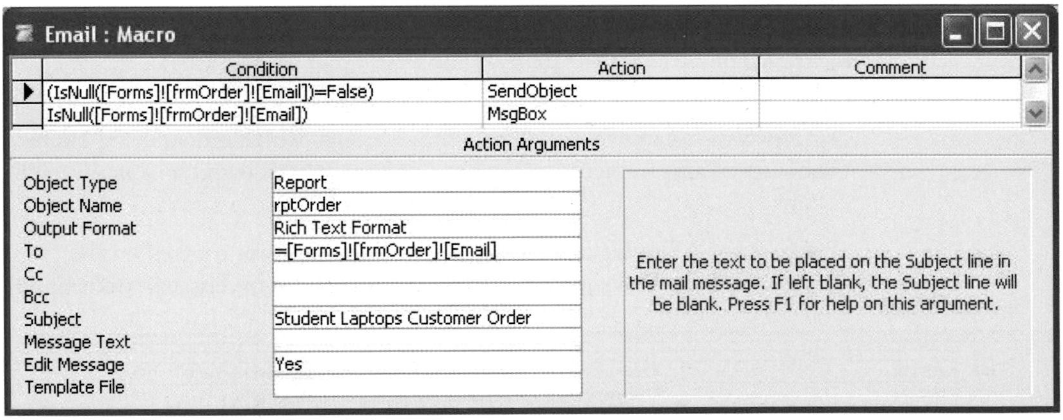

The **IsNull** function is used to check that an email address is displayed on the form and if it is sends the report called **rptOrder** to the email address shown.

If an email address is not present then the **MsgBox** Action is used to display a simple message as shown.

Figure 2.6.29 ▶

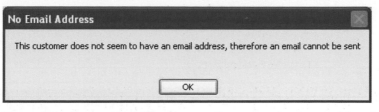

The email is sent in Rich Text Format. So you need to be careful in the design of the order. If you wish to send graphics and retain formatting you will need to send in Snapshot Viewer.

70. Using Tab Controls

You can use a **Tab Control** to present several forms on a single form as shown below. This is useful if you find yourself running out of room on screen.

Figure 2.6.30 ▶

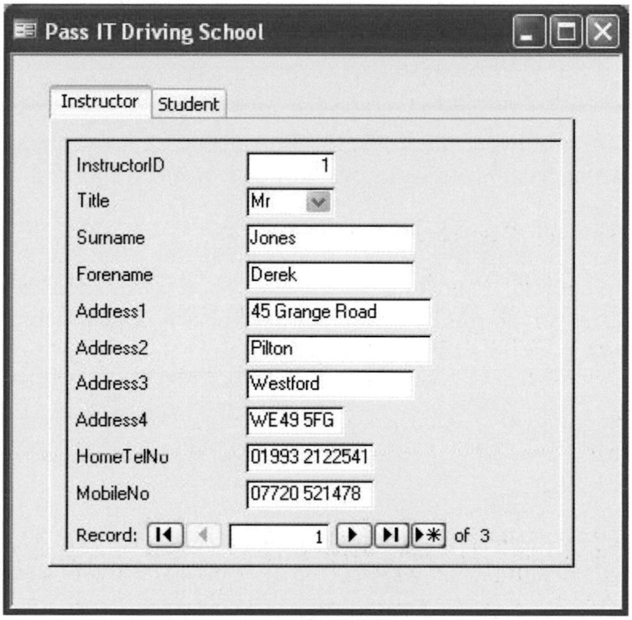

Open a new form in Design View. From the Toolbox choose the Tab Control and drag out a rectangle across the screen.

Double click on the Page Tab to display the properties. You can change the caption, name etc.

A right click on the Page Tab will display further options including deleting and inserting a new page.

There are many ways to build tabbed pages. Starting from scratch you can base the form on a table and from the Field List drag the fields required onto the page.

If your forms are already set up you can press F11 to display the Database Window and drag the form required on to the page as shown on the next page.

Figure 2.6.31 ▼

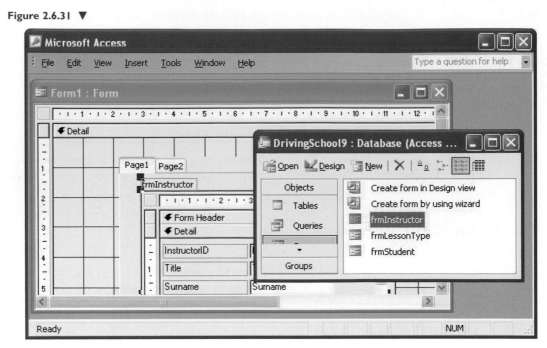

Quite often you will decide to add a tabbed form to an existing form. The existing form has become overcrowded with controls and you are running out of room.

If you are using this method it is vital you don't use drag and drop but use CTRL X to cut and CTRL V to paste the control on to the correctly selected page tab. If you do not do this carefully your controls will appear behind the Tab Control and appear on every page.

3 | Starting points

1: Bouncy Castle Hire

Bounce-a-Lot is a bouncy castle
hire company based in Westford.

The owner Kerry Williams hires
out bouncy castles to companies,
children's birthday parties,
weddings and other large social events.

She currently has ten different bouncy castles available for hire. Details of
castles and costs are shown below. Delivery is free and the castles are erected by
the delivery team. Hires can be from 1 to 14 days.

Castle Code	Castle Type	Size	Cost/Day
BB01	Bouncy Boxing	15'w × 15'd × 9'h	£80.00
BR02	Bungee Run	12'w × 35'd × 12'h	£150.00
CB03	Clown Bouncer	12'w × 15'd × 10'h	£50.00
FB05	Flinstone Bouncer	15'w × 15'd × 9'h	£45.00
FB06	Forest Bouncer	13'w × 16'd × 8'h	£45.00
G07	Gladiators	15'w × 20'd × 9'h	£80.00
GS08	Giant Slide	15'w × 25'd × 35'h	£125.00
JB09	Jungle Bouncer	15'w × 16'd × 10'h	£45.00
KB010	Kangaroo Bouncer	10'w × 12'd × 10'h	£40.00
RB11	Rainbow Bouncer	12'w × 10'd × 12'h	£35.00

Kerry currently keeps her records in a notepad and issues little in the way of
paperwork with each hire. Kerry has found business increasing steadily and feels
the need to computerise her record keeping, to deal with hiring, keeping
timetables and providing professional invoices with each hire.

Setting up the solution

The solution will consist of the three tables as shown: **tblBouncyCastle**, **tblCustomer** and **tblHire**.

The **Bouncy Castle Table** contains the seven fields shown. It includes a Picture of the Castle, a brief Description of the Castle to help the customer and a Status field set to Yes/No which will be used to indicate if the castle is available or not. The castles are coded as above with the Bouncy Castle Code as the key field.

Figure 3.1.1 ▶

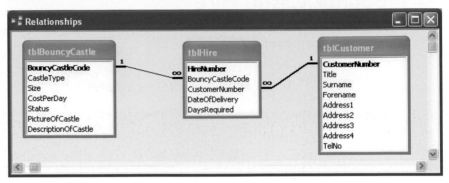

The **Customer Table** contains the usual fields Title, Forename and Surname with Address Lines 1 to 4 and Tel No.

The **Hire Table** contains details of Hire Number, Customer Number and Bouncy Castle Code which will link to the other tables.

The **Hire Table** also contains the fields **DateOfDelivery** and **DaysRequired**.

Task 1 — Setting up the Relationships

1 Load the file **BouncyCastle** from the **Access Support CD-ROM**. The file contains the tables and data already set up. You will need to set up the **Relationships** as shown above.

Task 2 — Setting up the Forms for Customers and Bouncy Castles

1 Use the **Form Wizards** to set up a **Bouncy Castle Form** based on **tblBouncyCastle**. Save the form as **frmBouncyCastle**.

Figure 3.1.2 ▶

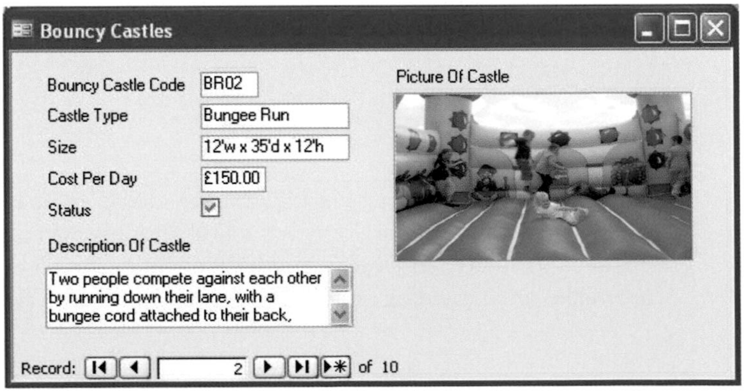

2 Go into its **Form Properties** and remove the **Scroll Bars**, **Record Selectors** and **Dividing Lines** in the usual way. Customise as you wish. Your completed form should appear something like the one shown above.

3 You need also to set up the **Customer Form** based on **tblCustomer**. Save as **frmCustomer**.

Task 3 Setting up the Query on which to base the Hire Form

You now need to design a multi-table query on which to base the **Hire Form**.

1 Set up the **qryHire** as shown below. Select the **HireNumber** and **BouncyCastleCode** from **tblHire** and then from **tblBouncyCastle** the fields **CastleType**, **Size**, **CostPerDay** and **Status**.

Figure 3.1.3 ▼

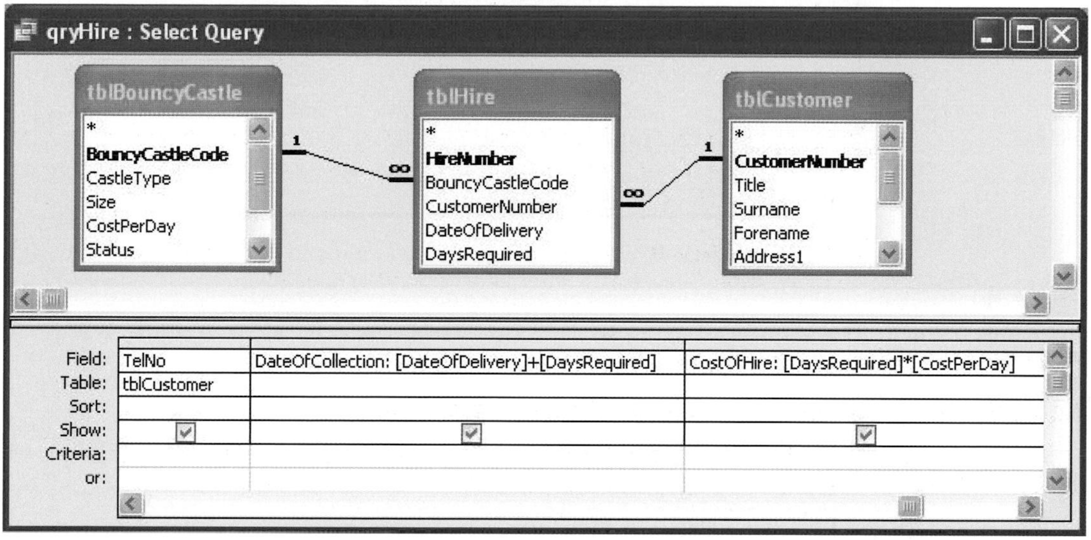

2 Select **DateOfDelivery** and **DaysRequired** from **tblHire**. Select the **CustomerNumber** from **tblHire** and then from **tblCustomer** the fields **Title** to Address4.

3 You will need to add two calculated fields as shown above:
DateOfCollection: [DateOfDelivery] + [DaysRequired]
and
CostOfHire: [DaysRequired]*[CostPerDay].

239

Task 4

Setting up the Hire Form

1 You now need to set up the **Hire Form** based on **qryHire**. Use the Wizard and select all fields. It will look a little untidy, customise as shown. Add the **Bouncy Castle Logo** from the Access Support CD-ROM. Save as **frmHire**.

Figure 3.1.4 ▶

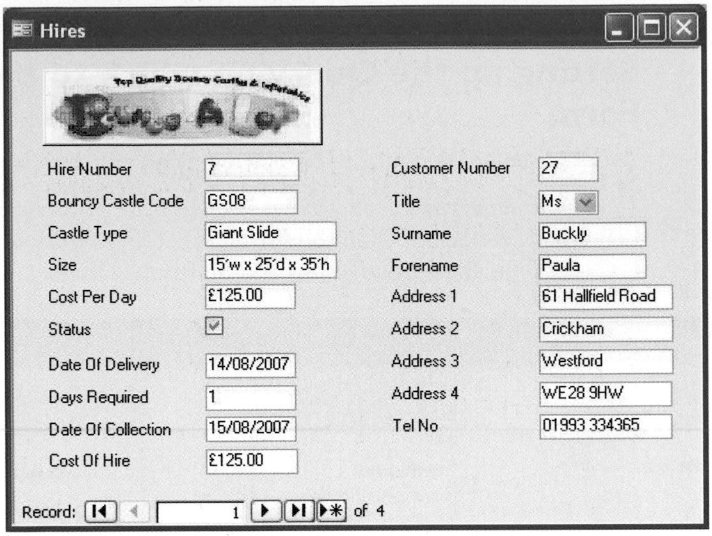

2 Book out castle RB11 to Customer 3 for 3 days and check all the features are working.

The next stage is to make data entry a little easier by adding a combo box to drop down just the castles that are available for hire.

3 Set up a query based on **tblBouncyCastle** using the fields **BouncyCastleCode**, **CastleType** and **Status**. Add the criteria **–1** to the **Status** field. Save as **qryAvailable**. The query is shown below.

Note −1 is the way Access stores "Yes" in a Yes/No field showing whether the Castle is available.

Figure 3.1.5 ▶

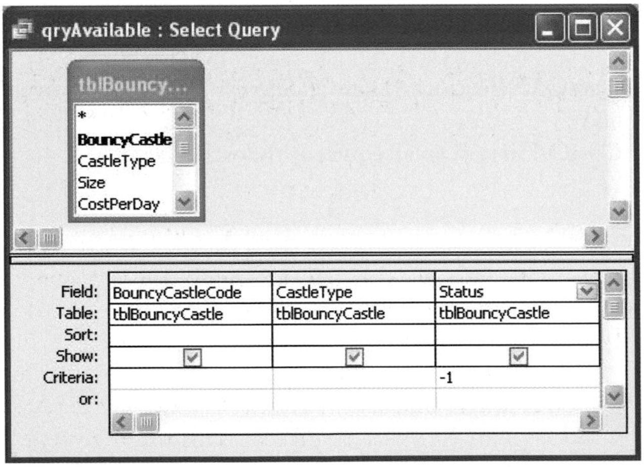

4 Open **frmHire** in Design View and add a combo box based on the **qryAvailable**.

5 Follow the Combo Box Wizard steps choosing to include all three fields in your combo box. Ignore sorting and hide options.

6 Select the key field **BouncyCastleCode** and select the '**Store that value in this field**' option to fill in the **BouncyCastleCode** on your form.

7 In much the same way add another combo box based on **tblCustomer** to drop down the Customer Numbers, Forenames and Surnames.

8 Choose to sort on **Surname** and remember to select the '**Store that value in this field**' option, choosing to fill in the **CustomerNumber** on your form. Your finished form will appear as below. The Confirm Hire option is added in Task 5.

Figure 3.1.6 ▶

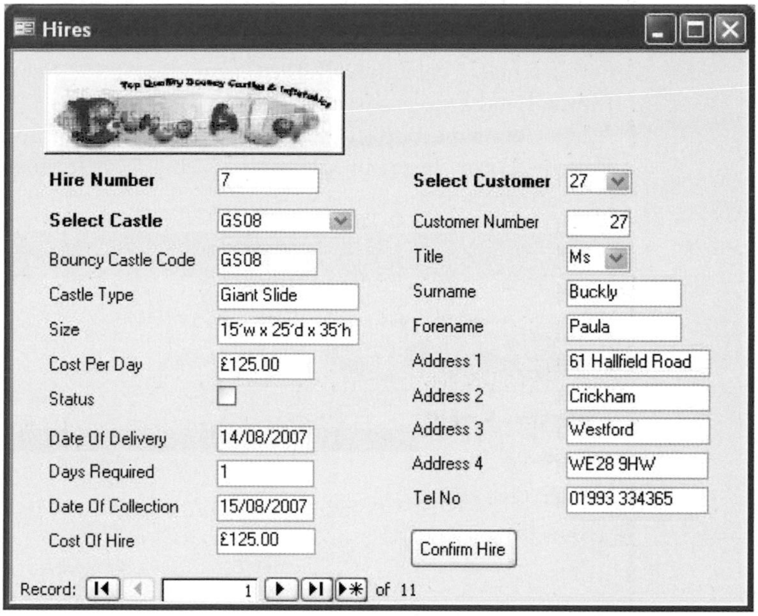

Task 5

Dealing with the Hire Process

The key to this solution is updating the **Status** field to **Out** (unchecked) when a castle is hired and **In** (checked) when the castle is collected and returned.

Figure 3.1.7 ▼

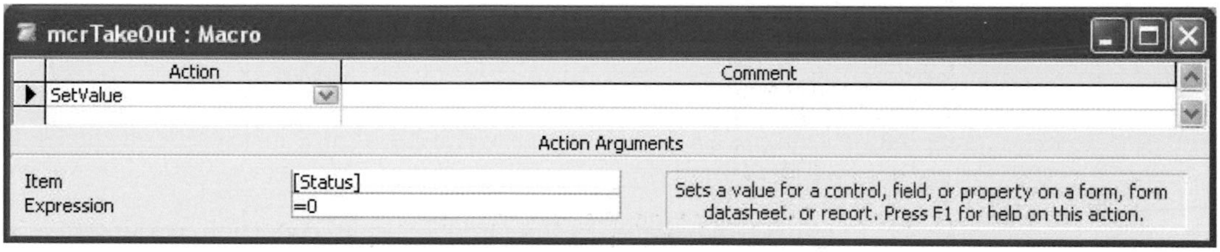

1 Set up a macro called **mcrTakeOut** using the Action **SetValue**. Set **Item** to **[Status]** and **Expression** to **=0**. (See Figure 3.1.7.)

2 Add the Action **GoToRecord** ready for adding a new hire. Add also the Action **Requery** and set the **Control Name** to the name of your combo box, it will be something like **Combo59**. This will refresh and update the records it drops down.

3 Add a Command Button to the Hire Form to run the macro. See Figure 3.1.6 above.

Task 6

Dealing with the Return Process

We now need to set up a form to deal with returns. We want to be able to call up the hire and set the status of the castle back to –1 to show that it has been returned and is available for hire again.

1 To save time make a copy of **qryHire** and call it **qryReturn**. Set up a Returns Form called **frmReturns** based on **qryReturn**.
2 Use the Wizard to add a combo box to **"Find a record on my form based on the value I selected in my combo box"**. Select to drop down the fields **HireNumber**, **CastleCode** and **Surname**. Label the combo box **Select Hire Number** as shown.
3 Set up a macro called **mcrReturn** using the Action **SetValue**. Set **Item** to **[Status]** and **Expression** to **= –1**.
4 Add a Command Button called **Confirm Return** to run the macro from the **Returns Form**. Test your solution by hiring a castle, checking its status and then returning it.

Figure 3.1.8 ▶

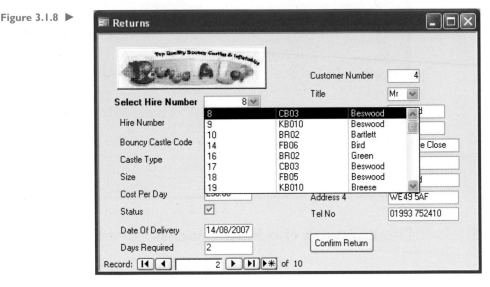

Note There are a number of issues at this point that we leave to the reader to solve. You clearly need to know the Hire Number to enable the return. There are certainly ways we could make that easier.

On the returns form it might be a way forward just to drop down the hires that are out on loan, in the same way that we dropped down the castles available for hire on the hires form.

Clearly the hires will build up over a period of time. A possible key to the solution is to clear hires from the solution on their return in a way that keeps track of active hires and returned hires.

2: Cricket Bat Orders

John Spalton makes handmade cricket bats from the finest English willow. He has worked for Buckston and Spalton in Somerset for 15 years.

Each bat is handmade to the purchaser's precise specification. He makes cricket bats on request by taking orders from local cricketers and cricket clubs.

He produces two styles of bat:

The Excalibur: a shape designed with a deceptively light pick up. This comes in Short or Long Handle and weighs from 2 lb 7oz to 2 lb 10oz.

The Sword: a shape designed for the player who likes a heavier bat. This comes in Short or Long Handle and weighs from 2 lb 11oz to 3 lb 4oz.

In addition a **Bat Cover** can be supplied for £8.99.

Bats can be collected from the workshop or delivered via courier with a **Postage & Packing** charge of £10.00.

John currently stores all information about orders in a handwritten diary and post-it notes on his notice board. He would like to computerise his jobs, sales and orders to improve his record keeping and build up a customer database.

Setting up the solution

The solution will consist of three tables: **tblBat**, **tblCustomer** and **tblOrder**.

The **Bat Table** contains the five fields shown. The data for the bat table is shown also.

Rather than use a number as a key field we have decided to code each type of bat. For example **ELH207** is a **Long Handle, Excalibur** weighing 2 lb 7 oz.

Figure 3.2.1 ▶

	BatStockCode	BatName	HandleSize	Weight	Price
▶ +	ESH207	Excalibur	Short Handle	2lb 7ozs	£90.00
+	ELH207	Excalibur	Long Handle	2lb 7ozs	£95.00
+	ESH208	Excalibur	Short Handle	2lb 8ozs	£100.00
+	ELH208	Excalibur	Long Handle	2lb 8ozs	£105.00
+	SSH211	Sword	Short Handle	2lb 11ozs	£110.00
+	SLH211	Sword	Long Handle	2lb 11ozs	£115.00
+	ESH209	Excalibur	Short Handle	2lb 9ozs	£115.00

tblBat : Table
Record: 1 of 12

The **Customer Table** contains the usual fields **Title**, **Forename** and **Surname** with **Address** lines 1 to 4 and **TelNo**.

The **Order Table** contains the fields **OrderNumber**, **CustomerNumber** and **BatStockCode** which will link to the other tables.

Figure 3.2.2 ▶

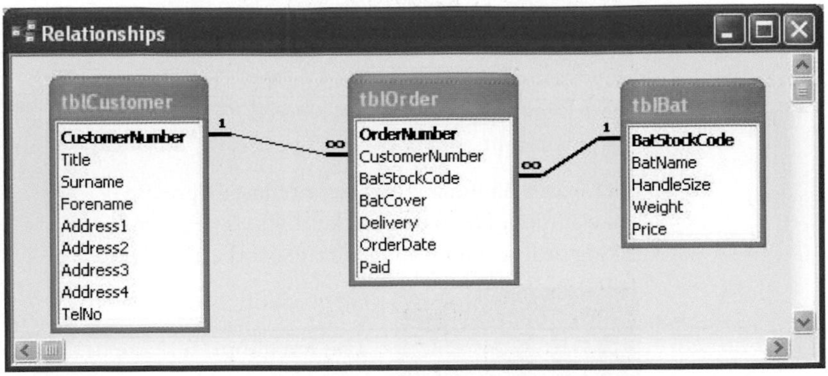

The fields **BatCover** and **Delivery** have been set to **Yes/No** depending on whether they are required or not.

A **Paid** field has been added also as **Yes/No** to determine when payment is made for the bat.

Task 1

Setting up the Relationships

1 Load the file **Bats** from the **Access Support CD-ROM**. The file contains the tables and data already set up. You will need to set up the **Relationships** as shown.

Task 2

Setting up the Customer and Bat Forms

1 Use the **Form Wizard** to set up a **Bat Form** based on **tblBat**. Go into its **Form Properties** and remove the **Scroll Bars**, **Record Selectors** and **Dividing Lines**.
2 You need also to set up the **Customer Form** based on **tblCustomer**. Save your forms as **frmBat** and **frmCustomer**.
3 Customise the forms further by editing and aligning the labels and controls. Your completed forms should appear something like those shown.

Figure 3.2.3 ▶

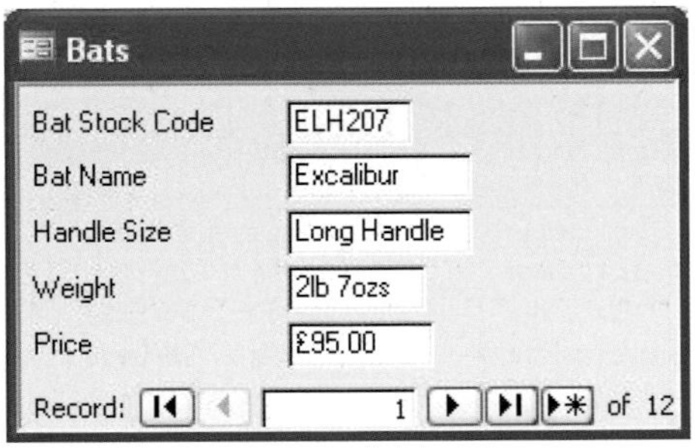

Bats

Bat Stock Code	ELH207
Bat Name	Excalibur
Handle Size	Long Handle
Weight	2lb 7ozs
Price	£95.00

Record: 1 of 12

Figure 3.2.4 ▶

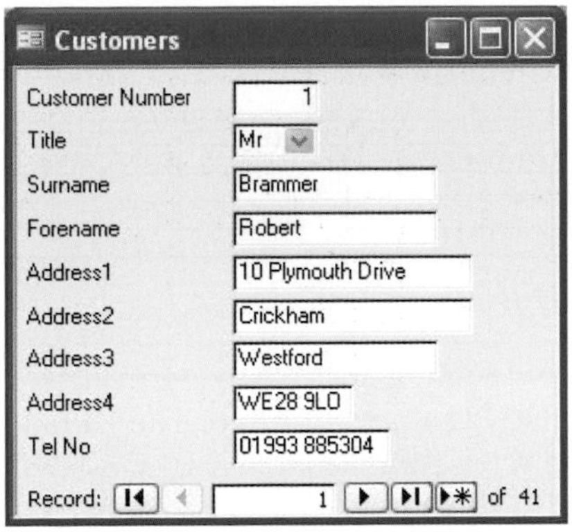

Task 3 — Setting up the Query to develop the Order Form

You now need to design a multi-table query on which to base the **Order Form**. You have seen how queries have been used to make calculations; in this example we are going to use the **IIf** function to make decisions.

1 Set up the query as shown with **OrderNumber** and **CustomerNumber** from **tblOrder**. It is vital you select the fields from the correct table and in the right order.

Figure 3.2.5 ▼

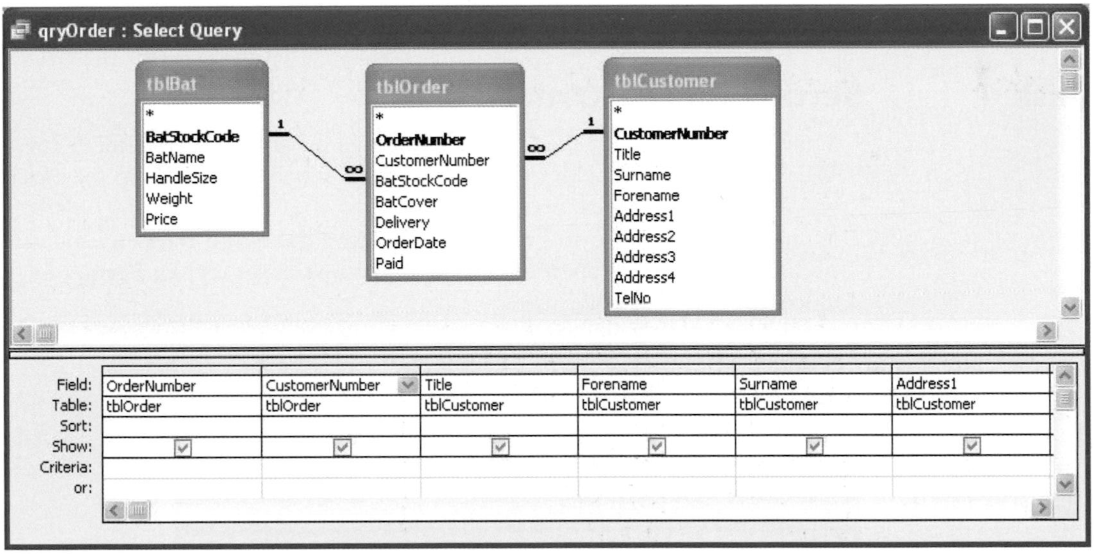

2 From **tblCustomer** add the Fields **Title** to **Address4**. Select **BatStockCode** from **tblOrder** and then all the other fields from **tblBat**. Add all the remaining four fields from **tblOrder.**

3 You will need to insert columns after the field **BatCover** and **Delivery** to add the **IIf** function as shown below.

Figure 3.2.6 ▼

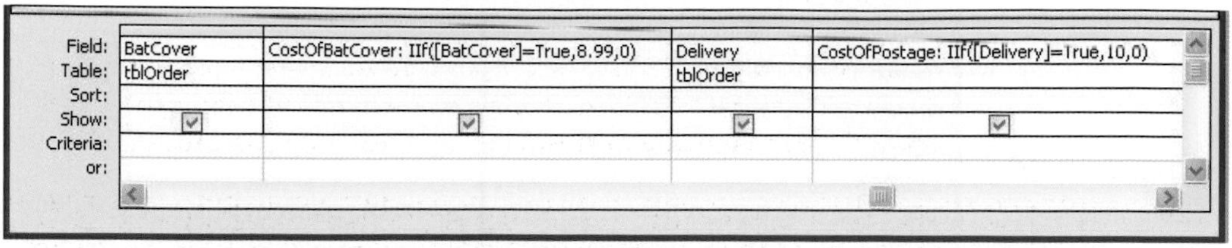

Field:	BatCover	CostOfBatCover: IIf([BatCover]=True,8.99,0)	Delivery	CostOfPostage: IIf([Delivery]=True,10,0)
Table:	tblOrder		tblOrder	
Sort:				
Show:	✓	✓	✓	✓
Criteria:				
or:				

4 The **BatCover** field has been set to **Yes/No**. The **IIf** function will look to see if the **BatCover** field is checked (True) and set **CostOfBatCover** to £8.99 else leave it at £0.00. The function deals with **Delivery** and **CostOfPostage** in the same way as shown below.

Figure 3.2.7 ▼

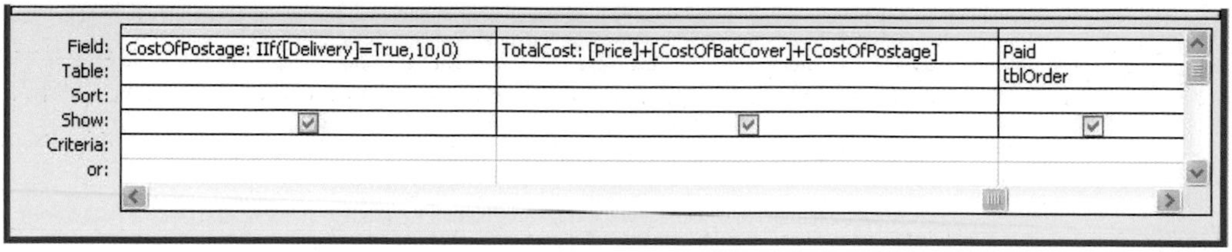

Field:	CostOfPostage: IIf([Delivery]=True,10,0)	TotalCost: [Price]+[CostOfBatCover]+[CostOfPostage]	Paid
Table:			tblOrder
Sort:			
Show:	✓	✓	✓
Criteria:			
or:			

5 Set up the **CostOfBat Cover** and **CostOf Postage** fields as shown above. Add also a calculated field **TotalCost: [Price]+[CostOfBatCover]+[CostOfPostage]**

6 Save the query as **qryOrder**.

Task 4   Setting up the Order Form

1 You now need to set up the **Order Form** based on **qryOrder**. Use the Form Wizard and select all fields from the **qryOrder**. Choose the fields in the order you want them to appear on the form.

2 You will need to use **Form Properties** to remove the **Scroll Bars** etc. You will need to go into the **Properties** of some of the text boxes and set **Format** to **Currency** and **Text Align** as required.

3 Labels and controls will need aligning and resizing to produce the **Order Form** as shown below. Save as **frmOrder**.

4 Enter an order to check it is working, e.g. Customer 2 - Bat ESH207 with all extras chosen. It is not easy to enter data as you need to know the **BatStockCode** and **CustomerNumber**.

Figure 3.2.8 ▶

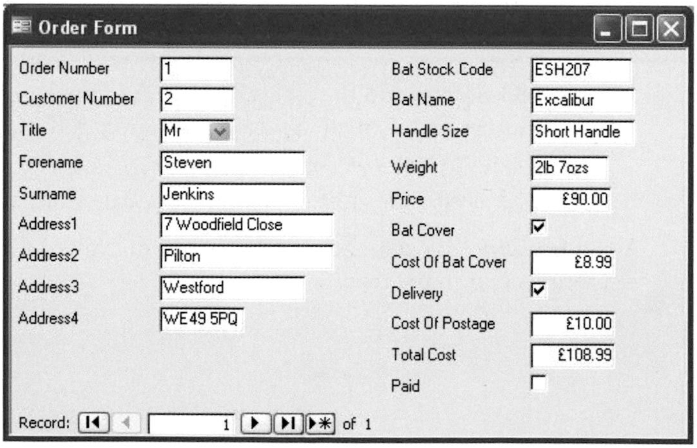

Order Form

Order Number	1	Bat Stock Code	ESH207
Customer Number	2	Bat Name	Excalibur
Title	Mr	Handle Size	Short Handle
Forename	Steven	Weight	2lb 7ozs
Surname	Jenkins	Price	£90.00
Address1	7 Woodfield Close	Bat Cover	✓
Address2	Pilton	Cost Of Bat Cover	£8.99
Address3	Westford	Delivery	✓
Address4	WE49 5PQ	Cost Of Postage	£10.00
		Total Cost	£108.99
		Paid	☐

Record: 1 of 1

Task 5   Making Data Entry easier

1 Set up a simple select query based on **tblBat** using all fields, name it **qryDropDown**.

2 Remove the **BatStockCode** field from **frmOrder** and replace it with a combo box based on **qryDropDown**. Follow the Wizard steps through. Remember to click **"Store that value in this field"** and select the **BatStockCode** field.

Figure 3.2.9 ▼

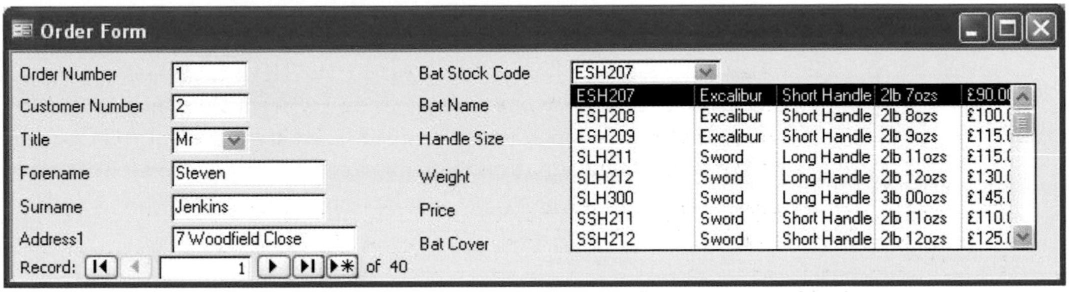

3 In the same way a combo box can be set up to drop down the **Customer** details.

Task 6   Producing the Hard Copy Order

To produce a hard copy order we would normally design a parameter query to ask for the order number and then base a report on that query.

We are going to use a technique called **Form Referencing** which makes the process a little slicker. You can refer to the value of any control on a form using Form Referencing.

For example, the identifier: **Forms![frmOrder]![OrderNumber]** refers to the value of the **OrderNumber** control on the **Form** named **frmOrder**.

1 In the **Database Window** make a copy of **qryOrder** and call it **qryPrintOrder**

Figure 3.2.10 ▼

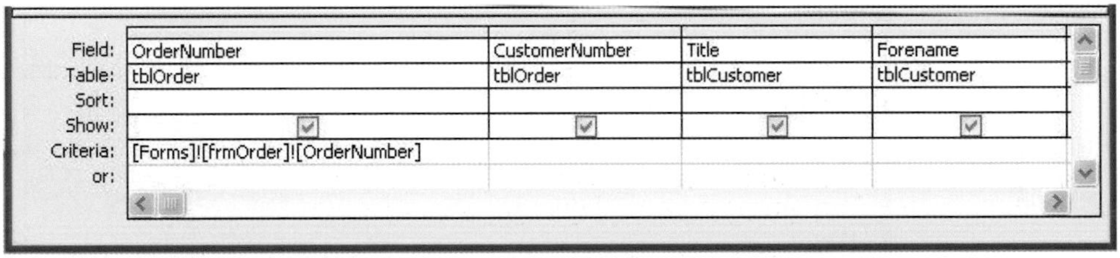

2 Add the form reference as shown above in the **OrderNumber** field: **[Forms]![frmOrder]![OrderNumber]**

3 Now use the **Report Wizard** to set up a **Report** based on **qryPrintOrder**. Select all fields except **Paid** and follow the Wizard default choices.

4 The report will try to run but will only display after this step. Set up a **Command Button** on **frmOrder** to run the Report in Preview Mode.

When **frmOrder** is open, the reference takes the value of the **OrderNumber** and returns that to the report.

Figure 3.2.11 ▼

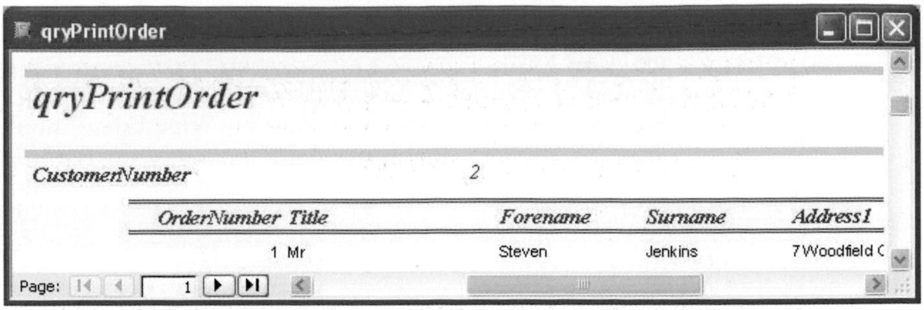

5 The report as ever is untidy and time needs spending tidying it up. Go into Design View and drag and drop the controls and labels needed for the report in to the Detail area. Remove any headers leaving just the Report Header and Footer.

The report will probably spread across 2 or 3 pages; you will need to get everything on to one page and drag the margins in. You will have to delete the lines Access inserts.

Figure 3.2.12 ▼

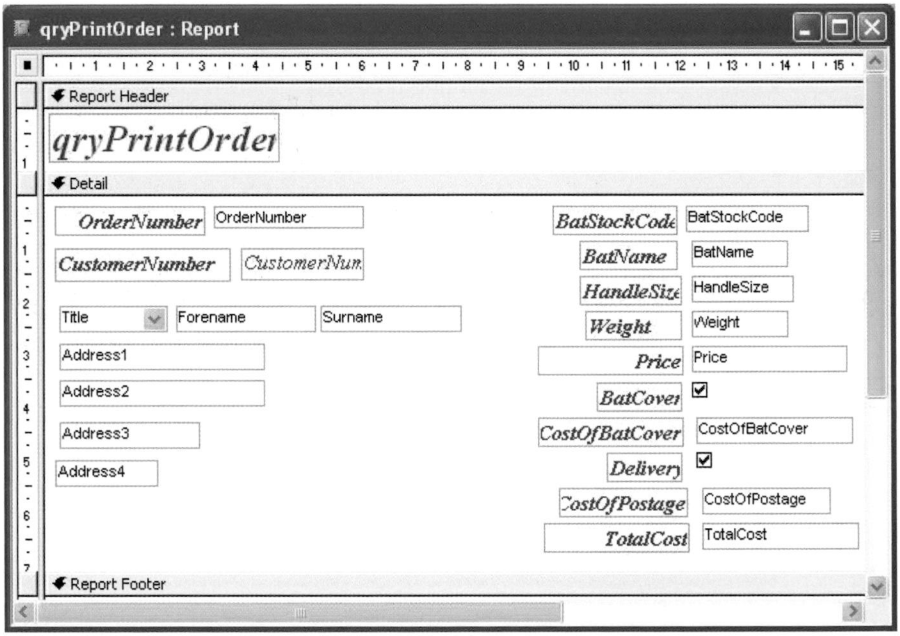

6 Select a suitable font for the Detail area controls and labels. Add the Company details and logo to the Header as required, as shown below.

Figure 3.2.13 ▼

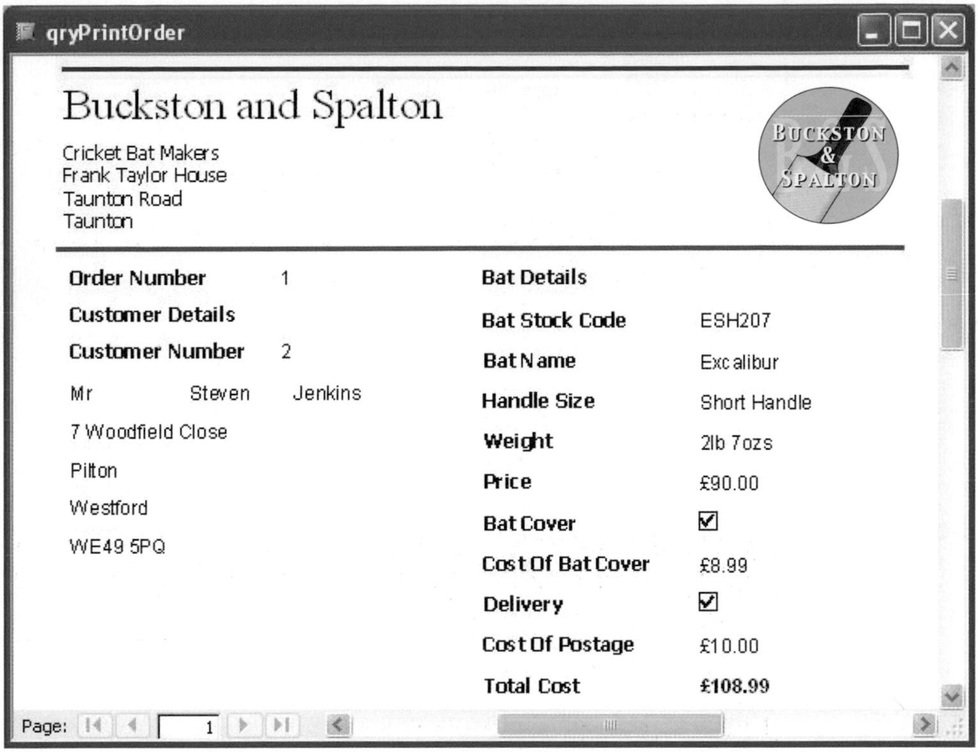

Hint Use Concatenate found in the **Tricks and Tips** No. 42 to further tidy up the layout.

3: The Stationery Store

The Irongate Copy and Stationery Store, situated in the centre of Westford, provides a comprehensive range of stationery, office supplies and computer consumables to local business.

Customers are able to phone orders through to the store and expect free delivery within 24 hours.

At present customers phone up and make an order. The shop assistant writes down the customer and order details in the shop diary.

The store would like to improve their ordering process. They would like an easier and more efficient way to store details of customers and orders.

Setting up the solution

The table for the stationery products is set out as shown. Each product has a product code.

Details of the products are stored along with typical units and the price, e.g. pens come in packs of 10 @ £0.73 per pack.

Figure 3.3.1 ▶

tblProduct : Table

	ProductCode	ProductDetails	ProductUnit	ProductPrice
	24	Buff manilla folders A4	100	£1.81
	25	A4 Plastic pockets	100	£0.93
	26	Budget pencils HB	12	£0.37
	27	Coloured pencils assorted	12	£0.95
	28	Bic Ballpoint pens medium point - black	10	£0.73
	29	Bic Ballpoint pens medium point - blue	10	£0.73
	30	Bic Ballpoint pens medium point - red	10	£0.73
	31	Spirit Jumbo markers - black	Each	£0.62

Record: ◄◄ ◄ 1 ► ►► ►✱ of 95

A **tblOrder** stores details of the OrderNo, CustomerNo and OrderDate. For example Order 4 is for Customer 7.

Figure 3.3.2 ▶

tblOrder : Table

		OrderNo	CustomerNo	OrderDate
	+	2	5	11/04/2007
	+	3	3	12/04/2007
►	+	4	7	27/04/2007
	+	5	8	02/05/2007

Record: ◄◄ ◄ 4 ► ►► ►✱ of 8

Another **tblOrderedProduct** is used to store details of the products attached to each order. For example Order 4 has three products listed

Figure 3.3.3 ▶

OrderNo	ProductCode	QuantityOrdered
3	66	1
3	71	1
4	14	5
4	25	2
4	51	6
5	31	6
5	32	6

Record: ◀◀ ◀ 1 ▶ ▶◀ ▶✱ of 113

Figure 3.3.4 ▼ The relationships are set up as shown below.

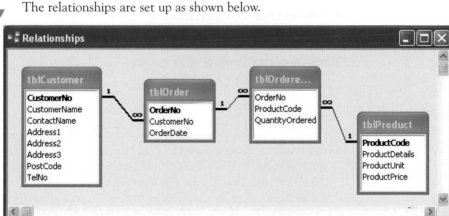

Task 1

Setting up the Relationships, Product and Customer Forms

1 Load the file **StationeryStore** from the **Access Support CD-ROM**. The file contains the tables and data already set up.
2 Set up the **Relationships** as shown previously.
3 Use the Form Wizard to set up a **frmProduct** based on **tblProduct**.

Figure 3.3.5 ▶

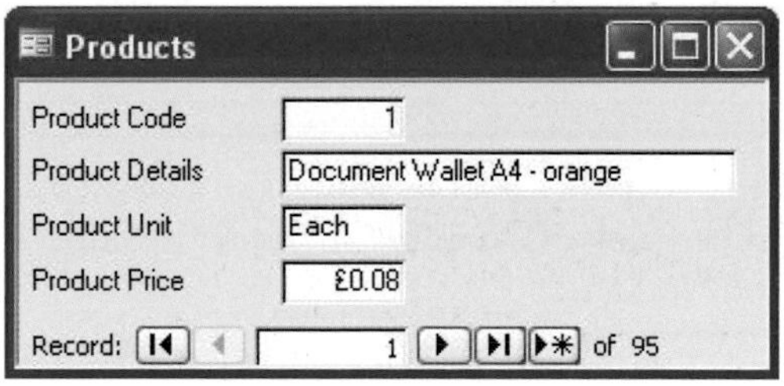

Products

Product Code	1
Product Details	Document Wallet A4 - orange
Product Unit	Each
Product Price	£0.08

Record: ◀◀ ◀ 1 ▶ ▶◀ ▶✱ of 95

4 In Design View use Form Properties to remove the **Scroll Bars, Dividing Line** and **Record Selector.**
5 Edit the Labels and resize the Controls as shown above. Change the **Caption** to **Products**.

6 You need also to set up **frmCustomer** based on the **tblCustomer**. Your completed form should appear something like the one shown below.

Figure 3.3.6 ▶

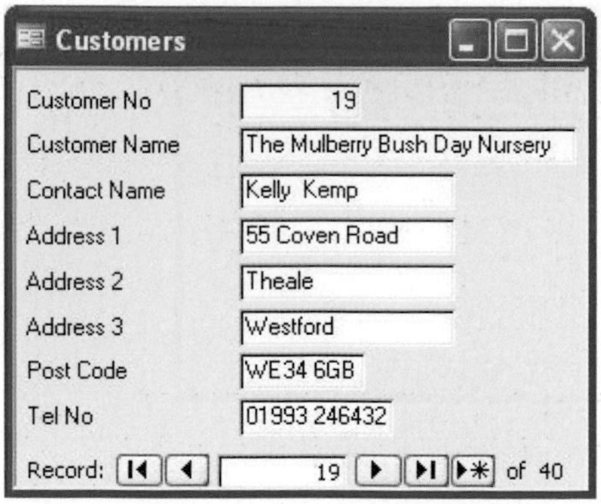

```
Customers                        [_][□][X]

Customer No          |        19        |
Customer Name        |The Mulberry Bush Day Nursery|
Contact Name         |Kelly  Kemp       |
Address 1            |55 Coven Road     |
Address 2            |Theale            |
Address 3            |Westford          |
Post Code            |WE34 6GB          |
Tel No               |01993 246432      |

Record: [I◀][◀]        19   [▶][▶I][▶*] of 40
```

Task 2   Setting up the SubForm

To set up the **frmOrder** we need to use a Main Form/SubForm approach.

The Main Form will be based on **tblCustomer** and **tblOrder**. The SubForm will display the products ordered with each order.

1 To set up the SubForm, design a query using the tables **tblOrderedProduct** and **tblProduct**. Select the fields **OrderNo, ProductCode** and **QuantityOrdered** from the **tblOrderedProduct**. Select all the fields from **tblProduct** except **ProductCode**. Arrange as shown below.

Figure 3.3.7 ▼

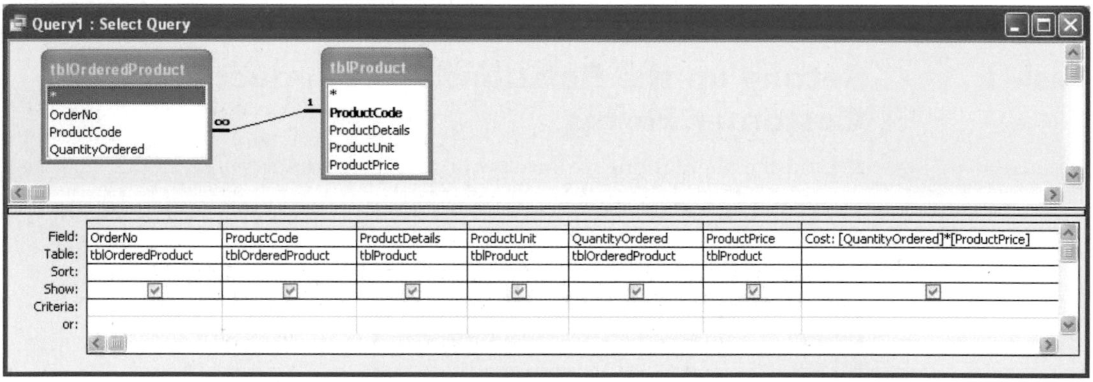

Field:	OrderNo	ProductCode	ProductDetails	ProductUnit	QuantityOrdered	ProductPrice	Cost: [QuantityOrdered]*[ProductPrice]
Table:	tblOrderedProduct	tblOrderedProduct	tblProduct	tblProduct	tblOrderedProduct	tblProduct	
Sort:							
Show:	☑	☑	☑	☑	☑	☑	☑
Criteria:							
or:							

2 We need to calculate the cost of each product ordered so add a calculated field to the query: **Cost: [QuantityOrdered]*[ProductPrice]** Save the query as **qryOrderedProduct**.

Task 3   Setting up the Main Form

1 Use the Form Wizard to set up a form based on **tblOrder**. Select the fields **OrderNo** and **CustomerNo**. Switch to **tblCustomer** and select all fields except **TelNo** and **CustomerNo**. Then select the **OrderDate** field from the **tblOrder**.

2 Do not click Next but from the drop-down select the **qryOrderedProduct**, select all fields and then click on **Next**.

3 Access detects this is a Form with subForm(s), click **Next**. Select **Tabular** and **Standard** from the dialogue boxes and name the forms **frmOrderMain** and **fsubProductItem**. Your completed Order Form should appear as below.

Figure 3.3.8 ▶

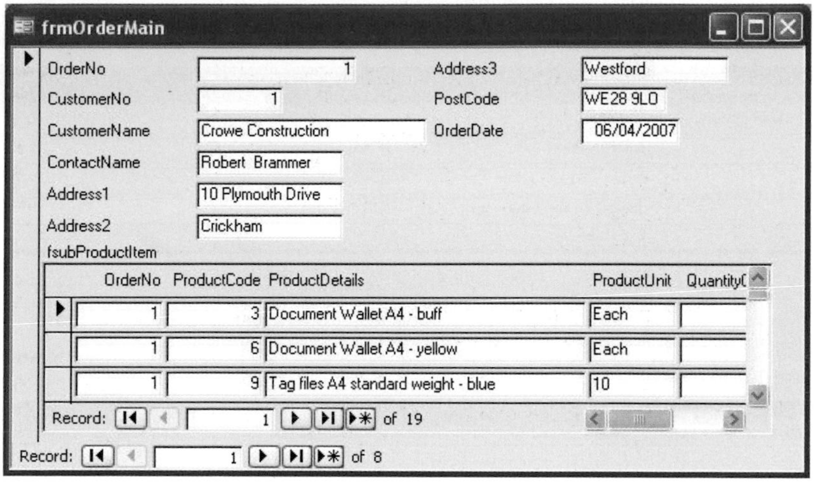

4 Test the solution by setting up an order. You do not have to enter the OrderNo in the SubForm. Access will do that for you after you have entered a ProductCode.

Note You do not need to display the OrderNo in the SubForm. It has been left in to show the relationships.

Task 4a

Tidying up the Main Order form

You will notice immediately that the Main Form and SubForm need tidying up.

1 Drop into Design View, go into **Form Properties** and remove the **Scroll Bars**, **Record Selectors** and **Dividing Lines**. Change the **Caption** to **Order**.
2 Move the controls so that the address is grouped together on the right. Edit the Control Labels with spaces as shown.
3 Some controls will need resizing and aligning e.g. Order No and Customer No.

Figure 3.3.9 ▶

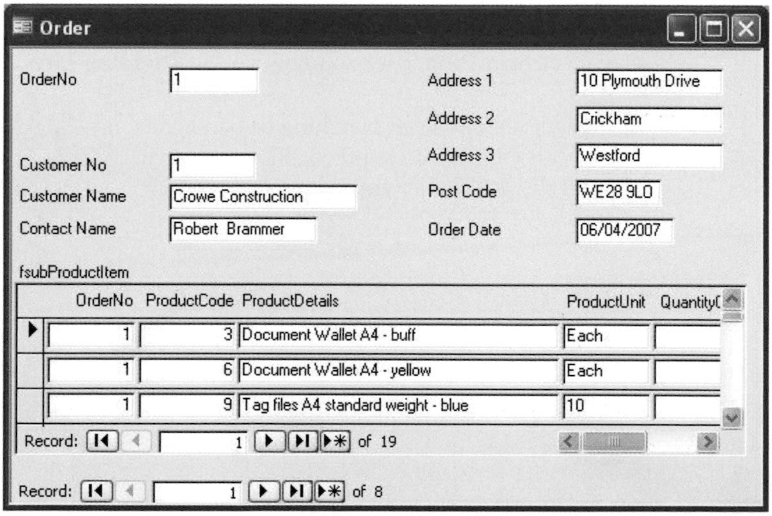

Task 4b   Tidying up the Order SubForm

1   Open the SubForm from the Database Window as shown. A number of controls need to be centre aligned, resized and positioned under their heading labels.

Figure 3.3.10 ▼

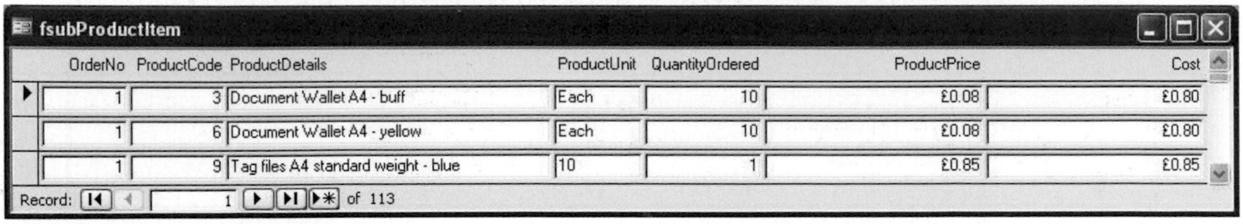

fsubProductItem							
OrderNo	ProductCode	ProductDetails	ProductUnit	QuantityOrdered		ProductPrice	Cost
1	3	Document Wallet A4 - buff	Each	10		£0.08	£0.80
1	6	Document Wallet A4 - yellow	Each	10		£0.08	£0.80
1	9	Tag files A4 standard weight - blue	10	1		£0.85	£0.85

Record: 1 of 113

2   Go into Design View as shown below. Some of the controls in the Detail area need centre aligning. The **Cost** and **ProductPrice** controls need resizing.

Figure 3.3.11 ▼

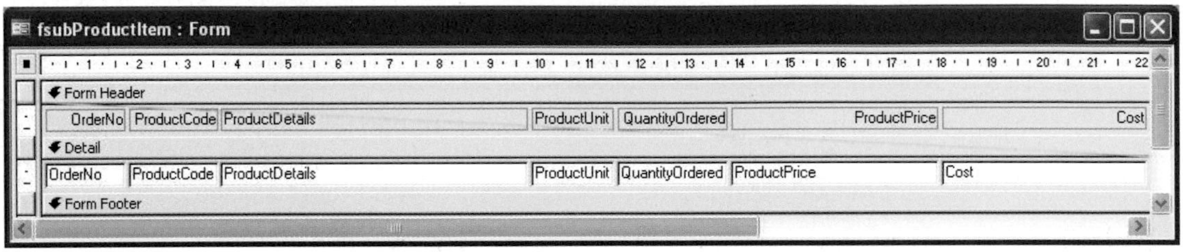

fsubProductItem : Form
✦ Form Header
OrderNo ProductCode ProductDetails   ProductUnit QuantityOrdered   ProductPrice   Cost
✦ Detail
OrderNo ProductCode ProductDetails   ProductUnit QuantityOrdered ProductPrice   Cost
✦ Form Footer

3   Edit the **Labels** in the **Form Header** and align and position above the **Detail** controls.

Figure 3.3.12 ▼

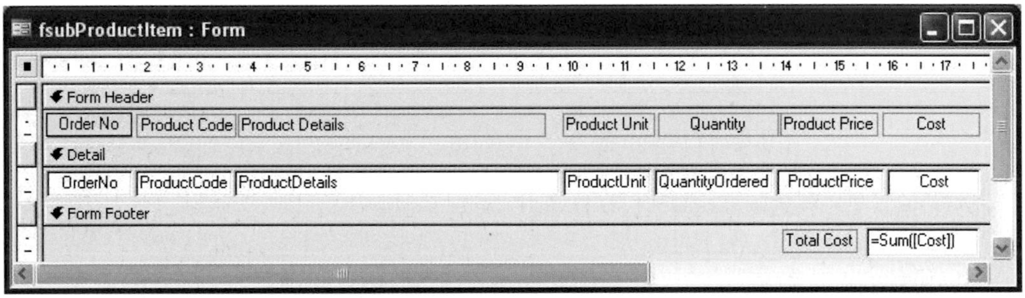

fsubProductItem : Form
✦ Form Header
Order No Product Code Product Details   Product Unit Quantity Product Price Cost
✦ Detail
OrderNo ProductCode ProductDetails   ProductUnit QuantityOrdered ProductPrice Cost
✦ Form Footer
Total Cost =Sum([Cost])

4   Select **Form Properties** and remove the **Dividing Line** and **Horizontal Scroll Bar**.

5   You will need to keep switching to Form View and back to the Main Form to see how it looks. Widen the subForm to show all the controls. Drag down the Form Footer about 1 cm.

6 We need to add a calculated field to the Form Footer area of the subForm. Add a **Text Box** and enter the formula **=Sum([Cost])** This will also need aligning and formatting to **Currency**. The finished form appears below.

Figure 3.3.13 ▼

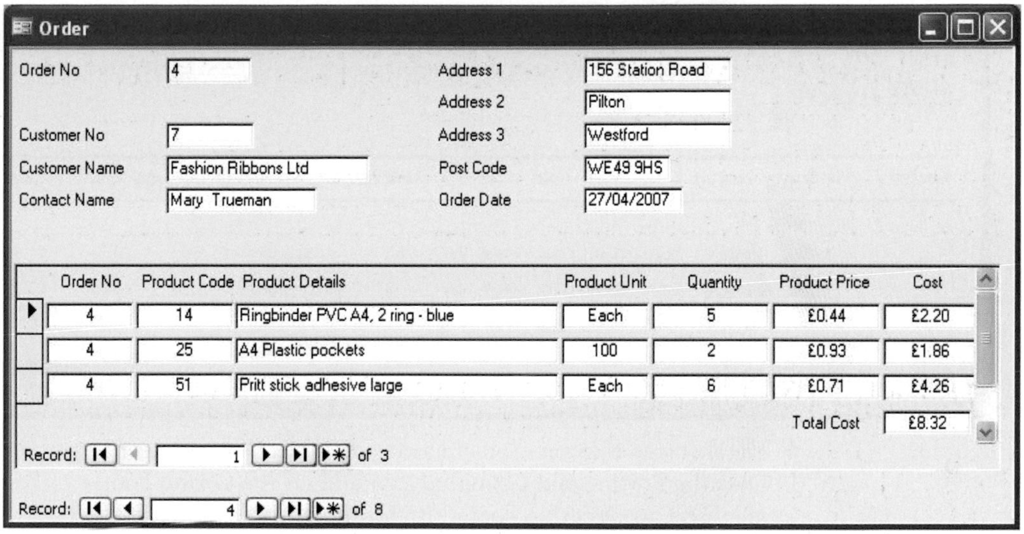

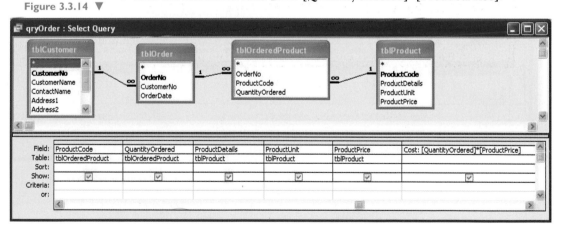

Task 5

Producing and Printing the Order

Presenting the final order takes a lot of patience! Set up a multi-table query using all the tables.

1 Select the **OrderNo, CustomerNo** and **OrderDate** from the **tblOrder** and the Customer details(not CustomerNo and TelNo) from the **tblCustomer**.
2 Select the fields **ProductCode** and **QuantityOrdered** from the **tblOrderedProduct** and the remaining fields in the **tblProduct**.
3 Add the calculated field **Cost: [QuantityOrdered]*[ProductPrice].**

Figure 3.3.14 ▼

4 Save the query as **qryOrder.** Use the **Report Wizard** to set up a report based on this query.

5 Select all fields. Group by **OrderNo** (not **CustomerNo**) and select a **Stepped, Corporate** layout. Save the report as **rptOrder**. The report will print all the orders in the format shown below.

Figure 3.3.15 ▼

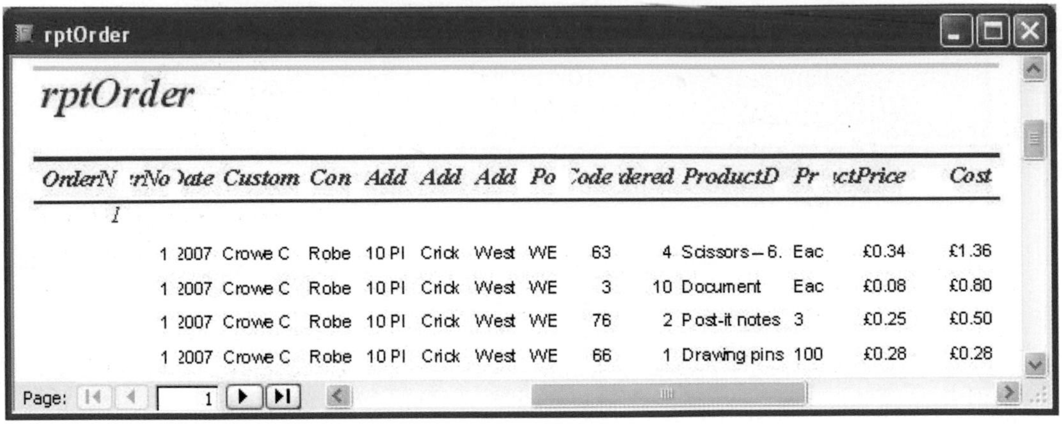

6 The first step is to get each order on a new page. Drop into Design View. Click the **Sorting and Grouping** icon and set the **Group Footer** to **Yes**. This will insert an **OrderNo Footer**. Right Click in the **Footer** and select **Properties**. Set **Force New Page** to **After Section**.

Figure 3.3.16 ▼

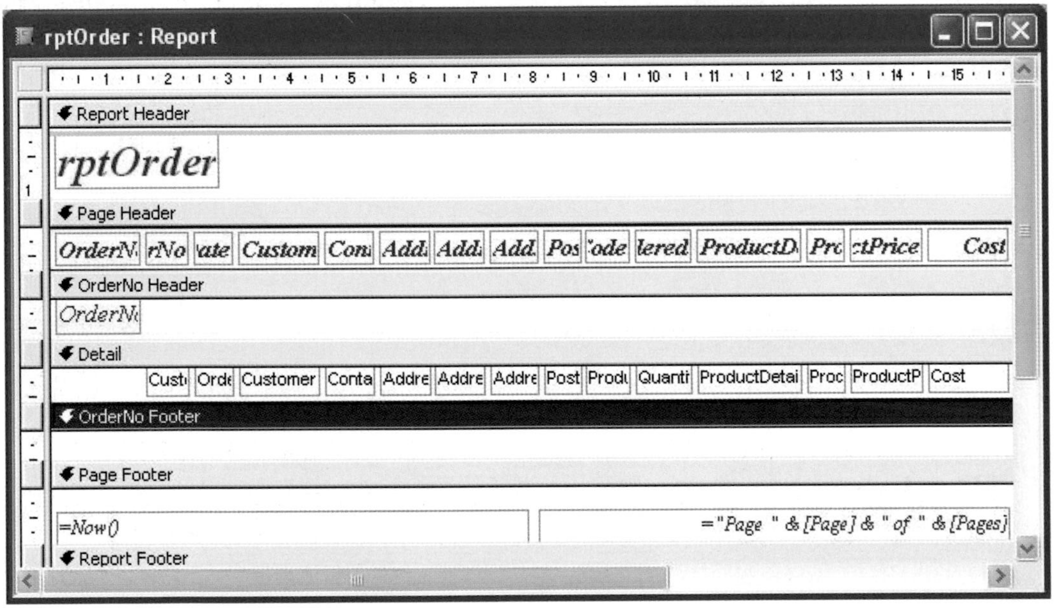

7 In the Page Header we want each order to have the company logo and company details. In Design View, click **View**, **Report/Header** to remove the **Report Header**. Remove all the **Labels** in the **Page Header** but retain the two horizontal lines.

8 Expand the **Page Header** a little to add a company logo. Add a **Label** and enter the company details as shown. Change the **Border Width** of the **Lines** to **1pt** and **Border Color** to **Black**.

Figure 3.3.17 ▼

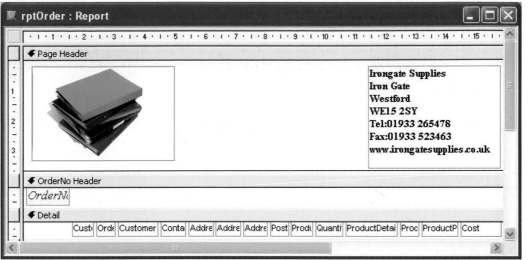

9 Expand the **OrderNo Header** by about 4 or 5 cm. Move the **Customer** details and **Order Date** to the **OrderNo Header**. Arrange with appropriate fonts and labels as shown.

Figure 3.3.18 ▼

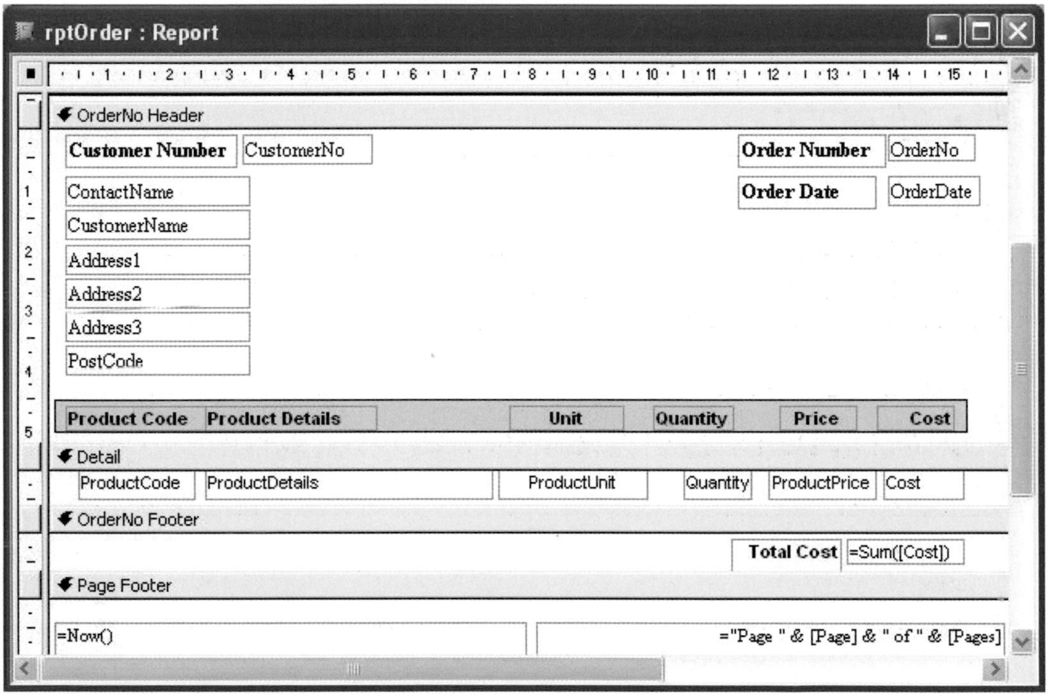

10 Just above the Detail section add a rectangle and choose a grey color fill. Position labels on the rectangle as shown. You now need to position and align the controls in the Detail area to sit underneath their respective headings. This is tricky!

11 In the **OrderNo Footer** add a **Text Box**. Edit the **Label** to read **Total Cost**. Add the formula **=Sum([Cost])** to the control and set the format to **Currency**.

Figure 3.3.19 ▼

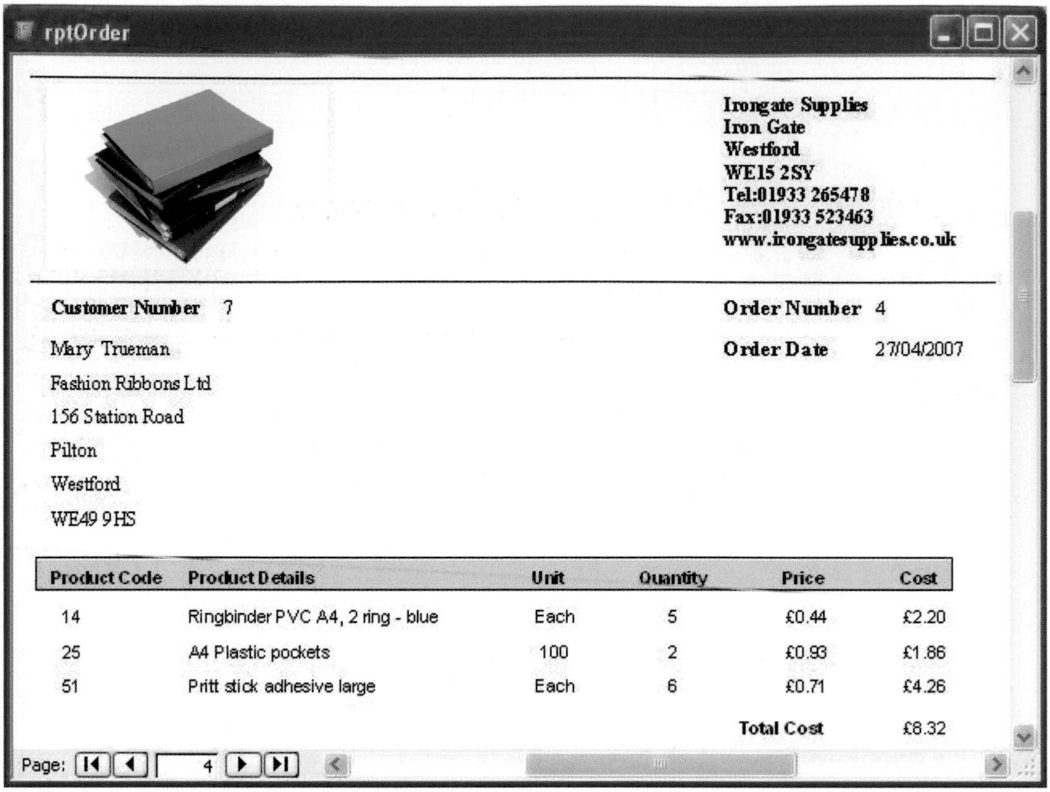
rptOrder

Irongate Supplies
Iron Gate
Westford
WE15 2SY
Tel:01933 265478
Fax:01933 523463
www.irongatesupplies.co.uk

Customer Number 7

Mary Trueman
Fashion Ribbons Ltd
156 Station Road
Pilton
Westford
WE49 9HS

Order Number 4
Order Date 27/04/2007

Product Code	Product Details	Unit	Quantity	Price	Cost
14	Ringbinder PVC A4, 2 ring - blue	Each	5	£0.44	£2.20
25	A4 Plastic pockets	100	2	£0.93	£1.86
51	Pritt stick adhesive large	Each	6	£0.71	£4.26
				Total Cost	£8.32

Page: 4

Note If you wish just to print the Current Order on screen you will need to use the Form Referencing techniques previously shown and add a button to the Main Order form.

4 Project ideas

1: Abbey Window Cleaning Services

Kate Reeves organises her husband Ken's window cleaning business from home.

Two other window cleaners are employed as the business grows.

The business serves two or three small villages on the outskirts of a large East Midlands town. Ken is always on the lookout for new business and adding properties to his rounds.

He does this by calling door to door or distributing flyers. A number of customers are added by word of mouth. He bases his charges on the size of property which in turn reflects the number of windows.

Category	House Type	Charge
A	Large Detached	£9.50
B	Detached	£8.00
C	Bungalow	£5.00
D	Semi-Detached	£6.00
E	Cottage	£5.00
F	Other	TBN

He tries to categorise jobs as simply as possible to help the customer. He reserves category F for individually negotiated prices.

Details of rounds are held in a file. Each round is numbered and contains the addresses of the properties in each round along with their charge category. Some properties contain additional notes detailing special requirements or requests, e.g. conservatory also.

Rounds are allocated to window cleaners weekly who receive a photocopied work list. A calling card is left requesting payment and to let the customer know the window cleaner has been. If payment is received on the day, the work list is updated and handed back to Kate. She updates records and then produces work lists to collect payments.

Kate wishes to computerise her and Ken's business. She wants to be able to:
■ store and easily update details of rounds
■ produce work lists for window cleaners
■ store details of payments and jobs
■ produce payment request lists
■ issue payment requests
■ produce income reports.

2: Albion Away Travel

Dave Shaw organises the away travel for supporters of Burton Albion Football Club.

He lays on coaches for all 23 league games and FA Cup games as required. Usually only one 60 seater coach is needed for a game but there will be occasions in a season when he needs to lay on two or more coaches.

He keeps a chart of the fixtures over the season. Two or three weeks prior to each game he will discuss with the coach company the estimated price, departure and return times for each trip.

He will then set the price of the journey and publish details in the match day programme and club shop as shown below.

Match No	Opponents	Date	Dept Time	Return Time	Price
1	Halifax Town	16/08/08	4.30 pm	12.30 am	£10.00
2	Woking	20/08/08	10.30 am	8.00 pm	£12.00
3	Southport	29/08/08	11.00 am	7.30 pm	£10.00

Supporters book their places by phoning Dave and requesting seats for their chosen match. Dave keeps a seating plan for each coach, takes down their name and contact number, the number of seats required and pencils in details on his plan. Payment is made on the day. Any profit made goes to the supporters club and helps keep the cost of travel down.

Dave wishes to computerise this job and provide an improved service to the customer.

He would like to:

■ store details of bookings and seat allocation
■ have quick access to seat availability
■ produce reports on bookings and income for each match
■ produce reports on income over the season
■ develop a customer mailing list.

3: Bouncy Castle Hire

Bounce-a-Lot is a bouncy castle hire company based in Westford

The owner Kerry Williams hires out bouncy castles to companies, children's birthday parties, weddings and other large social events.

She currently has 10 different bouncy castles available for hire. Details of castles and costs are shown below. Delivery is free and the castles are erected by the delivery team. Hires can be from 1 to 14 days.

Castle Code	Castle Type	Size	Cost/Day
BB01	Bouncy Boxing	15'w × 15'd × 9'h	£80.00
BR02	Bungee Run	12'w × 35'd × 12'h	£150.00
CB03	Clown Bouncer	12'w × 15'd × 10'h	£50.00
FB05	Flintstone Bouncer	15'w × 15'd × 9'h	£45.00
FB06	Forest Bouncer	13'w × 16'd × 8'h	£45.00
G07	Gladiators	15'w × 20'd × 9'h	£80.00
GS08	Giant Slide	15'w × 25'd × 35'h	£125.00
JB09	Jungle Bouncer	15'w × 16'd × 10'h	£45.00
KB010	Kangaroo Bouncer	10'w × 12'd × 10'h	£40.00
RB11	Rainbow Bouncer	12'w × 10'd × 12'h	£35.00

Kerry currently keeps her records in a notepad and issues little in the way of paperwork with each hire. Kerry has found business increasing steadily and feels the need to computerise her record keeping.

She wants her computerised solution to:

- improve her record keeping and manage the castle hires
- book out castle hires
- issue daily delivery and collection details
- issue an invoice with each hire
- develop a customer database
- manage income and hire statistics
- produce a catalogue of bouncy castles.

4: Cake Making

Kirsty Wright makes a variety of cakes for all occasions, such as birthdays, anniversaries and weddings.

If it is possible then she can make it. She has been trading since 2003 and has many satisfied customers, who return to her again and again.

Cakes come in set sizes and prices as shown below.

The prices shown are inclusive of VAT, packaging, stands and delivery.

Kirsty keeps details of all her prices and customers in a diary.

Sponge Cakes	Basic Price
Round (6" or 10")	£2.00, £3.00
Square (6" or 10")	£2.50, £3.50

Fruit Cakes	
Round (6" or 10")	£2.50, £3.50
Square (6" or 10")	£3.00, £4.00

At present customers phone up and make an order. Kirsty writes down the customer details, the cake they require and the delivery date in her diary.

Kirtsy would like to improve her current cake-ordering process. She would like an easier and more efficient way to store details of her customers and orders.

She has a new PC and would like a solution provided to offer her:

■ quick access to a customer database and contact numbers
■ quick access to a pricing catalogue for customer mailing
■ a diary of cakes to be made and delivered
■ access to orders past and present
■ a professional looking receipt to accompany payment for each cake
■ order history to help her with her future planning.

5: Charity Xmas Cards

Jane Sanders is a Breast Cancer Care volunteer.

Each year, in the run up to Xmas she delivers catalogues of charity Christmas cards to families in and around the village of Twerton.

She bases some of her deliveries on a mailing list of families registered with Breast Cancer Care and individual requests from local volunteer groups who help promote the charity.

She keeps a record of her deliveries and details of collection times so she can pick up unwanted catalogues and/or orders.

Customers requiring cards are invited to complete an order form enclosed in the catalogue and return it to Jane.

Jane compiles her orders on a spreadsheet grid as shown below.

Customer	Address	Cat No	Description	Quantity	Price	Date
Wenn	21 Heathway	A456	Snowmen	2	3.99	11/11/08
		C387	Xmas Trees	3	2.75	
Pedley	37 Station Rd	A233	Assorted	5	4.99	13/11/08
		C546	Snow Scenes	2	3.75	
		A463	Baubles	1	2.75	

Jane wishes to enter her orders on to her PC and organise her collection and deliveries.

She would like the system to:

■ help her build up a committed customer mailing list
■ track unwanted catalogues
■ keep details of orders and requests
■ monitor money raised for return to the charity.

6: Conferences @ The Bird in the Hand Hotel

The Bird in the Hand Hotel is situated in South West Derbyshire. It offers conference facilities for local business.

It has three conference rooms available: Suite 1, Suite 2 and Suite 3. Daily hire charges are shown below.

Room	Price per day	Max no of delegates
Suite 1	£150	15
Suite 2	£150	20
Suite 3	£200	30

Rooms can be arranged by request in classroom or U-shape style. Further equipment can be hired for the day at the rates shown below.

Equipment	Price per day	Equipment	Price per day
TV	£30	Flip Chart	£10
OHP	£15	Data Projector	£40
Screen	£15	Lectern	£10

Catering is charged @ £21.00 per delegate. This includes hot/cold buffet and tea/coffee/mineral water throughout the day.

Andrew Corbett is the conference manager. Requests for conference facilities are taken by phone or letter.

Andrew will take down the customer details, the conference date, the number of delegates and the facilities they require. He will allocate a suite for the conference and confirm by letter the details and costs. On the day of the conference the company are given an invoice which they are expected to pay within 28 days.

Although it is a small business Andrew wants to run the operation from his computer. He wishes to be able to:

- store details of bookings and issue letters of confirmation
- invoice the company on the day of the event
- produce weekly/daily rotas and suite requirements for the hotel staff
- build up a customer database of local business
- produce management reports on use and income
- issue flyers with updated details of facilities offered.

7: Cricket Bat Orders

John Spalton makes handmade cricket bats from the finest English willow.

He has worked for Buckston and Spalton in Somerset for 15 years.

Each bat is handmade to the purchaser's precise specification. He makes cricket bats on request by taking orders from local cricketers and cricket clubs.

He produces two styles of bat:

The Excalibur: a shape designed for the ultimate in power, with a deceptively light pick up. This comes in Short or Long Handle and weighs from 2 lb 7 oz to 2 lb 10 oz.

The Sword: a shape designed for the player who likes a heavier bat with a great pick up. This comes in Short or Long Handle and weighs from 2 lb 11 oz to 3 lb 4 oz.

In addition a Toe Guard can be fitted to each bat for £5.00 and a Bat Cover supplied for £8.50.

Bats can be collected from the workshop or dispatched via courier with a Postage and Packing charge of £10.00.

John currently stores all information about orders in a handwritten diary and post-it notes on his notice board. He would like to computerise his jobs, sales and orders to improve his record keeping and build up a customer database. He needs to be able to:

- store and access orders
- issue delivery notes and order details
- provide information on jobs to be completed this week
- develop a customer database
- circulate all customers pre season with flyers and price lists
- keep track of paid and unpaid orders
- produce details of annual income.

8: The Derwentdale Fun Run

Sue Spalton organises an annual Fun Run in May of each year, called The Derwentdale Dash. It is in aid of The National Trust and Marie Curie Cancer Care.

The venue is the picturesque area around the village of Thorpe and Dovedale in the south of the Derbyshire Peak District.

It is a series of cross-country races of between 1 and 5 miles, run by about 600 people of all abilities.

There are three race categories. There is a 1 mile fun run for children under the age of 12, scheduled to start at 10 am. It is followed by a 3 mile fun run for people of all ages at 10.30 am and then starting at 11.30 am is the 5 mile event for serious runners.

Each runner must pay an entrance fee. The fees for this year are shown in the table below.

Under 12 Yrs	12-18 Yrs	OAP	Adult
£5	£7	£9	£12

All runners are invited to fill in an application form.

Applicants are invited to enter for one of three race categories.

For each runner, the organising committee need to know their name, date of birth, gender, telephone number, date of application, race category and category of payment (Under 12, 12–18, 'Old Age Pensioner' (OAP), Adult).

A unique four-digit number will be allocated to each runner.

If the application is received before 1 April 2008 then a £1.00 discount is applied.

Sue wishes to use her PC to computerise the organisation of the event. She wishes to be able to:

- store details of entry and entry fees
- issue confirmation of entry automatically
- issue race lists
- enter results and times
- invite runners to the following year's event.

9: Hair on the Move

Hair on the Move is a mobile hairdressing service run by Karen Sirrel in rural Derbyshire.

She employs two trainees and offers a wide range of services in the comfort of your home at more convenient times and affordable prices.

Karen's business is expanding and demand is high. She is adding to her customer base on a weekly basis.

Customers ring Karen to arrange an appointment and service. Karen takes down their details and allocates a hairdresser to the service. Customers tend to want to keep the same hairdresser.

Her prices are shown below. Additional services such as colouring are available on request.

Service	Price
Ladies Cut & Finish	£20.00
Ladies Wet Cut	£10.00
Gents Cut & Finish	£15.00
Gents Wet Cut	£10.00

Karen wants a solution set up on her PC to deal with the appointments, income and services.

She would like to be able to:

- keep records of her customers to provide a better service
- organise her appointments more efficiently
- keep records of payments and income
- manage the work of her assistants.

10: Hotel Room Booking @ The Broadway Hotel

The Broadway Hotel is situated in South West Derbyshire. It offers bar, catering, conference facilities and room booking.

The hotel has ten bedrooms numbered 101 to 111. Rooms 101 to 107 are Twin, 108 to 111 are Double En-Suite.

A Twin room can be booked at £44.95 per night with a £10.00 supplement for a second person.

A Double En-Suite costs £54.95 per night with a £15.00 supplement for a second person. Breakfast is included in the cost.

Bookings are made by phone, letter or email.

The hotel manager Alan Currie records the customer details along with dates, room number and the number of nights required.

A letter of confirmation is sent to the customer. On departure the customer receives an invoice detailing the costs. Payment is made on departure.

During the stay at the hotel all meals, drinks at the bar, newspapers and telephone calls are charged to the customer's bill and added to the invoice.

Alan wishes to computerise this part of the hotel operation. He wishes to be able to:

- store details of bookings and issue letters of confirmation
- have quick access to room availability
- invoice the customer on departure to include details of all additional expenditure
- produce daily lists of arrivals for the cleaning staff
- build up a customer database
- produce management reports on use and income
- produce daily lists of departures for the cleaning staff.

11: Peak Cycle Hire

Richard James has been hiring-out cycles in the Peak District National Park for many years.

He runs this from part of a small café he owns near the entrance to the park. He has cycles to suit all sizes, ages and abilities.

Pumps, puncture repair kits, locks, carriers and a map are available and are included in the cost of hire.

A deposit of £20 is required on all bikes. A £50 deposit is payable on a tandem.

Peak Cycle Hire

Deposits are withheld in the event of damage or late return.

The hire charges are shown below, payment is by cash only.

Type of Bike	Up to 3 hours	Whole Day	No of Bikes
Mountain/Trails Bike	£9.00	£13.00	10
Junior Bike	£6.50	£8.50	10
Tandem	£22.00	£30.00	2

Availability is from 9.30 am to 4.30 pm, later in summer. Last hire is 2 hours 30 minutes before closing. It is not possible to reserve bikes in advance; they are available on a first come first served basis.

10% discount is offered for students and OAPs.

Richard keeps details of hires in a diary on a daily basis. He writes down the customer details, the type of bike hired, the time it was hired and the payments due.

Increasingly during the summer months he is very busy and all bikes are out on hire regularly.

He wants to computerise his record keeping to:

- store details of daily hires and times
- record details of deposits and payments
- issue a receipt to the customer on payment
- produce reports on daily hires, demand and income
- produce reports on bike usage.

12: School Stationery Orders

Christine Taylor works at Westford School and is in charge of ordering stationery from suppliers. Stationery can include anything from paper, document wallets to sellotape and board pens.

She deals in the main with three suppliers: Derbys CC, Esco and F. Lee & Co.

At the end of each school year she phones around the key suppliers for best current prices and keeps details in a spreadsheet of each item, along with the best price and supplier.

The school has nine faculties: Maths, English, Science and so on. Each faculty has a budget holder who is responsible for completing stationery orders. Usually there will be a major order at the start of the year and then a number of minor ones throughout the school year.

At the start of the new school year the budget holder for each faculty is allocated a sum of money for stationery based on numbers of students. Christine issues a stationery price list and order form to all budget holders. This has to be completed before the start of the school year.

Christine currently keeps all her records on a spreadsheet but thinks a database solution may improve processing. She wants to:

- maintain a database of suppliers
- maintain a database of products and best prices
- keep track of faculty ordering and improve her record keeping
- produce reports analysing faculty expenditure
- produce reports analysing usage e.g. paper
- use the information to better plan needs
- provide better information to faculties and management on expenditure.

13: Village Hall Auctions

Stanton on the Hill Village Hall runs 80 : 20 auctions every three months. Items are submitted for auction, the customer takes 80% of the sale price with 20% going to the Village Hall Fund. The organiser is Beryl Hartley.

Typically auctions are attended by 200 or so people offering over 400 lots.

At the auction you will find furniture, household items, memorabilia, and objets d'art and many other items, all at knock-down prices.

Sellers wanting to offer lots for auction are invited to submit details by at least 28 days before the next published auction date. This enables Beryl to publish catalogues.

Sellers offering lots give Beryl their name and contact details. They also provide details of the lot and requested reserve price. Beryl logs these details into a spreadsheet as shown.

Lot No	Lot Details	Reserve	Seller	Contact No
00017	Beatles Yellow Submarine	£100	Don Buxton	01283 734562
00018	Smokers items and pipes	£40	Charles Alman	01283 534892
00019	Brass Carriage Clock	£20	Marie Thomas	01332 775344
00020	Wind-up Gramophone	£90	Don Buxton	01283 734562

On the day of the auction bidders pay a small entry fee, give their contact name and phone number to the organiser and in turn are issued with a Bidder ID Number.

When a lot is sold, the auctioneer notes the Lot No, the winning Bidder ID Number and the actual selling price. Collection and payments are then dealt with whilst the auction continues.

Beryl wants to run the auctions from her PC. She would like to:

- store details of lots and sellers
- produce pre auction catalogues
- store details of bidders and issue ID numbers
- record sales and issue confirmation receipts
- access records and reports on sales, sellers and income.

14: Westford Community Bus

David Griffiths is responsible for the Westford Community Bus Scheme in Mid-Somerset. The 20-seater bus is funded by the local parish council. It provides a weekly service for the local community to the three major towns in the area.

The bus leaves on the same day each week, at the same time and picks up and drops off at the home of the passenger. A nominal fee is charged.

David keeps a register of volunteers who are trained in driving the bus. He allocates a driver to each journey, each week.

Day	Date	Destination	Cost	Driver
Tuesday	21/11/08	Taunton	£1.00	David Griffiths
Wednesday	22/11/08	Street	£0.50	Pete Wilson
Thursday	23/11/08	Weston-Super-Mare	£1.00	Claire Griffiths

To take advantage of the scheme residents have to register for a permit with the local council for which a fee of £2.00 is charged annually. David keeps a file of residents who participate in the scheme.

To book a seat on the bus residents have to phone David and simply give their name, the bus service required and pick up point. David keeps a seating plan for each trip and merely allocates a customer to a seat on a first come first served basis. The service is immensely popular and David feels a computer solution will improve the service and his record-keeping.

He would like the solution to offer the following features.

- store details of residents with permits
- store details of volunteer drivers
- improve the booking process
- give quick access to seat availability
- produce timetables and seating plans
- produce annual reports on income and use to the local parish council.

15: Westford Toy Library

Westford Toy Library is based in the local community centre in Westford. The library is affiliated to the Early Years Library Network. It hires out toys to parents, child minders and playgroups.

It has built up a stock of over 1000 toys details of which are stored in a ring-bound folder.

Toys are coded and allocated a category: Activity, Basic, Co-ordination, Electronic, Fun and Games, Jigsaws, Music and Special Needs. Toys are also catalogued by a target age range 0–1, 2–3, 4–5 and 6–7 years old.

Toy Code	Description	Category	Age Range	Value £
T1	Farm playmat	Activity	2-3 yrs	£10.00
T29	Flutterfly	Activity	2-3 yrs	£7.50
T67	Super Scribbler	Co-ordination	0-1 yrs	£15.00
T156	Coloured Clown	Basic	2-3 yrs	£10.00
T234	Crazy Guitar	Electronic	6-7 yrs	£25.00
T256	Train Set	Electronic	6-7 yrs	£35.00

To join the library there is an annual subscription fee as shown below. Toys can be borrowed on a weekly basis for up to a month at 30p per toy per week. Members can borrow as many toys as they wish. Fines are paid on a basis of 30p per day overdue.

Type	Fees
Parents	£2.00
Childminders	£3.00
Playgroups	£5.00

The library is run by volunteers who feel a computerised solution would improve record keeping. The solution should offer:

- a detailed and up-to-date catalogue of toys
- to store details of members and fees payable
- to record details of loans and overdues
- to manage loan and overdue payments
- to provide a range of reports on loans, members and income.

Index

Abbey Window Cleaning Services,
    project idea 259
Access
    application icon, changing 225–6
    caption text, changing 224–5
    compacting size of 228
    components of 7–11
    creating new database 13
    password protecting 226
    starting 9–10
    startup options 131, 178, 187
    Status Bar, customising 226–7
action queries 166–72
Albion Away Travel, project idea 260
append queries 166, 167–9
archiving data using action queries
    167–71
AutoExec macro 220
Autokeys (hot-keys), creating 221
AutoNumber 27
    adding a code prefix to 192
    restart numbering of 192

Bouncy Castle Hire, database project
    237–42, 261
business cards, creating 216–18
buttons see command buttons

Cake Making, project idea 262
calculated fields
    adding to a form 202
    expression builder 202–3
    in queries 57–8, 196–200, 201
    in reports 153–9
calendar controls 228–9
Charity Xmas Cards, project idea 263
clock, adding to a form 180–1
colours, selecting for forms 70–1
combo boxes 83
    alphabetic ordering of names in
        87–8
    for entering student gender 83–5
    to enter student details 148–51
    to look up student details 85–7
command buttons
    adding to forms 79–82
    button images, designing 206–7
    creating from graphic images 207
    customising Exit/Quit button 208
    default button, setting 203–4
    running macros from 121–3
compacting database size 228
concatenation of text 197, 214–15

Conferences @ The Bird in the Hand
    Hotel, project idea 264
controls on forms 67–8
    see also command buttons
    adding tool tips 212
    borders and special effects 206
    calendar controls 228–9
    combo boxes 83–8, 148–51
    control panel, adding 82–3
    framing 73, 82–3
    moving focus of 205–6
    multiple changes 204
    option buttons/radio controls 209
    option groups 210–11, 233
    properties, setting 73–4
    selecting multiple 67, 73
    spinner controls 229–30
    tab controls 139–42, 146–7,
        235–6
Cricket Bat Orders, database project
    243–9, 265
cross field validation 223–4

data entry
    forms 64, 83–5, 247
    input masks 28–9
    tables 23–7, 192
data types 15–16, 27
Database Window 10–11
    hiding and unhiding 220–1
Date() function 29, 50–1, 56–7, 230
DateAdd() function 200
DateDiff() function 199
dates
    calendar controls 228–9
    as criteria in queries 38, 42–3
    Date() function 50–1, 56–7, 230
    Default Value property, using to
        enter 29, 191
    difference between dates, calculating
        199
    formatting on forms and reports
        203
    future dates, calculating 200
    month, extracting from a date 199
    in multi-table queries 56–7
    in parameter queries 48–9
    SetValue action, macros 230
    weekday, extracting from date 198
default values 19, 29, 191
delete queries 166, 169–71
Derwentdale Fun Run, project idea
    266

error messages
    duplicate values 193
    setting up table relationships 190–1
    validation text 22, 28
Excel, importing data from 194–5
exiting application, confirmation
    message 179–80, 208
expression builder, using 202–3

field properties 28
    default values, setting 19, 29
    field size 17, 19
    format field 29, 198
    input masks 20–1, 28–9
    Lookup Wizard 17–18
    validation rules 22, 29–30
fields 12
    see also field properties
    AutoNumber 15, 23, 27, 192
    creating read-only on forms 204–5
    editing table structure 16–17
    names and data types, defining
        15–16
filters, adding to a form 146–7
Format() function 203, 216
forms 8
    see also controls on forms; SubForms
    adding a real time clock 180–1
    based on more than one table 88–91
    calculated fields 202
    colours 70
    creating from scratch 213–14
    creating using wizards 59–62
    datasheet view 63
    dates, formatting 203
    design view 63, 65–6
    developing 68–70, 71–2
    expression builder, using 202–3
    filters, adding 146–7
    form view 63, 64, 66
    formatting 70–1
    graphics, adding 77–8
    menu bar, removing 213
    modal and pop up 212–13
    positioning of 208–9
    printing without buttons 211
    properties, setting 74–6, 208–9
    read-only fields 204–5
    sizing of 208–9
    sort options, adding 147–8
    special effects 71, 73, 77, 78, 82,
        206
    splashscreens 176–8

tidying up 175–6
toolbox 65, 66, 71, 72, 77, 83
front-end menus *see* switchboards

graphic imagess
    adding to forms 77–8
    adding to reports 102
    creating command buttons from 207
    designing for buttons 206–7
grouping data in reports 107–18,
        155–6, 256

Hair on the Move, project idea 267
hot-keys, setting up 221
Hotel Room Booking, project idea 268

icons
    adding/removing from toolbars
        182–4
    changing application icon 225–6
IIf() function and IIf statement 201,
        215, 245–6
Import Spreadsheet Wizard 194–5
Income report 153–60
indexes preventing data duplication
        193
input masks 20–1, 28–9
Instructor Contact Details report
        97–103
Instructor form 60–2, 78, 132
Instructor table 6, 25
Instructors' Timetable report 107–12
Is Null operator, queries 196

Lesson Analysis report 160–4
Lesson Booking form 89–91
Lesson table 6
    archiving old data 167–71
    setting up 26–7
LessonType form, setting up 62
LessonType table 6, 26, 172
LIKE operator, queries 195–6
list boxes 85
    see also combo boxes
Lookup Wizard 17–18

macros 9
    About message box 120–1
    archiving lesson records 171
    AutoExec macro 220
    Autokeys (hot-keys) 221
    checking for no data 164–5
    closing splashscreen 177–8
    conditions in 223
    copy and paste 151–2, 222–3
    cross field validation 223–4
    emailing a report 234–5
    formatting text in message boxes
        219
    opening forms 119–10
    printing multiple copies 224

printing reports 121
sorting records on forms 147–8
switchboards, customising 121–3
mailing labels, creating 216–18
make-table queries 200–1
menus, customising 184–7
message boxes
    About message box 120–1
    formatting text in 219
    setting up with macros 120–1,
        164–5
    visual basic code for 208
modal versus pop up forms 212–13
Month() function 199
multi-table queries 52–8

option buttons 209
option group controls 210–11, 233

parameter queries 46–9, 232
Pass IT Driving School system 5–6
    data entry 23–30
    forms 59–91, 175–81
    macros 119–23
    menus and toolbars 181–7
    queries 36–58, 166–72
    relationships 31–5
    reports 92–118, 153–65
    search and sort options 146–52
    SubForms 132–45
    submitting as coursework 2–3
    switchboard 124–31, 173–5
    tables 12–22
password protection 226
Peak Cycle Hire, project idea 269
pop up versus modal forms 212–13
primary key field 15, 17
progress meter, adding to Status Bar
        226–7
project ideas
    Abbey Window Cleaning Services
        259
    Albion Away Travel 260
    Bouncy Castle Hire 261
    Cake Making 262
    Charity Xmas Cards 263
    Conferences @ The Bird in the
        Hand Hotel 264
    Cricket Bat Orders 265
    Derwentdale Fun Run 266
    Hair on the Move 267
    Hotel Room Booking @ The
        Broadway Hotel 268
    Peak Cycle Hire 269
    School Stationery Orders 270
    Village Hall Auctions 271
    Westford Community Bus 272
    Westford Toy Library 273

queries 8
    action queries 166–72

adding and removing tables 40
append queries 166, 167–9
calculated fields in 57–8
changing field order 40
concatenation of text fields 197
creating in Design View 36–9
creating using the Wizard 41–2
delete queries 166, 169–71
deleting fields from 38
forms using 88–91
IIf function 201, 245–6
make-table queries 200–1
multi-table queries 52–8
parameter queries 46–9
renaming field headings 40
running 38
select queries 36–45
sort order, changing 42, 88
update queries 166, 172
using Date() function 50–1
quit button, customising 179–80, 208

radio controls 209
records
    adding using a form 80
    copying and pasting using macros
        222–3
    navigation on forms 81–3
    preventing changes to 204
referential integrity 34–5, 190–1
relationships
    adding tables 31–3
    cascading updates and deletes 33,
        35
    deleting 35
    error messages 190–1
    referential integrity 34–5, 190–1
    setting links 33 4
reports 8–9, 92
    adding graphics 102
    calculating totals 153–60
    check boxes and coded fields,
        replacing with text 215–16
    concatenating text strings 214–15
    controls, formatting 102–3
    counting records 158–9
    creating using a wizard 92–3, 103–6
    customising layout 97–101
    dates, formatting 203
    Design View 95
    displaying error messages if no data
        164–5
    emailing using a macro 234–5
    forcing page breaks 110–12, 214
    formatting dates on 203
    formatting invoice numbers 216
    from currently displayed record
        233–4
    grouping data 107–18
    images, adding 102
    Layout Preview 97

lesson analysis 160–4
mailing labels, creating 216–18
orientation of 96–7
Print Preview 93–4
printing from option group control 233
printing multiple copies 224
professional looking 101–3
toolbars 95–6

School Stationery Orders, project idea 270
select queries 8
  creating new 36–9
  date criteria 38
  for a date range 42–3
  multiple criteria 43–5
  Yes/No criteria 39–40
sort options, adding to forms 147–8
sort order in queries 42, 88
Sorting and Grouping option, reports 107–18
special effects 71, 73, 77, 78, 82, 206
spinner controls 229–30
splashscreen, setting up 176–8
startup options 131, 178, 187, 225
Stationery Store, database project 250–8
Status Bar
  adding a loading progress meter 226–7
  customising information displayed in 227
string handling
  queries 195–6, 197–8
  reports 214–15
Student form
  combo boxes, adding 83–7

command buttons, adding 79–82
control panel, adding 82–3
control properties, setting 73–4
creating using form wizard 59–60
developing in design view 71–2
form properties, setting 74–5
opening with a macro 119–20
Student Lesson reports 103–6, 112–15, 121
Student table 6, 13–22, 23–4
SubForms 132
  created using drag and drop 138–9
  creating using wizard 132–7
  displaying SubForm totals on main form 231
  for Pass IT Driving School system 139–44
  to display Weekly Timetable 145
Switch statement, reports 216
switchboards 124
  adding Report switchboard 129–31
  creating using Switchboard Manager 124–8
  creating with macros 121–3
  customising 128–9
  startup options, setting 131
  updating 173–5

tab controls 139–42, 146–7, 235–6
tables 7
  see also fields; field properties
  copying and pasting data into 195
  creating new 14
  data entry 23–7, 192
  importing data into 194–5
  indexes preventing data duplication 193
  naming conventions 16

relationships between 31–5, 190–1
  structure of, editing 16–17
text strings, concatenating 197, 214–15
timers
  adding a clock to a form 74–5
  setting for splashscreen 178
tool tips (screen tips) 212
toolbars 10–11
  customising 181–4
  reports 95–6
toolbox, form design 65, 66, 71, 72, 77, 83

update queries 166, 172

validation rules 22, 29–30
Village Hall Auctions, project idea 271
Visual Basic (VB) 181, 207, 208, 227, 229–30

weekday, extracting from a date 198
Weekly Timetable
  report, producing 116–18
  SubForm to display 145
Westford Community Bus, project idea 272
Westford Toy Library, project idea 273
wildcard searches 195–6
Wizards
  Combo Box Wizard 83–8, 148–51
  Command Button Wizard 79–82
  Form Wizard 59–62
  Import Spreadsheet Wizard 194–5
  Lookup Wizard 17–18
  Query Wizard 41–2
  Report Wizard 92–3